# THE POPULATION CRISIS

## Implications and Plans for Action

*Edited by Larry K. Y. Ng*

*Stuart Mudd, Co-Editor*

*Associate Editors: Hugo Boyko, Robert C. Cook,*
*Frank J. Ditter, James E. McLennan,*
*and W. Taylor Thom, Jr.*

BLOOMINGTON & LONDON

*Indiana University Press*

The present volume is abridged and revised from *The Population Crisis and the Use of World Resources,* issued under the auspices of the World Academy of Art and Science, edited by Stuart Mudd, published in 1964 by Dr. W. Junk, Publishers, The Hague, and in the United States by Indiana University Press

SECOND PRINTING 1966

# THE POPULATION CRISIS

*Implications and Plans for Action*

## PREFACE

THIS BOOK REPRESENTS the culmination of two separate efforts. The World Academy of Art and Science more than three years ago decided that the topic of their second volume should be the global population problem, considering it "the most critical subject with which we could deal." It was probably no coincidence that at about the same time a group of undergraduate students at Stanford University, during an informal discussion, expressed concern over the world's population situation. It was certainly not expertise that led us to our expression of concern. Rather, it was prompted by a somewhat reluctant realization that our generation will be the one which will experience the effects of the population explosion, and any action that has to be taken must ultimately come from this particular generation. But intelligent action presumes knowledge and understanding of the situation, both of which we found to be conspicuously lacking. Clearly something should be done about this, but what?

Individual research and consultation with faculty members at Stanford convinced us that the most effective action would be to publish a collection of articles, written by leading authorities. In publishing such a collection, an unique effort will have been realized. In its idealistic aspect, such a book should represent the collaborative efforts of both the expert and the beginner working together on a common human problem. In its more pragmatic aspect, the book should serve to acquaint the student with the situation and hopefully to stimulate thought on the subject.

Such are the separate beginnings of both the World Academy of Art and Science and student projects. One soon came to learn of the other's undertaking. A meeting clearly disclosed the wisdom of pooling our assets. Our conclusion was that in so doing we would be using the manuscripts that we have to the best possible advantage. In this joint effort, we hope that the original purpose underlying our endeavour will not be forgotten: namely, that the younger generation is indeed concerned with the rapid expansion of population, and is doing something about it.

## PREFACE

A more detailed and comprehensive volume has appeared in hardback, under the title *The Population Crisis and the Use of World Resources* (Stuart Mudd, Ed.), published by Dr. W. Junk, Publishers, The Hague, 1964, and by the Indiana University Press, Bloomington, Indiana, 1964. The present paperback volume represents a condensed and reorganized version of that hardback, and some new articles have been added. The basic orientation of the two editions is somewhat different: the hardback presents a balanced discussion of population and world resources, in the hope that it may offer guidelines toward rational policies; the paperback aims rather to kindle the imagination and challenge the thinking of young people, particularly students. It is hoped that this book may serve as a helpful reference for student seminars on population problems and that through such use a stimulation to action will be provided.

Indeed one of youth's historic roles has been to provide the enthusiasm—if not the leadership—for change. Few areas challenge our imagination and audacity of thought more than our need to confront the population dilemma. We are confident that an informed generation will arise to meet this challenge.

LARRY NG

# PREFACE

AMONG THE DRAMATIC changes in human ecology which have been brought about by the unprecedented and accelerating growth of the sciences and technology, two stand out as presenting problems of peculiar scope and urgency. First, of course, are those resulting from the liberation of fission and fusion energies of the atom; these are the subjects of daily discussion, anxiety and hope, and will not be further considered here beyond pointing out that they are intimately, if subtly, interwoven with the second great category of change. This category comprises the profound ecological disequilibrium brought about by the world-wide application of scientific medicine and public health to reduction of death rates without corresponding reduction of birth rates. The resulting explosive increase in populations, in particular in the developing regions of the world, which is outpacing any practicable increase of resources, is a cause of grave concern to every thoughtful observer of human ecology. The two categories are interwoven because the pressure of population growth on natural resources has throughout history been an exciting cause of aggressive and often military expansion and warfare.

We are well aware that much has been said and written both on population and on natural resources. We offer no royal road out of the wilderness. However, we do dare hope that a balanced discussion of both facets of the question by authors of highest experience and competence may offer some useful guide lines toward rational policies.

It is a curious fact that the profound ecological disequilibrium we are facing is in large measure an unforeseen consequence of the very triumphs of the sciences and their application to human welfare by the great international agencies such as WHO and UNICEF, the philanthropic foundations and progressive governments. Must we suppose that these same beneficent agencies and persons will pass by this crisis of our time with averted eyes? The editors refuse to accept so defeatist a view. There is hope if we will openly face the problems.

STUART MUDD

# CONTENTS

PREFACE on behalf of Student Group, by LARRY K. Y. NG      v
PREFACE on behalf of World Academy of Art and Science,
  by STUART MUDD      vii
*Introduction*
  1. Sir JULIAN HUXLEY: The Impending Crisis      3

PART ONE. THE POPULATION CRISIS

*The Facts of Population Growth*
  2. C. LANGDON WHITE: Geography and the World's Population      11
  3. ANNABELLE DESMOND:
     How Many People Have Ever Lived on Earth?      20

*Economic, Social and Political Analysis*
  4. EUGENE R. BLACK: Address to the Economic
     and Social Council of the United Nations      39
  5. J. MAYONE STYCOS: Problems of Fertility Control
     in Underdeveloped Areas      44
  6. PHILIP M. HAUSER: Demographic Dimensions of World Politics      58

*Regional Statements*
  7. IRENE B. TAEUBER: Asian Populations. The Critical Decades      72
  8. ROBERT C. NORTH: Communist China and the Population Problem      88
  9. EDGAR SNOW: Population Control in China:
     An Interview with Chou-En-lai      99
10. RONALD HILTON: The Population Explosion in Latin America      104
11. ROBERT C. COOK and KAVAL GULHATI: Housing and
     Population Growth in Africa, Asia, and Latin America      114
12. LINCOLN H. DAY: The American Fertility Cult      124

*Resources and Population*
13. ARNOLD J. TOYNBEE: Man and Hunger. The Perspectives of History      133
14. FOOD AND AGRICULTURAL ORGANIZATION REPORT:
     Food Supplies and Population      149
15. C. S. CHRISTIAN: The Use and Abuse of Land and Water      157
16. W. TAYLOR THOM, JR.: The Constructive Use of World Resources      177

PART TWO.   IMPLICATIONS OF THE POPULATION EXPLOSION

*Biological and Psychological Considerations*
17. WARREN O. NELSON: Current Approaches
        to the Biological Control of Fertility                                    191
18. ALAN F. GUTTMACHER: The Place of Sterilization                      201
19. JEROME M. KUMMER, M.D.: The Problems of Abortion.
        The Personal Population Explosion                                     207

*Eugenic and Genetic Considerations*
20. FREDERICK OSBORN: The Protection and Improvement
        of Man's Genetic Inheritance                                           215
21. HERMANN J. MULLER: Better Genes for Tomorrow                    223

*Public Health Considerations*
22. JOHN E. GORDON and HAZEL ELKINGTON: Public Health
        in an Overpopulated World                                              248

*Cultural Considerations*
23. HENRY B. VAN LOON: Population, Space, and Human Culture      258
24. F. L. LUCAS: The Writer in an Overpopulated World                  267


PART THREE.   ACTION PROGRAMS

25. BROCK CHISHOLM: The Problem of New Problems                    279
26. UNITED NATIONS GENERAL ASSEMBLY RESOLUTION
        ON POPULATION GROWTH AND ECONOMIC DEVELOPMENT       282
27. RICHARD N. GARDNER: The Politics of Population:
        A Blueprint for International Cooperation                            285
28. ANNABELLE DESMOND: The Asian Population Conference         297
29. ALAN F. GUTTMACHER, M.D.: Planned Parenthood
        —World Population Report                                               304
30. CLARENCE J. GAMBLE: The Initiation of Contraceptive Services  312
31. THE AMERICAN ASSEMBLY: Final Report
        on the Population Dilemma                                               317

Appendix: Voluntary Organizations and Research Programs            323
Notes                                                                                337
Bibliography                                                                         347
List of Contributors                                                                351
Index                                                                                355

# LIST OF FIGURES

### 2. *Geography and the World's Population*

Fig. 1. Areas of the world hospitable and hostile to man's occupance.    13
Fig. 2. Foodcrop and non-foodcrop zones of the world.    14

### 3. *How Many People Have Ever Lived on Earth?*

Fig. 1. Growth of human numbers.    26
Fig. 2. A thousand years of world population growth.    33
Fig. 3. Life expectancy over the ages.    36

### 13. *Man and Hunger. The Perspectives of History*

Fig. 1. Distribution of the population of the world according to
       daily intake of calories.    144
Fig. 2. Estimated population increases for various regions
       of the world, 1960-2000.    145

### 14. *Food Supplies and Population*

Fig. 1. Overall index of needs in total food supplies, 1970-2000.    152
Fig. 2. Index of needs in total food supplies
       by selected major food groups.    155

### 16. *The Constructive Use of World Resources*

Fig. 1. Relative populations and per capita work potentials
       of particular nations and regions.    179
Fig. 2. Diagram representing differences between a profit-motive
       economy and an earnings-motive economy.    187

### 19. *The Problems of Abortion. The Personal Population Explosion*

Fig. 1. Percentage of pregnancies terminating in induced abortion
       according to order of pregnancy.    209
Fig. 2. Percentage of pregnancies terminating in induced abortion
       for women currently or previously married at age of abortion. 209

### 28. *The Asian Population Conference*

Fig. 1. Population growth in Europe and Asia, 1900-2000.    298

# THE POPULATION CRISIS

*Implications and Plans for Action*

# Introduction

❦ ❦ ❦

## 1.

## THE IMPENDING CRISIS

### by Sir Julian Huxley

I shall try to take the broad view of an evolutionary biologist, who must try to look at things in the light of the enduring process of evolution of which we all form a part. Seen in this light, the population crisis is part of a very critical period in the history of the world.

Thanks to the new vision which we have attained through the knowledge explosion which has gone on parallel with the population explosion in the last half-century, we have a new vision of our destiny. We may say that today evolution in the person of man is now becoming conscious of itself.

I do not want to amplify this at great length. I would remind you, however, that all reality is, in a perfectly genuine sense, evolution; that biological evolution on this planet has been going on for nearly three billion years, and that in the course of that period life has advanced (not only increased in variety, but advanced in organization) so that its highest forms, instead of being submicroscopic, tiny pre-amoebic units, became larger and more powerful, and after hundreds of millions of years vertebrates, and then land vertebrates; and eventually the final dominant type, now spreading over the world . . . man.

And man is now, whether he likes it or not, and indeed whether he knows it or not (but it is important that he is beginning to know it), he is now the sole agent for the future of the whole evolutionary process on this earth. He is responsible for the future of this planet.

Now to come back to the present crisis. I would describe the present crisis as one in which quantity is threatening quality, and also, if you like, one in which the present is threatening the future. Before we make up our minds what we ought to do in the present crisis—it is no good just getting into a flap and saying that we ought to do something—we must try to find what our ultimate aim is as agent or leader of evolution here.

Surely, it isn't just power. Surely, it isn't just to eat, drink, and be merry, and say, "Well, what's posterity done for us? To hell with posterity!" It isn't just mere quantity of possessions or mere quantity of people. Nor is it just preparation for some rather shadowy after-life. I would assert that it must be to hold in trust, to conserve and to cultivate the

3

resources of the earth and the resources of our own nature. And so our aim should be to increase the richness of life and enhance its quality.

"Fulfillment" is probably the embracing word; more fulfillment and less frustration for more human beings. We want more varied and fuller achievement in human societies, as against drabness and shrinkage. We want more variety as against monotony. We want more enjoyment and less suffering. We want more beauty and less ugliness. We want more adventure and disciplined freedom, as against routine and slavishness. We want more knowledge, more interest, more wonder, as against ignorance and apathy.

We want more sense of participation in something enduring and worthwhile, some embracing project, as against a competitive rat-race, whether with the Russians or our neighbours on the next street. In the most general terms, we want more transcendence of self in the fruitful development of personality, and more human dignity not only as against human degradation, but as against more self-imprisonment in the human ego or mere escapism.

If we look at the present scene in the light of some such vision as this, what do we see? I might begin by telling a little of what I have seen in Africa. I was sent there to report to UNESCO on the conservation of wildlife and natural habitats. And in the wonderful Queen Elizabeth National Park in Uganda the animals had been so well preserved that the hippos were overmultiplying and had trampled down the margins of the lakes and the channels; they had eaten up all the surplus food, and in fact were destroying their own habitat. The point I want to make is that man is now busy destroying his own habitat.

Man has been over-exploiting the natural resources of this planet and has been ruining its soils and doing all sorts of other unpleasant things to it. He has wasted enormous amounts of resources which he ought to have conserved. He has cut down the forests and caused floods and erosion. As Fairfield Osborn put it in the title of his book, he has plundered our planet. (Can we expect we might have another book from him, with the title *Our Blundered Planet?*) And so we are well on the way to ruining our own material habitat.

The further point I want to make is that we are beginning to ruin our own spiritual and mental habitat. Not content with destroying or squandering our resources of material things, we are beginning to destroy the resources of true enjoyment—spiritual, esthetic, intellectual, emotional. We are spreading great masses of human habitation over the face of the land, neither cities nor suburbs nor towns nor villages, just a vast mass of urban sprawl or subtopia. And to escape from this, people are spilling out further and further into the wilder parts and so destroying them.

And we are making our cities so big as to be monstrous. They are growing to such a size that they are becoming impossible to live in. Just as there is a maximum possible size for an efficient land animal—you can't have a land animal more than about twice as large as an elephant—so there is a maximum possible efficient size for a city. I think that London, New York, and Tokyo have already got beyond that size.

Ambassador Chagla of India has said that civilization has already imposed a grievous burden on the future. I entirely agree. We have to try to lighten that burden and prevent its getting heavier. To take another metaphor, man is in danger of losing his claim to be the lord of creation, and of becoming the cancer of the whole planet: Not a very nice prospect, but a perfectly genuine one. In the message which Australian scientists have prepared, they made a profound and depressing remark that unless we took some care, the people of all countries all over the world would soon become under-privileged.

To look at the crisis more specifically, first of all there are nearly three billion people on earth. Whatever happens, there will be about six billion people by the end of the century, well within the lifetime of many of our children already living. Even at the present moment, over half the world's population are under-fed, under-healthy, under-housed, under-wealthy, under-educated and in general under-privileged. There is an immense gap between the "haves" and the "have-nots," the privileged and the under-privileged; and the gap is widening instead of narrowing.

The world's present rate of population increase is something phenomenal. It is about fifty million a year, and increasing every year, both for simply arithmetical reasons and because the compound interest rate of increase is still itself increasing. That means the equivalent of one good-sized town every 24 hours—a hundred and forty thousand odd. If you like to think of it in terms of minutes, it is the equivalent of ten baseball teams complete with coach every minute. And yet there are people who have so little quantitative sense that they talk of getting rid of our surplus population by sending them off to other planets!

Then there is the other great myth of the present day, that this crisis can be solved by Science—"Science" with a "S"—a sort of mystical magician. "Science will find a way." Well, it's not finding its way very well at the moment; Japan, for instance, has done a wonderful job in bringing its rate of population increase down, but it is still increasing at nearly 1% per annum and is already bursting at the seams. Science is not finding a way to make our traffic problems in big cities much easier. And it is completely unable to cope with the appalling problems of health and housing in great over-large cities in under-privileged countries, such as Calcutta.

Then there is the point with reference to what Mr. Eugene Black has recently said—the point that science cannot find a way of successfully industrializing an under-developed country if its birth-rate is too high. That is one of the important points that has emerged from careful economic studies. In order to industrialize an under-developed country, you need a great deal of capital and you need a great deal of human skill and expertise. If you have too many human beings to feed, house, educate, service, and all the rest of it, that capital and skill will be used up in looking after the growing generation, and you won't be able to industrialize.

This came out very clearly in the study of possible industrialization in India by Professors Coale and Hoover in which they pointed out that unless India got its birth-rate down by about 50% in the next 35 or 40 years, it would never be able to break through to a successful, advanced, industrialized economy.

The same sort of thing applies even to developed countries. You can't develop your educational system adequately if too many children are coming along. I have noticed that the classroom deficit in the United States had not been reduced but had actually increased in the last year of the last administration. I was once Director-General of UNESCO, and there we are all the time struggling to keep up with the enormous deficiencies of educational systems all over the world; how can we do this when floods of new children are coming along every year?

One thing that science *could* do would be to discover better methods of birth control. That is the key to the whole matter. Physiological and medical science has already brought about what we call "death-control," with the result that population is exploding; but it has not done the necessary converse of this—discovering what to do about birth-control. I would say categorically that the control of population, birth-control applied on a large scale, is a prerequisite for anything that you can call progress and advance in human evolution, even in the immediate future.

The time has now come to think seriously about population policy. We want every country to have a population policy, just as it has an economic policy or a foreign policy. We want the United Nations to have a population policy. We want all the international agencies of the UN to have a population policy.

When I say a population policy, I don't mean that anybody is going to tell every woman how many children she may have, any more than a country which has an economic policy will say how much money an individual businessman is going to make and exactly how he should do it. It means that you recognize population as a major problem of national life, that you have a general aim in regard to it, and that you try to devise methods for realizing this aim. And if you have an international population policy, again it doesn't mean dictating to backward countries or anything of that sort; it means not depriving them of the right (which I should assert is a fundamental human right) to scientific information on birth-control and help in regulating and controlling their increase and planning their families.

It is said that there are three countries which have already a population policy. I think it depends actually upon how you define a country, but if you include colonial territories or areas of similar scope, there are at least four: India, Pakistan, Barbados and Puerto Rico. They have official population policies, and in some cases they have been reasonably successful. It is most important that these countries should be given every aid in pursuing these policies. [Note July 1963: China is now a fifth.]

When it comes to United Nations agencies, one of the great scandals of the present century is that owing to pressure, mainly from Roman Catholic countries, the World Health Organization has not been allowed even to consider the effects of population density on health in its deliberations. This must be reversed.

There is great frustration in the minds of medical men all over the world, especially those interested in international affairs, who, thanks to their devoted labors, have succeeded in giving people information on how to control or avoid disease. Malaria is a striking example. As a result of all this wonderful science and goodwill, population has exploded, and new diseases, new frustrations, new miseries are arising. Meanwhile medical men are not allowed to try to cope with these new troubles on an international scale—and indeed sometimes not even on a national scale. I think I am correct in saying that even in an advanced and civilized country, the United States, there are two States in which the giving of birth-control information, even on medical grounds, is illegal.

I would say that it is essential that this whole question of population policy should be raised in the United Nations itself. (In this connection see United Nations General Assembly Resolution 1838, adopted 18 December, 1962, republished in this volume as a chapter in Part III, Action Programs.) The UN Assembly should be a forum for airing this major problem of our times. It is already a forum for airing other problems—disarmament, atomic warfare, and so on. We must not, out of deference to religious or national or political prejudice, put our heads in the sand or pretend that the problem does not exist. We must get it discussed in the most public way in the world's greatest forums.

We must look at the whole question of population increase not merely as an immediate problem to be dealt with ad hoc, here and now. We must look at it in the light of the new vision of human destiny which human science and learning has revealed to us. We must look at it in the light of the glorious possibilities that are still latent in man, not merely in the light of the obvious fact that the world could be made a little better than it is. We must also look at it in the light of the appalling possibilities for evil and misery that still remain in human life.

I would say that this vision of the possibilities of fruitful fulfillment on the one hand as against frustration resembles the Christian view of salvation as against damnation. And I would indeed say that this new point of view that we are reaching, the vision of evolutionary humanity is essentially a religious one, and that we can and should devote ourselves with truly religious devotion to the cause of ensuring greater fulfillment for the human race in its future destiny. And this involves an all-out attack on the problem of population; for the control of population is, I am quite certain, a prerequisite for any radical improvement in the human lot.

## Part One

# THE POPULATION CRISIS

❍ ❍ ❍ ❍

# The Facts of Population Growth

❍ ❍ ❍

## 2.

## GEOGRAPHY AND THE
## WORLD'S POPULATION

*by C. Langdon White*

The distribution of the world's more than 3 billion people is strikingly uneven. Some areas literally swarm with humanity, others are empty or nearly so, while still others run the gamut between these two extremes. In brief, about one-half of the world's people are concentrated on a mere 5% of the earth's surface whereas 57% of the land supports only 5% of the people.

Why is it that human beings have not scattered themselves more widely and more evenly over the earth? Is this a matter of human preference or does the natural environment invite here and repel there? If man can make a living anywhere on earth and still if so much of it is virtually empty, is there any reason to be greatly concerned over the world's so-called population problem? The answer to the question—*where man is in what total numbers and why*—is undeniably the most important, the most significant in the field of human geography. In the long run, the limiting factor to population growth is the amount of arable land. Too many people forget that despite the fantastic contributions of science and technology *everything* man uses comes from the earth. The size of the arable area and the size and quality of the natural resources are more or less definite and limited. Man must begin here!

Hence human geography is vitally concerned with the problem of population. The purpose of this chapter is to 1) point out why certain areas support a disproportionate number of the world's total population, 2) explain why huge segments of the earth are empty or nearly so, and 3) suggest reasons why man will experience difficulty feeding his increasing numbers (150,000 per day) unless he does something about his birthrate. The startling increase in world population has resulted not from higher birthrates, but from falling deathrates, particularly since World War II.

### A BRIEF LOOK AT THE LAND

The earth's land surface from the standpoint of terrain is divisible into four principal classes: *plains,* which comprise 41%, *plateaus,* which

11

make up 33%, *hill country*, which constitutes 14%, and *mountains*, which cover 12%. If topography were the sole criterion of land use, we would have little to worry about, for two-thirds of the land area would be adapted to agriculture—95% of the plains, 75% of the plateaus, 25% of the hill country, even 5% of the mountains. *But topography is not the sole determinant:* climate and soil must be considered also for they restrict significantly the land suitable for farming to a startling one-fourth of the earths total land area *(Fig. 1)*. Thus many plains are unable to support agriculture and hence any considerable number of people because of cold, aridity, inaccessibility, or swamps; while the hot humid lands cannot be regarded as non-food crop lands, large segments remain unproductive and sparsely populated, and they are regarded as "problem lands." Whereas the Philippines and Java are densely populated, interior Brazil and New Guinea are nearly empty. These notable contrasts invite inquiry into their causes and into the food crop potential of enormous areas now almost unpopulated but apparently well suited climatically to food crop production and capable of supporting dense populations.[1]

If crops are to do well, there must be at least 15 inches of precipitation in middle latitudes and 40 inches in the tropics, where evaporation is high. Length of the frostless season also definitely limits the areas of the earth suitable for crops. Even where topography and climate are favorable, enormous areas are sub-marginal for agriculture because of infertile soils; witness the vast reaches of podzol soils in the North American and Eurasian taiga, of the extensive lateritic soils in the rainy tropics, and of raw sand in the Sahara, in Arabia, and elsewhere.

### THE POPULOUS LANDS

Man is most densely settled on lands below 1500 feet—that is, on expansive plains and flood plains and even on low plateaus and hills. These lands are to be found in middle latitudes, in the subtropics and in a few areas in the tropics. The lands that support the largest numbers of human beings are Asia, Africa and Latin America. These lands, which contain two-thirds of mankind, have very high birthrates, and the masses of the people have an extremely low level of living. In recent years as a result of medical science and sanitation, the death rates have fallen sharply. In fact this is the main reason for the world population explosion. Population is dense too in Western Europe and eastern North America and reasonably dense in parts of Australasia. Together these lands contain about one-fifth of the world's people. All have low death rates: birth rates, however, are high in some areas, but low in others. Nowhere is there concern currently regarding the ability of the people to produce the essentials of life. These are the lands where nature is kind and provides climatic, topographic, and soil conditions more directly suitable to the production of food crops.

Comprising the third group are the countries of eastern and south-eastern Europe, Spain, Japan, and several South American nations. They too contain about one-fifth of the world's population. They have moderate death rates but high enough birth rates to yield a rather high rate of

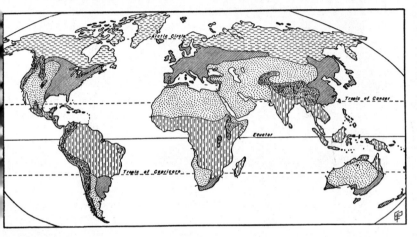

LEGEND

FAVORABLE

TOO COLD
Arctic & Subarctic

TOO DRY
Desert & Semi-desert

TOO HOT
Wet Tropics & Savanna

TOO HIGH
MT. Climates

FIG. 1. Areas of the world hospitable and hostile to man's occupance.
(From R. H. Fifield & G. S. Pearcy, *Geopolitics in Principle and Practice,* Boston: Ginn and Company.)

increase. Recently Japan and Hungary, in this group, have ranked among those nations with the lowest human fertility.

### THE SPARSELY SETTLED LANDS

Figure 2 shows the parts of the world regarded as non-food-producing. With three notable exceptions,[2] they are in the so-called restrictive environments—high mountains, deserts, ice caps, and tundras. Any increase in population (native and foreign) in these areas encounters serious obstacles, some at present insuperable. For the most part, man has here only outposts.

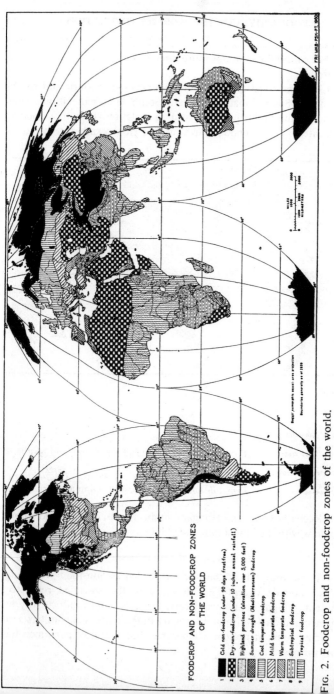

FOODCROP AND NON-FOODCROP ZONES
OF THE WORLD

1  Cold non-foodcrop (under 90 days frost-free)
2  Dry non-foodcrop (under 10 inches annual rainfall)
3  Highland provinces (elevation over 5,000 feet)
4  Summer drought (Mediterranean) foodcrop
5  Cool temperate foodcrop
6  Mild temperate foodcrop
7  Warm temperate foodcrop
8  Subtropical foodcrop
9  Tropical foodcrop

Boggy homographic equal-area projection

Boundaries generally as of 1939

FIG. 2.  Foodcrop and non-foodcrop zones of the world.

(Reprinted from "*A World Map of Food Crop Climates*," pp. 285-295. Food Research Institute Studies, Vol. I, No. 3, November 1960, with permission of the publishers, Food Research Institute, Stanford University. © Copyright 1960 by the Board of Trustees of the Leland Stanford Junior University).

*High mountains.* Rugged surfaces, shallow stony soils, and limited flat land, conspire to restrict arable land in the mountain parts of the earth to 5%. Inhospitable climate due to high altitude, keeps population to very small numbers. The tropics are an exception, for there elevation lifts the people into a temperate climate; e.g., mile-high Mexico City. Even in Peru's Sierra, which man has occupied for centuries, the Indians are living mostly in valleys and high plateaus rather than on high mountains; nowhere are the Indians growing crops, even hardy ones, above 14,000 feet. Above this elevation, human beings live only by grazing sheep, llamas, and alpacas. The highest permanent habitation on earth is in Peru at an altitude of 17,100 feet; and the farther man goes from the equator, the more inhospitable high mountains become; in high latitudes they are wholly unoccupied.

*Deserts.* The world's deserts are presently among the most sparsely populated of all lands. Only a minuscule portion of most deserts is under cultivation, a situation that bids fair to persist, since water is scarce and in the desert it is water that means life. So expansive are these lands that food production is ruled out from about one-fifth of the land surfaces of the globe. Even when the small "islands" made productive by irrigation are added, the world's deserts probably have not more than 2 to 5% of their total areas cultivable. It is estimated that deserts comprise 17% of the world's land area and 2.6% of the world's population.

No one at this time really knows what the freshening of sea water may mean to reclamation of the world desert lands; however, if such water is to be utilized for irrigation, the price must be reduced from the present $1.25 per 1000 gallons to about 25 cents. In the United States even should the cost of desalinated water be reduced to 25 cents per 1000 gallons, it would cost farmers $80 an acre foot for irrigation against the current price (the highest price) of about $5.

*The Cold Lands.* These comprise two categories, the ice caps and the tundras. Together they cover about 29% of the world's land surface but have a mere 0.7% of the world's population.

*The Ice Caps.* Antarctica, most of Greenland, and several smaller ice-covered areas are empty of population. Though Antarctica is almost twice the size of the United States, it *has not one single permanent human inhabitant!* Since it is the coldest place on earth (the lowest surface temperature ever recorded was at the South Pole, −102° F), and since it is covered with ice and snow, it is indeed difficult to see how any economic basis for settlement ever can be established there. Yet these ice caps make up one-fifth of the land surface thus ruling out food production there.

*Tundras.* Tundras cover millions of square miles in the Arctic, but human numbers are small. Agriculture is next to impossible, for the frostless season is too short for the majority of crops to reach the harvestable stage, most soils are infertile, drainage in summer is unbelievably bad, and isolation is appalling. The growing of crops is expected to inch slowly poleward into the southern fringe of the tundra but the intrusion will be small.

Up to the present time, neither the United States nor Canada has deemed it worthwhile to invest heavily in tundra agricultural enterprises. Their lands are in wilderness and are utilized by natives, chiefly Eskimos, for hunting and trapping. The widely scattered population, averaging less than one person to the square mile, is costly to maintain. In 1962 Canada announced that the most expensive citizens in the world were her Eskimos. In northern Fennoscandia the Lapps in small numbers live by grazing reindeer. The Soviet Union, conversely, makes spectacular claims regarding her achievements in the tundra at advanced agricultural experiment stations. Yet the *Great Soviet Atlas* shows no settlement of as many as 50,000 acres north of the northern limit of agriculture established in 1913. To be sure some farming is being carried on along the coasts of the Barents Sea and near the mouths of the larger rivers —the Ob and Yenesei and on areas once regarded as waste land north of the Arctic Circle on the Lena, the Kolyma, and the Indigarka. However, spots must be carefully selected by farmers thoroughly familiar with the vagaries of the climate so as to be protected from cold north winds. Moreover, only quick-ripening crops can be grown—cabbage, broccoli, turnips, spinach, radishes, lettuce, etc. In Finland and Sweden, farmers are plowing land that had lain under ice for centuries. In 1956, coastal Greenland began to experiment with the Inca cereal, quinua, which grows higher than any other grain in the Andes of Bolivia and Peru, and recently the United Nations announced that more than 1 million acres of Arctic lands are now producing food crops by scientific methods. Yet this is little more than a speck on the great tundra wilderness. In this habitat, man is primarily a hunter, trapper, or fisher, occupations that require much land—70 to 200 square miles to sustain a single person. Because the pastures are poor and need resting, even graziers must be nomadic.

*Wet Tropical Lowlands.*[3] Enormous portions of these lands are empty or almost so. The Amazon Basin averages less than one person to the square mile; even this small population can scarcely feed itself. Java, on the other hand, is one of the most densely populated areas on earth. But it possesses volcanic soils of high nutrient status and the Dutch introduced scientific agriculture.

The sparsity of people over sizeable areas of the Wet Tropics result from many circumstances: disease, enervating climate, poor water supply, infertile soils, dense forest cover, poverty, dearth of implements, lack of incentive, and reluctance to change their ways.[4]

Too poor to learn, too ignorant to improve, too frightened to try, a large mass of tropical peasantry is seemingly doomed to an endless round of inadequacy. Here and there a spark may be kindled, now and then an improvement made; but in spite of a growing awareness of the outside world, such people may still present a considerable drag to any progressive force.[5]

As the eminent French geographer and authority on the tropics, Pierre Gourou, has emphasized, it will not be easy for tropical natives to raise their level of living even if they obey nature's directions; it will be utterly impossible, however, for them to do so if they disregard them. In short, we do not yet know how to handle these lands.

For the most part, the hot wet lands have repelled the white man: perhaps he may win them in time but even this is problematical. Such lands are too hot and too humid for comfort and progress; many of the same obstacles that impede the native populations are applicable also to the white population.

Many of the diseases are in the process of being conquered, however. Tropical medicine is making sensational progress. Since World War II the World Health Organization has treated and cured millions. It is attempting to stamp out 50 million cases of yaws from the world—half of them from Africa. It is also fighting a war against malaria—the world's costliest disease and its greatest cause of disablement. As a result of this war, the number of people who annually fall ill from malaria has dropped from 250 million to 140 million. WHO experts believe that within 10 years malaria can be eradicated from the earth (tropical Africa excepted· for the time being). Along with several other agencies, WHO is slowly but surely driving the tsetse fly, slayer of cattle and killer of men, from the huge sweep of Africa where it has prevailed for ages—an area half as large again as the entire continent of Australia.

No great numbers of people are expected to migrate to the Rainy Tropics until life there can be much improved. Betterment involves progress in transport and communication, public health, food, water supply, and an over-all improvement in level of living. Such progress would require capital of a size possessed by no tropical governments. The job is positively staggering and probably will continue to be so for decades, perhaps forever.

Much of the ill health results from poor food and contaminated water and ill health contributes to low economic status. When people are ill and weak from starvation or near-starvation, they cannot work and produce as they could if well and sustained by a satisfactory diet.

Probably the strongest argument against the wet tropics as a permanent home for white people is the current trend in pioneering. Even if science and medicine should be successful in banishing diseases that presently impede progress, white people *prefer* a cool climate to a hot one. What emigrants *desire* and not what they can or could do, determines the trend of population.

## OVERPOPULATION AND UNDERPOPULATION

In discussions of population, much is heard regarding overpopulation and underpopulation. Persons who do not tunnel under the surface in their thinking tend to be of the opinion that the sparsely populated lands afford the safety valve for the densely populated ones and hence that there is no serious problem. Density *per se,* however, does not necessarily imply overpopulation nor does sparsity guarantee underpopulation. If the degree and skill in the sparsely populated country be low, that country possibly is overpopulated; conversely, if the skill be high and the natural resources base strong, very high densities may occur without overpopulation. Moreover, the sparsely settled and virtually empty lands are those whose climates particularly make even subsistence agriculture highly speculative and often impossible.

## INDUSTRIALIZATION: THE PANACEA?

The answer to population pressure by encroachment onto and development of new lands does not appear promising: all the best grasslands are already occupied. As already noted, lands in restrictive environments show little promise at least for the immediate future (Fig. 1), and the lands already densely occupied may reach a saturation point—at least. those in the under-developed category such as China, India, and Pakistan.

What then can be done? Many regard industrialization as the way out. The literature dealing with population and underdeveloped lands invariably preaches this credo. But is industrialization the magic wand? The writer does not think so. Modern industry cannot be superimposed upon the feudalistic society of underdeveloped lands. Many of these countries are limited by a lack, or at least a paucity, of fuel and power, by low wages, dearth of skilled workers, poorly developed transport, scarcity of capital, hostile or at least unfavorable climates, lean raw materials base, and all kinds of social obstacles and man-made economic difficulties. Neither undue ambition nor unbridled enthusiasm by political and social leaders can supply bases for industrialization if these are wanting. Many times underdeveloped nations have embarked on ambitious projects without adequate information, disregarding the bases operative in the scientific location of industry upon which success depends. The sporadic voices of caution invariably are ignored.[6] Those in power are extremely sensitive to any criticism of their programs. Undeniably the industrial fetish dies hard. However with the years, the weaknesses and strengths of hothouse industrialization are becoming more apparent.

Industrialization in nearly all underdeveloped countries faces five major difficulties:

1) The prevailing biting poverty and widespread illiteracy of the people which restrict the market for fabricated products and reduce the supply of skilled workers to man the plants.

2) Scarcity of local capital. Capital from the masses is an illusion; the majority of the people live too close to the level of bare subsistence to have funds for creating new real capital. Accordingly, for many years to come industrialization must depend to a very considerable degree upon foreign capital. However, for foreign capital to enter a given country, the investment climate must be good and the political situation must be reasonably stable. Elmer W. Pehrson, authority on mineral economics, states that very few underdeveloped countries have realistic laws and regulations that encourage private capital to invest in the development of minerals.[7]

3) The prevalent concept of national self-sufficiency—that a country must have industrial plants and that these must make use of domestic raw materials even at high cost. It is difficult, for example, to understand how countries like Argentina and Egypt can justify from an economic standpoint, integrated iron and steel plants.

4) Inadequate transportation. With few exceptions railroads are so poorly integrated with the settlement pattern that the movement of goods is extremely costly. In some countries the railroads may be of several gauges.

5) The scarcity of technological know-how. In many countries this deficiency is being corrected. Hundreds of young men are learning skills in the United States, Western Europe, and the USSR. It must be remembered, however, that industrialization is not spontaneous but is a process of social change that takes place over a considerable period of time.

### SUMMARY AND OUTLOOK

It has been pointed out that only about 25% of the earth's land surface possesses geographic conditions suitable for human life and for the production of food for human consumption. If it be true that human population will probably double by the year 2000 and if now two-thirds of the world's people are hungry, then the future points to trouble—deep trouble, for in the great world race food supply is no match for population.

Even the foreign aid programs are threatened by the intolerable living standards of the two-thirds of humanity in large parts of Asia, Africa, and Latin America constantly in want. They are the product of a sharp decline in the death rate unaccompanied by a sharp decline in the birth rate.

The writer does not agree with the proponents of the cornucopia school that whenever mankind gets into trouble—even deep trouble— science and technology will rescue him. The major problem currently is to feed adequately, both in number of calories and nutritionally, all peoples on this earth. The intensity of production will increase and yet there is indisputably a maximum, measureable extent of the cultivable area. Geography's great contribution could be a world land-use survey. As L. Dudley Stamp has pointed out, the problem of the underdeveloped lands is not one to be solved by government decree; rather it is a problem that will persist for decades, generations, perhaps centuries.

There is no measurability available for man's multiplication. His numbers in the final analysis thus will depend upon the carrying capacity of the earth. Man must learn to get along with what nature has provided. He will be able to increase his numbers greatly but with a falling level of living. One of man's biggest jobs is to learn to control himself. Unless he can do this, all his accomplishments will be for naught. The path of life is strewn with the bones of those who failed to make the necessary adjustments to the times. We do know that man is capable of making the adjustments to his time. What we do not know is whether he will do so before it is too late.

3.

# HOW MANY PEOPLE HAVE EVER LIVED ON EARTH?

*by Annabelle Desmond*

How many people have ever been born since the beginning of the human race?

Reprinted from February 1962 issue of the *Population Bulletin*, published by Population Reference Bureau, 1755 Massachusetts Ave., N.W., Washington 36, D.C. (This article was based on a research report prepared by Fletcher Wellemeyer with the technical assistance of Frank Lorimer, and on supplemental research by Georgine Ogden. The *Bulletin*, which represents a unique cooperative undertaking, makes available to the general reader various aspects of the world population crisis.)

What percentage does the present world population of three billion represent of the total number of people who have ever lived?

These questions are frequently asked the Population Reference Bureau's Information Service. Because of the perennial interest and because of the credence sometimes given to what would seem to be unrealistic appraisals, this issue presents an estimate prepared by Fletcher Wellemeyer, Manpower, Education and Personnel Consultant, Washington, D.C., with Frank Lorimer of American University, Washington, D.C., acting as advisor. This estimate, based on a certain statistical, historic and demographic assumptions set forth in an appendix, should be regarded as no more than a reasonable guess. It assumes that man first appeared about 600,000 years ago, a date which has been proposed for the dawn of the prehistoric era. However, this date obviously is a compromise, anthropologically speaking, between varying extremes.

Since then, it is estimated that about 77 billion babies have been born. Thus, today's population of approximately three billion is about 4.0% of that number.

Absolutely no information exists as to the size and distribution of prehistoric populations. Presumably they were not large, nor very widely distributed. If the 600,000 B.C. date is accepted as a sound compromise, then only about 12 billion people—less than one sixth of the total number ever born—are estimated to have lived before 6,000 B.C.

Anthropologists and paleontologists differ by hundreds of thousands of years as to when man first walked this earth. Recent discoveries strongly suggest that the life-span of the human species might date back as much as two million years. However, this time-scale has not yet been accepted by all anthropologists.

If the "beginning" actually extended a million years prior to 600,000 B.C., the estimated number of births prior to 6,000 B.C. would be 32 billion, and the estimated total number, about 96 billion.

Prior to 1650, historical population data are very scanty for every part of the world. Despite this lack of knowledge, ancillary evidence exists which reveals the general pattern of human growth. Throughout the thousands of centuries which preceded the present technological age, human survival was such a touch-and-go affair that high fertility was essential to balance brutally high mortality. The human female—a relatively slow breeder, even among mammals—had to reproduce somewhere near her physiological limit in order for the family, the clan, the tribe and the nation to survive.

As human culture developed over the ages, the chances of survival tended to improve. When the invention of agriculture provided a more stable food supply, the base was laid for the maintenance of large populations and for their spread into new areas. However, high death rates continued to check population growth.

Until recently, at least a half of all babies born died before reaching maturity. Man's quest for some formula to avert death included magic, incantations and prayers, but none of these had shown any efficacy against the major killers. Then, with the advance of modern science, the mortality pattern of a million years was broken.

Jenner's dramatic discovery of vaccination for smallpox was the first of a multitude of discoveries destined to defer death, especially in infancy and childhood. This brilliant application of the scientific method to biology and medicine, together with improved agricultural technology, better transportation and the vast and complex nexus of an emerging industrial culture, set in motion forces which drastically lowered death rates and thereby greatly increased the efficiency of reproduction. In some countries, the birth rate declined also, although more slowly than the death rate. During the 19th century, the industrial countries of the West were the first to experience the transition from high to low birth and death rates. The transition took about 150 years.

These epochal changes profoundly altered the patterns of survival and population growth. In those countries of northern Europe and North America which were the first to exploit effectively the new medical discoveries, life expectancy at birth rose rapidly from 30 years to 40, then to 50, and, by 1960, to 70 years and more. Infant mortality declined drastically: now, 95 out of every 100 babies born in Western industrial countries live to reach adulthood.

Although the power to defer death is one of the greatest advances in man's long history, it has been the principal factor in the acceleration in the rate of population growth during the past century. Now, public health programs reach even the world's remote villages, and death rates in the less developed areas are falling rapidly. But the traditionally high birth rates—so essential to offset the high death rates of even the very recent past—remain high. Thus, population growth soars.

Therefore, over the long span of history, the rate of population growth has tended to accelerate—almost imperceptibly at first; then slowly; and recently, at a rapid clip. By the beginning of the Christian era, 200-300 million people are believed to have lived on earth. That number had grown to some 500 million by 1650. Then the growth curve took a sharp upward trend. By 1850, the world population was more than 1 billion. Today, it is over 3 billion.

The quickening tempo of growth is even more dramatically expressed in doubling time. It took hundreds of thousands of years for world population to reach the quarter-billion mark, at about the beginning of the

Christian era. Over 16 centuries more passed before that number reached an estimated half-billion. It took only 200 additional years to reach one billion, and only 80 more years—to about 1930—to reach two billion. Population growth rates are still going up. During all of the eons of time —perhaps as long as two million years—the human race grew to its present total of three billion. But it will take only 40 years to add the next three billion, according to United Nations estimates. In certain nations and larger areas, populations will double in 25 years or even less, if growth rates remain unchanged.

This historical review traces the proliferation of the human species through three very broad time-spans: Period I extends from 600,000 B.C. to 6,000 B.C.; Period II extends to 1650 A.D.; and Period III, to 1962. These time periods are chosen because the dates mark important epochs in man's cultural development.

It should be emphasized, however, that not all portions of the globe experienced simultaneously the cultural and technological advances which mark these different stages of man's history. When the first European settlement was established in Australia in 1788, the aborigines there were in the Stone Age. Even today, some tribes living in New Guinea and elsewhere still remain at that level.

### PERIOD I—THE OLD STONE AGE

Period I extends from 600,000 to 6,000 B.C. It begins early in the Paleolithic or Old Stone Age and continues to the beginning of the Neolithic or New Stone Age. It is estimated that during this period numbers grew to about five million, that man's birth rate was close to 50 per thousand, and that there was an approximate total of 12 billion births.

Little, if anything, is known about population size during this hunting and gathering stage of man's existence. The total land area of the earth is approximately 58 million square miles. It seems reasonable to assume that not more than 20 million square miles could have been used successfully by the relatively few who inhabited the earth at that time. The consensus of competent opinion indicates that, on moderately fertile soil in a temperate climate, about two square miles per person would be needed for a hunting and gathering economy.

It must be assumed that there were severe limitations on man's numbers during this period; and that his life cycle and average generation were much shorter than they are today. Man existed for the most part in wandering bands in order to survive. Our ancient ancestors were completely subject to all the vagaries of the weather and the ecological cycle of the game animals on which their existence depended. Food shortages were usually endemic, and the ravages of epidemics were routine—although the wide dispersal of the population tended to localize these hazards. Nevertheless, the picture that emerges is one in which births and deaths were roughly balanced, with births perhaps holding a narrow margin.

## The Long Time-Span of Prehistory

Anthropologists and paleontologists are gradually putting together, piece by piece, the great jigsaw puzzle that is the history of early man. Dr. T. D. Stewart, Head Curator of the Department of Anthropology, National Museum in Washington, D.C., points out that only a few fossils of humans who lived in this period have been found. Nevertheless, man's long time-scale is known today with far greater accuracy than ever before, mainly because of the new radioactive dating techniques. According to Dr. Stewart, new discoveries demand new theories or that existing theories be adjusted.

The remains of *Zinjanthropus,* recently found in the Olduvai gorge of Tanganyika by L. S. B. Leakey, Curator of the Coryndon Museum, Nairobi, Kenya, which Leakey believes date back almost two million years, probably do not represent the beginning of the line. *Zinjanthropus* has been called man because he was a toolmaker, in the crudest sense. Since his physical form represents a very early stage of human evolution, it is not advisable to assume so early a beginning for purposes of estimating human population growth.

However, it is generally believed that "man" had reached the point of being able to make simple tools and to talk by a half million or even a million years ago. Though he presumably emerged much earlier, *Homo sapiens* first appeared with great force in Europe sometime between 25,000 and 30,000 years ago. Very little is known about where he came from or about his connection with the Neanderthal people who were one of many types of man to precede him. By 20,000 B.C., he had created the first great art in human history: the magnificent paintings and other artifacts found in certain caves in southern France and northern Spain. He engraved and carved bone and ivory with faithful representations of his women and of the animals he knew so well: the mammoth, the bison and others. These were believed to have had magic significance—to bring fertility to the clan and success to the hunter.

No birth rates or death rates have ever been found on the walls of the prehistoric caves. Thus, what is the puzzle of man to the anthropologist and the paleontologist becomes the engima of man to the demographer. A United Nations Report, *The Determinants and Consequences of Population Trends,* published in 1953, presents a comprehensive survey of world population through the whole of man's history. Readers are referred to it for a more complete historical survey than this limited space permits. The Report states:

That men, using tools, have been living on this planet for at least one hundred thousand years, and possibly for over a million years, is proved by various types of evidence. For example, the definitely human skeletal remains found at Choukoutien, China, in association with artificial stone and bone implements and possible indications of the use of fire, were deposited during the second interglacial period, or earlier. There is evidence, also, that several divergent types of men emerged, some of whom had specialized characteristics which place them outside the ancestral line of all living races today. The Neanderthal people, who were dominant in Europe during the last (Würm) glaciation, were apparently such a divergent race.

### PERIOD II—6000 B.C. TO 1650 A.D.

Starting with the beginning of the New Stone Age, this period extends through the Bronze and Iron periods, through classical antiquity and the Dark Ages, the Renaissance and the Reformation. It is estimated that world population increased one hundredfold during the period, growing from five million to half a billion, and that about 42 billion births occurred.

It is believed that at the beginning of the era the earth was still very sparsely settled and population was widely dispersed. Vast areas of the globe were not inhabited, partly because the last glaciations had just receded.

It was during this period that man began to *produce* food instead of simply consuming what nature had laid before him. In the Near East, he had already passed the stage of the most primitive village-farming communities which grew out of the earliest agriculture with its domestication of animals. Some of these ancient communities developed into the earliest known urban settlements. The development of agriculture with its settled farming community spread to other areas of the earth during this period. Eventually, it was to change drastically man's pattern of survival and his way of life.

The earliest scene of settled village-farming communities appears to have been in the Near East. Robert J. Braidwood, Professor of the Oriental Institute of Chicago, and Field Director of the Jarmo Project, a recently studied archeological site in Iraq, says: "It is probably very difficult for us now to conceptualize fully (or to exaggerate) the consequences of the first appearance of effective food production. The whole range of human existence, from the biological (including diet, demography, disease, and so on) through the cultural (social organization,

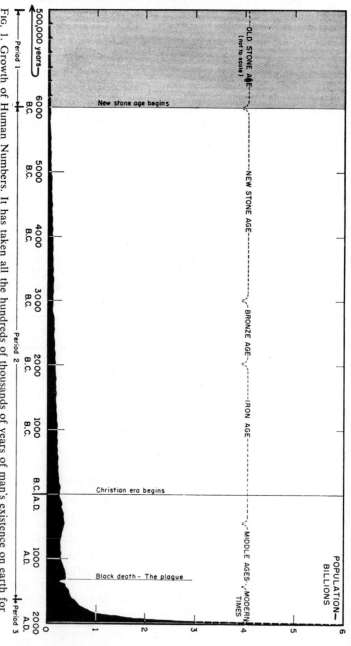

FIG. 1. Growth of Human Numbers. It has taken all the hundreds of thousands of years of man's existence on earth for his numbers to reach three billion. But in only 40 more years population will grow to six billion, if current growth rates remain unchanged. If the Old Stone Age were in scale, its base line would extend 35 feet to the left!

politics, religion, esthetics, and so forth) bands of the spectrum took on completely new dimensions."

Braidwood described the hilly piedmont and intermontane regions surrounding the great "Fertile Crescent" which starts in the valleys of the Tigris and Euphrates Rivers, sweeps around to the north to touch southern Turkey and Syria, then curves south to the shores of the Mediterranean and into Egypt. One radioactive-carbon date suggests that this development was well advanced by 4000 B.C.

Sheep, goats, pigs, cattle and some kind of horse-like animal were used by those living in the area. Their plants were wheat and barley. Braidwood notes that some sort of hybridization or mutation, particularly in domesticated plants, must have taken place before certain species could have been moved to other areas. However, they seem to have moved into the Danube Valley by 4000 B.C., and into western Europe by 2500 B.C.

In other words, man was learning to utilize his environment more efficiently; thus it could support more people than ever before. But numbers were still regulated by the food-producing quality of the land. Population grew in times of plenty and declined when food became scarce and when disease decimated large populations, as it did in Europe during the Dark Ages.

During the Bronze Age, man began to use copper and bronze and to build towns, cities and states. Kings, advanced religions, social classes, writing, and enduring monuments, such as the Nile pyramids, appeared during this period. The Iron Age brought iron metallurgy, the invention of the alphabet, the use of coined money, and the spread of commerce and navigation.

The early and great empires and cultures developed: those of Egypt, Rome and Greece; of King Asoka in India; of the Han dynasty in China; and, later, the empires of the Mayas and the Incas in the New World. The Hindu, Confucian, Buddhist, Jewish, Christian, Muslim and other great religions emerged.

### The City—Period II

The great cities of ancient times rose in rich valleys adjacent to the Mediterranean, the Red Sea and the Persian Gulf, along the Indus and the Nile, and along the Yangtze in China. The first great urban civilization arose about 3500 B.C. in Mesopotamia, along the Tigris and Euphrates. Another grew up in Egypt before 3000 B.C. and still another in Crete. A fourth arose along the banks of the Indus in western India, but whether this grew directly out of Neolithic beginnings or was a transplant of the Sumerian culture of Mesopotamia is a matter of dispute. Urban civilizations developed in China at a later date, and still later in some areas of tropical Central America and in Peru.

The urban societies of Mesopotamia, China and Egypt maintained complex centralized control of soil and water resources in order to provide irrigation and to control floods. These "hydraulic" civilizations supported very dense populations with highly integrated social systems. The individual peasant was allowed a small land area which produced more food than his family needed. Such civilizations have persisted in Egypt, India, China and elsewhere to the present day, with little change in the economic basis of life but with periodic rises and declines.

The ancient Mediterranean, Asian and American urban civilizations appear to have been isolated flowerings of human culture which culminated in "golden ages" and then declined. The archeological record abundantly reveals their wave-like nature. For additional information, readers are referred to an earlier issue of *Population Bulletin*, "The World's Great Cities: Evolution or Devolution?" (September 1960).

## The A.D. Era of Period II

The United Nations study previously mentioned states that, at the beginning of the Christian era, the world's population was likely to have been between 200 and 300 million people. Discussing the lack of historic demographic information, the Report states:

Various kinds of evidence indicate that man's numbers became adjusted to the food-producing capacity of the land in ancient times—increasing as it rose and declining as it fell. Unfortunately little of this evidence is of a census type, and most of the remainder does not provide a basis for estimating the number of inhabitants of an area. Large parts of the world's population were subject to some sort of census enumeration near the beginning of the Christian era, but the information available from these census has limited value. Roman censuses were taken for administrative purposes and were restricted to "citizens," an expanding category as citizenship rights were extended to outlying regions. Moreover only adult males were included in some of these censuses, while all household members except "children" were included in others. Chinese censuses at about this time provided reports on total population but interpretation of the results involves many difficulties. Elaborate records were kept by the ancient Incas, but their meaning is obscure.

J. C. Russell, Professor of History at the University of New Mexico, who has contributed much to the demographic history of the West, has traced the population changes within the Roman Empire from the second century A.D. to the year A.D. 543, a period he characterizes generally as one of imperial decline:

. . . However, within the general picture there are great differences in the trends. Actually most of the decrease occurred in western Mediterranean lands: Italy, Gaul, Iberia, and North Africa, together with Greece and Egypt.

In Syria the population seems to have held even while in Gaul and Britain something like recovery must have occurred at the end of the period. Eastern Asia Minor and the Slavic area probably increased markedly. The German and Scandinavian spheres apparently held even in spite of emigration. The information about the central, eastern, and northern parts of Europe is so vague and uncertain that there may have been a considerable increase in population. The general rise in temperature should certainly have reduced the semiglacial conditions of the northern countries and made them attractive for grain-growing groups.

In the second and third centuries A.D., Rome suffered two devastating epidemics which have not been identified but their virulence suggests bubonic plague. According to Dr. Russell:

The period from A.D. 543 to 950 probably marks the lowest ebb of population in Europe since the early Roman Empire. It covers the first great attack of the plague, the worst epidemic to strike the area with which we are concerned. Following it came the Mohammedan invasions from the semi-nomadic areas of the lands surrounding the Mediterranean. From the east in the tenth century the Hungarians scourged most of Europe and what they missed was visited by the terrible raids of the Vikings from the north. Some measure of the weakness of the European population is indicated by the feeble defense put up against these invaders by the governments of Europe. . . .

Endemic diseases such as malaria and tuberculosis were prevalent, and the latter was particularly fatal among young people. In fact, the combination of both diseases occurred quite frequently and was highly fatal. Dr. Russell speculates that during the periods of population decline in early medieval Europe, much carefully tilled and drained acreage lapsed into breeding grounds for mosquitoes; and that a period of wet, warm weather about 800-900 A.D. greatly increased the incidence of malaria.

The span of life (extreme length of life) seems to have been around 100 years, as it is now. Those who could avoid infection were likely to live to considerable ages. According to John Durand, Assistant Director in Charge of Population, the United Nations Bureau of Social Affairs, the best basis for making mortality estimates of the Roman period is a study of tombstone inscriptions for males dying between the ages of 15 and 42. This method corrects the exaggeration of years that humans are apt to indulge in, even on tombstones, and allows for the under-representation of children's deaths. On this basis, Durand concludes that life expectancy at birth for the whole population of the Roman Empire was probably only about 25 or 30 years.

After the year 1000, it appears that population began to increase; and, between 1000 and 1348, that growth was phenomenal, particularly in northern Europe. The Empire of Charlemagne had already capitalized on the upward population movement, and stronger governments began to develop in Germany, Scandinavia and even in Russia. The Crusades spread Christianity throughout the Middle East and brought contact between the Muslim and Christian worlds.

Then in 1348, the bubonic plague, which seems to have first appeared in the sixth century in Egypt, suddenly erupted in Europe in a more virulent form, táking a frightful toll of lives. Russell states that "the years 1348-1350 saw a very heavy loss of life, 20 to 25% in most European countries. The decline continued with later epidemics until the population of about 1400 was near 60% of the pre-plague figures. . . ."

TABLE I

*Approximate Population of the World and Its Subdivisions, 1000-1600*
*(in millions)*

| Year | World | Europe | Asiatic Russia | South West Asia | India | China Major* | Japan | South East Asia, Oceania | Africa | The Americas |
|------|-------|--------|----------------|-----------------|-------|--------------|-------|--------------------------|--------|--------------|
| 1000 | 275 | 42 | 5 | 32 | 48 | 70 | 4 | 11 | 50 | 13 |
| 1100 | 306 | 48 | 6 | 33 | 50 | 79 | 6 | 12 | 55 | 17 |
| 1200 | 348 | 61 | 7 | 34 | 51 | 89 | 8 | 14 | 61 | 23 |
| 1300 | 384 | 73 | 8 | 33 | 50 | 99 | 11 | 15 | 67 | 28 |
| 1400 | 373 | 45 | 9 | 27 | 46 | 112 | 14 | 16 | 74 | 30 |
| 1500 | 446 | 69 | 11 | 29 | 54 | 125 | 16 | 19 | 82 | 41 |
| 1600 | 486 | 89 | 13 | 30 | 68 | 140 | 20 | 21 | 90 | 15 |

* China proper, plus Manchuria and Korea, Outer Mongolia, Sinkiang and Formosa.
Source: M. K. Bennett, *The World's Food,* 1954.

Between 1500 and 1700, far-ranging social, economic and intellectual revolutions began which formed the basis for the modern world. The era of medieval authority was first challenged in northern Italy, at the time of the Renaissance. This was followed by the age of discovery, with voyages around Africa and to the New World. At the same time, the Reformation set the stage for the revival of intellectual development in northern Europe. For the first time since the Golden Age of Greece, the human intellect began to look at the world objectively. This led to the birth of the scientific method: new concepts of the nature of matter, energy and, ultimately, of life began to capture the minds of men. Out of this intellectual revolution came powerful new insights which were eventually to greatly change man's pattern of living and dying.

In Europe about the middle of the 17th century—after the end of the Thirty Years' War and the period of peace and stability which followed—agricultural methods improved, slowly at first and then rapidly. New crops were introduced and crops were rotated; manure and fertilizers were used more generally; and the soil was cultivated more extensively.

Even though these more advanced methods increased food production, the margin of plenty continued to be precarious, especially for those who lived in cities. A comparable agricultural expansion seems to have occurred in China at about the same time.

Unfortunately, little is known about population growth and decline during this period for the vast continent of Asia, particularly for India and China. M. K. Bennett, Director of the Food Research Institute, Stanford University, has recognized the need for a continent-by-continent or region-by-region survey. He estimates that world population in 1000 A.D. was somewhere around 275 million, or "probably less than half of the population of Europe in 1949; . . . that there has been one century, the fourteenth, [the century of the Black Death in Europe] in which world population did not increase at all, but declined. . . ."·

The earlier "hydraulic" civilizations became subject to disorders which checked and, in some cases, reversed their population growth.

The Americas had an estimated population of 16 million at the time of their discovery by Columbus. Julian Steward, Research Professor of Anthropology, University of Illinois, has estimated the population of the different regions of the American Hemisphere in 1492 as follows:

| | |
|---|---:|
| North America: | |
| North Mexico | 1,000,000 |
| Mexico | 4,500,000 |
| West Indies | 225,000 |
| Central America | 736,000 |
| South America: | |
| Andean Area | 6,131,000 |
| Remainder | 2,898,000 |
| Total | 15,490,000 |

### PERIOD III—1650—1962 A.D.

If man's existence on earth is viewed as a day, this period is less than a minute. But a fourth or more of all human beings ever born have lived during this brief span.

The period brought a sixfold increase in human numbers: from an estimated half-billion in 1650 to over three billion in 1962. There were approximately 23 billion births during this period—over half as many as in the preceding 76 centuries!

World population doubled between 1650 and 1850, growing beyond the one-billion mark. It doubled again, to reach two billion by 1930, in only 80 years. Since that time, the rate of growth has accelerated steadily. Now over 50 million more people are added each year. If the current rate remains unchanged, today's population will double again in less than 40 years.

A steadily falling death rate, especially during the last century, is mainly responsible for the very rapid acceleration in population growth. It is estimated that during 1650-1750, population was growing at about 0.3% a year; during 1750-1850, at about 0.5%; 1850-1950, at 0.8%. Currently, the rate is somewhere between 1.6 and 1.9%.

This period brings man through to the modern agricultural-industrial age with its tremendous scientific and technological discoveries which have greatly speeded up the rate of social change in the Western world and which have revolutionized agriculture, industry, communication, transportation, etc. These developments have made possible the support of the mammoth populations in numerous areas of the world. However, many of those technological advances are only beginning to touch the less developed areas where living levels for over half of the world's people are only a little, if any, above what they were during much of the earlier history of the race.

For the world as a whole, the mid-17th century is a bench mark in the pattern of population growth. Then, the upward surge in the numbers of people began. Just why the response to the early stirrings of the modern age was so rapid is not entirely clear, though many of the major factors which stimulated the increase in human numbers can be recognized. In Europe, the frightful famines and epidemics that marked the Dark Ages seem to have decreased, although hunger and disease were still endemic. The discovery of the New World opened the way for great transatlantic migrations to the rich, sparsely settled lands of the Americas. To some extent, this relieved the growing population pressure in Europe and provided a new source of food for the Old World. It also gave impetus to the tremendous growth of populations of European origin—at home and in European colonies—which amounted to a ninefold increase during the period.

The development of the scientific method and the application of this new knowledge to technology stimulated the Industrial and Vital Revolutions which so greatly changed man's way of life throughout the Western world. The industrial Revolution brought the transition from agrarian to industrial societies—a transition which is beginning only now for large areas of Africa, Asia and Latin America. The Vital Revolution brought the Western industrial nations through the demographic transition: from high birth and death rates to low birth and death rates.

More facts and learned estimates concerning world population are available for this period since census-taking began during the 17th cen-

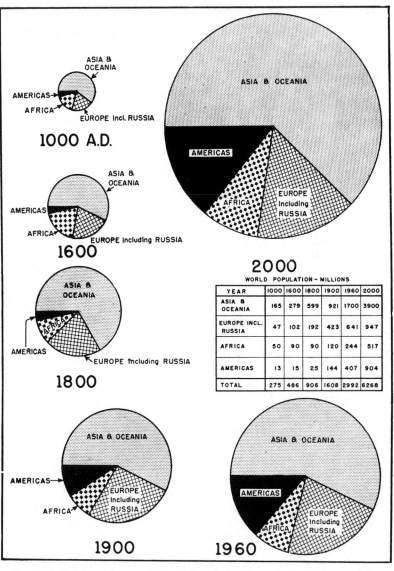

WORLD POPULATION — MILLIONS

| YEAR | 1000 | 1600 | 1800 | 1900 | 1960 | 2000 |
|---|---|---|---|---|---|---|
| ASIA & OCEANIA | 165 | 279 | 599 | 921 | 1700 | 3900 |
| EUROPE INCL. RUSSIA | 47 | 102 | 192 | 423 | 641 | 947 |
| AFRICA | 50 | 90 | 90 | 120 | 244 | 517 |
| AMERICAS | 13 | 15 | 25 | 144 | 407 | 904 |
| TOTAL | 275 | 486 | 906 | 1608 | 2992 | 6268 |

FIG. 2. A Thousand Years of World Population Growth. In 1000 A.D., Asia accounted for 60% of the world's population, Europe, including Russia, for about 17%, Africa, 18% and the Americas, 4%. By 1960, Asia's percentage had declined to somewhat under 60, that of Europe and the USSR had increased to 22% and the Americas, to 14%. Africa's portion declined to 8%. By 2000, Asia may comprise about 65% of the total, Europe and the USSR, 15%, the Americas, 15% and Africa, 8%. Russia includes Asiatic and European Russia.

tury. The first censuses were conducted in 1655 by the French and British in their Canadian colonies. Iceland took a count in 1703, Sweden in 1748 and Denmark in 1769. The United States took its first national census in 1790. Great Britian took its first in 1801.

The first estimate of world population ever to be compiled was published in the 17th century by a Jesuit priest named Riccioli who estimated that one billion people then inhabited the earth: 100 million in Europe,

TABLE II

*Estimates of World Population by Regions, 1650-1960*

| | Estimated population in millions | | | | | | |
|---|---|---|---|---|---|---|---|
| Source of estimates and date | World | Africa | Northern America[a] | Latin America[b] | Asia (excl. USSR)[c] | Europe and Asiatic USSR[e] | Oceania | Area of European Settlement[d] |
| Willcox's estimates: | | | | | | | | |
| 1650 | 470 | 100 | 1 | 7 | 257 | 103 | 2 | 113 |
| 1750 | 694 | 100 | 1 | 10 | 437 | 144 | 2 | 157 |
| 1800 | 919 | 100 | 6 | 23 | 595 | 193 | 2 | 224 |
| 1850 | 1,091 | 100 | 26 | 33 | 656 | 274 | 2 | 335 |
| 1900 | 1,571 | 141 | 81 | 63 | 857 | 423 | 6 | 573 |
| Carr-Saunders' estimates: | | | | | | | | |
| 1650 | 545 | 100 | 1 | 12 | 327 | 103 | 2 | 118 |
| 1750 | 728 | 95 | 1 | 11 | 475 | 144 | 2 | 158 |
| 1800 | 906 | 90 | 6 | 19 | 597 | 192 | 2 | 219 |
| 1850 | 1,171 | 95 | 26 | 33 | 741 | 274 | 2 | 335 |
| 1900 | 1,608 | 120 | 81 | 63 | 915 | 423 | 6 | 573 |
| United Nations estimates: | | | | | | | | |
| 1920 | 1,810 | 140 | 117 | 91 | 966 | 487 | 9 | 704 |
| 1930 | 2,013 | 155 | 135 | 109 | 1,072 | 532 | 10 | 786 |
| 1940 | 2,246 | 172 | 146 | 131 | 1,212 | 573 | 11 | 861 |
| 1950 | 2,495 | 200 | 167 | 163 | 1,376 | 576 | 13 | 919 |
| 1960 | 2,972 | 244 | 200 | 207 | 1,665 | 641 | 16 | 1,064 |

[a] United States, Canada, Alaska, St. Pierre and Miquelon.
[b] Central and South America and Caribbean Islands.
[c] Estimates for Asia and Europe in Willcox's and Carr-Saunders' series have been adjusted so as to include the population of the Asiatic USSR with that of Europe.
[d] Includes northern America, Latin America, Europe and the Asiatic USSR and Oceania.
Source: United Nations, *The Determinants and Consequences of Population Trends*, 1953.

500 million in Asia, 100 million in Africa, 200 million in America and 100 million in Oceania. It appears that Riccioli reported the conjectures of others rather than his own. Other contemporary estimates of the 17th century all range below Riccioli's and one as low as 320 million.

G. King, a 17th-century English scholar, estimating population densities for the various continents, allocated 17 acres per head for Europe, 20 for Asia, 64 for Africa and 129 for America. This yielded a total of 700 million for the world, or 600 million, rejecting a hypothetical southern continent. If correct land areas as now known are substituted, the estimate would be 874 million. It should be noted that this estimate is two thirds higher than the estimate of approximately 500 million accepted by modern scholars.

Even though Asia's population continued to increase during the period, its proportion of world population declined from about 58% in 1650 to 53% in 1920 (excluding the Asiatic part of the USSR). Africa's proportion also declined, from 20% to 8%. But the proportion for Europe, including all of the USSR, rose from 20% to 27%. Since 1920, the proportion for Asia and Africa has again increased, while that for Europe has declined.

Today, the combined population of the Americas is about 400 million. Their proportion of world population increased from approximately 2% in 1650 to 14% at the present time. As previously mentioned, the indigenous American populations were heavily decimated by diseases brought in by Europeans and by wars with early colonizers. Much of the subsequent increase was due to immigration and to the proliferation of the immigrant groups. More recently, the descendants of the indigenous Americans have been increasing rapidly.

## The Demographic Transition of Period III

Application of the scientific method to medical technology brought man the ability to defer death. In the Western industrial countries, this has changed his pattern of survival far more rapidly than any other major social development throughout his long history. Similarly, in the Western world, knowledge about the control of fertility is widespread. As the traditional pattern of high birth and death rates changed to one of low birth and death rates, man's reproductive process has become much more efficient.

In the heavily populated, less developed countries of Africa, Asia and Latin America, the application of scientific techniques to defer death is generally accepted and quite widely practiced; but the control of fertility has not begun to be practiced extensively enough to affect birth rates. As a result, rapidly falling death rates combined with traditionally high birth rates have touched off a surge in the rate of population growth.

Modern public health methods have cut death rates by one third or more in a single year in some countries. With the drastic decline in infant and child mortality, the proportion of the population under 15 years of age tends to increase. It is now over 40% in many of these countries, as compared with about 20% in some countries of western and northern Europe.

It is expected that the growth rate will increase even further in many areas of Africa, Asia and Latin America, as death rates continue to decline. This will surely happen unless effective measures can be devised

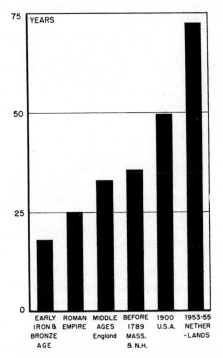

FIG. 3. Life Expectancy Over the Ages. Life expectancy at birth is believed to have been about 18 years in prehistoric times. It has quadrupled today in some of the Western industrialized countries.

(Source: Louis I. Dublin, Alfred J. Lotka and Mortimer Spiegelman, *Length of Life: A Study of the Life Table,* and United Nations, *Demographic Yearbook,* 1960.)

which will speed up the demographic transition and the rate of social change. Simply stated, acceptable measures must be found to bring birth rates into balance with modern low death rates, thereby completing the demographic transition. Unless birth rates are reduced, population growth rates will continue upward until they are checked eventually by a rise in the death rate.

Discussing the present rapid rate of population growth, the latest

United Nations *Demographic Yearbook* points out that approximately one half of the world's population lives in only four countries—China (mainland), India, the USSR and the USA—and that the reliability of world population estimates depends largely on the accuracy of the information available about the population of these countries:

Similarly the 1950-59 average rate of increase, estimated in the range of 1.5 to 2.0% per annum for the four largest populations and 1.6 to 1.9% per annum for the remainder of the world, can be placed, in view of possibly compensating errors, between 1.6 and 1.9% per annum for the world as a whole. . . .

Actually in view of declining mortality, it is virtually certain that the rate of world population growth has now surpassed 1.5% per annum, and quite possible that it has attained 2.0%. Because of this decline of mortality, world population certainly increased in the year 1959 by at least 45 million, and possibly by as much as 55 million. Again it is evident that much of the uncertainty is caused by the lack of precise knowledge regarding the population of China (mainland). Large margins of error must also be allowed for in the estimated annual increases in India, in other parts of Asia, and in Africa.

TABLE III

*Estimated Population and Vital Rates for the World by Region, 1950-1975*

| Continent & Region | Midyear population (millions) 1959 | Annual rate of increase (percent) 1950-1959 | Vital Rates 1955-1959 Birth Rate | Vital Rates 1955-1959 Death Rate | Medium Projection to 1975 (millions) |
|---|---|---|---|---|---|
| WORLD TOTAL | 2,907 | 1.7 | 36 | 19 | 3,830 |
| AFRICA | 237 | 1.9 | 46 | 27 | 303 |
| Northern Africa | 78 | 1.9 | 45 | 26 | 76* |
| Tropical & Southern Africa | 159 | 1.9 | 47 | 28 | 226 |
| AMERICA | 398 | 2.1 | 34 | 14 | 543 |
| Northern America | 196 | 1.8 | 25 | 9 | 240 |
| Middle America | 65 | 2.7 | 45 | 18 | 99 |
| South America | 137 | 2.3 | 42 | 19 | 204 |
| ASIA | 1,622 | 1.8 | 42 | 23 | 2,210 |
| South West Asia | 74 | 2.5 | 46 | 21 | 116 |
| South Central Asia | 546 | 1.8 | 44 | 26 | 737 |
| South East Asia | 208 | 2.1 | 44 | 23 | 280 |
| East Asia | 794 | 1.8 | 39 | 21 | 1,075 |
| EUROPE | 423 | 0.8 | 19 | 10 | 476 |
| Northern & Western Europe | 141 | 0.7 | 18 | 11 | 154 |
| Central Europe | 137 | 0.8 | 19 | 10 | 156 |
| Southern Europe | 145 | 0.9 | 21 | 10 | 166 |
| OCEANIA | 16 | 2.4 | 25 | 9 | 21 |
| UNION OF SOVIET SOCIALIST REPUBLICS | 211 | 1.7 | 25 | 8 | 275 |

* The United Nations estimate for 1975 was surpassed by 1959; and it has issued no new projections for this area.
Source: United Nations, *Demographic Yearbook*, 1960, and *The Future Growth of World Population*, 1958.

The Chinese census of 1953 is very difficult to appraise and might introduce an error of as much as 90 million in the present world population!

## What is Past is Prologue

Since man first appeared on earth, human arithmetic has moved from a relatively simple exercise in addition to a complicated one of geometric progression. It took all of the vast reaches of time to build today's population of slightly over three billion. But it will take only 40 more years for population to reach six billion, if the present growth rates remain unchanged.

It is noteworthy that the desire to control fertility has never had the emotional imperatives which brought the power over death. Only modest efforts have been made thus far to discover effective methods of fertility control which would be acceptable to the people of all cultures and religions. Less than modest efforts have been made to disseminate what knowledge is now available to all of the world's people who would benefit from that knowledge. Consequently, during the past decade of rapid death-rate decline in the less developed countries, there has been no measurable reduction in high birth rates; so population growth has increased.

Rapid population growth cannot be maintained indefinitely in any part of the world. If birth rates do not decline in overcrowded lands, death rates eventually will rise to check growth.

The gulf which exists today between the peoples of the world has widened: life is better than ever before for those who live in the Western industrial countries. But the majority of the world's people still live close to the subsistence level, in poverty and squalor reminiscent of the Middle Ages. If the demographic transition to a balance between low birth and death rates could be hastened in the less developed countries, this gulf might yet be bridged in time to avert a Malthusian disaster.

# Economic, Social and Political Analysis

❍ ❍ ❍

4.

## ADDRESS TO THE ECONOMIC AND SOCIAL COUNCIL OF THE UNITED NATIONS

*by Eugene R. Black*

I am making my annual report to you in a period when world tensions are particularly acute. Like millions of other people, I have been following events in this United Nations building with deep and anxious concern over the past 12 months. I am aware, of course—as all of us are—that the political difficulties with which the United Nations is struggling are reflections in many cases of economic problems; no lasting political solutions can be expected until much more is done to remedy the economic ills which afflict so many countries.

In these circumstances it is all the more important that the Economic and Social Council should continue to seek cooperation among nations to deal with the financial problems of our time. It is now acknowledged everywhere that much more assistance must be rendered to the less developed countries by those more fortunately placed. . . . But there is a limit to the funds that capital-exporting countries are willing to provide. There are also movements in the less developed countries themselves which vitiate all efforts to raise world living standards. One of the most massive of these obstacles is the tremendous rise in the populations of already crowded countries.

Three hundred years ago there were probably no more than 500 million people alive in the world, and the total was increasing only slowly. This stability was maintained by an uneasy balance between high birth rates and death rates. Many babies were born, but many also died. Living conditions were such that many of the remaining children failed to survive beyond the age of thirty.

In Europe, the picture began to change in the late eighteenth century.

This is the major portion of an address to the Economic and Social Council of the United Nations, New York City, April 24, 1961, by Eugene R. Black, then President of the World Bank. The full text of the address is given in the original hardback edition of this book, *The Population Crisis and the Use of World Resources,* Stuart Mudd, Editor, The Hague, Dr. W. Junk Publishers, 1964, and Bloomington, Indiana University Press, 1964, pp. 63-72.

Populations began to grow, sometimes very fast. Elsewhere the balance of new lives against deaths has been upset largely in our own lifetime. The pattern has been a steep fall in death rates, with birth rates little changed. But the circumstances have been somewhat different from the earlier European experience. The population revolution has often been achieved very cheaply. In Ceylon, to take the best-known example, the expenditure of $2 a head on a public health campaign with the prime purpose of eradicating malaria reduced the death rate by three-quarters over a single decade. Similar stories can already be told of public health programs undertaken in other countries, and there will undoubtedly be more in the future.

Of course we welcome this trend, whatever the problems it may set for us. We all want to reduce the suffering and waste involved in premature death or disabling disease, and we can expect death rates to go on falling in the developing countries. Medical science continues to discover increasingly effective ways of promoting public health, and since governments can usually act on behalf of the community in putting these new techniques to work, we may expect them to be applied as soon as the money can be found to pay the accompanying bill. People will live longer in the future.

But if only 20 people—or even fewer—in every thousand are henceforth to die each year, then a birth rate of 40 per thousand, which formerly just kept the population steady, will bring an explosive growth in numbers. And there is little reason to suppose that birth rates will soon decline to match the fall in death rates. It is much simpler to attack disease than it is to alter the reproductive pattern of a society. Medicine has yet to make available a cheap and easy method of regulating births. And not everyone wants fewer children.

*          *

What view are we to take of all this?

I am not convinced that population growth will eventually outrun the development of the world's resources. It is true that at present rates of consumptions we will use up the known reserves of several important fuels and minerals within a few decades. Heavy demands will certainly be made on our agricultural resources, and there may be acute difficulty in organizing the movement of food and other necessities about the world on the scale required to meet the needs of a population twice its present size. But I am inclined to think that those prophets who forecast the exhaustion of the earth's resources, underestimate the ingenuity of man and the potentialities of science. And I am not too disturbed about the long-run problems of feeding the extra persons we expect, although I find myself a little out of sympathy with some of our professional agricultural optimists—it seems to me Utopian to expect that every country will be cultivated as efficiently as Denmark, and that thereby, the world could easily feed twice its present population.

But all this does not mean that we ought to welcome population growth on the scale that we see it today.

Some people argue that a big population implies a good market for the businessman's product: he can use mass production techniques and charge low prices. They insist, too, that with a growing population, the businessman constantly finds demand exceeding his estimates. Optimism and production run high; new products win ready acceptance, while obsolete industries die painlessly; the incentive to invest is strong; and social mobility and change are encouraged. The burden of social costs is spread widely. By contrast, they suggest, a declining or even stationary population brings pessimism and economic stagnation; there is insufficient reward for private enterprise, and the state is thereby forced to intervene increasingly in fields better left to the private citizen.

This body of theory may conceivably be true in the circumstances of a rich country with resources to spare. But it is wildly irrelevant to the problems of most developing countries today.

It is, of course, a fact that some of the poorer countries do not have domestic markets big enough to support mass production industries. But it is clearly ridiculous to suggest that inadequate population is holding back the development of, say, India, which packs more than twice the population of the United States into less than half the space. Where most people go barefoot for lack of shoes, industry is not failing to grow because its products are not wanted. Where the agricultural laborer can find work to occupy him for only half the year, no further pressure is needed to make him wish for a different occupation. Where two-thirds of every dollar of income must be spent on food, where manufacturing industry is almost nonexistent, one need not worry that excessive saving will lead to under-employment of resources. The lash of further poverty is not required to drive these people to action. The developing countries need many things—not only capital, but the skills and health to make good use of it. By no means do all of them need population growth.

\*        \*

But need it or not, they have it. They should ask themselves if they can afford it. In Asia, in the Middle East, in Latin America, in Africa, the population of most countries is growing at the rate of 2% annually—and sometimes 3½% or more. In most of Latin America and Africa there is fortunately room for the extra people. In the long run, although not now, there should also be adequate resources available to feed, clothe and house them. But in many parts of Asia and the Middle East, resources are few, and there is not nearly enough room. Agricultural land which once sufficed to support a stationary and much smaller population has already been divided and subdivided beyond the limits of effective cultivation. Cities are crowded to bursting, and are still getting bigger.

Population growth on this scale would be a serious challenge to a country with adequate living standards. Where incomes are very low, and economic development is a desperate need, such growth can be a crippling handicap.

The speed at which a country develops depends largely upon its ability to direct its growing resources to investment rather than to consumption, to uses which will raise tomorrow's output rather than satisfy today's demands. A poor society finds it difficult to save at all, and will be doing well if it can set aside 10% of its income. At this rate, if its population is growing, it will barely be investing enough to stay where it is. Yet the likelihood must be that it will invest not more than 10%, but less: a growing population with a high proportion of dependent children will find it increasingly difficult to spare any of its income from consumption.

Unless foreign aid can be increased, a country in this position is faced with a stark alternative. It must reduce its savings, or lower its living standards—although both are already inadequate.

The industrialized countries have shown their willingness to help. Common humanity and self-interest alike impel them to do so. All the evidence points to a greater flow of aid in the coming years. But I find myself increasingly doubtful whether domestic savings and foreign aid together will be sufficient to allow real progress, if present rates of population growth continue for long.

Figures are hard to come by in this field. But it may be possible to indicate some orders of magnitude.

Some calculations have been made about the cost of providing houses in India during the next generation, if the population continues to grow at its present rate of about 2% a year. If you disregard the cost of rural housing, on the somewhat optimistic assumption that it can be carried out entirely with local materials and labor, then you still have to pay for the homes of nearly 200 million extra people who, it is expected, will be living in India's cities 25 years hence. Making full allowance for the fact that many of the extra persons will be children needing not new houses, but simply more space in existing households, a sober estimate of the cost suggests that in the 30 years between 1956 and 1986 a total investment in housing of the order of 118 billion rupees, or roughly $25 billion, will be needed. If you find a figure like that difficult to grasp, I may say that it is well over four times the total lent by the World Bank in all countries since it started business 15 years ago. Put another way, it is more than 30 times the initial resources of the International Development Association—and those resources are supposed to cover IDA's first five years of operations.

My cost estimate takes no account of the need to improve existing housing in such cities as Calcutta. It leaves out the cost of roads, sewage systems, water supplies and other services. Yet the problems of urban growth form only a small part of the challenge presented when economic development is attempted in the context of a vast expansion in population.

In the social field, many more new hospitals and clinics will be needed, simply to maintain present standards—standards which by common consent are sadly inadequate. Far more must be spent on education. Here look again at India, not because its problems are unusual, but because they are well documented. In 1956, about 31 million Indian children were getting an education—less than 40% of those of school age. It is mathematically certain that if the population grows as expected, a three or fourfold increase in educational investment will be needed if all children are to be receiving an education by 1976. When you come to productive investment, the story is similar. Enormous investments will be needed. But population growth does not only tend to reduce the flow of investment funds. It also means that the capital invested in industry must be spread increasingly thinly over the labor force: each pair of hands is backed by fewer dollars of capital. Productivity suffers, and the gap in living standards between the developing and the industrialized countries widens, instead of narrowing.

I must be blunt. Population growth threatens to nullify all our efforts to raise living standards in many of the poorer countries. We are coming to a situation in which the optimist will be the man who thinks that present living standards can be maintained. The pessimist will not look even for that. Unless population growth can be restrained, we may have to abandon for this generation our hopes of economic progress in the crowded lands of Asia and the Middle East. This is not a field in which international agencies can do much. But there is scope for governments to act: it is time that they gave earnest attention to this threat to their aspirations.

\* \*

Population growth does not alter the rules for successful economic development. On the contrary, it reinforces their strength by increasing the penalties for breaking them. In relation to the need, capital is short, and must be stretched as far as it can possibly go. In the developing countries, therefore, the first question to be asked of any economic policy must be: "Is this the road to maximum economic growth?", and if the answer is

"No" we must look very closely at any doctrines which are put forward to excuse this sacrifice of economic advancement.

For the providers of economic aid, this situation implies a duty not only to see that the money is properly and efficiently applied, but also to guard against the temptation to use development assistance to achieve their own commercial or short-term political objectives, rather than to serve the priority needs of the recipient countries. For the developing countries themselves, it implies that they must realize that they least of all can afford to accept low returns on their investments. They cannot afford to waste scarce resources by putting prestige ahead of real need, by ignoring hard economic calculations, by refusing to accept productive capital while they debate for years the respective roles of public and private enterprise.

At best, and even if real sacrifices are made by the industrialized nations to increase the flow of aid, there is grave danger that, in the face of existing rates of population growth, the resources available for economic development will fall short of the needs of the developing countries. We bear a heavy responsibility toward succeeding generations to make the best use of all our resources.

5.

# PROBLEMS OF FERTILITY CONTROL IN UNDERDEVELOPED AREAS

*by J. Mayone Stycos*

Because the size, distribution and rate of increase of population are closely related to questions of national power and economic development, population has long been a topic of interest for most nations. The science of demography, moveover, has a long and distinguished history within the social sciences. It is all the more surprising, then, that until the past few years scientific research on motivational aspects of demographic problems has been virtually nonexistent. In a science dealing with three of the most basic human events and processes—birth, death, and migration—psychological, social, and cultural factors have been all but ignored as objects of scientific inquiry. It is probably fair to say, even

Reprinted from "Marriage and Family Living," February 1963, by kind permission of the editor.

now, that we know more about what people expect, want, and do with respect to planting wheat or purchasing TV sets than with respect to having babies.

Part of the explanation lies in the fact that demographers have tended to ignore or minimize certain types of data. The field has recruited many of its personnel from economics, actuarial science, and statistics, disciplines highly suspicious of "soft" data collected in the area of attitudes and opinions; and has relied almost exclusively on the "hard" data provided by national censuses and vital statistics. Since these data are not collected primarily for social scientists, and since they are subject to a number of inadequacies, an important aspect of the role of demographer is ingenuity at upgrading data (often from poor to fair) by conceptual and statistical manipulation. In a sense demographers have been seduced by the enormous volume of free data provided them by national governments, and have been lulled into asking limited questions of these data, rather than raising new questions which can only be answered by collecting other types of information. Demographers tend to be disdainful, on the one hand, of the social scientist who collects superb original data on his Sociology 101 students, and on the other, of the grand theorist who requires little empirical data for reaching conclusions.[1]

With respect to fertility research there have been special obstacles. Demographers are part of a general culture which has regarded the sexual sphere as an intensely private and personal affair. As most social scientists, demographers have not only been members of the middle class, the major bastion of restrictive sexual norms, but in their very role of social scientists, have perhaps been overly sensitive to taboos in the sexual sphere. Inquiry into sexual matters has, until recently, been largely within the confines of the psychiatrist's couch, and it is of interest that it took a zoologist (Kinsey) to crack the myth that *normal* people will not talk about their sexual behavior to a social investigator.

Fortunately, for the field as a whole, if not for population experts in particular, practical exigencies have forced demographers to stick their necks out in a way rarely demanded of social scientists.[2] They have been repeatedly asked to *predict* future population, and, more recently, are being asked what to do about it. On both counts the field has been found deficient and this discovery has in large measure been responsible for a rather sudden spate of motivational studies in a wide variety of countries.

As is usually the case in the early stages of research, the studies have been generally marked by an absence of theoretical sophistication, and by a failure to build in comparability with investigations of a similar nature done elsewhere. Nevertheless, they have provided an invaluable baseline of information from which a number of crude hypotheses is emerging. It is not the objective of this paper to summarize or evaluate these studies in any systematic fashion. Rather, these studies will be drawn upon, along with the personal experience of the writer, to outline some of the real and mythical obstacles in the way of planned programs of fertility control.

At the most general level, the explanation for a durable demographic gap (a discrepancy between low death rates and high birth rates) goes something like this. Until recently, most under-developed areas had very high death rates, perhaps forty or more per thousand population. In order to survive, such societies *had* to have comparably high birth rates. Any cultures which did not develop mechanisms for maintaining high fertility in the face of high mortality have disappeared. Consequently, customs such as early marriage emerged and survived along with various beliefs and values emphasizing the desirability of maximum fertility. The introduction of fertility control techniques into such societies runs counter, therefore, to some of the most basic customs and values, and can be expected to meet with considerable resistance or indifference.

At the same time, good health and long life are almost universal values, so that modern technology for saving lives is readily accepted. Moreover, unlike birth control, many public health measures do not require individual commitment, but can be carried out by draining swamps, improving sewage disposal, purifying the water supply, etc. Consequently, death rates can be expected to decline rapidly wherever the technological means are made available.

This general explanation is quite plausible and may even be valid. However, the well-known fact that fertility can be expected to decline very slowly by "natural" means would seem to argue the necessity for public programs to speed up the process. Why have so few governments in areas of high growth rates introduced such programs? Obviously, democratic governments are reluctant to introduce policies they believe contrary to the values of the majority of the people; but this would not be so serious a consideration for totalitarian societies, or for democracies where opposition parties are weak. In order to understand the typical reluctance of governments, it would be useful to discuss in some detail the attitudes of the elite and of the masses toward population growth and fertility control.

### ELITE ATTITUDES

We can discuss reasons for the reluctance of governments to introduce family planning programs under three major headings: (1) ideas about population and population control closely related to nationalism; (2)

naive faith in the "demographic miracle"; (3) erroneous theories about the causes of high fertility.

## Nationalism

Throughout the world, under-developed societies are experiencing waves of nationalism. Perhaps an essential condition of significant economic development, it is actively fostered by national leaders. Several common ingredients of nationalism present obstacles to programs of fertility control.

*Pride in Numbers.* A large population, while not guaranteeing international power, is probably a necessary condition of power. Giant armies and industries both require large population bases, and the total national product of a nation is greatly influenced by the sheer weight of numbers. Chinese leaders have even suggested maximizing their population size to guarantee survival in strength following an atomic decimation. Mixed with such more or less rational beliefs are more sentimental notions. Leaders of the new nation, Nuvela, become passionately convinced that there is something valuable in being a Nuvelian. More of a good thing— more Nuvelians for the world—emerges as a goal or at least a vague feeling obstructing policies for reduction of numbers. Low birth rates may even be viewed as a sign of the decadence of nations surfeited with "civilization" and approaching cultural senescence. Views similar to these have been current among leaders in nations as disparate as Mexico and the Soviet Union.

*Anti-colonialism.* An almost invariable aspect of nationalism is the channelling of aggressions toward a common scapegoat, usually the foreign country which has historically exercised the greatest degree of political or economic control. Any lever for pinning responsibility on this country for a host of local ills will receive maximum exploitation. If the suggestion of a population control program can be in any way linked to the "imperialist" nation, an unusually powerful and effective anti-colonialist charge can be advanced—that the colonial power wishes to "do away with" Nuvelians or at least inhibit their growth, a subtle and insidious form of genocide.

*Faith in Economic Policies.* The new government also wishes to show that its past backwardness was due to the economic and political policies of the imperialist nation. Freed of such tyrannical shackles, its new program of economic and social reform can provide adequately for its present and future population. Admission of a population problem may sound like an admission of programmatic defeat. Marxist ideology, and to a large extent Roman Catholic ideology, regard "population problems" as smokescreens concealing inadequacies of the economic and social system; but the argument has great appeal (as well as a certain amount of truth) in areas where neither Marxism nor Catholicism reigns.

Where democratic forms of government are emerging, the party in power is wary of population programs, since many of these same arguments used against the colonial powers can be used against it by the opposition party. Within the West Indies, cleavages of color (black versus white), ethnicity (East Indian versus colored West Indian), and class (rich versus poor) have variously been used by politicians when family planning programs have been publicly discussed. In addition to charges of genocide, admission of a population problem by the majority party has been used as evidence of the inadequacy of the party's reform policies. In China, a major governmental program of family limitation was short-lived, partly because orthodox groups regarded it as an admission of weakness of the nation's economic policies. In other communist countries, birth control programs are carefully labeled as maternal health programs.

*Population Pressure as an Instrument of Nationalism.* Population growth is typically viewed as a phenomenon which is not influenced but which influences other things. In its most extreme form it has been used as a rationale for territorial expansion, as in the case of Japan, Italy, and Germany prior to World War II. Currently, under-developed nations use population growth to justify the necessity for new markets, the need for more foreign aid, etc., and to stir up national enthusiasm for expensive programs of education, social and medical services, and industrialization. Programs for more houses, jobs, land, schools, and hospitals are intrinsically more appealing than programs for less babies. The former programs become even more appealing if it can be shown that there are more babies every day who need and deserve such services.

### The Demographic Miracle

It is common knowledge that western countries once had high fertility and that following their industrial revolution fertility declined to "modern" levels. Faced with high birth rates and high rates of population growth, many leaders of under-developed areas place their trust in the magic of economic development. If we invest in schools, factories and cities, they argue, the population problem will take care of itself. The argument is subject to at least two important limitations.

First, demographers do not know exactly why or how fertility rates have declined. In the absence of such knowledge there is no guarantee that what happened in one set of societies in the past will happen to a quite different set in the future. Indeed, under certain conditions, improved economic circumstances and the breakdown of traditional patterns can cause increases in fertility. For example, such changes might bring about greater marital stability to non-legal unions which now have decidedly lower fertility than more stable legal unions; or, as in India, the breakdown on taboos on the remarriage of widows could lengthen the average reproductive period. A growing body of evidence indicates that fertility did in fact increase among western nations in the early periods of industrialization, as a result of such changes as increased and earlier marriage and reduced maternal mortality.

Second, mortality in the western nations declined much more rapidly than fertility, and closure of the ensuing "demographic gap" took some nations up to two-hundred years. It was during the industrial revolution that Europe's great population increases occurred. Because of modern medical technology, mortality among contemporary under-developed nations is declining far more rapidly than has ever been the case in the past, with little indication that fertility will show a similarly accelerated decline.[3] Even assuming that the decline will occur *eventually*, how long can a society afford to wait when annual rates of increase are such that the population will double in thirty or forty years?

Another comfortable belief about the population problem stems from the theories of Josue de Castro. In *The Geography of Hunger*, de Castro popularized the notion that protein deficiency accounts for the high fertility of the lower classes. Despite the disrepute with which this theory is regarded by demographers, it has captured the imagination of many of the educated elite in a number of countries. It has the familiar twin advantage of simplicity and of avoidance of the real problem. With economic development, the population will eat better and therefore bear fewer children. No direct attack on the problem is necessary.

### Elite Theories about Lower Class Fertility

Upper class explanations for the high fertility of lower class groups are similar in most societies with which the writer is acquainted. It is argued that the lower classes want many children or it is argued that they do not care how many they have. Religious values are also viewed as major obstacles to fertility control. In addition, the lower classes have certain needs such as an unusually high drive for sexual relations which are uninhibited by a sense of morality or social responsibility. In the face of such values and biological drives, birth control programs are doomed to failure, and might even increase the immorality of these classes. In any event, the problem should be attacked more directly by teaching "self-control," reducing sexual frequency by state-provided avenues for sublimation, and the reduction of illegitimacy by legal, religious, and social pressures.

*The Desire for Large Families.* Because the typical couple in under-developed areas in fact produces a large family, it is tempting to conclude that this is the desired state of affairs. The available evidence, while not entirely satisfactory, would suggest the contrary. When asked to name the ideal number of children, or when asked whether or not they want more children, lower class women in societies as different as Peru, Lebanon, Puerto Rico, Jamaica and India do not regard the question as meaningless, and do not favor very large families. Three or four children is generally seen as the ideal number, and most women who have four children do not want any more.

*Religious Values.* The major religions of the East do not contain explicit ideologies with respect to fertility control. While there are certain aspects of the philosophy of such faiths which encourage the having of large families, respondents in surveys rarely cite religious objections to family planning; and it is generally agreed that religious ideology is not a major factor in resistance to population control for non-Christian religious groups.

While the Catholic religion strongly and explicitly condemns most forms of birth control, and while the Church as an organization can be highly influential in the determination of international, national and local policies with respect to population control, the weight of the evidence suggests that its impact on attitudes and behavior of individual couples is small. Studies comparing Catholic and non-Catholic beliefs and behavior with respect to family planning have been conducted in countries where Catholics are in the majority (Puerto Rico), minority (Jamaica), or evenly balanced (Lebanon). In none of these areas is there any significant difference in attitudes or behavior with respect to family planning.[4] Such results almost invariably astonish national leaders, who tend to assume that the teachings of the Church are followed by its members.

*Sex Relations and Fertility.* Just as it is tempting to deduce attitudes from behavior, so it is tempting to deduce a high frequency of sex relations from high fertility, since sex relations are a necessary antecedent to fertility. The temptation is made all the more attractive by the generally condescending and patronizing attitudes of the upper classes toward the lower classes. The latter are variously viewed as 'children,' as primitive or animal-like, or as amoral or immoral. Thus, biological urges are stronger and inhibitions are weaker than among the upper classes. Finally, lacking electric lights and civilized means of diversion, the lower classes retire early. The entire complex is expressed in a saying, "Procreation is the poor man's recreation."

Again, the available evidence, while unfortunately limited, points in the opposite direction. First, there is no assurance that high sexual frequency increases fertility: indeed, there is a current plausible hypothesis suggesting that it inhibits it because of lower sperm counts per act of coitus. Second, there is no reason to believe that lower class sexual frequency is higher than that of upper class and, because of malnutrition and fatigue, it may well be lower. In limited studies in the United States, Lebanon and India, lower educational groups have not been found to have higher sexual frequencies than better educated groups. Third, the notion that night baseball will substitute for sex seems somewhat naive. Lest the reader think we are building straw men, let us recall the advice of the ex-Governor General of Ceylon:

"He who goes to bed early to save candles begets twins," said Viscount Soulbury . . . Ceylon's former Governor General quoted this ancient Chinese proverb to illustrate what he considers the cause for the alarming increase in Ceylon's population. He said he had advised Ceylon's Pime Minister to introduce electric lighting to the villages to counter the population rise. . . . "There has been a lot of glib talk about family planning," said the Viscount, "but that was not very easy—electric lights are the solution."[5]

Such notions are not limited to Europeans. In an opening speech to an international Planned Parenthood Conference, Prime Minister Nehru announced, "I was told only today about the possible consequences of, let us say, electricity going to a rural area. . . . the period for which they can work or amuse themselves or do other things is enormously lengthened and thereby, indirectly perhaps, it effects even this family planning business."[6] A vice-president of India has publicly commented that "Sex is the only indoor sport open to us, and large families are produced. It is the poor people that produce large families and not the rich ones."[7] In recommending the rhythm method for India's masses, another high-ranking Indian official pointed to its salutary effects on "self-indulgence:" "The task is essentially that of educating the individual in a manner which will enable him to sublimate his sexual urge into channels of activity which are productive of gain to the community . . . instead of yielding without even a thought of self-restraint to the desire for self-indulgence."[8]

*Illegitimacy and Promiscuity.* A frequent phrase heard in the West Indies is "irresponsible paternity," referring to the common pattern of having children out of wedlock. The fact that a large proportion of children are born illegitimate in the West Indies leads the middle classes to make a causal connection with high fertility rates. Religious leaders and social reformers appear to view males as casting their seeds indiscriminately throughout the female population. The young are therefore exhorted to marry as a curb to irresponsible paternity and high fertility.

In point of fact, most illegitimate births are the produce of common-law or consensual unions rather than of promiscuity. Moreover, if the young entered legal unions as recommended, there is good reason to believe that their fertility would show marked increases, since they would be changing from transitory relationships to more permanent ones. In short, the relation between legitimacy and fertility in the West Indies, and perhaps in many regions of the world, is the opposite of what is usually assumed.

#### PROGRAMS OF FERTILITY CONTROL

If middle-class notions have deflected attentions from the real problems and solutions, they have also profoundly affected the programs of fertility control where these have occurred in under-developed areas. This is the case because private programs are largely controlled by urban middle class women, and because the basic philosophy and methods of such programs have been borrowed from American and British experience. The latter programs were formed by crusading middle class women battling simultaneously against the shackles of puritanism and the tyranny of men. What have been the implications of this historical background and how appropriate are western patterns for non-western countries?

### The Dominance of Feminism

As most voluntary organizations, planned parenthood groups have been led by women. Unlike most voluntary organizations, however, they adopted explicit and implicit female policies because they were part of the whole movement to emancipate the women. Specifically, they were aimed at freeing the woman from the pain and drudgery of child bearing and child rearing as well as from the consequences of male sexual exploitation. It is no surprise, therefore, that a major intent of the movement, perhaps only partly conscious, has been to wrest control of fertility from males and give it to females. We say "wrest control" since there is overwhelming evidence that insofar as western fertility declines are due to contraceptive techniques, these techniques have been predominantly male methods. In their almost exclusive concern with female methods and female audiences, planned parenthood groups have been swimming upstream.

In under-developed areas, the emphasis may be even more misplaced, since male dominance in general and specifically in the sexual sphere is much more marked than in the modern western societies. In justification of its position, planned parenthood advocates repeat their plaints about the irresponsibility of males, and the lack of male motivation for controlling fertility. However, in western nations of low or moderate fertility the evidence is against this hypothesis; and in under-developed nations, while the evidence is scanty, male sentiments favoring small families do not seem markedly different from female and, in certain aspects, may be stronger. Interestingly enough, a major reason for the scantiness of the evidence is that the typical survey concentrates on females and never elicits the opinions of the male.

## The Clinical Approach

Partly because of the medical orientation of Margaret Sanger, and primarily because of the legal difficulties under which the movement in this country has labored, a very strong medical bias dominates the Planned Parenthood movement in the United States. Among other things, this has meant a concern with "maximum protection" methods and concentration on the individual case rather than a mass approach utilizing less effective but simpler techniques. It has meant the clinical system which waits for patients to come to it, and it has meant examination rooms, case histories and white coats. It has also meant a highly conservative attitude toward abortion, sterilization, publicity and non-medical personnel.

While a good case can be made for the tactical necessity for medical sponsorship in puritanical nations, no such necessity exists in most underdeveloped areas, a fact which makes examination of the efficacy of the clinical system quite relevant.

An important limitation of birth control clinics is that they are not used. In England, according to a recent national sample, only 6% of those who have used birth control have even received family planning advice from a clinic.[9] In Japan, where over 800 health centers include family planning, an experienced observer estimates that: "Of the families utilizing birth control in Japan, not more than 10% have received instruction or material from government services."[10] In Puerto Rico, despite the existence of an extensive network of birth control clinics for two decades, less than one in ten families has ever obtained birth control materials from a clinic. In less developed areas, wherever clinics exist they show pitifully small case-loads.

The explanations of clinical services probably lie on several levels only some of which have to do with the clinics *per se*. For the time being let us enumerate three.

(1) The methods typically offered by the clinics are not those most popular with most people. Neither male methods nor abortion are ordinarily offered in private or public clinics.

(2) The clinical atmosphere discourages many women and all but the

most stout-hearted of men. On the one hand, it is too public in the sense that to be seen there may be embarrassing. On the other hand, the intimate private examination and case-histories rituals frighten and embarrass many women in cultures where female modesty is an important value.

(3) Being under-publicized, clinics are not known about by large groups of the population. The very people who most need their services are least likely to know about them. Moreover, the clinics' emphasis on child *spacing* and on the advantages to health of family limitation are not the most effective appeals in under-developed areas at this time. Among lower class and peasant populations, the having of children is the most natural thing in the world. Women do not become concerned until they have four or five children and then want to *stop* having children for reasons that have less to do with health than with economics.

### The Chimerical Contraceptive

Hardly a planned parenthood conference goes by without at least one speaker accounting for the failure of birth control programs in the following terms: "Because of crowded living conditions and the absence of privacy, and due to the lack of running water and sanitary facilities, a cheap, simple contraceptive must be developed appropriate for use under such conditions." In the light of the number of bodily and household functions which are daily performed without running water in lower class houses, we feel that the concern over this matter is somewhat excessive. Further, one can only conclude that the same lower class ingenuity which manages such "prodigious" sexual frequencies in the face of such strong needs for privacy could also deal with the "problem" of privacy for birth control. Curiously, while the middle class ascribes sexual attitudes and behavior to the lower class different from its own, it projects its own attitudes with respect to needs for privacy and sanitary facilities. This is not to say that simpler contraceptives are not desirable; it is merely to point out that inadequacies in organization, educational techniques, and basic approach should not be concealed by fanciful explanations for programmatic failure.

A cheap, safe, and relatively simple contraceptive will soon be generally available in the form of an oral pill. It will prove more popular than any other female method, but whether it will solve by itself the kind of problems outlined below is questionable. As well phrased by one writer, ". . . the governments of underdeveloped areas that have launched such programs seem to have fallen into the 'technological fallacy' which has long marked Western thinking in this area. They have adopted, in

other words, a kind of blind faith in the gadgetry of contraception. . . .[11]
(Since Dr. Stycos' article was written, "the loop," or intra-uterine coil,
has come to appear even more promising.—Ed.)

## SOME REAL PROBLEMS

We have discounted a number of popular explanations for the failure of
birth control programs. Are there no real problems? There are, and they
are at least as numerous as the fallacious ones. Let us summarize a few.

### Ignorance

Wherever studies have probed lower class knowledge of sexual physiology, including the United States, the degree of ignorance has been startling. Maintained by strong taboos on discussion of sexual matters in
many countries, this basic ignorance extends to the area of modern contraceptive techniques. While it is generally known that *something* can be
done, only vague notions exist about *what*. "Birth control" or "family
planning" is often confused with abortion, with the permanent stopping
of child bearing, or with something done by prostitutes to avoid pregnancy or by men to avoid venereal disease. In the light of such ignorance
and misinformation it is little wonder that people stay away from clinics,
the functions of which must seem mysterious and faintly nefarious.

### Indifference

In the absence of information about contraceptive means, commitment to
small family goals should not be expected to be strong. While we have
seen that the average woman wants only three or four children, in studies
conducted by the writer high proportions of these same women say they
have never *thought of the matter before*. In the absence of information
on means, questions on ideal size must be interpreted carefully. Most of
these women would probably reply positively if asked whether they
would like to own Cadillacs—but lacking the remotest chance of doing
so, they have never seriously considered the matter before. Desiring
three children may be in the same category for women ignorant of anything but sexual abstention as a contraceptive technique.

### Ambivalence

While women or men may express sentiments generally favorable to
small families, it is not difficult to get them to admit favorable sentiments
toward large families as well. Because of the fear of high infant mortality,
the need for support in old age, and the emotional satisfaction of children, parents can simultaneously favor small and large families. More-

over, in the absence of knowledge for achieving small families, large ones are achieved and are *post hoc* likely to be rationalized as a good thing, especially in public situations.

## Late Motivation

Analysis of the data from almost any birth control clinic in the world will show that the average woman seeks family planning assistance only after she has had several children. Sample surveys also disclose that women become seriously interested in birth control only after several births and then want to *stop* having children. However, contraceptive activity at this late date tends to be relatively inefficient because of lack of experience and because sexual patterns have become fairly routinized and difficult to change. Thus, even if birth control is introduced at this point, its impact on fertility is relatively minor.

### SOLUTIONS

The initial and perhaps major hurdle of programs for fertility control in under-developed areas is the elite ruling classes. These groups must be informed about the gravity of the population problem, disabused of comfortable beliefs about the problem taking care of itself, and educated concerning the values, attitudes and behavior of the lower classes in the population. The programs themselves should be government sponsored rather than private for several reasons. Private programs cannot marshall the economic and human resources necessary to make a major impact on the birth rate. Moreover, the prestige of government backing is highly important in an area which is characterized by ambivalent attitudes. Finally, and perhaps most important, such programs should be taken out of the hands of do-gooding amateurs and put in the hands of professionals. While medical aspects and personnel may be included in such a program, basic policies and administration should be turned over to non-medical professionals—social scientists, community development experts and communications media specialists.[12] What might the broad outlines of such a program be?

(1) It would give at least as much attention to males as to females, and, possibly more attention. Given the fact of male dominance and the fact that fertility declines have historically been accomplished by means of male contraceptive techniques in many countries, males cannot be ignored. Moreover, because of their generally higher literacy, prestige, sophistication, and range of social relationships, they would not only be accessible to more new ideas but more effective disseminators of these ideas.

(2) Far more resources, and probably the bulk of them, should be put into non-clinical systems of education and contraceptive distribution. Normal retail channels should be maximized by education and subsidization of key shopkeepers, druggists, healers, midwives, barbers, etc. Most of these would be dealing with men in the normal atmosphere of economic transaction rather than the strange world of the clinic. Insofar as possible, local organizations should be formed, with volunteer and paid workers serving as agents for distribution of materials and ideas. Extension workers, home economists, and community development and public health personnel should receive special educational programs.

(3) The mass media, especially the printed word, should be given much more emphasis than is usual in such programs. Experimental programs in Puerto Rico and Jamaica have shown pamphlets to be as effective as personal visits or group meetings in getting people to adopt birth control. In Japan, according to recent studies, half of the women knowledgeable about birth control learned of it through magazines, nearly 20% through newspapers, and nearly 10% through books.[13] Even in nations of high illiteracy, written materials can be utilized with much greater effectiveness than is usually supposed.

(4) Every effort should be made to reach young couples with the object of initiating contraceptive practice at an early date for child-spacing purposes. Relatively simple techniques such as coitus interruptus should be encouraged, with no great expectations of high individual effectiveness. This will have the advantage of effecting a significant reduction in fertility on a mass basis and of preparing couples for more efficient but difficult contraceptive techniques after they have as many children as they desire.

(5) Particularly with younger couples, the reputedly deleterious effects to health of rapid child bearing should be ignored or minimized, and social and economic disadvantages of excessive child bearing stressed.

(6) For women and men who have had all the children they desire, sterilization facilities should be provided. Female sterilization in Puerto Rico has enjoyed enormous popularity and in India and Puerto Rico male sterilizations, especially where subsidized, are gaining rapidly. Legalized abortion programs similar to the Japanese should receive careful consideration. Programs such as these which are often viewed as immoral or at least "drastic" in western eyes, do not appear so to many other populations where they tend to be considered safer, more efficient and less troublesome than contraception. At the very least, such programs could be viewed as interim measures until efficient contraceptive practice becomes widespread.[14]

CONCLUSIONS

As demonstrated by several of the articles in this volume, the population problem in many under-developed areas is serious and can be expected to grow worse. Slowing the rate of population increase is no substitute for economic development, but can make possible, assist, or accelerate that development. Programs of fertility control are entirely feasible but face major obstacles in elite attitudes and beliefs about population dynamics and lower class culture; as well as in the dominance of ideas about family planning programs imported from the United States and England. There are also problems associated with informing and motivating the mass of the population, but, in the writer's opinion, these are less serious than of informing, motivating and activating ruling groups into creating careful and intelligent programs. Given the seriousness of the consequences of continued population growth in under-developed areas, optimism about the possibilities of fertility control programs is a necessity—and *cautious* optimism is justified.

6.

# DEMOGRAPHIC DIMENSIONS OF WORLD POLITICS

## *by Philip M. Hauser*

Politics in general, as well as world politics, is a branch of engineering—social engineering—not of science. Yet the consideration of the demographic aspects of world politics is not an inappropriate subject to be treated in this book. It is the purpose of this chapter to point to ways in which the findings of the science of demography illuminate various aspects of the world political scene.

There are various ways in which this subject can be developed, but I have arbitrarily chosen to discuss population factors in relation to politics, broadly conceived, on the global and on the international levels, respectively. By "global" problems I mean those that concern the earth as a whole; by "international" problems I mean those that arise among the various political subdivisions of the globe.

Reprinted from *Science* by permission.

## GLOBAL CONSIDERATIONS

There is no world government charged with the task of achieving world order and performing other civil governmental functions for the earth as a whole. This, however, does not mean that there are no political problems of a global, as distinguished from an international, character. Some such global problems are in fact dealt with by the United Nations and its specialized agencies, which are, of course, organizations of individual sovereign nations rather than organs of world government. Examples of global problems—problems which transcend and cannot be contained within national boundaries—include health, weather, fallout, and the newly emergent problems of outer space. It is easy to demonstrate that the contemporary rate of world population growth also constitutes a global problem—one which would be of great concern to a world government if we had one, and one which is of increasing concern to various organs of the United Nations and the specialized agencies.

Although the first complete census of mankind has yet to be taken, it is possible to reconstruct, with reasonable accuracy, the history of world population growth. This history may be encapsulated in the following estimates of the population of the earth: at the end of the Neolithic period in Europe (8000 to 7000 B.C.),[1] perhaps 10 million; at the beginning of the Christian era, 200 to 300 million; at the beginning of the modern era (1650), 500 million; in 1950, 2.5 billion.

These four numbers constitute a measurement of one of the most dramatic aspects of man's existence on the globe, and they explain the purple language of the demographer in describing the changes in rates of population growth during the modern era as a "demographic revolution" or "population explosion".[2]

The demographer's concern is not based only on considerations of the past. It is even more justified by postwar developments in population growth.

Since the end of World War II the rate of population increase has continued to accelerate and has reached a level of about 1.7% per year. There is justification, indeed, for pointing to a new population explosion in the wake of World War II of a great magnitude than that previously observed. At the rate of world population increase for the period 1800-1850, for example, the present population would double in 135 years; at the 1900-1950 rate, in 67 years; and at the postwar rate, in only 42 years.

Projection of the post-World War II rate of increase gives a population of one person per square foot of the land surface of the earth in less than 800 years. It gives a population of 50 billions (the highest estimate of the population-carrying capacity of the globe ever calculated by a responsible

TABLE I.

*Population, income, and energy consumed per capita, by continent, about 1950. Source of data: United Nations, except where otherwise indicated.*

| Area | Total Population No. (millions) | (%) | Aggregate income Dollars* (billions) | (%) | Per capita income ($) | Energy consumed per capita (kw-hr)** |
|------|------|------|------|------|------|------|
| World | 2497 | 100.0 | 556 | 100.0 | 223 | 1676 |
| Africa | 199 | 8.0 | 15 | 2.7 | 75 | 686 |
| Northern America*** | 219 | 8.8 | 241 | 43.3 | 1100 | 10,074 |
| South America | 112 | 4.5 | 19 | 3.4 | 170 | 741 |
| Asia | 1380 | 55.3 | 69 | 12.4 | 50 | 286 |
| Europe (exclusive of U.S.S.R.) | 393 | 15.7 | 149 | 26.8 | 380 | 3117 |
| U.S.S.R. | 181 | 7.2 | 56 | 10.1 | 310 | 1873 |
| Oceania | 13 | 0.5 | 7 | 1.3 | 560 | 3543 |

* See (8, 9).    ** See (33).    *** Central America included.

scholar) in less than 200 years! This estimate, by geochemist Harrison Brown,[3] is based on the assumptions that developments in the capturing of solar or nuclear energy will produce energy at a cost so low that it would be feasible to obtain all the "things" we need from rock, sea, and air, and that mankind would be content to subsist largely on food products from "algae farms and yeast factories!"

Moreover, the United Nations estimates of future world population indicate even further acceleration in the rate of world population growth during the remainder of this century. Between 1950 and 1975 the average annual percentage of increase, according to the United Nations "medium" assumptions, may be 2.1%, and between 1975 and 2000, almost 2.6%.[4] Such rates of increase would double the population about every 33 and 27 years, respectively.

It is considerations of this type that would make it necessary for a world government to exercise forethought and planning, which constitute rational decision making, in facing the future. This, of course, is the purpose of the projections. The figures do not show what the future population of the world will be—for the world could not support such populations. They do demonstrate that man, as a culture-building animal, has created an environment in which the rhythm of his own reproduction has been modified in such a manner as to point to crisis possibilities.

## CRISIS POSSIBILITIES

The crisis possibilities are of several forms, each posing major world political problems. The first, we may note, is the ultimate crisis, which would result from the fact that the globe is finite[5] and that living space would be exhausted. Unless one is prepared to argue that future technological developments will enable man to colonize other globes,[6] it is clear that present rates of population increase must come to a halt by reason of lack of space. No facts or hopes as to man's ability to increase his food production and to increase other types of goods and services can indefinitely increase man's *Lebensraum* (or could do so even if we accept the absurd assumption that man, at terrific cost, could burrow into the earth, live in man-made layers above it, or live on the seas).

In the short run, let us say to 1975 or to 2000, world population will be confined to much more manageable numbers. The United Nations projects, on the basis of its medium assumptions, a world population of about 3.8 billion by 1975 and 6.3 billion by 2000.[7]

In the short run there is no problem of exhausting the space on the globe, nor is there reason to fear serious decreases in world per capita food supply, as is evidenced by projections of The Food and Agricultural Organization, and others concerning foodstuffs.[8] But there is great reason to be pessimistic about the possibility of greatly increasing the average world level of living during the remainder of this century.

In 1950, world per capita income was estimated at $223.[9] In North America, per capita income was $1100. Had each person on the globe enjoyed the North American level of living in 1950, as measured by per capita income, the aggregate world product in 1950 would have supported only 500 million persons, as contrasted with the actual world population of 2.5 billion. For average world income to have matched income in North America, aggregate income would have had to be increased about fivefold. To bring world per capita income by 1975 to the level enjoyed in North America in 1950 would require about a 7.5-fold increase of the 1950 level in 25 years. To do the same by 2000 would require a 12-fold increase in the 1950 world income within 50 years.

Even if the more modest income level of Europe ($380 per capita in 1950) were set as the target, great increases in productivity would be necessary, because of prospective rates of population increase, to raise average world income to the required level by 1975 or 2000. To achieve this goal by 1975, world income would have to be increased 2.5-fold over the 1950 level, and to achieve it by 2000, the required increase would be greater than fourfold. A decline in the rate of world population growth to that of the period 1800 to 1850—namely, to 0.5%—would decrease by three-fourths and four-fifths, respectively, the projected world-income requirements for attaining this goal by 1975 or 2000.

These considerations not only show the enormous difficulty of materially increasing the world level of living on the basis of present rates of population increase but indicate, also, the weakness of the argument that a solution to the population problem is to be found in more equitable distribution of the world's food supply or of goods and services in general.[10] The equitable distribution of world income in 1950 would, to be sure, have raised the per capita income of Latin America by 31%; of Africa, almost threefold, and of Asia, four- to fivefold, but it would still have produced a per capita income per annum of $223, only one-fifth that in North America and only three-fifths that in Europe (exclusive of the U.S.S.R.). The miserably low level of living of most of the world's population is attributable not so much to maldistribution as to low aggregate product, the result of the low productivity of most of the world's peoples.

These political problems of a global character may perhaps be better understood through consideration of their international aspects, special attention being given to the plight of the two-thirds of the world's population resident in the underdeveloped areas of the world, in Asia, Africa, and Latin America.

### INTERNATIONAL CONSIDERATIONS

The short-run implications of present rates of world population growth are manifest in specific forms and in varying degrees of intensity among the various regional and national subdivisions of the globe. The distribution of the world's population and of the world's utilized resources, manifest in differentials in levels of living, is the result, of course, of millenia of human history. The demographic dimensions of international politics may best be comprehended against the background of differences among peoples in levels of living and the significance of these differences at this juncture in world history[11] (Table I).

To note the extremes, North America in 1950, with about 16% of the earth's land surface, contained less than 9% of the world's population but about 43% of the world's income. Asia, in contrast, with about the same proportion of the world's land surface (18%), had 55% of the world's population but only 12% of the world's income. Per capita income in Asia was at a level of about $50 per year as contrasted with a level of $1100 in North America. Despite the fact that such comparisons are subject to considerable error,[12] there is no doubt that a tremendous difference in per capita income existed, of a magnitude perhaps as great as 20 to 1.

The major factor underlying this difference is indicated by the contrast in the difference in nonhuman energy consumed in North America and Asia, respectively—over 10,000 kilowatt-hours per capita per year for the former in contrast to less than 300 for the latter. The availability of nonhuman energy for the production of goods and services is perhaps

the best single measurement available of differences in capital investment, know-how, and technology which account for the great differences
in productivity and, consequently, in the size of the aggregate product
available for distribution.

The other relatively underdeveloped continents of the world also had
relatively low shares of world income as compared with their proportions
of world population. Africa, with a per capita income of about $75 per
year, and South America, with $170, were also well below not only the
level for North America but also the levels for Europe (exclusive of the
U.S.S.R.), the U.S.S.R. and Oceania. There is a high correlation among
these areas between per capita income and amount of non-human energy
consumed (Table I).

These differences in levels of living, as it turns out, are in general in-
versely related to present and prospective rates of population increase.
The populations of the relatively underdeveloped continents of the world
are increasing at a more rapid rate than those of the economically advanced continent.[13] Between 1950 and 1975, to use the medium projections of the United Nations, while the population of Northern America is
increasing at an average annual rate of 1.7% and that of Europe, at
1.2%, that of Asia will be growing at an average annual rate of 2.4%,
that of Africa at 2.1%, and that of Latin America at 3.4%. Between
1975 and 2000, while the rate of increase for Northern America will
average 1.2% per year and that for Europe, 1.0%, the rate for Asia will
be 3.0%, that for Africa 2.8%, and that for Latin America 3.8%, a rate
at which the population would double about every 18 years.

As I have indicated above, rapid increase in world population imposes a severe burden on efforts to raise levels of living. It is easy to
demonstrate that the burden would become an impossible one for the
economically underdeveloped areas should their rates of population increase follow the trends indicated in the United Nations projections.

For example, Asia, merely to maintain her present low level of living,
must increase her aggregate product by 60% between 1950 and 1975,
and by an additional 75% between 1975 and 2000. To raise her per
capita income to the European level for 1950 while continuing to experience her rapid population growth, Asia would have to increase her 1950
aggregate income 12-fold by 1975 and 21-fold by 2000. Africa, to do the
same, must increase her aggregate income eight-fold by 1975 and 13-fold
by 2000, and Latin America would have to increase her aggregate income
fourfold by 1975 and eightfold by 2000.[14]

To achieve a per capita income equal to that of Northern America in
1950 while experiencing the projected population growth, Asia would
have to increase her aggregate income 35-fold by 1975 and 62-fold by

2000. Africa, to achieve a similar goal, would require 22-fold and 38-fold increases, respectively, in aggregate income, and Latin America, 12-fold and 23-fold increases.

TABLE II.

*Summary of projections of urban population for the world and for Asia, 1975 (18).*

| Cities (category) | Population (millions) | | | Estimate of increase in population 1950-1975 (millions) | | Estimate of increase in population 1950-1975 (%) | | Proportion of total population in cities | |
|---|---|---|---|---|---|---|---|---|---|
| | Projection for 1975 | | 1950 | | | | | Projection | |
| | Upper | Lower | | Upper | Lower | Upper | Lower | 1975* | 1950 |
| *The World* | | | | | | | | | |
| 100,000 and over | 745 | 488 | 314 | 431 | 174 | 138 | 55 | 19 | 13 |
| 20,000 and over | 1155 | 779 | 502 | 653 | 277 | 130 | 55 | 30 | 21 |
| *Asia* | | | | | | | | | |
| 100,000 and over | 340 | 176 | 106 | 234 | 70 | 222 | 66 | 15 | 8 |
| 20,000 and over | 544 | 283 | 170 | 374 | 113 | 220 | 66 | 25 | 13 |

* Figures are based on the "upper" projection, which assumes urbanization of an increasing proportion of the population.

These considerations provide additional justification for the use by the demographer of the phrase *population explosion*; and they certainly indicate the hopeless task which confronts the underdeveloped areas in their efforts to achieve higher levels of living while experiencing rapid population growth. The control of rates of population growth would unquestionably decrease the magnitude of the task of achieving higher levels of living in the under-developed areas, especially in those with populations that are large relative to resources.[15]

Increasingly large proportions of the population in the underdeveloped areas of the world are becoming concentrated in urban places. The continued acceleration in the rate of world urbanization during the first half of this century was mainly attributable to urbanization in the underdeveloped areas, which proceeded at a pace considerably above that in the developed areas.[16] I have had occasion to make projections of the urban population of the world and of Asia to 1975; these are presented in Table II as illustrative of what is in prospect in the underdeveloped areas of the globe.[17] For the rate or urbanization in Latin America and Africa is, also, accelerating.

The projections for Asia indicate that in the 25 years between 1950 and 1975, in cities either of 100,000 and over or of 20,000 and over, urban population will increase by at least two-thirds and may perhaps triple.

The lower projection is based on the assumption that the proportion of urban population in Asia will be the same in 1975 as it was in 1950. Under this assumption the projected increase would result from total population growth alone. But if it is assumed that the rate of urbanization in Asia will increase as it did between 1900 and 1950 while the total population continues to grow at the rate projected by the United Nations, then tripling of Asia's urban population is indicated.

Thus, while the nations of Asia are attempting to improve their miserable urban living conditions, their urban populations will continue to increase explosively—perhaps to triple within a period of less than one generation.

In the economically more advanced nations of the world, urbanization is both an antecedent and a consequent of technological advance and of a high level of living—a symbol of man's mastery over nature. In the underdeveloped nations, however, urbanization represents instead the transfer of rural poverty from an over-populated and unsettled countryside to a mass urban setting. In the economically underdeveloped areas of the world, urbanization is outpacing economic development and the city is more a symbol of mass misery and political instability than of man's conquest of nature.[18]

The prospect for individual nations, while variable, is in general the same—one of explosive growth. Between 1955 and 1975, according to the United Nations medium projections, the population of China will increase by 294 million persons and that of India, by 177 million.[19] That of Pakistan will increase by 45 million persons, and that of Indonesia, by 40 million, in these 20 years. To confine our attention to the Far East for the moment, smaller countries with the most explosive increases include South Korea, Taiwan, and Ceylon. Each of these nations is faced with a task of tremendous proportions merely to maintain her present level of living, let alone to greatly increase it while continuing to grow at the projected rates.

### POLITICAL INSTABILITY

What will happen if the underdeveloped areas in Asia are frustrated in their efforts to attain a higher standard of living?

Warren S. Thompson devotes his latest book to providing an answer to this question.[20] The larger of these nations are not apt to remain hungry and frustrated without noting the relatively sparsely settled areas in their vicinities—the nations in the South-East Asia peninsula: Burma, Thailand, and the newly formed free countries of Indochina, Laos, Cambodia, and Vietnam. (Vietminh, that is North Vietnam, is already engulfed by Communist China.) Even parts of thinly settled Africa may be subject to the aggressive action of the larger and hungrier nations as feelings of population pressure mount. Moreover, Communist China, the largest nation in the world by far, faced with the greatest absolute population increases to add to her already heavy burdens in striving for economic development, may not confine her attention only to the smaller nations within her reach. Her present actions relative to her boundaries with India and possible tensions over her boundaries with the U.S.S.R. contain explosive possibilities.

It is Thompson's conclusion that the larger nations in the Far East, including Japan, India, and Pakistan as well as China, may resort to force to achieve access to additional resources under sufficient population pressure. The smaller countries may not be able to resort to force but are almost certain to require outside aid to prevent chaos. Futhermore, Indonesia and the Philippines, under mounting population pressures, are likely to continue to experience growing internal political instability.

Population pressure as a factor in political instability is not confined to the Far East. Populations of the Middle East and North Africa—the Muslim area (exclusive of Pakistan)—may increase from 119 million in 1955 to 192 million by 1975, an increase of 73 million or 61% in 20 years.[21] As Irene Taeuber has noted, this is an area "where internal instabilities and conflicts of religious and ethnic groups create recurrent crises for the region and world." Taeuber observes that the immediate political instabilities in this area are attributable more to "diversities among the peoples and the nations than to population pressure or population growth."[22] But she points to the importance, in the decades that lie ahead, of economic advances to lessen tension in this region and to the barrier that rapid population growth may contribute to that development.

Latin America, although in large part still a sparsely settled area of the world, is already experiencing problems associated with rapid population growth which give promise of worsening. For Latin America, as has been reported above, is faced with a population increase of 86% between 1950 and 1975 and of 95%, almost a doubling, between 1975 and 2000.[23] Especially difficult in Latin America are the problems posed by accelerating rates of urbanization. Recent measurements of rate of urban growth in Latin America indicated that of 15 countries for which data were available, urban population in one, Venezuela, was increasing at 7% per year, a rate which produces a doubling about every 10 years; seven had growth rates which would double their population in less than 18 years; and only two (Chile and Bolivia) had rates of urban growth of less than 1% per year.[24] Growth rates (total and urban) of the magnitude which Latin America is experiencing are likely to add appreciably to the difficulty of raising living levels and are likely to worsen already existent political instabilities that threaten internal order and may affect world peace.

Finally, a fourth region of political instability to which the population factor is a contributing element, and one where it will be increasingly manifest, is sub-Saharan Africa.[25] Middle Africa is sparsely settled, but increasing knowledge about the area indicates high birth rates, decreasing death rates, and explosive growth. The United Nations projections indicate a population increase from 154 million in 1955 to about 202 million in 1975, or an increase of 31%. The familiar syndrome of underdeveloped areas—malnutrition, disease, and urban and rural squalor on the one hand and aspirations for independence and economic development on the other—are now emergent in this most primitive continent of the globe. And here, as in the other underdeveloped areas, rapid population growth is likely to intensify political unrest.

In southern Africa another type of population problem is also a major element in a political problem that has grave implications for world order as well as for the stability of the Republic of South Africa. This is the problem arising from the conflict between the indigenous people and European settlers manifest in apartheid. Rapid and differential rates of growth of native and European populations are likely to intensify rather than to allay conflict in southern Africa.

The tensions and political instabilities generated by explosive population growth in the economically underdeveloped nations have a special significance in the contemporary world, characterized by the bipolar conflict between the Western and Communist blocs and the efforts on the part of each to win the allegiance of the uncommitted nations of the world. This conflict has several demographic dimensions of importance.

### THE WESTERN AND COMMUNIST BLOCS

The first of these dimensions is evident in the way in which population is distributed among the three political blocs into which the world is divided. For in 1955 each of these political groups—the Western nations, the Communist nations, and the uncommitted nations—had approximately the same population. The Western and the Communist blocs, respectively, each have much to gain in the struggle to win the allegiance of the uncommitted third of the world's people. This titanic competition is focused primarily on South and Southeast Asia at the present time, because the bulk of the world's politically uncommitted population is located there.

In this war for men's minds, the competition between Western-world and Communist ideologies, each of the contestants has powerful weapons. Apart from military power which I will leave out on the assumption that a nuclear stalemate exists, the key weapons of the Communists, as is daily attested to by their propaganda, are the exploitation of the wide gap between the levels of living of the "have" and "have-not" nations and the attribution of blame for the misery of the "have not" nations on the imperialistic and colonial practices of the "have" powers. Needless to say, the fire of this propaganda is effectively fed by the frustration of the underdeveloped areas in their efforts to advance their levels of living, or in their efforts to win independence from imperial powers, where this is not yet accomplished.

The Communist bloc, with relatively little, but with increasing, surplus product, is attempting more and more to help the uncommitted nations in economic development. The U.S.S.R. may perhaps be departing from its postwar cold-war policy of trying to persuade uncommitted nations to accept its ideology by means either of internal coups or direct external aggression.

The chief weapon of the western nations, apart from the example of their free way of life is, undoubtedly, the provision of assistance to the underdeveloped nations to help them achieve their economic goals.

Thus, the success or failure of underdeveloped areas to raise their levels of living has the most profound world political implications. The most important immediate international political question is the question of whether the Western-world approach or the Communist approach is the more effective one for achieving economic development.

It is to be emphasized that this is not a rhetorical or hypothetical question. It is being answered by the course of events, the definitive test of achievement. It is being answered by what may be regarded as the most important experiments of all time—experiments under way in each of the three blocs of nations. A great race is on among the economically underprivileged nations to attain higher living levels—some by relatively free, and some by totalitarian and Communist, methods. The contests involve nations within each of which both economically advanced and underdeveloped areas are to be found.[26]

The greatest single race under way is undoubtedly the race between the leaders of the Western and Communist blocs, respectively—that is, the United States and the U.S.S.R. The U.S.S.R. has certainly served notice that, by its methods, it hopes to surpass the level of living attained by the United States, and in the not too distant future. Overshadowed only by the direct contest between the United States and the U.S.S.R. is the race between India and Communist China,[27] a race of special and direct immediate interest to the underdeveloped areas. For these mammoth nations, the two largest in the world, are bending every effort to achieve higher living standards—one through the Communist approach and the other by democratic methods. The outcome of this race will be of great interest not only to the underdeveloped nations in the uncommitted bloc but also to those in the Western bloc—the underdeveloped nations in Latin America as well as those committed to the Western bloc in Asia and in Africa.

The international political situation, then, as described above, gives a special significance to explosive population growth. For present and future rates of population growth may, indeed, prevent underdeveloped nations from raising their levels of living. Simon Kuznets' examination of the evidence indicates that the gap between "have" and "have-not" nations is increasing rather than decreasing. To the extent that underdeveloped nations are frustrated in their efforts to advance their living standards, they will, it may be presumed, be more open to the blandishments of the Communist bloc. Furthermore, if the underdeveloped Communist nations demonstrate that they can achieve more rapid economic progress than the underdeveloped Western nations, the free way of life may well be doomed. Success or failure in this fateful contest may well hinge on the ability of the nations involved to decrease their rates of population growth.[28]

### THE ALTERNATIVES

The "why" of the population increase, in an immediate sense, is readily identifiable. It is to be found in the great increase in "natural increase"— in the gap between fertility and mortality. Quite apart from the precise timing of changes in the relations between mortality and fertility, it is clear that explosive growth can be dampened only by decreasing natural increase. This is true for the world as a whole in the ultimate sense, with differences in timing for different parts of the world. For suggested solutions to the problems of present and prospective rates of population growth in the various subdivisions of the world through migration, foreign trade, redistribution of wealth, and similar means hold forth little promise, if any, even in the short run.

There are only three ways to decrease natural increase: (i) by increasing death rate; (ii) by decreasing the birth rate; and (iii) by some combination of the two.

Although it is true that decreased death rates were largely responsible for the population explosion in the past and are foreseen to be a large factor in the future, the adoption of a policy to increase mortality, or to diminish efforts to increase longevity, is unthinkable. Unless one is prepared to debate this, two of the three ways of decreasing natural increase are ruled out. For two of them involve an increase in death rates.

If longevity gains are to be retained, then, the only way to reduce explosive population growth is to decrease the birth rate. That is, the "death control" mankind has achieved can be retained only if it is accompanied by birth control. This proposition, even though it flows directly from the demographic facts of life, in view of prevalent value systems provokes heated debate of the type manifest in the press. Birth control has recently, indeed, made the front pages of the world press.

What is important about the value controversy under way is that it definitely affects global and international policy and action on matters of population and, therefore, on the crucial political problems involved. The most significant thing about all the available methods of birth control—a fact mainly obscured in the present public controversy—is that they are by no means adequate to the task of slowing down explosive world population increase, especially that in the underdeveloped areas. The great mass of mankind in the economically less advanced nations which are faced with accelerating rates of growth fail to limit their birth rates not because of the factors at issue in the controversy we are witnessing but because they do not have the desire, the know-how, or the means to do so. The desire to control fertility, arising from recognition of the problem, is, however, increasing. Japan is already well down the road to controlling its birth rate, although by methods which are not enthusiastically endorsed either by the Japanese themselves of by other peoples. China, India, Pakistan, and Egypt[29] have population limitation programs under way or under serious consideration, and other underdeveloped areas are showing increasing interest in this problem.[30] The changes in value systems which will create mass motivation to adopt methods of family limitation are not easily brought about,[31] but they are at least under way.

Birth control methods in use in the economically more advanced nations are not, in the main, well adapted for use in the underdeveloped areas. But the results of increased research and experimentation with oral contraceptives are encouraging,[32] and there may soon be a breakthrough on obtaining adequate means for the task of limiting population growth in the underdeveloped areas.

### CONCLUSION

The demographer and the increasing number of his allies, in directing attention to the implications of world population growth, are in fact pointing to major global and international political problems—problems that cannot be ignored. Needless to say, the solution to the problems is not to be found in appeals to the traditions of the past, sacred or secular.

The solution is to be found in the policies and actions which man himself, as a rational animal, must work out and implement. The mind of man, which has conceived remarkable methods for increasing life expectancy, is probably ingenious enough to devise methods by which the population explosion can be controlled within the framework of man's diverse value systems.

# Regional Statements

❂ ❂ ❂

### 7.

## ASIAN POPULATIONS:
## THE CRITICAL DECADES

### by Irene B. Taeuber

In the middle of the 17th century there were some 250 million people in that portion of the Asian Continent that lies below the present boundary of the U.S.S.R. In the two centuries from 1650 to 1850 Asia's population more than doubled. Growth was increasing in regularity and in pace, whether associated directly with colonial rule or indirectly with the crops, the economic techniques, and the social codes that came along with European expansion. In the 80 years of classic colonial rule, roughly from 1850 to 1930, population grew from 650 million to 1 billion. Then in the three decades of the Japanese drive for a continent of Asia for the Asians, the Pacific war, the nationalist struggles, and the revolutions that made half of Asia Communist, population increased a further 500 million to reach 1.5 billion in 1960.

Thus Asia begins its modernization, not with the 250 million people of 1650, or the 650 million people of 1850, but the 1.5 billion people of today. The tragedy of the period of European expansion for Asian countries inheres in this simple demographic fact. Populations multiplied again and again; once empty lands were filled, and once occupied lands were occupied even more densely. But economies remained primarily subsistence agricultural, people remained illiterate, and living and values alike remained traditional. Birth rates remained at the high levels appropriate to ancestral-oriented cultures where the succession of sons was essential and life was precarious. Social, economic, and demographic transformations that might have come slowly over centuries must come swiftly over decades if the good and the reasonably long lives that are the aspirations of Asian peoples become realities.

Asian populations total about 1½ billion people today.

What is the expectation for the future?

There is no precise answer to this question for individual countries, certainly not for the continent. Birth rates have not been reduced, nor can

Presented to the Committee on the Judiciary, House of Representatives, the United States of America, September 13, 1962.

they be reduced quickly without major changes in the institutions of the peasant societies. If economic development and public health activities can be sustained so that there is food, shelter, and health protection for the increasing people, death rates will continue to decline. If family life remains traditional, illiteracy yields only slowly to advancing education, and the contraceptives appropriate to Asian peasant societies remain ideals rather than scientific achievements, birth rates may decline slowly in the cities and the modernizing areas. Declines in national birth rates will be slow indeed, though, unless rates decline swiftly and sharply in the rural areas.

Given declining death rates and unchanging birth rates, the 1½ billion people in the Asia of 1960 will increase to more than 2 billion in 1975.[1] Then given continuities in the decline of death rates and lethargic stabilities in birth rates, numbers will exceed 4 billion by the end of the century. If this should occur, the net addition to the population of Asia below the Soviet boundary in the half century from 1950 to the year 2,000 would be larger than the population of the entire earth including Asia, in 1950.

The growth back of 1962 has occurred, but future numbers are conjectures. Moreover, the interpretation of the numbers that may exist in future decades is difficult. Their social, economic, and political significance depends on many developments—in economic growth, in social change, in educational achievements. And on these associated developments depend also the future of family life and aspirations and hence the future of the birth rate.

Analysis of the population growth and the population problems of the future is complex. We who failed to predict the growth of recent decades can hardly assert competence to predict the growth of future decades. Nor do theories and ideologies help particularly. Malthusianism proclaims imminent catastrophe while Marxism-Leninism asserts the value of the increasing hands and denies the problems of the increasing mouths. The relevance of either to analysis, policy formulation, or assessment of the future is limited. Malthusianism derived from dire expectations of the futures of European peoples, in Europe or elsewhere. Marxism-Leninism persists as theory while the U.S.S.R. undergoes a demographic transition quite similar to that in capitalist countries. The experiences of the Peoples Republic of China demonstrate that the population problems of Asian lands can neither be ignored with safety nor safely solved through defining hands as assets in great leaps and commune reconstructions.

A series of probing questions must be asked if the population growth of Asian countries is approached with a focus toward problems of resolution. There will be resolution, and it will involve economic, social, and political transformations, but the direction of movement may involve advance or retrogression. The demographic process may include declining birth rates, increasing death rates, or some combination of the two.

The first question is a series of questions. What happened to quicken growth rates? Why were governmental planners in countries and in international organizations so oblivious to the problems of growth? Why were there no plans for population development along with those for agricultural and industrial development, labor, education, and health?

The second question is a simple one. What are the dimensions of the problems of growth in the individual countries?

The third question is again a series, this time involving the future. What are the processes of resolution, and what are countries now doing or planning to do to secure that balance of low birth and death rates that reduces growth to manageable proportions? What is the role of migration, in this resolution, whether international or internal, whether planned or unplanned? What is the role of migration if population-resources relations remain acute and there is relative failure to move forward in peaceful internal solutions to economic-demographic difficulties?

### SCIENCE, TECHNOLOGY, AND IMBALANCE IN GROWTH

Prior to the medical and public health breakthroughs that yielded the miracle-working chemicals and the antibiotics, death rates were tied inexorably to ways and means of living. It was natural, therefore, that the early planning of national governments and international organizations involved economic development and public health but not education concerning social change and family planning. It was argued that increases in per capita food production and income would surpass rates of population growth. Since it was also argued that birth rates would decline slowly in response to economic advance and rising expectations, no major problems of growth were anticipated, either in the long or the short run.

The postwar developments differed from those anticipated in the midforties. The major force of change was neither economic nor ideological but scientific and technological. In late 1946 and early 1947 the public health services of Ceylon had the houses of the island sprayed with DDT. The death rate was cut 40% within a single year. The miracles of modern public health were realities. In the short run, the ties that bound death rates to levels of living and ways of living were snapped. Death rates dropped, the rate of population growth moved upward. There were no economic developments to provide additional employment for the increasing labor force. There were no social changes in village life to stimulate declining family size.

Ceylon was the omen for the Asian future. Death rates declined rapidly in country after country as national governments and international organizations cooperated in public health programs. Rates of population growth moved upward as increasing numbers of countries and increasing proportions of people maintained the birth rates of ancient times alongside the death rates of new times. The successive estimates of future populations that were made by the United Nations Secretariat soon became antiquated, for the high projections of one series were too low for the populations that existed within a few years. The censuses of 1960 and 1961 indicate that India, Pakistan, the Philippines, and other countries underestimated the rates at which their populations were growing.[2]

The advances of science and technology in the public health field made theories of automatic transitions to low birth rates as antiquated as those of traditional Malthusianism. If a country is reasonably successful in its health and agricultural programs, its rates of population growth should be, or should soon become, 3, 3½, or even 4% a year. Computations of future populations based on rates of growth such as these yield numbers difficult to comprehend, whether the areas are coral atolls or continental countries. Yet, given continuing progress in national and international activities to provide freedom from hunger and disease, these are the rates of growth that must be assumed for the future subject to three essential reservations:

1) That there is continuity in public order and public health activities.
2) That food produced or available is sufficient for the maintenance of the increasing populations.
3) That there are no increases in the control of fertility.

In simplest terms, the increasing rate of population growth reflects a lack of balance in scientific and technological developments. Scientific advances have freed death rates temporarily from the age-old ties with nutritional deficiencies and evironmental hazards. There have been no comparable scientific advances to free birth rates from their intimate links with traditional social structures, sex roles, and value systems. Is the villain then science, the solution simply more science? The seemingly obvious conclusion is enticing, but it is insufficient either as explanation or as sole policy directive.

Today's rates of growth, as those of earlier centuries, are products of reduced death rates. Most men view the prolongation of life with favor, and they have always viewed it thus. A solution to the problems of population growth through increasing death rates is rejected. But if death rates are to decline to ever lower levels in a finite world, birth rates must also decline. There is no alternative. But declining birth rates mean controlled fertility, and there is neither a universal good called the small family nor a universal ethic that interprets parental responsibilities as including limitation of offspring.

Thus there is approval of science, technology, and action programs that contribute to the health and longevity of people, and that provide increasing material goods. There is ambivalance to research and action programs in the field of human fertility. And this is true despite the increasing realization that the long and abundant physical life which is the goal of development activities can be preserved only if birth rates also decline.

A summary statement may be in order. The force that led to increasing rates of population growth was declining mortality. The demographic crisis is created by the failure of birth rates to decline along with death rates. Within a period of time whose duration no man can now foresee, the decline of birth rates becomes the only alternative to the increase of death rates.

The demographic, political, and other complexities of the Asian population situation can be reduced to one simple question: Will growth be reduced through the humane processes of declining birth rates or the ruthless processes of increasing death rates?

### THE DIMENSIONS OF THE PROBLEMS

Two summary tables may serve as prelude to later discussion. In table I, the population of Asia east of Iran and south of the U.S.S.R. is compared with that in other regions. In table II, past and possible future growth are sketched for the Asian region.

Asia, as defined to exclude the southwestern region and the northern half of the geographic continent, includes extraordinary concentrations of people. More than half the earth's total population live on this one-sixth of earth's land surface.

The area of the south-central and eastern Asian region is comparable in size to that of the U.S.S.R., Northern America, or Latin America. The population is many times greater than that in any one of these other regions. The Soviet Union is relatively empty; so, too, is Northern America. These are advanced industrial areas, with educated and predominantly urban populations, with scientific and technological components that push knowledge ever forward and continually transform earth's environment and extend its horizons. In Latin America there is poverty, malnutrition, and illiteracy, and there are rates of population growth generally more rapid than those in Asia. But resources are immense, while people are sparse in relation to land and other resources. The problems of development are those of organization and management, not the niggardliness of nature or the huge population increases of past periods. The world's population problems, as its people, are concentrated in Asia.

The population growth that was described previously for continental Asia below the boundaries of the Soviet Union is given for the subregion the United Nations designates incongruously as "Asia and the Far East" in table II. A glance at this corroborates the fact of acceleration in the rates

TABLE I.

*World population in major regions, 1957*

| Region | Land area (in thousands of square kilometers) | Population, 1957 (in millions) | Percent of world total | |
|---|---|---|---|---|
| | | | Land area | Population |
| Total | 135,535 | 2,795 | 100.0 | 100.0 |
| Asia and the Far East[1] | 21,178 | 1,483 | 15.6 | 53.0 |
| Soviet Union | 22,403 | 205 | 16.6 | 7.3 |
| Northern America[2] | 21,483 | 189 | 15.9 | 6.8 |
| Latin America[3] | 20,501 | 192 | 15.1 | 6.9 |
| Rest of the world[4] | 49,770 | 726 | 36.8 | 26.0 |

[1] Asia south of the Soviet Union and east of Iran, without New Guinea.
[2] Canada, Greenland, and the United States.
[3] America south of the United States.
[4] Africa, southwest Asia, Europe west of the Soviet Union, Oceania, and New Guinea.
Source: United Nations. Department of Economic and Social Affairs. "The Population of Asia and the Far East, 1950-80." Future Population Estimates by Sex and Age, Rept. IV, Population Studies No. 31. ST/SOA/Series A/31. New York, 1959. Table 1. From: "Demographic Yearbook, 1958," table 2.

of population increase among Asian populations and adds the further fact that growth is prevalent throughout the region. It also indicated that there were substantial differences in rates of growth among the subregions from 1920 to 1950 and suggests the possibility of similar differences from 1950 to 1980.

The depth of the Asian population problems is apparent, some of the dimensions measurable, if attention is turned to individual countries. We have selected five whose fates are highly significant for Asia and the world: India, Pakistan, Indonesia, Communist China, and Japan. The first four are underdeveloped, but the last is urban and industrial, with an educated citizenry, a rate of economic growth among the highest in the world, and a birth rate far below that of the United States.

The time span is limited to the near future, roughly the 15 years from 1960 to 1975. The nature of uncertainty is altered thereby, for all persons who will be aged 13 or above in the year 1975 are already born. If the basic data on population size and age structure in 1960 were correct, actual populations aged 13 and above in 1975 could be altered from those projected only by death rates different from those assumed in the projections. Populations already born cannot have their numbers altered by changes in birth rates.

TABLE II.

*Population trends in Asia and the Far East, 1920-50*

| | | [Populations in millions] | | | |
| | | Regions[1] | | | |
| Year | Total | Central-south | Southeast | Continental east | Maritime east |
|---|---|---|---|---|---|
| Estimated: | | | | | |
| 1920 | 991 | 326 | 110 | 478 | 77 |
| 1930 | 1,074 | 362 | 128 | 496 | 88 |
| 1940 | 1,181 | 410 | 155 | 515 | 101 |
| 1950 | 1,317 | 466 | 172 | 559 | 120 |
| Projected:[2] | | | | | |
| 1960 | 1,572 | 555 | 210 | 670 | 137 |
| 1970 | 1,906 | 681 | 268 | 799 | 158 |
| 1980 | 2,268 | 833 | 348 | 906 | 181 |
| Increase, amount | | | | | |
| 1920 to 1950 | 326 | 140 | 62 | 81 | 43 |
| 1950 to 1980 | 696 | 278 | 138 | 236 | 44 |
| Increase, percent: | | | | | |
| 1920 to 1950 | 33 | 43 | 56 | 17 | 56 |
| 1950 to 1980 | 72 | 79 | 103 | 62 | 51 |

[1] The United Nations region designated as Asia and the Far East excludes southwest Asia and the Asian portion of the U.S.S.R. The regional groupings are as follows: Central-south Asia—Afghanistan, Bhutan, Ceylon, India, the Maldive Island, Nepal, Portuguese India, and Pakistan; southeast Asia—Cambodia, Burma, Indonesia, Laos, Malaya, the Philippines, Timor, Singapore, Thailand, and Vietnam; continental east Asia—Peoples Republic of China, Hong Kong, Macau, and the Mongolian Peoples Republic; maritime east Asia—Taiwan, Japan, Korea, and the Ryukyu Islands. Vietnam and Korea are the undivided countries.

[2] The projected populations for the individual countries, and hence for the regions and the ECAFE area as a whole, are those regarded as most reasonable by the analysts of the United Nations.

Source of data: United Nations, Department of Economic and Social Affairs, *The Population of Asia and the Far East, 1950-1980*. Future Population Estimates by Sex and Age, Rept. IV, Population Studies No. 31. ST/SAO/Series A/31. New York, 1959. Tables 4 and 6.

The conjectural "if" as to the accuracy of present knowledge is an immense one, for the largest of the populations of Asia is that of the Peoples Republic of China. A registration and investigation of the population in late 1953 and early 1954 yielded a population of 582 million for the mainland area. If the birth rate was 41.6 at this time and the death rate 20.4, and if the death rate declined in the general Asian pattern while the birth rate remained unchanged, population increased from 582 million in 1953 to 733 million in 1963. If the population had been 733 million in

1963 and the trends had continued for the 15 years from 1963 to 1978, the population would have exceeded 1 billion by 1978.

The construct for mainland China is an artifact already divorced from the realities of life in Communist China, though the extent of the departure is not measurable for a country where demographic ignorance or secretiveness on the part of the government creates and perpetuates levels of ignorance unparalleled in the modern world. Estimates and projections for Communist China are included, however, for the analysis of Asian populations cannot exclude the Chinese. Discussion may be highly conjectural, but discussion there must be. The projections for the underdeveloped countries other than China are also constructs whose relations to realities in the coming years may be impaired or shattered by the sudden mortality of cataclysm or the slowly increasing death rates that could accompany economic and political failures. This is neither a prediction nor an anticipation of tragic deteriorioration in conditions of living. It is, rather, an affirmation of the awful vulnerability of most Asian populations, whether in India, Pakistan, Indonesia, mainland China, or elsewhere.

The projections of future populations for India, Pakistan, and Indonesia are similar to those for mainland China. All involve assumptions of unchanging fertility and declining mortality. These assumptions permit significant analysis of the problems of the near future. It is unlikely that there will be major declines in birth rates in the period of little more than a decade that separates late 1962 from 1975. If there is economic development and continuing public health expansion, death rates will decline. Thus the projected populations are those likely to exist unless there are failures in the plans of the countries, the international organizations, and the United States.

The problems of population growth are unavoidable components in ongoing economic and social developments. They are indicators of progress not of failures.

### Total populations

The total populations, the amounts of the increases, and the percentages of those increases are given in table III. The figures are staggering in their magnitudes. India must provide for an increase of 177 million within the next 15 years. Pakistan's increase will be 50 million.

East Pakistan's population was estimated at 53 million in 1961; in 1976, under the assumed conditions, it will be 84 million. More than 30 million people will be added in 15 years in a region without cities, industrial development, or substantial known resources for industrialization. If this growth occurs, the people of East Pakistan will be settled 600 to the square kilometre. Quoting conclusions from the United Nations: "The problems of economic development posed by East Pakistan's rapidly growing population are of a kind and dimension hardly encountered in any other part of the world at this time."[3]

Indonesia's projections are largely constructs built on reasoned assumptions.[4] Here, too, present living is difficult. People are vulnerable to interruptions in food supply, whether episodically through crop failures or continuously through economic deterioration. However, if mortality should decline to relatively low levels, population would increase from 93 million in 1961 to 137 million in 1975.

TABLE III.

*Populations in selected Asian countries, 1960 and 1975.*

| Country | Population (in thousands) | | Increase | |
|---|---|---|---|---|
| | 1960-65 | 1975-78 | Amount (in thousands) | Percent |
| India[1] | 423,600 | 600,600 | 177,000 | 41.8 |
| Pakistan[1] | 95,387 | 145,630 | 50,243 | 52.7 |
| Indonesia[1] | 93,344 | 137,376 | 44,032 | 47.2 |
| Mainland China[1] | 732,900 | 1,112,700 | 379,800 | 51.8 |
| Japan | 93,371 | 102,729 | 9,358 | 10.0 |

[1] India, 1961-76; Pakistan, 1961-76; Indonesia, 1960-75; Mainland China, 1963-78.
Sources of data: United Nations, *The Population of Asia and the Far East*, 1950-80. India, high fertility projection, table VIII; Pakistan, low mortality projection, table XVII; mainland China, high fertility projection, table II; Japan, medium projection, table XI. United Nations, *The Population of Southeast Asia (Including Ceylon and China: Taiwan)*, 1950-80. Indonesia, low mortality projection, table III, pp. 138-139.

The island of Java is the world's classic illustration of population growth. Lord Raffles estimated the population as 4.5 million in 1815. Even then there was concern over the pressures of people on limited land. In 1960 there were more than 60 million people on the island of Java. If growth continues as projected, the population of this small island will exceed 100 million by 1975. Whether the Javan economy can absorb an additional 44 million people within the next 15 years is indeed debatable. The possibilities for population transfers from crowded Java to relatively empty Sumatra will be noted later.

In relative terms, the populations of these Asian giants were increasing in similar fashion in the past and, given continuities in development, they will do so in the future. Projected growth in the next 15 years ranges from a low of 42% in India to a high of 53% in Pakistan. The hypothetical progression of mainland China to its population of more than a billion in 1978 implies rates of growth comparable to those assumed for the other underdeveloped countries.

That there are resolutions to growth and the problems of growth is apparent in the figure for Japan—an anticipated growth of only 10% in the 15 years from 1960 to 1975.

## The productive ages

Is it correct to assume that rates of population growth of 40 to 50% within a 15-year period constitute major population problems in these great Asian countries? The answer is unequivocal and it is affirmative. In Table IV, populations in the productive ages from 15 to 59 are given for the years 1960 and 1975, together with increases and rates of increase in numbers in this 15-year period.

TABLE IV.

*Populations in the productive ages, 1960 and 1975.*

| Country | Population aged 15 to 59 (in thousands) | | Increase | |
|---|---|---|---|---|
| | 1960-1963 | 1975-1978 | Amount (in thousands) | Percent |
| India | 233,300 | 316,600 | 83,300 | 35.7 |
| Pakistan | 50,137 | 74,036 | 23,899 | 47.7 |
| Indonesia | 51,521 | 72,289 | 20,768 | 40.3 |
| Mainland China | 376,800 | 551,300 | 174,500 | 46.3 |
| Japan | 57,529 | 70,206 | 12,677 | 22.0 |

For notes and source references, see table III.

The span of years from age 15 through age 59 is a long one. The activities of men in these years are defined as labor, whatever the culture and whether that labor involves working in the rice fields of the monsoon lands, in the iron and steel works that are appearing in the new Asia, or in the service and distribution sectors of the traditional societies. The activities of women are more diverse, for these are the years that include marriage, homemaking, childbearing, and childrearing, and some form of participation in economic activities. Overall, though, men and women in the central 45 years of the life-span maintain themselves and persons in the younger and the older ages. This is the economic responsibility. They produce the younger generation for which they provide—thus fulfilling an essential demographic responsibility. And then they provide for the aging and the aged—thus fulfilling the familial responsibilities that are essential in modern as in ancient societies.

If time and space were available, trends in the adult population would be considered for finer age groups and separately for men and women.

In broad generality, though, the potentialities, the requirements, and the problems of development were apparent in the crude figures of table IV.[5]

The difficulties of an economic development sufficient to provide more adequate employment and income for the existing labor force are compounded immensely if that labor force increases in numbers some 35 to 50% in a decade and a half. This relation of the increasing labor force to modernization is so critical that it merits statement in another form. If there were no economic expansion, there would be two to three claimants for each economic position vacated by death or retirement. For the years from 1965 to 1970, the ratio of additions to departures from labor force ages is 229 for India, 285 for Pakistan, 262 for mainland China, and 283 for Indonesia. This is a rough index of the dynamism required in the economies.

### Women and families

It is gross and perhaps unpardonable simplicity to move directly from population figures to the economic relations and the institutional structures of nations. The population facts place boundaries and impose directions of movement, however, and so they may be used as indicative of the extent of the dynamics required for continuing adjustment in the future.

In the years from 1960 to 1975, girls in their 'teens will increase by 50% or more in the underdeveloped Asian countries. If marriage ages and marriage frequencies remain unchanged, new families formed in 1975 will be half again as numerous as those formed in 1960. Given equal rates of childbearing, annual numbers of births in the late seventies will be 1½ times as great as annual numbers in the early sixties. It should be noted that this does not imply a rise in fertility; it is an increase in numbers of births due to the fact that more women are marrying and having children at the same rates.

Constancy in birth rates combined with declining death rates and increasing numbers of women in the childbearing ages would produce the following numbers of children below age 5 in the specific countries, numbers being in thousands:

| Country | 1960-63 | 1975-78 |
|---------|---------|---------|
| India | 68,300 | 98,500 |
| Pakistan | 16,651 | 25,597 |
| Indonesia | 15,441 | 21,773 |
| Mainland China | 122,100 | 193,100 |
| Japan | 7,357 | 7,326 |

It may be noted that the projected numbers of young children increase at more rapid rates than the projected numbers of adults in the productive ages. The reason is a simple one; young women in the major ages of child-bearing will be increasing more rapidly than the older women, for the reductions in mortality to which they have been subjected will have been greater. And numbers of young children will have had their numbers increased in even higher proportions by the assumed declines in mortality. This characteristic pattern of mortality change compounds the increase in the numbers and the proportions of children and thus increases the relative burdens of dependent on productive age groups.

### The dependent ages

In populations with high birth rates, there are high proportions of youth, small proportions of the aged. The ratios of total dependent to total productive age groups are high. And, given constant fertility and declining mortality, these dependency ratios increase. The picture of table V needs no elaboration beyond the figures themselves. Advancing consumption levels, personal development, opportunities for children, savings—all these are difficult when family maintenance requirements are so great.

TABLE V.

*Dependent and productive age groups, 1960 and 1975*

| Country | Dependent ages | | Productive ages | | Dependent ages per 1,000 in productive ages | |
|---|---|---|---|---|---|---|
| | 1960-63 | 1975-78 | 1960-63 | 1975-78 | 1960-63 | 1975-78 |
| India | 190,300 | 284,000 | 233,300 | 316,600 | 816 | 897 |
| Pakistan | 45,250 | 71,594 | 50,137 | 74,036 | 903 | 967 |
| Indonesia | 41,823 | 65,087 | 51,521 | 72,289 | 812 | 900 |
| Mainland China | 356,100 | 561,400 | 376,800 | 551,300 | 945 | 1,018 |
| Japan | 35,842 | 32,525 | 57,529 | 70,206 | 623 | 463 |

For notes and source references, see table III.

### Education and the oncoming generation

Increasing numbers of men and women in the central ages, increasing numbers of families and households, growing burdens of youth and aged—these are the processes of past, present, and future. Numbers of children in elementary school ages are also increasing (table VI). There are a hundred million children aged 5 to 14 in Indian now; there will be 150 million in 15 years. Pakistan's 24 million children will increase to almost

40 million, the Indonesia's 21 million to 35 million. Given the achievement of the projected numbers, China's 180 million would increase to almost 300 million. The increase in children in school ages in India, Pakistan, Indonesia, and mainland China would amount to 187 million in the 15 years from 1960 to 1975.

Schools, teachers, and maintenance should be provided for the 300 million children now aged 5 to 14—and then further schools, teachers, and maintenance should be provided for an additional number close to 200 million. While this drive for general elementary education is proceeding, higher schools, colleges, technical institutions, and universities are needed for the intermediate, technical, managerial and scientific personnel so essential to the future development of economies, societies, and political institutions.

TABLE VI.

*Children in elementary school ages, 1960 and 1975*

| Country | Number (age 5 to 14) (in thousands) | | Increase | |
|---|---|---|---|---|
| | 1960-63 | 1975-78 | Amount (in thousands) | Percent |
| India[1] | 100,100 | 150,300 | 50,200 | 50.1 |
| Pakistan[1] | 24,323 | 38,752 | 14,429 | 59.3 |
| Indonesia[1] | 21,363 | 34,666 | 13,303 | 62.3 |
| Mainland China[1] | 182,800 | 292,700 | 109,900 | 60.1 |
| Japan | 20,242 | 13,300 | —6,942 | —34.3 |

For notes and source references, see table III.

In 1975, children now below age 5 will be aged 15 to 19. The numbers of youth in the late teens and the increases in their numbers are given in table VII. If someway the breakthrough could be achieved and the young men and women who will be aged 15 to 19, 15 years from now could spend the major portion of these years in educational activities, if not in the types of school systems accepted as normal in developed countries, modernization could be accepted as a probability for the future. If the youth of 1975 are not educated, the workers and the parents of the following decades will not be educated, and the struggle against the manifold problems of ill-trained human resources will continue.

The advance of education is perhaps the single most critical factor beyond economic viability itself. The self-perpetuating mechanisms of traditional societies are nowhere more apparent and more serious than here, for the large families, the severe burdens on families and communities and the deterrents to economic growth are part of a complex of forces that preserve the traditionalism and the illiteracy—as these in turn perpetuate the early marriages, the abundant childbearing, and the high rates of population growth.

TABLE VII.

*Youth aged 15 to 19, 1960 and 1975.*

| Country | Numbers (in thousands) | | Increase | |
|---|---|---|---|---|
| | 1960-63 | 1975-78 | Amount (in thousands) | Percent |
| India[1] | 41,500 | 60,000 | 18,500 | 44.6 |
| Pakistan[1] | 9,517 | 15,035 | 5,518 | 58.0 |
| Indonesia[1] | 8,416 | 14,275 | 5,859 | 69.6 |
| Mainland China[1] | 62,000 | 113,500 | 51,500 | 83.1 |
| Japan | 9,552 | 7,251 | —2,301 | —24.1 |

For notes and source references, see table III.

### RESOLUTION: PROBLEMS AND PROCESSES

The outline of the problems of population and the growth of population yields a somber picture. So also does any projection of growth in a single component into the future. So also did estimates of the European population future in the late 18th and early 19th centuries and the estimates of the Japanese population future in the late 19th and early 20th centuries. Projection to catastrophe is simple. It might even be valid if science and technology remained constant, if people did not strive creatively to improve their own destinies and those of their children, and if governments did not develop their policies in some relationship to the realities of their problems.

Given the magnitude of the problems and the uncertainties concerning their resolutions, summary and conjecture in outline form seem the most feasible procedure.

1. The population growth now occurring is a measure of the greatest humanitarian achievement of all times. The maladjustment is not the advance of science that permitted the saving of life but the failures of a scientific development that would yield comparable reductions in birth rates.

2. The problems of population growth and the urgency involved in the reduction of birth rates are major concerns among many Asian governments. There are Government policies in India and Pakistan; there have been and there may again be policies in Communist China. The great questions concern means and motivations, not the goals of governments.

3. The rapid increases in persons in the productive ages, in families, and in youth in school ages will continue for the next 15 years, whatever the course of birth rates. The numbers of those already born can be altered by shifting death rates, not by shifting birth rates.

4. Any assumption of or arguments concerning the priorities in economic development, social change, and population control are artifacts. All are essential to the achievement of modernization in the individual countries, as in the region as a whole. Success is not possible in any one without roughly parallel success in the others.

5. Urbanization, the expansion of the cultivated acreage, and the more intensive and more productive use of land already cultivated are essential to the modernization of economies and populations. Given the size of the populations, the high rates of growth, the paucity of prime lands now unused, and the density of settlement on existing lands, modernization is not likely to follow as byproduct of urban growth. The increase in the productivity of agriculture, the induction of social change in the villages, and the reduction of birth rates among rural people must be approached as urgent problems of modernization in the contemporary Asian setting.

6. There are possibilities for expansion in some Asian countries, particularly in southeast Asia. The availability of unused areas should ease the transition to modernization if the new resources are developed along with the transformation of the economies. If such areas are occupied in traditional ways, the only contribution of the occupation is an increase in the numbers of people and the extension of the areas of poverty.

7. Given the achieved size of the base populations and the rapidity of the growth, planned transfers of population are not feasible as solutions to problems of population pressure and population growth. The Governments of the Netherlands and Indonesia alike emphasized assisted movements from crowded Java to relatively empty Sumatra. The concept is illusory, for prohibitive investments of capital would be required to transport and resettle Java's increase. . . . The transfer of 20,000 households a year during each of the 30 years from 1950 to 1980 would reduce the population projected for Java in 1980 from 92 million to 87 million; 12% of the population increase of Java would have been transferred to Sumatra, but 88% would remain in Java.

8. International migrations can be neither solutions nor major palliatives to the problems of population growth and economic development in Asian countries. The Asian future differs from the European past in four critical aspects:

(*a*) There are no empty hemispheres awaiting development by the modernizing Asians.

(*b*) The base populations in Asia are so huge and the rates of population growth are so high that European size movement would have little demographic effect, even if they were possible. The United States received 34 million migrants from Europe in the years from 1820 to 1955. This number of migrants would represent less than a single year's population growth in Asia.

(c) The nationalism of the current period is a barrier both to the movement of emigrants and to the willingness of countries to receive immigrants.

(d) Emigration can be a demographic safety valve for countries in process of modernization, with increasing industrialization and urbanization, expanding education, and declining birth rates. It offers only transitory relief to the premodern country where modernization is hope rather than ongoing process and birth rates are intact at ancient levels.

9. Given the absence of international boundaries, there would be major migrations and population redistributions within the the Asian region. The potentialities of the slightly used river deltas of southeast Asia and the fabulous resources of the outer islands of Indonesia would not long remain simply potentialities to be developed at leisure by their present holders.

10. The greatest of the many "danger spots" in the world population of the coming century is the long, fortified, and already vacated frontier zone that separates the Asian peoples of the southern portion of the geographic continent of Asia from the European peoples of the northern portion of that continent. The wall against migrants from a developing Asia is already erected by the Soviet Union; the critical confrontation is already fact. The shape of the outcome depends on the rate of development of the Asian peoples.

11. Expansionism, militarism, and the associated migrations of peoples have characterized nations midway in their modernization. This which has been true of the European and the Japanese pasts may also be true of the Asian futures.

8.

# COMMUNIST CHINA
## AND THE POPULATION PROBLEM

### by Robert C. North

Human beings, in order to survive, must constantly adapt themselves to their environment—or alter the environment to meet their needs or to suit their purposes.

Whether a given population or society adapts relatively more or alters its surroundings relatively more will depend to a considerable degree upon the "hostility" or "friendliness" of the environment and also upon the level of organization the people have achieved when they confront it.

If the environment is extremely hostile the people will be engrossed in extracting a minimal living from it and will not easily accumulate the spare energy necessary for organizing themselves sufficiently to make large changes in their surroundings. On the other hand, if the environment is extremely benign, with fruit falling into the lap, so to speak, the people may perceive no need for changing the world about them, and consequently their efforts at self-organization are not likely to go beyond the minimal demands of the community.

Human beings living somewhere between such extremes of environment will be continually challenged by what appear to be the shortcomings or undesirable characteristics of the world immediately about them. Over the years and decades and centuries they will try to "reorganize" the environment to suit their purposes, and these efforts, in turn, will stimulate them to devise more effective and efficient forms of self-organization.

This self-organization will tend to be political insofar as it involves relationships that are essentially interpersonal—and economic insofar as it involves the allocation and exchange of resources. The physical alteration, the re-shaping, the reorganization, and the transformation of the environment, on the other hand, tends to be considered technological rather than political or economic.

Whether the alteration of the environment is relatively easy or relatively difficult will depend to a large degree upon the distribution of certain vital resources such as the proximity of fertile land and a supply of water or the sequential arrangement on the earth's surface of timber (or coal), a navigable river, and deposits of iron.

It is a probable, therefore, that people in areas where the resources are easy—but not too easy—to obtain and conveniently—but not too conveniently—distributed will be stimulated to greater organizational effort than people elsewhere.

Whether a given environment is essentially "hostile" or "benign" will depend to some extent, of course, upon the ratio between the resources and the numbers of people. If the population is too small, there will not be the manpower to manipulate the environment, and if the population is too large, a mass of the population will be poor and there will be neither the reservoir of human energy nor the "capital" or minimal stockpile of resources necessary for reorganization of the surroundings.

It should be clear, however, that a highly organized people operating from a highly organized—or "reorganized"—base environment can move into an extremely hostile environment, a desert, for example, and reshape it. Also, a relatively unorganized people in a hostile environment can borrow organizational techniques and organized resources (tools, capital, and the like) from a highly organized people with a highly organized base.

Much of the world-wide conflict today concerns first of all the allocation of the world's resources and also the means by which relatively unorganized people in relatively "hostile" environments shall be equipped to alter and even transform, their surroundings.

In this conflict there is not much disagreement on the technical level, but in the political and economic spheres the controversy is heated and sometimes violent. What systems of allocation and exchange will bring about the necessary technological transformation most effectively and efficiently, and what patterns of interpersonal relationships are needed or best suited to ensure the economic and technological undertakings? It is over these issues that much of the cold war is being fought.

There is one problem, however, that appears to be political, economic, and technological all at once, and that is the population issue.

If the numbers of people are too large for the environment as it stands, what is the most effective course of action? Can the imbalance be redressed by a reorganization of the environment? In some circumstances the answer is clearly affirmative. A population problem in an arid region, for example, can frequently be solved by a large-scale importation of water.

But is it always possible to alter the environment rapidly enough and continuously enough to meet the needs of a population that grows rapidly and continuously? Or is it sometimes necessary—for sheer lack of resources or even space—to think about limiting the population? Can such an exploding population alter the environment to meet its requirements, or must the population adjust within certain limits of the environment?

This is a question which confronts many people in the world today, including Communist China, and it is in Communist China, perhaps, that the issue has been associated with the most bitter political controversy.

The usual Marxist-Leninist view has always been that a country or a region is "over-populated" only because of a gap between the technological level of the society and the appropriateness and effectiveness of the political and economic systems.

In capitalistic society, therefore, the population difficulty is seen by communists as inevitably rooted in the conflict between capitalist production relations—how the economic system is organized—and the labor or productive force. This clash between capital and labor must inescapably give rise to a state of relative underemployment and over-population. The only solution for the population problem of a capitalist country is the seizure of state power by the proletariat.

But what about the population in a generally non-capitalist, pre-industrial society such as China?

The Bolshevik revolution in Russia was scarcely a test of Marxist-Leninist population theories. Even today the resources and vast spaces of the Soviet Union are being used by only about two hundred million people, and the problem is more of man power shortage than of over-population. It was the communist seizure of power in China that put Marxism-Leninism face-to-face with the challenge of a vast population.

At first the Chinese Communists seemed intent on controlling their rate of population growth, but then a number of ambiguities appeared in the official attitudes, and in time a loud and spirited debate ensued.

In dealing with Chinese population problems, the communists have identified two incompatible approaches—the Malthusian and the Marxist. According to Malthusian theory one might expect the needs of a rapidly expanding population to increase at a greater rate than production and supply. "But Marxists," according to Wang Ya-nan, the President of Amoy University, "do not approach the problem in this way. Marxists admit that in a certain stage of society the relatively large or small population produces a definite influence over the improvement of the economic life or the development of the economy of the society. But they first of all affirm that human labor, at any stage of society, remains the most valuable wealth, or the source of wealth."

The question hinges, according to Wang, on the capacity of the social system to make rational utilization of and arrangements for its existing labor power. Capitalism and private enterprise "waste" human labor power and thus render a given population "excessive." Under such circumstances a "population problem" is frequently inescapable. This injurious social system, moreover, and particularly the evil influences it leaves behind, cannot be wholly eradicated all at once, and hence a certain transition period is inevitable in a pre-industrial society such as China.

During this development from capitalism to Marxist-Leninist-Maoist socialism "millions and tens of millions of the laboring masses" may have been basically rid of poverty and exploitation, but it was inevitable that some of the disabilities of the earlier period of capitalism and imperialism should persist and that the people would have to endure great difficulties and sacrifices including even unemployment and severe food shortages. Yet these sacrifices were of a wholly different and fundamentally optimistic nature since they paved the way for new and unprecedented progress and development.

The surplus of population, according to the communist viewpoint, had been a dangerous phenomenon under conditions which existed previously in China. In those days vast numbers of people were unemployed, impoverished and destitute. There was wide-spread suffering from pestilence, and the mortality rate was high. Under such circumstances the rapid growth of the Chinese population had been a serious menace.

But the communist victory in China had created a wholly different situation, according to Wang Ya-nan. For once they had achieved power, Mao Tse-tung and his colleagues had been able to alter the proportionate shares of the different sectors of the economy. In short order the state sector was rendered significantly larger than the private sector, and the industrial sector was increased relative to the agricultural sector. Productivity could now be raised, and the living conditions of the people—even the living conditions of a population that was rapidly expanding—could be steadily improved. It was possible, now, to abolish unemployment, poverty, vagrancy, hunger, pestilence, war and untimely death and to put the increasing numbers of people into productive work.[1]

Early in 1957 a controversy emerged between Chinese Communist spokesmen, on the one hand, and non-Party scholars and intellectuals, many of these "population experts" of many years standing. While confessing certain "errors" of the past and disassociating themselves from Malthusianism—or even the "New Malthusianism" of which they were charged—these non-Party intellectuals insisted that the rapidly rising population in China was still a serious problem. In presenting their arguments, these men differed somewhat among themselves, but it was clear that all of them were taking serious issue with the Party policy on population.

"In pre-liberation days I wrote many articles on the problem of the population of China," confessed Wu Ching-ch'ao, professor in the China People's University and a member of the China Democratic League. A sociologist, Wu had taken his Ph.D. at the University of Chicago years before. "When I go over these articles today, I immediately find that many of the points I brought up before were incorrect."[2]

Wu had maintained in the days of the pre-communist era that "the large population of China is the main cause of the poverty of the majority of people in China." Now it was clear, however, that poverty and the large population had been two different phenomena, and that there was "no connection whatsoever between them," or—if there had been any connection—it was entirely "accidental." The truth of the matter was that unemployment and poverty and misery and untimely death had been the consequence of the social system, and not of the expanding population.

Wu Ching-ch'ao now realized that he had been guilty of another error. ". . . I dreamed that China's birth rate would one day drop considerably . . . This is an idealist point of view. Experience teaches us that never in an industrialized nation has the number of population been reduced as a result of the practice of birth control."[3]

"The cause of my errors," Wu Ching-ch'ao admitted, "was that I did not study the problem from the standpoint and method of historical materialism."[4] As a consequence of this carelessness he had "covered up the crime of the reactionary ruling class and had confused the masses about the nature of the revolutionary struggle. The basic task is not to achieve birth control, Wu conceded, but to increase labor productivity—though "too high a birthrate," he insisted, would impede capital accumulation even under socialism.

Honesty forced Wu Ching-ch'ao, after confessing his errors, to come back to the birth rate problem. On the one hand, China should undoubtedly strive to accelerate socialist industrialization so that the country's technical level could be steadily raised. On the other hand, however, it was inescapable that the rate of population increase should be kept down so that the number of people asking for employment should be reduced gradually. "In introducing birth control to China," he asserted, "our goal is to reduce the present birth rate of 3.7% to 1.7%."[5]

Having blurted out the unpleasant truth as he saw it, Wu hastened to disassociate himself from any taint of Malthusianism.

"There are among us those who are inclined to make criticism which is unwarranted," he complained. "The moment they hear people talk about birth control, they consider it an attempt to promote New Malthusianism . . . [which] seems to have something in common with our policy. This view is incorrect . . . There is a fundamental difference between us and the New Malthusianists. In the first place, the New Malthusianists generally take a pessimistic attitude toward agricultural production, constantly worrying about food shortage for the population. We are not at all pessimistic about this point . . . even if the present rate of population did not drop, we could still produce more than enough to feed our people. We promote birth control, not for the shortage of food."

The purpose of promoting birth control, according to Wu Ching-ch'ao, was to improve the health of mothers and babies and to "make our production fall in line with the basic economic law of socialism and the law of development according to ratio and plan, so that we may fulfill without any difficulty the general task of the transition period."[6]

At the July 3, 1957 meeting of the fourth session of the First National People's Congress in Peking Dr. Ma Yin-ch'u, a distinguished Chinese economist with a Ph.D. from Columbia University and the President of Peking University, issued a paper entitled "A New Theory of Population."

While carefully disassociating himself from the Malthusian approach, Ma asserted that the biggest contradiction in China was between overpopulation and an inadequate supply of capital and identified the large population of the country and its rapid rate of increase as major problems and chief obstacles to economic development.

In order to improve living conditions, Ma declared, it was necessary to increase the supply of capital as a prerequisite to production expansion. "As we have a big poulation," he pointed out, "our consumption expenditure is enormous and not much national income can be saved for capital accumulation, which must be distributed among many production departments. Thus the amount of capital a department can receive is too small."[7] China's vast population had become a stumbling block to the country's industrialization. The need was to bring the Chinese population under control in order to lower the ratio of consumption expenditure to capital accumulation.

Unless such measures were taken, Ma warned, the drive for industrialization would move forward only at the extreme expense of the people, who might well retaliate by violence—as the people of Poland and Hungary had done, ". . . if we do not try to tackle the problem of population as soon as possible, the kindness we have rendered the peasants will inevitably be translated into disappointment and dissatisfaction. Although they will not follow the footsteps of the Poles and Hungarians, they will give the government a great deal of trouble."[8]

Communist spokesmen were quick to take issue with the proponents of birth control—even though the government had made extensive, though largely ineffective, efforts of its own to reduce the rate of population growth. The "rightists," according to the Party, had intentionally taken advantage of the population problem "to oppose the Party and socialism." They had seized the problem as "an excuse for the restoration of the bourgeois sociology as well as of capitalism." These "rightists," in fact, "were really old hands in class struggle and, therefore, could avail themselves of this problem in the pitch of class struggle and political struggle."[9]

The theory which considers population a fundamental problem of the society, according to government and Party spokesmen, had been one of the most powerful weapons used to paralyze the revolutionary consciousness of the working class. Imperialism and the reactionary factions in China had used the problem all along, and now it was proving useful to the new group of rightists who wanted to prove that China, by the fact of its great population, could not be built into a socialist country.[10]

Perhaps the rightists would "craftily attempt to deny" their intent to create ideological confusion and to make the masses lose confidence in socialism and industrialization. "We have," they might say, "committed theoretical mistakes at most. Our intention is good. We act so only to popularize birth control." Yet the outcome of the rightist arguments, Party spokesmen declared, was to assert "that China is over-populated now and cannot be built into a socialist country." Beyond this, ". . . you yourselves understand clearly that birth control cannot be carried out immediately. Even though we may enforce it throughout China right now, in a perfectly strict way conformable to our ideal, it will take effect only after more than a decade."[11]

Perhaps the technical difficulties associated with attempts at population control lay at the heart of the Party attitude. Perhaps they were trying to hide a program that had failed, to make an asset out of a discouraging reality. In any case, according to the Party viewpoint, the rightists wanted to take a capitalist road out of the population difficulty. (Even the Party admitted that there was a difficulty.)

"Opinion differs as to how the population problem of our country can be tackled and solved," an early 1958 Jen Min Jih Pao article asserted. "One kind of view is 'leftist.' Those who maintain this point of view think that our large population and high rate of population growth is positively a good thing. From their point of view, the birth control campaign is making mountains out of mole hills. When tackling problems and laying down plans they seldom based their thinking on the population of 600,000,000, but are often concerned with absolute magnitudes and speed with no regard whatever for reality."[12]

Opposed to this viewpoint, Party spokesmen charged, the rightists "think that our huge population and high rate of population growth are absolutely a bad thing. From their point of view, all difficulties may be attributed to the size of our population . . . They pin their hope on an unrealistic birth control program aimed to keep the population from going beyond the 600,000,000 mark."[13]

Both the "leftist" and "rightist" viewpoints were condemned as erroneous. Ideologically and practically both were absolutist from the Party standpoint. "To them a huge population is either absolutely good or absolutely bad."[14]

"Our Party has pointed out that our large population is a good thing . . ." one spokesman recalled. "But our Party has also pointed out the difficulties arising from a big population. These are difficulties of development, and we are already prepared for overcoming these difficulties."

The correct Party way to solve the population problem was by means of a basically multi-pronged approach: "The concrete content of this way is to encourage planned birth-giving and propagandize and popularize birth control, and to make unified arrangements for production, labor and pay or allotment on the basis of 600,000,000 people. The most fundamental means, however, is to develop vigorously our industrial and agricultural production and increase our social productivity."[16]

During the transition period the People's Republic—while encouraging birth control—must expand industrial and agricultural production as rapidly as possible; allot rewards "according to labor," that is, lengthen apprenticeships and avoid excessive pay to young men in order to discourage early marriage and large families; and make unified arrangements for raising the level of technical capability in order to hasten the achievement of socialism.[17]

"The venerable Doctor Ma always claims himself to be different from Malthus," two critics charged at a Seminar on the History of Chinese Revolutions at Peking University. "And we sincerely hope that he is not a Malthusian. Yet, in his masterpiece "The New Population Theory," the venerable Doctor Ma did really and actually disseminate Malthus' views. This is indeed to be regretted."[18] Like Malthus, Ma had perceived the population problem, as the "root of all social problems."

The central problem, as the Party saw it, was this: "As our country is densely populated and has a weak economic foundation, can we rely on our own strength to build up socialism? Or can we rely on our own strength to guarantee a high rate of development of productivity in society?"[19]

A large population would be not only an outstanding, but also an advantageous characteristic of China with the potential for "generating a tremendous energy for the building of socialism."[20] But the bourgeois rightists, hitherto having nursed "an inveterate hatred" of the working people, did not miss an opportunity "to curse" the large population of China. Previously these mischief makers had held the large population responsible for evils actually emanating from imperialism. Now, hiding behind a new phraseology, they were insulting and slandering the Chinese people by contending that it would be exceedingly difficult to build socialism in the face of a rapidly expanding population.[21]

There was one basic difference between Malthusians and Marxists. "They [the Malthusians] regard the population problem as the fundamental problem underlying the solution of all the problems relating to human society: only if birth control is practiced, population is reduced and poor people are restrained from producing more children, then all the problems will vanish and society can make smooth progress. We believe that such a view is incongruous with the materialist conception of history. The fundamental problem of the development of human society lies in whether the nature of production relations meets the demand of productivity."[22]

Dr. Ma had failed to perceive these realities.

"Our point of view is dramatically opposed to his," wrote Min Tzu, putting forward the Party viewpoint a few weeks later. "We believe that it is a very good thing for China to have a large population. Since the liberation we have made extremely brilliant achievements in economic and cultural construction. The reason why we can do this is inseparable from the great creative labor of the 600 million people."[23]

"As all of us know, the national income is the material wealth newly produced by the toiling people in the process of production," Min Tzu wrote. "When the 600 million people give full play to their production enthusiasm, it will increase the national income considerably. When the absolute amount of national income is increased, it is possible for us to speed up capital accumulation, which in turn will guarantee the development of the national economy, increase our consumption to a definite extent, and thus improve our people's livelihood."[24]

What should particularly be pointed out here, according to Min Tzu, is that "the labor of the broad masses is itself a kind of investment."

"Is a large population really contradictory to mechanization and automation?" asked Min Tzu. "Ma's thesis was based on the following point: "What it took a thousand men to do before can now be done by, say, 50 after mechanization and automation. Then, what shall we do with the 950 persons who have been laid idle?" Obviously, he took mechanization and automation as the factor responsible for over-population and unemployment. Thus, to avert overpopulation and unemployment he thought it necessary for us to slow down mechanization and automation. This is an extremely erroneous theory which inflexibly applies to socialist society the law of relative over-population applicable under capitalist conditions."[25]

In contrast to the limited productive possibilities of capitalism, Min Tzu asserted, a socialist society would open up wholly new productive relations with the capacity for "infinitely broad" development of productive forces. ". . . the large population in China is not in contradiction with mechanization and automation, but instead may speed up mechanization and automation."[26]

"Why is there so big a difference between Ma Yin-ch'u's view and ours?" Min Tzu asked. "This is because he took the bourgeois stand, observing problems in the light of metaphysics and through a non-realistic approach. Thus he failed to reflect upon the objective actuality, a fact which led his discussion in the wrong direction."[27]

Labor productivity, according to Min Tzu, is determined by the number of workers and output per worker. If we see more workers employed, but lose sight of their larger output, the conclusion is bound to be that the labor productivity tends to be lower with more workers employed. If we are aware that in this socialist society industrial and agricultural development is speedy, and becomes even speedier than the growth of population, we may understand that socialism can raise productivity to a high level."[28]

Any apparent similarity between Party policy and the New Population Theory was illusory and false, according to the Party viewpoint. "Our efforts to publicize and popularize birth control and to control appropriately the rate of increase of population aim at abating the difficulties confronting us in the large-scale economic construction resulted from the large population and the inherent economic backwardness. However, we never regard the control of the rate of increase of population as the prerequisite for the construction of socialism. On the contrary, we believe that our 600,000,000 population is the capital for socialist construction, and we must rely on the mass of hard working and gallant people to erect a magnificent edifice of socialism."[29]

The official Chinese Communist attitude was summed up by Liu Shao-ch'i, who made it clear that the population of China—in line with Marxist-Leninist-Maoist theory—was expected to transform the environment rather than to adapt itself through a limitation of its numbers.

"We have a population of more than 600 million," Liu told the Second Session of the C.C.P. Eighth National Congress on May 5, 1958, "and our Party has ties of flesh and blood with this vast population. By relying on this great force we can or soon can do anything within the realms of human possibility."[30] The vast population was an asset and not a liability. Man—Chinese man—need not limit his numbers. Chinese man could do anything.

Liu admitted that "for the time being" the people were economically poor and "culturally like a clean sheet of paper." But his colleague, Mao Tse-Tung, had already described well the true implications of these circumstances: "Poor people want change, to work hard and to make a revolution. A clean sheet of white paper has nothing written on it and is therefore well suited for writing the newest and most beautiful words on it and for drawing the newest and most beautiful pictures." Precisely because the people were poor and unsophisticated, Liu maintained, they would exert the vigor to transform their environment into a proper place and find ways for developing its productivity faster than the needs and demands of the increasing numbers of people.

In mid-1962 these optimistic attitudes toward population were abruptly altered.

With the faltering of the Great Leap Forward, Chinese Communist leaders fell back on a "campaign against early marriages" and the discouragement of too many children in the early years as oblique approaches to the problem of birth control. The minimum age for marriage, according to the Marriage Law, was twenty for men and eighteen for women. "From a medical point of view," it was asserted, these ages were the absolute lower limit for "physical and intellectual growth" and "psychological well-being."[31] Later marriages were encouraged, and unmarried young people were especially cautioned against premature unions motivated by "bourgeois affection" and similar emotions rather than by the requirements of society.[32]

Under the new Chinese Communist policy "family planners"—themselves under attack only a short time earlier—were also warning young wives against endangering their health and the effectiveness of their work by having too many children in the early years of marriage.[33] Pressures began to be applied through trade unions and other organizations for limiting the size of individual families. Sterilization was made easier,[34] contraception was encouraged, and abortions were considered permissible under certain circumstances. Government spokesmen admitted the desirability, even the necessity, of lowering the nation's birth rate,[35] and began to express interest in the development of oral contraception.

It remains to be seen whether, objectively, the Chinese Communists will be capable of their Herculean task or whether the plans of Liu, Mao, and their colleagues emerge only as "most beautiful pictures" on a clean sheet of paper. In the meantime a bitter race continues between efforts to raise production, on the one hand, and the exploding population on the other. It is difficult to foresee a satisfactory outcome. With every advance —in food production, in sanitation, in housing—the population takes a further leap. And with each discrepancy between accomplishment and demand, the society will be subject to further stresses and strains—no matter what the nature of the governing system.

9.

# POPULATION CONTROL IN CHINA: AN INTERVIEW WITH CHOU-EN-LAI

## by Edgar Snow

On January 23, 1964, shortly before France recognized the People's Republic of China, Edgar Snow was given a five-hour interview by Premier Chou En-lai in Conakry, Guinea. The long colloquy was published in Paris in its entirety in three issues of *Le Nouveau Candide* (January 30, February 6, February 13) and in full or abridged form in other continental newspapers, in the London publication *Arts and Sciences in China,* and in *The New York Times.* The portion of this interview which dealt with the population question is included in this aritcle. To provide some background for this interview, it is preceded by an extract from Mr. Snow's book. *The Other Side of the River: Red China Today* (Random House, 1962) pp. 414-416.

*     *

Contraceptives are on sale for both men and women. At various hospitals and clinics I found that standard devices were available at the equivalents of twenty to thirty American cents. I was told that they are supplied gratis when necessary. In remote Szechuan at a rather primitive clinic I was shown charts, demonstration equipment and plentiful supplies but was also told that the demand for instruction was "light." A pessary there cost thirty cents. Existing supplies would doubtless prove inadequate if the population applied en masse, but for those who presently "plan" there seemed to be no shortage.

Both abortion and sterilization were as easily available in China in 1956 during the "family planning campaign" as advice on contraception. While the advice is still disseminated through radio talks and literature, sterilization is now obtainable only through a doctor's recommendation and abortion is discouraged although still performed on the same condition. The extent to which people may submit to sterilization is indicated by experience in India, where significant cash inducements were offered together with free surgery. By 1960 only 22,000 cases were reported, or about one in 20,000.

A British-educated Indian demographer, S. Chandrasekhar, of the Institute of Population Studies of Madras, visited China in 1959. Like most travelers, he was "continually impressed by how clean and neat everything was," but he drew attention to the consequences for China's food economy. In the *Atlantic Monthly* of December, 1961, Mr. Chandrasekhar wrote that in 1959 the birth rate had attained forty per thousand while the death rate had been reduced to "twelve per thousand, an incredibly low figure for an Asian country. The infant mortality rate, a sensitive index to a community's level of public health, environmental hygiene, and total cultural milieu, was around fifty per thousand births per year." Mr. Chandrasekhar elsewhere says in effect that this represents a reduction of about 75 percent as compared to prerevolution estimates.

Mr. Chandrasekhar's figures would not apply to the country as a whole; as stated above, China's annual increase is about 2 per cent, if the 1953 census was correct. This figure was also given to me as "average" by Chou En-lai in 1960. Even if China's increase dropped to as low as the current Japanese rate (1.01 percent; the United States rate is 40 percent higher than Japan's) the result would be six to seven million more Chinese annually. India faces an even more serious problem than China, however, with the gap between her food output and the minimal survival needs of a third of her population widening each year. According to the Ford Foundation report already cited, India will by 1966 have 25 percent more people than she can adequately feed.

The dismissal of Ma Yin-ch'u from his post as president of Peking University in 1960 was attributed abroad to his espousal of birth control. The Peking authorities said he was retired because of "old age." He was seventy-six, but he had one of China's most active and independent minds and was in good health. A Yale graduate and a famous economist, Ma had made a deep impression on intellectuals when he decided to collaborate with the Communists. He did advocate birth control but he was not a Malthusian. In 1956 he published an original theory of "overall balance and proportional development" in economic planning which stressed the danger of retrogression by overdevelopment of industry at the expense of agriculture. For that he was strongly attacked, but he held his ground until party stalwarts forced his resignation. It is interesting that Mao Tse-tung nevertheless not only praised Ma's "eight point charter for agriculture" but had the party adopt it. In 1961 Ma still retained his seat in the National Congress. It was also significant that in 1961, Ma Yin-ch'u's "original theory" still remained unanswered.

Literature and radio broadcasts continue to publicize techniques of birth control and periodicals urge young people to use contraceptives for family planning. Many workers and peasants I questioned, as well as the college girls I have mentioned, said that they were "planning" for no more than two or three children. Party members told me that within the party "undisciplined" procreation is frowned upon. Most high-ranking party members have small families, although I know at least one who (somewhat embarrassedly) last year celebrated the birth of his seventh child in quest of a son! The two-child family is regarded as ideal and party functionaries receive no extra allowances for more children.

A means of "planning" which might not work in another society but has produced a noticeable effect in China is the officially sponsored social approval for late marriages. For an ambitious student, early marriage can be a handicap, as in the West, and today everybody is supposed to be an ambitious student. The prestige of the party and the press behind marriage for men at twenty-five to twenty-seven and for women at twenty-one to twenty-three as "ideal" has made it stylish among the closely party-led youths. Their examples may eventually impress the "outer-directed" peasant masses, who also do not like to be found behind the times or "old-fashioned." The party does not "select brides and grooms," as reported abroad, but young people often consult group leaders as well as parents before they marry.

\*     \*

*Snow*: Recently I read in the Chinese press an interview between you, Premier Chou, and a factory worker, a husband and father of two children, who had been sterilized to avoid further increase. Is that practice now widely fostered?

*Premier Chou*: (Laughing) I'm afraid your question will give people the impression that I am a Marxist who advocates having no offspring. This is of course absurd. What you referred to was something I said on a specific occasion. We do believe in planned parenthood, but it is not easy to introduce all at once in China and it is more difficult to achieve in the rural areas, where most of our people live, than in the cities. The first thing is to encourage late marriages. The years 20 to 30 are very important to mental and physical development—years when scientific and artistic growth often occur most rapidly. Among various means of referred parenthood, sterilization is only the last, and only applies to those already burdened by too many children. *(Newly married couples are advised to try to limit their offspring to two. Among party members the small state subsidy for help in child support is limited to two children —as has been true at least since 1960—E.S.)* Sterilization is practiced in many countries of the world, but heretofore mainly on women, not men. That not only imposes inequality on women but what is more, as I have been told by many doctors, sterilization is simple and harmless for men while more complicated for women. However, in China, which has just freed itself from semi-feudalism, there is great resistance among men to the practice of sterilization to curtail excessive reproduction. Others are likely to say that such a man has been castrated; he has become a eunuch!

That is why I was particularly interested in encountering a factory worker who had subjected himself to sterilization. It happened that Chen Yi and I were visiting a factory where we found that a great many workers were encumbered by large families. Then I came upon a woman worker holding a child in her arms. *(Nursing mothers in China often place their infants in factory creches during working hours, where they visit and care for them intermittently.)* I asked her how many children she had, she replied that she had two, and I then asked if she approved of family planning. When she replied that her husband had beeen sterilized, I asked to meet him and discovered that he was a deputy manager of the plant. He had simply decided that it was a good means and had adopted it; his factory superiors were not even aware of it. *(The magazine article referred to quoted the father as saying that sterilization had in no way impaired his health and that his normal married life continued satisfactorily.)*

*Snow:* By these and other means now being encouraged could one expect to see China's population growth rate reduced to as low a percentage as that of Japan, or even lower, by 1970?

*Premier Chou:* Since the Second War Japan has achieved remarkable decline to about 1%. We have sent people to Japan to study means used there and the results. Our present target is to reduce the population increase to below 2%; for the future we aim at an even lower rate. However, I do not believe that it will be possible for us to equal the Japanese rate by 1970—for some of the reasons mentioned. For example, as a result of the improved living conditions over the past two years, our rate rose again to 2.5%! Therefore, China's purpose in carrying out planned parenthood is entirely positive. Planned parenthood, on the basis of increased production for consumption, is conducive to raising the living standard of the people. This is a matter of fundamental importance. That is why we have been studying it very carefully during the past two years.

*Snow:* Some time ago I read that Chinese scientists were working on a simple and effective oral contraceptive. What has happened to it? Secondly, are you aware that such a contraceptive has been tested and approved by the United States health bureau and may soon be, or already is, on public sale? Would you be interested in mass distribution of such means in China?

*Premier Chou*: It is true that our scientists have been experimenting along such lines but we have not yet produced a satisfactory oral contraceptive. I also have read of the American product. We should be very interested to know more about it.

(Chou En-lai said that he would be prepared to discuss the whole subject of planned parenthood at greater length, if time permitted. Obviously now "demographic-minded," he has been consulting with experts. His remarks indicated that his government has adopted a much more serious and systematic approach to means of curtailing population growth than was apparent during my visit to China late in 1960. The latest official national census taken in China, in 1957, showed a total population of 656 million inhabitants, including those on Taiwan. At an average annual increase of 2% since then the total would now exceed 700 million, not including some 16 to 18 million Overseas Chinese, chiefly in Southeast Asia.

# Latin America

❂ ❂ ❂

## 10.

# THE POPULATION' EXPLOSION IN
# LATIN AMERICA

### by Ronald Hilton

Much has been made, and rightly, of the population explosion in Latin America. There is an abundant literature on the statistical aspects of the problem, together with the usual sociological considerations.[1] This paper will, therefore, concentrate on some highly significant but neglected aspects of the question.

A glance at the map of Latin America shows that the population is concentrated in the highlands, or temperate zone, and along the coastlines. The deep substratum of the population in the highlands is Indian, although the top layers may, to varying degrees, have been modified by miscegenation with white immigrants, and in very rare cases with Negroes who have wandered up from the coastal areas. These coastal areas have a population which is primarily white south of the Tropic of Capricorn, Negro in the areas such as northeastern Brazil where a plantation economy flourished, and mixed Indian, white and Negro in the remaining sectors. In general the highlands provided a better environment than the lowlands for the development of Indian civilizations. The Indians who lived at sea level were usually the victims of internecine warfare. While it is absurd to repeat that the Spaniards killed off literally all of the Indians in the Caribbean islands, it is true that they virtually annihilated them and completed the "destruction of the Indies" with even more success than the Caribs, who were busy annihilating the Arawaks when the Spaniards arrived.

From this general description several considerations derive. The first is that, conspicuously in South America, there is a large empty area between the coastal zone and the highlands. The immediate response is to say that this area should be filled up and that it provides a built-in safety valve for the continent's population explosion. This is largely the motivation behind the transferral of Brazil's capital from Rio de Janeiro to Brasília. It remains to be seen whether the creation of Brasília will lead to the opening up of the Brazilian plateau, which has a much better climate than the coastal zone but which seems to have been denuded by centuries of destructive fire-agriculture. Moreover, the soils in the Brasília area are not in general satisfactory for agriculture, and the Belcher Associates of Ithaca, New York, the consultants for the Brasília project, did not answer satisfactorily the questions on this subject asked by the *Hispanic American Report*.

Indeed, much of the unoccupied area of South America suffers from edaphological difficulties. The Guianese and Brazilian shields have practically no humus. In the Guianas there is a fertile strip of alluvial soil along the coast, but the forests of the interior hide extremely poor soils. Where the rains are excessively heavy (and a characteristic of Latin America is that most areas suffer from an extremely high or conversely an extremely low rainfall), the soils are leached, and even apparently good grazing land lacks mineral content and can support only the most miserable herds of cattle. These considerations were the basis for the pessimism expressed by Isaiah Bowman in his *Limits of Land Settlement* (*New York*, 1937). As a result of the efforts of the U.S. Government to develop techniques to make the desalinization of sea water feasible, certain arid areas of Mexico, Chile and Brazil will be opened up, but topography will be a major obstacle to irrigation.

Then there is the basic fact that the tropical rivers of South America still do more harm than good. It has been calculated that the Amazon alone provides about one-fifth of all the water entering the world's oceans. The damp winds from the Atlantic striking against the Andes produce three great river systems—the Amazon, the Orinoco, and the Magdalena—and if one sees them on a rampage one can realize why in classical antiquity the bull was the symbol of a roaring torrent; Hercules wrenching off a bull's horn, out of which flowed water producing the cornucopia or horn of plenty, is a symbol of man's conquest of rivers. Latin America needs lots of Hercules to bring the Amazon, the Orinoco, and the Magdalena systems within fixed channels, just as at long last the United States is finally taming the Mississippi system.

There still remain in the interior of South America certain fairly fertile areas at medium elevation which would be excellent centers of colonization providing the difficult problem of communications could be overcome. In an unpretentious book, *The Conquest of Brazil*, which has become a classic and has been translated into Portuguese, Roy Nash has expounded the thesis that these highland areas must be colonized first and that from them the great river basins, especially Amazonian, can slowly be reduced to submission.

Is it possible then to make Amazonia an effective center of human activity? There is a manic-depressive answer to this question. Ellsworth Huntington said no, since the area does not provide the climatic stimuli without which no civilization can develop. Preston James believes that this is an old wives' tale, with about as much substance as the belief of ancient geographers that Germania could never become civilized because of the excessive cold. It may be that, just as developments in heating made Germania habitable, so progress in airconditioning will make life in Amazonia tolerable. In any case, no spot in Amazonia has a climate as unbearable as New York or Washington in summer. Some Latin American writers, like the Mexican José Vasconcelos and the Colombian Luis Enrique Osorio, have developed an almost mystical theory according to which civilization, which began in the tropics, will return there in due course, and Amazonia will become a great center of culture. This area of conjecture does not lend itself to scientific speculation, but rightly or wrongly most disinterested observers state that there is little likelihood of Amazonia becoming a center of dense population and creative activity in the foreseeable future.

Indeed, who will inhabit regions like Amazonia? In *La raza cósmica*, Vasconcelos expresses the idea that Latin America's lack of racial purity, far from being a handicap as was earlier thought, may allow Latin America to create the "cosmic race," the mixture of white, Indian, and Negro, which will represent the culmination of human evolution. Miscegenation, regarded in the past as creating half-breeds, who combined the defects of the racially "pure" parents and in some mysterious way destroyed their qualities, will, according to modern genetic theories, create new and superior types, just as hybrid maize is superior to more elementary species.

This theory may appear to be attractive scientifically and even philosophically, but who indeed is peopling the empty spaces of Latin America? The hard fact that the present occupants are tending to move off the land and to add to the population of the capitals, making Latin America a continent of megapoles.[2] As typical manifestations of macrocephalia, greater Buenos Aires has about a quarter of Argentina's population, while Montevideo comprises almost a half of the population of Uruguay. It is common to lament this trend, but the economist Lauchlin Currie has propounded a scheme by which much of the population of Colombia would be moved off the land and established in the big cities to make possible a rationalization of Colombian agriculture.

It is, in fact, becoming harder and harder to find immigrants who will settle on the land and face the conditions prevailing there. The Italians who opened up the countryside of southern Brazil, Uruguay, and Argentina have been succeeded by a generation which can find good jobs in the area of the European Common Market. Many of those who migrated to Brazil, revolted at being expected to undertake tasks the Brazilians themselves would not do, demanded that they be repatriated to Italy. There was in the past century a free migration of Spaniards to and from Latin America, but, despite the population pressure resultant from the rise of the Spanish population to 30 million, the Franco government discourages this loss of manpower. In any case, Spaniards like Italians today prefer to find work in France, Germany, or one of the other Common Market countries. The Chinese and Syrian-Lebanese are not wanted in Latin America since they tend to congregate in the cities as small tradesmen. It is startling, for example, to see how much of the trade of Paramaribo, Surinam, is in Chinese hands.

By the default of others, the Japanese have become priority immigrants. Not only do Brazil and Paraguay in particular welcome them, but the Japanese Government, determined to maintain the island's population at 90 million, regards migration to South America, in addition to birth control and abortion, as being an important means to this end. Although nationalism and terrorism still infect the Japanese colonies in Brazil, the Japanese immigrants are welcomed, but it remains to be seen if the second generation of Japanese will be content to stay on the farm as their fathers did. Be that as it may, it was the Japanese farmers who opened such important areas as western São Paulo and Paraná. In any case, the population explosion of Latin America is the result of internal growth rather than of immigration.

Why should there be a startling growth of the native population? Undoubtedly the elimination in large areas of such diseases as malaria and yellow fever has been a contributing factor, as has the decline in the death rate and especially in the infant mortality rate because of generally improved health conditions. While such improvements would benefit primarily the underprivileged Indians and Negroes, it would seem correct to say that the greatest increase occurs among the mixed breeds, whose dynamism and fertility contrasts with the lack of will to live and reproduce among the pure Indians. In countries like Haiti there is a sharp rivalry between the mulattoes and the pure Negroes; it appears that the former are reproducing more rapidly.

Two other explanations of the population increase in Latin America deserve to be examined more critically. The first is that the Catholic Church has effectively banned birth control. It is true that Latin America is rapidly becoming the greatest concentration of Roman Catholics in the world, thus establishing an embarrassing correlation between Catholicism, backwardness, and social unrest. It is equally true that the Catholic Church is promoting rather grotesque methods of birth control and is playing Russian roulette with fertility. It is a fact that Argentina, officially a Catholic country which has presented such a disgraceful spectacle of military and ecclesiastical tyranny, has felt moved, through its delegation in the United Nations, to fight any attempt to promote the study of birth control as being incompatible with the Latin American heritage as though the fight against birth-control and divorce were its essential features! It is a fact that the United States Government, in the whole of the Alliance for Progress program, has not felt free to make any serious reference to the problem of birth control.[3]

At the same time, Catholic Argentina which so vigorously fights birth control, has about the lowest birth rate in Latin America. Many nominal Catholics pay about as much attention to the Catholic Church's stand on birth control as Baptists and other low church groups in this country do to the prohibition against liquor. Indeed, it has been suggested that just as prohibition did much to undermine Fundamentalist Protestantism in this country, so hostility to effective birth control will undermine fundamental Catholicism in Latin America. This is already happening in Puerto Rico, where the supposedly Catholic women of the people would sooner face the ire of the priests than a·lifetime of misery brought about by the bearing of excessively large families.[4]

Among the intellectuals and government officials, there has been a growing willingness to disregard the Church's interdiction of a serious discussion of birth control problems. The liberal, anti-clerical Mexican publishing house, the Fondo de Cultura Económica, took the lead a few years ago when it translated Malthus into Spanish. Since then there has been an increasing candor regarding this controversial issue. The military dictatorships which plague Latin America willingly ally themselves for practical reasons with the Catholic Church, which can so easily become an instrument of thought-control, yet they usually do not share the Church's puritanical attitude in sexual matters. With a strange and picturesque inconsistency, at the same time as Argentine dictator Juan Perón was promoting his claim that his dead wife Evita should be made a saint, he was sponsoring legalized prostitution, which the Catholic Church disapproves of, although with none of the vigor it displays in fighting birth control. El Salvador is one of the most Catholic countries in Latin America, but it is reported that the military clique at present ruling El Salvador is quietly promoting birth control to fight the problems brought about by El Salvador's population density, one of the highest in Latin America.

Whatever the actual influence of the Catholic Church may be in these matters, it is certain that the Church's vehement stand on this issue, in sharp contrast with its indifference to matters of poverty, tyranny, and social injustice, is undermining the prestige of the Catholic Church in Latin America. Indeed, the feeling is spreading that the Catholic Church is a nuisance and a hindrance to the development of decent living standards in Latin America. The Christian Socialist movement, which under Eduardo Frei has grown markedly in Chile, is trying to transform the social role of the Catholic Church, but it too has refused to adopt a realistic attitude in matters of birth control.

Besides the theory that the Catholic veto on birth control is an important factor in the population explosion of Latin America, we should mention the explanation given by the Brazilian Josué de Castro in his *Geography of Hunger*. de Castro is a nutritionist whose theories have won him such wide respect that he was appointed director general of the United Nations Food and Agricultural Organization. Baldly stated, his theory is that mammals, and indeed other organisms, when they are starved, become unusually fertile and reproduce vigorously, as a biological assertion of the need to survive. Thus it is, according to Josué de Castro, that there is a population explosion among the starving people of Brazil's Northeast.

This theory is ingenious and attractive, but obviously it involves some highly technical biological considerations. The distinguished biochemist Professor James Murray Luck does not hesitate to dismiss Josué de Castro's thesis as worthless. According to Professor Luck, it is based on deductions irresponsibly drawn from unverified experiments carried out years ago at Stanford.[5]

It has not been suggested elsewhere, but it seems evident that population concentrations in Latin America are the result of economic activities. Once these activities decline, the population may not be reduced as fast as the circumstances would warrant. While this may be a universal law, it would seem to be especially applicable to Latin America, where national boundaries prevent free migrations. The population density of Haiti, where there are almost twice as many people as in the Dominican Republic, which has almost twice the area of Haiti,[6] is in part the result of the former prosperity of the French plantations, which were wrecked during the wars of independence. The result has been a phenomenon similar to that of the wetbacks coming from Mexico into the United States. Haitians moved in as farm workers onto the Dominican sugar plantations. In part because of cultural differences (the Haitians speak creole French patois, the Dominicans, Spanish), tensions built up to such a point that dictator Trujillo in 1932 ordered the massacre of the Haitian immigrants. In this disgraceful episode, which Albert C. Hicks has described in *Blood in the Streets*, some 30,000 were killed, a small indication of the dangers with which the population explosion is fraught.

A geographical inspection of Haiti and the Dominican Republic provides no clues as to the population distribution. Indeed, geographically one would expect the Dominican Republic, which has some excellent farmland, to have a much greater population than eroded, worn-out Haiti. Some suggest that the rate of reproduction is larger among the relatively pure Negroes of Haiti than among the light mulattoes of the Dominican Republic. It is impossible to provide scientific evidence for this hypothesis. It might be argued that, perhaps in accord with the theories of Josué de Castro, the impoverished Haitians breed faster than the somewhat less poor Dominicans. A differential in birth rate based on income levels would be hard to verify, since the Dominicans have not reached the economic level at which the rate of reproduction seems to decline.

The answer seems to be historical and to be related to the economy of coffee plantations which require an unusual number of workers—far more than do sugar or other plantations. For geographical reasons, Haiti has produced primarily coffee, the Dominican Republic, sugar. During the colonial period, the French ran Haiti with remarkable efficiency, and its plantations made it possibly the wealthiest agricultural community in the New World—what a far cry from present-day Haiti! These efficient plantations attracted large numbers of farm workers. When, with independence, the plantation economy collapsed (what a lesson for those who believe that independence from "colonialism" is the solution to the woes of tropical countries!), the population remained, and indeed went on breeding, even though there was now no economic basis for the numerous population. It would seem that economic activity stimulates population growth which continues under its own momentum after the need for the population has disappeared.

There is a similar case in Central America. El Salvador, with a very high density of population, is surrounded by three countries with much lower population densities. In particular, there is a striking contrast between El Salvador and the adjoining areas of Honduras, which are almost empty. Racially the Salvadoreños are mestizos pretty much like the Hondureños, so that a differential in reproduction rate based on race would seem to have no basis.

The only satisfactory explanation is that El Salvador, like Haiti, is for geographical reasons good coffee country. The plantation economy has attracted a dense concentration of farm laborers, who have reproduced more than the local economy will justify, with the result that recently Salvadorean peasants began to settle on the Honduran side of the boundary, creating an international issue between the two Central American republics.

The most peculiar case is that of Costa Rica, which has today the highest annual rate of population growth in the world. It was recently placed at 4%, as opposed to 3.6% for Communist China and 2.6% for Latin America as a whole. Costa Rica is, however, a very special case. Whereas it is estimated that a third of the population of Paraguay has left the country because of a series of dictatorships culminating in the Stroessner regime, Costa Rica is a peaceful democracy which attracts the victims of neighboring dictatorships. We hear much of the conflict between the oligarchy and the masses in Latin America, but Costa Rica has a classless society without grinding poverty and with a very low death rate. In much of Latin America life is a continual struggle between man and his telluric environment. Costa Rica is one of the few countries about which one may properly use the trite expression "eternal Spring." Costa Rica has a combination of plantation agriculture and small industries which together provide a good economic basis for a growing population. The Pan American Highway is opening up the western section of the country, and a startling development is taking place there. In brief, it would be as incorrect to regard Costa Rica as being typical of Latin America as it would be to view Florida or California as typical of the United States.

A variety of factors, including geographical barriers and the lack of social cohesiveness in the traditional Spanish way of life, brought about the fragmentation of Spanish America into 18 republics. Improved communications and increased travel are bringing about a common realization of their cultural unity. There is a growing linguistic unity, and even those who hate the Spanish tradition are attempting to spread, together with literacy, the use of the Spanish language. American anthropologists are trying to push the study of Indian languages on the grounds that the population of "Indoamerica" is increasing, but the argument is almost certainly fallacious. Those who know Paraguay, for example, can testify to the decline in the use of guaraní over the past twenty years.

Regardless of these considerations of detail, it is evident that there is a population explosion in Latin America. There is wide discrepancy among anthropologists about the Indian population of the New World at the time of the Conquest. Certainly the Peruvian Julio Tello, who was both an Indian and an Indianist, was being romantic when he placed the population of the Inca empire at 80 million. Anthropologists tend to be pro-Indian and anti-Spanish, and this should be taken into account in assessing their estimates. The present trend is to raise the earlier calculations of the Indian population at the time of the Conquest and to suggest that war and disease decimated it. Then, according to the calculations of Sherburne F. Cook & Lesley B. Simpson, the population began to rise slowly until, in the 18th century, it reached the level of the late 15th century. Since that time, at first by immigration and more recently by the rapid growth of the mestizo group, the population has risen rapidly, and today "Latin" America has more people than "Anglo" America. Population projections have in general proved quite inaccurate, but it has been calculated that eventually Latin America will have double the population of Anglo America.

This is hardly a reason for saying "The more, the merrier." This juxtaposition of Anglo and Latin America will probably produce the same degree of cordiality which Russia displays toward China. There is already evidence that the spectacular anti-American demonstrations in Latin America are matched by a dour and growing if undemonstrative hostility toward Latin America in the United States. Gone are the silly days of facile declarations of Pan Americanism. There will be a continuing flow of migrants to the United States from a Latin America strained by population pressures and by political strife. In the eastern part of the United States the Puerto Ricans occupy the lowest social level. Even though they are white, they are outranked socially by the Negroes. The bitterness which this produces is kept in check by the realization that Puerto Rico enjoys an artificially favorable economic status.[7] On the side of the native Americans there is one significant demonstration of a hostility to Latin America sparked by the dislike of Puerto Ricans: it is almost impossible to sell movies, TV programs, or radio programs with a Latin American theme. This is presumably the reason why American financiers have dropped a much publicized plan to make a movie about the life of Simón Bolívar. It is not without significance that a movie about the Spanish hero, the Cid, was given a wide and successful circulation, and that all kinds of Puerto Ricans, Mexicans, and Cubans in the United States, as protective coloration, spread the story that they are really Spaniards. This will probably change with time, but it is too early to say what position the Puerto Ricans will finally occupy in the U.S. social structure.

In the western part of the United States there is a curious coincidence in that the area where the Bircher movement is strong—Southern California, Arizona, New Mexico, and Texas—has the highest concentration of Mexican population. There are significantly well-documented cases of teachers in that area being pressured by the Birchers into giving a strictly U.S. interpretation of the war with Mexico. Just as in the East, Puerto Ricans like Teodoro Moscoso have risen to positions of prominence, so Raymond L. Telles was the first Mexican to become mayor of El Paso and to serve as a U.S. Ambassador. The Bircher movement in the West seems to have been stimulated by the uneasy feeling of the native American population that they are being pressed from below by the Mexicans.[8] It is significant that Birchers favor dictatorships in Latin America which will keep the people in their place and make them subservient to the

United States. The feeling that the followers of Barry Goldwater are inimical to the Latin American population explains the hostility to his nomination by the Puerto Rican delegation to the San Francisco convention, and even by the ultra-conservative sector of the Mexican press. The Spaniards and the Portuguese in the area of high Mexican concentration often proclaim their admiration for Franco and Salazar in order to make it clear that they are Europeans not to be confused with Latin Americans. When Mexican American and Puerto Rican families climb socially in the United States, they frequently hide their real origin and refer to their alleged Spanish family ties.

One odd relic of the old Pan Americanism is that the United States set up a quota system after World War I to avoid an excessive migration of Latins from Europe and to preserve the north European character of the American population. The quota system was not applied to Latin America, but it is now apparent that the threat of "Latinization" comes not from the East but from the South. In the absence of a quota system a variety of economic tests are applied.

In view of the end of isolationism and the development of a global U.S. policy, this double standard should be abandoned, and immigration from all over the world strictly controlled. In the past, free international migration helped to open up empty areas of the globe. The problem now is not to fill up empty areas but to stabilize the population. The liberal dream of free migration is dangerously romantic. Because, for example, China fails to control its population, there is no reason why other countries should be asked to suffer the consequences and allow minorities to develop which will be a perennial social problem. Countries can function harmoniously only if they have a more or less homogeneous population. Immigration controls alone can make this possible, and countries like Haiti will simply have to accommodate their population realistically to the land and resources they have available. Only then can we have peaceful communities, and any institution which impedes this is a force for evil.[9] Since it is unlikely that Latin America will face up to the reality of the population problem, the future is grim.

(A very extensive bibliography on population in Latin America follows Professor Hilton's chapter in the hardback edition of *The Population Crisis and the Use of World Resources.*—Ed.)

11.

# HOUSING AND POPULATION GROWTH IN AFRICA, ASIA, AND LATIN AMERICA

*by Robert C. Cook and Kaval Gulhati*

### INTRODUCTION

This paper discusses the housing problem in Africa, Asia, and Latin America in relation to population growth and urban expansion. The main emphasis is on the present housing deficit and on the population growth which is likely to increase this deficit, especially in the urban areas.

### THE PROBLEM OF THE HOUSING DEFICIT

An accumulated housing deficit exists in African, Asian, and Latin American countries. This deficit is a reflection of the low standards of living and the high rates of population increase in these areas.

Most African, Asian, and Latin American countries have a small group of high-income families who occupy spacious—or at least modern—housing units. This tiny, well-housed minority is not the focus of the discussion that follows. The emphasis here is, necessarily, on the great majority of the population living in overcrowded, often primitive and unhygienic, conditions.

Millions of these low-income or "no income" persons in these areas who do not occupy conventional housing units live in "makeshift (improvised, rustic, nonpermanent) structures . . . made of such materials as mud, old boards, straw, scrap metal, etc." Others dwell in housing units which are dilapidated or which lack basic facilities, such as piped water, sanitary service, etc. Still others have no private dwelling and literally live on sidewalks or other public places, as in Calcutta or Hong Kong. According to a United Nations report, these persons are probably left out from both the housing and population censuses, and to make even an approximate estimate of their number is almost impossible.

However, a large proportion of those that do get enumerated are inadequately housed. A recent United Nations report on world housing estimated that over 900 million persons in Africa, Asia, and Latin America are without proper housing. More than 700 million of these people live in Asia. At a low estimate of $500 per unit, the total cost to eliminate this shortage in Asia would amount to $70 billion.

In the past, little or no gain was made in meeting the deficit. The reason for this is the economic inability of the nonindustrial nations to provide enough housing for their expanding populations. In the large-population countries, this is an enormous problem. As these populations grow bigger, the already appalling housing situation is likely to get worse.

### THE RATE OF POPULATION GROWTH IN RELATION TO THE HOUSING SITUATION

The impact of the high rate of population growth on the housing deficit is threefold:

(1) High birth rates and falling death rates result in larger family size. More babies mean more overcrowding in the already crowded dwellings of many Asian and Latin American countries. In Panama, for example, where the birth rate is about 40[1] and the death rate 18, the average number of persons per room is almost 3. Denmark, with a birth

TABLE I

*Number of persons per dwelling and per room in selected countries for latest available year*

| Country | Average number of persons per dwelling | Percentage of dwellings with following number of rooms | | | Percentage of dwellings with following number of persons per room | | | |
|---|---|---|---|---|---|---|---|---|
| | | 1-2 | 3-4 | 5 plus | Less than 1.5 | 1.5 and over | 2 and over | 3 and over |
| Argentina | 5-6 | 63 | 27 | 10 | 19 | 81 | 63 | 36 |
| Panama | 5 | 82 | 14 | 4 | 27 | 73 | 66 | 46 |
| Trinidad-Tobago | 4-5 | 57 | 36 | 7 | 42 | 58 | 48 | 24 |
| Mauritius | 5 | 74 | 18 | 8 | 28 | 72 | 62 | 33 |
| Ceylon | 5-6 | 76 | 19 | 5 | | | | |
| United States | 3.3 | 8 | 33 | 59 | | | | |
| Denmark | 3.1 | 4 | 58 | 38 | 96 | 4 | 1 | 0 |
| West Germany | 4.0 | 17 | 58 | 26 | 83 | 17 | 7 | 1 |

NOTE.—The data refer to dwellings only. A dwelling is a room or a suite of rooms and its accessories intended for private habitation with a separate access to the street. In some countries, the data include nonpermanent structures and improvised shelters.
Source: United Nations. Statistical Yearbook, New York, 1961.

rate of only 16.6 and a death rate of 9.5, has just about one person to every two rooms. These high rates of growth in Africa, Asia, and Latin America have resulted in a larger proportion of children in the population. For example, in the industrial countries where the low birth- and death-rate pattern is established, the ratio of children under 15 years to the total population is only about 20-30%. In the underdeveloped areas, this proportion is 40% or more of the total population. Table I gives statistics on the crowded housing conditions of some countries in the underdeveloped areas.

The table shows that these African, Asian, and Latin American countries average five to six persons per housing unit, whereas in the United States and Europe the average is about three to four persons. Further, about three-fourths of the dwellings in the underdeveloped countries have less than two rooms. And in three countries, Argentina, Panama, and Mauritius, nearly two-thirds of the dwellings have more than two persons per room. In contrast, the United States, Denmark, and Germany have over three rooms to almost every dwelling. And the overwhelmingly majority of dwellings have less than three persons to every two rooms.

(2) High birth rates and large family size mean more babies and more family expenditure. This adversely affects (a) the rate of family savings, and (b) the rate of increase of the national per capita income.

Unless these low-income families save, they cannot invest in private houses or hope to pay higher rents for better housing.

As it is, the current per capita income levels in Africa, Asia, and Latin America are extremely low, The average per capita income for Asia is a little over $100, and in India and Pakistan it is as low as $70-$80. The Latin American average of $298 is somewhat better. . . . The faster these income levels rise, the quicker will be the effect on living conditions. But, in the past, population increase has been so rapid that the relative increase in per capita income has been slight. (For data on income levels, see table III.)

(3) Future population growth: The current situation with respect to population growth and housing conditions is complicated. The prospect for future rapid growth adds to the gravity of the problem.

In terms of housing needed or of new housing required in the future, the rate of growth of the adult population (that is, changes in birth and death rates in prior periods) is the most relevant factor. By studying the age distribution of a population (and relating this to marriage, divorce, and widowhood rates, that is, rates of household formation), an estimate can be made of the number of housing units needed in the future.

Table II gives the population of Latin America by age for 1960 and projections to 1975.

The striking facts that emerge from the tables are:

(a) In absolute numbers, the age group 0-19 outstripped all other age groups in 1960. The current household forming age group of 20-44 was about one-third of the population;

TABLE II

*Estimated population of mainland Latin America, by age, 1960*

POPULATION

[In thousands]

| Age | Mainland Latin America | Mexico | Central America | Tropical South America | Temperate South America |
|---|---|---|---|---|---|
| 0 to 4 | 31,147 | 6,068 | 2,101 | 18,735 | 4,243 |
| 5 to 14 | 46,570 | 9,181 | 2,992 | 27,942 | 6,455 |
| 15 to 19 | 18,223 | 3,402 | 1,196 | 10,886 | 2,739 |
| 20 to 44 | 61,280 | 10,452 | 3,786 | 35,494 | 11,548 |
| 45 to 64 | 23,282 | 4,036 | 1,303 | 12,444 | 5,499 |
| 65 and over | 6,040 | 981 | 359 | 3,070 | 1,630 |
| Total population, 1960 | 186,542 | 34,119 | 11,737 | 108,572 | 32,114 |

PERCENT INCREASE, 1960-75

| Age | | | | | |
|---|---|---|---|---|---|
| 0 to 4 | 50.2 | 63.1 | 53.9 | 53.8 | 14.0 |
| 5 to 14 | 55.4 | 59.4 | 62.8 | 58.2 | 33.5 |
| 15 to 19 | 58.5 | 66.3 | 59.9 | 58.0 | 50.6 |
| 20 to 44 | 45.0 | 61.5 | 52.0 | 48.0 | 18.4 |
| 45 to 64 | 44.1 | 38.2 | 52.1 | 49.1 | 34.9 |
| 65 and over | 72.3 | 84.8 | 70.2 | 69.4 | 70.5 |
| Total increase, all ages | 50.5 | 59.6 | 56.4 | 53.4 | 29.0 |

Source: Population Reference Bureau, *Population Bulletin*, Vol. XVIII, No. 6, October 1962.

TABLE III

*Population and per capita gross national product in 1960*

| Region and country | GNP per capita (U.S. dollars) | Mid-1960 population (millions) | Region and country | GNP per capita (U.S. dollars) | Mid-1960 population (millions) |
|---|---|---|---|---|---|
| Total free world | 558 | 1,968 | Latin America-Con. | | |
| Africa | 128 | 225 | Bolivia | 62 | 4 |
| Asia | 111 | 969 | Mexico | 310 | 35 |
| India | 81 | 433 | Northern America | 2,720 | 199 |
| Pakistan | 68 | 92 | United States | 2,791 | 181 |
| Japan | 413 | 94 | Canada | 2,009 | 18 |
| Philippines | 144 | 28 | Western Europe | 917 | 354 |
| Latin America | 298 | 204 | France | 1,267 | 46 |
| Argentina | 439 | 21 | United Kingdom | 1,347 | 53 |
| Brazil | 196 | 66 | Oceania | 1,259 | 16 |

Source: U.S. Department of State, Agency for International Development, Statistics and Reports Division. *Estimate of Gross National Product*, March 1962.

(*b*) A little over half of the total population was under 19 years. These are the youngsters who will need independent housing during the next decade; and

(*c*) The expected percent increase during 1960-75 in all age groups is 50. In the age group 5-19, the expected increase is over 55%.

This mushrooming growth of young people who will soon be forming their own families will add more pressure to the current housing situation. Thus, any planning for housing programs must take into account the housing needs of the present population (that is, the current housing deficit), plus a continuing increase of these needs due to population growth.

A quotation from Dr. Irene Taeuber in a recent paper published in the *Population Bulletin* sums up the demographic outlook for Latin America:

"Increase is rapid in all age groups. Any planning in any aspect of social and economic development must involve a present population plus a continuing increase of that population. . . .

If age at marriage remains unchanged, new families formed in 1975 will be three-fifths again as numerous as those formed in 1960. There are potential markets here—but there are also major requirements for employment, and for investment in housing, equipment, and facilities. . . .

If fertility remains unchanging, the analysts of 1975 will compute ratios of growth from 1975 to 1990 as high as those that we have computed for the years from 1960 to 1975."

Calculations made by the United Nations show that in Africa, Asia, and Latin America, construction of over 7 million dwelling units is needed in 1960 to accommodate new households formed as a result of population increase. By 1975, the rate of construction must increase 75% over 1960 on account of accelerated population growth and associated changes in the age composition.

POPULATION GROWTH AND URBAN EXPANSION

The urban populations of Africa, Asia, and Latin America are growing at rates that are almost twice as high as the over-all population growth rates. The estimated rate of growth for urban Latin America is 4.2% per year. Urban Africa and urban Asia each has an annual rate of 4%[2] (European urban growth is at the rate of 1.6% a year.) These staggeringly high growth rates mean the addition of an increasingly larger number of people to the already overpacked, underhoused city populations.

Table IV shows that in 1960 an estimated 275 million Africans, Asians, and Latin Americans were living in cities of over 100,000 people. (This figure is over 50% higher than the entire 1960 U.S. population of about 180 million.) And by 1975 the number will more than double. Further, the proportion of the populations living in urban areas of 100,000 and over will be twice as high for Africa, almost twice as high for Asia, and about three-fifths as high for Latin America in 1975.

The reasons for growth rates of these proportions are: (*a*) The migration of large numbers of rural people from agriculture to industry, located in urban areas; and (*b*) the high rates of natural increase, that is, births minus deaths, of the city populations.

TABLE IV

*Estimated and projected urban population, by size groups, for Africa, Asia, and Latin America, 1960 and 1975*

|  | Population in places 100,000 and over (millions) | As percent of total population | Population in places 1,000,000 and over (millions) | As percent of total population |
|---|---|---|---|---|
| Year 1960: |  |  |  |  |
| Africa | 20 | 8 | 6 | 2 |
| Asia | 204 | 12 | 102 | 6 |
| Latin America | 51 | 25 | 25 | 12 |
| Year 1975: |  |  |  |  |
| Africa | 48 | 16 | 12 | 4 |
| Asia | 486 | 22 | 221 | 10 |
| Latin America | 118 | 39 | 61 | 20 |

Source: Urban Land Institute, World Urbanization, Technical Bulletin No. 43, April 1962.

The report of the United Nations Economic Commission for Europe Seminar on housing in October 1961 makes this comment: "While the housing requirements of developed countries originate in a normal population development and the need for a renewal of housing stock, those of countries in the process of rapid industrialization arise mainly from large-scale and intense urbanization."

Table V shows Latin American rural-urban population growth in 1950-60 and projections to 1970. This table indicates an urban population increase of 30 million (or about a 45% increase) in 1959-60. The estimated urban population of 138 million for 1970 will be more than double the 1950 figure of 66 million. In rural Latin America, the 1950-60 population growth was less than 15%. The estimated increase in rural numbers between 1950 and 1970 is about 29 million. The most striking fact is that, by 1970, Latin America's total population will jump by 60% over the 1950 figure. And over 70% of this increase is expected to be in urban areas.

TABLE V

*Latin America: Estimates and projections of the total, urban and rural population by country, midyear 1950, 1960, and 1970*

| Country | Total | | | Urban | | | Rural | | | Total | | Urban | | Rural | |
|---|---|---|---|---|---|---|---|---|---|---|---|---|---|---|---|
| | 1950 | 1960 | 1970 | 1950 | 1960 | 1970 | 1950 | 1960 | 1970 | 1950-60 | 1960-70 | 1950-60 | 1960-70 | 1950-60 | 1960-70 |
| Total | 155,570 | 199,235 | 257,040 | 65,469 | 95,870 | 138,300 | 90,101 | 103,365 | 118,740 | 28 | 29 | 46 | 44 | 15 | 15 |
| Argentina | 17,190 | 21,000 | 24,990 | 11,040 | 14,205 | 17,485 | 6,150 | 6,795 | 7,505 | 22 | 19 | 29 | 23 | 10 | 10 |
| Bolivia | 2,930 | 3,600 | 4,540 | 1,015 | 1,380 | 1,980 | 1,915 | 2,220 | 2,560 | 23 | 26 | 36 | 43 | 16 | 15 |
| Brazil | 51,975 | 65,860[1] | 84,440 | 18,815 | 27,380 | 39,780 | 33,160 | 38,480 | 44,660 | 27 | 28 | 46 | 45 | 16 | 16 |
| Dominican Republic | 2,130 | 2,845 | 3,895 | 505 | 865 | 1,480 | 1,625 | 1,980 | 2,415 | 34 | 37 | 71 | 71 | 22 | 22 |
| Colombia | 11,145 | 14,770 | 19,590 | 4,170 | 7,065 | 11,080 | 6,975 | 7,705 | 8,510 | 33 | 33 | 69 | 57 | 10 | 10 |
| Costa Rica | 800 | 1,145 | 1,560 | 265 | 460 | 685 | 535 | 685 | 875 | 43 | 36 | 74 | 49 | 28 | 28 |
| Cuba | 5,520 | 6,820 | 8,340 | 3,065 | 4,110 | 5,345 | 2,455 | 2,710 | 2,995 | 24 | 22 | 34 | 30 | 10 | 11 |
| Chile | 6,075 | 7,635 | 9,660 | 3,575 | 5,010 | 6,900 | 2,500 | 2,625 | 2,760 | 26 | 27 | 40 | 38 | 5 | 5 |
| Ecuador | 3,195 | 4,285 | 5,630 | 910 | 1,500 | 2,235 | 2,285 | 2,785 | 3,395 | 34 | 31 | 65 | 49 | 22 | 22 |
| El Salvador | 1,870 | 2,395 | 3,115 | 685 | 1,020 | 1,515 | 1,185 | 1,375 | 1,600 | 28 | 30 | 49 | 49 | 16 | 16 |
| Guatemala | 3,040 | 3,980 | 5,325 | 760 | 1,205 | 1,940 | 2,280 | 2,775 | 3,385 | 31 | 34 | 59 | 61 | 22 | 22 |
| Haiti | 3,110 | 3,725 | 4,620 | 380 | 710 | 1,290 | 2,730 | 3,015 | 3,330 | 20 | 24 | 87 | 82 | 10 | 10 |
| Honduras | 1,385 | 1,755 | 2,305 | 430 | 590 | 885 | 955 | 1,165 | 1,420 | 27 | 31 | 37 | 50 | 22 | 22 |
| Mexico | 26,435 | 35,115 | 47,330 | 11,265 | 17,510 | 26,900 | 15,170 | 17,605 | 20,430 | 33 | 35 | 55 | 54 | 16 | 16 |
| Nicaragua | 1,060 | 1,465 | 1,955 | 370 | 625 | 930 | 690 | 840 | 1,025 | 38 | 33 | 69 | 49 | 22 | 22 |
| Panama | 755 | 1,010 | 1,370 | 285 | 430 | 670 | 470 | 580 | 700 | 34 | 36 | 51 | 56 | 23 | 21 |
| Paraguay | 1,400 | 1,625 | 1,975 | 390 | 565 | 860 | 1,010 | 1,060 | 1,115 | 16 | 22 | 45 | 52 | 5 | 5 |
| Peru | 8,170 | 10,510 | 14,030 | 2,975 | 4,480 | 7,030 | 5,195 | 6,030 | 7,000 | 29 | 33 | 51 | 57 | 16 | 16 |
| Uruguay | 2,410 | 2,760 | 3,020 | 1,895 | 2,245 | 2,505 | 515 | 515 | 515 | 15 | 9 | 18 | 12 | .... | .... |
| Venezuela | 4,975 | 6,935 | 9,350 | 2,675 | 4,515 | 6,805 | 2,300 | 2,420 | 2,545 | 39 | 35 | 69 | 51 | 5 | 5 |

1 An estimate of Brazil's midyear population based on the provisional figure from the 1960 census is 70,600,000, or 4,700,000 greater than projected.

Source: United Nations, *Situación demográfica, económica, social y educativa de América Latina*, Conferencia sobre educación y desarrollo económico y social en América Latina, Santiago de Chile, 5 a 19 de Marzo de 1962, ST/ECLA/CONF. 10/L. 4; 10 de enero, 1962, table 1, p. 8.

In Asia, between 1900 and 1950, the population living in cities of 100,000 or more mounted from about 20 million to nearly 106 million (a gain of 444%). In Africa, there was a gain of 629%, from 1.4 million to 10.2 million.

A unique feature of Latin American urbanization is that about 10% of the total population in 13 out of the 20 countries lives in the largest city or metropolitan area, usually the capital city. In six countries, the largest city contains one-fifth or more of the population.

If 20% of the U.S. population lived in Washington, D.C., the Capital would have 36 million people.

These statistics explain why so much attention is directed to the urban housing situation. While rural housing, no doubt, poses problems, they remain pale in intensity as compared to urban conditions. Firstly, densities are less in rural areas and a lot of housing is put up on a self-basis. And, secondly, the rural exodus to urban areas relieves some of the pressure on the land.

In the cities, land prices are prohibitively high and most people cannot afford to own their homes. For example, in Manila, an acre of land costs $25,000 to $30,000. Some Asians and Latin Americans can pay the high rent for a decent house, but the vast majority who cannot, live in filthy concentrations of rubble, scrap, and human beings. These are the urban slums, a selected few of which are described below.[3]

*Bombay.*—The population of Bombay grew by almost 70% during 1950-60.

About one-half of the population lives in substandard housing and a large number live on footpaths. Bombay's slums contain over half a million persons living in 9,000 dilapidated units. Another million live in 200,000 single-room tenements scattered over the city. In some cases, 7 to 10 persons consisting of 2 or 3 families share 1 room.

*Calcutta.*[4]—With a population of nearly 6 million. Calcutta is one of the largest cities in the world. Between 1950 and 1960, Calcutta's population increased by 2.3 million.

About one-fourth of the total population lives in one-eighth of the city's land which constitutes the Calcutta slums. Nearly two-thirds of these slum families have no water supply and no proper lighting or ventilation. In some cases, as many as 45 persons share 1 latrine.

*Hong Kong.*—A population of 2.9 million, increasing at a rate of 4.1% a year, gives the island a density of over 7,000 persons per square mile. In 1957, a survey of regular housing showed that 79% of the households shared common facilities. About 40% were living in "cubicles, bed-spaces, cocklofts, and on verandas." Only 7.5% had a living room not used for sleeping.

The new resettlement blocks provide low-rent accommodation averaging 24 square feet per person.

*Rio de Janeiro*.—By 1960, Rio's population had added nearly 1 million people to the 1950 total of 3 million. In 1950, Rio's slums, known as "favelas," contained about 14.3% of the population. A 1948 survey showed that two-thirds of the "houses" were worth less than $108. Three-fourths had no toilets and about 90% had no piped water.

*Mexico City*.—The population of the federal district surrounding Mexico City grew by 160% between 1940 and 1950. The city proper grew by 53% during the same period.

A citywide housing survey in 1952 showed that 34% of the population lived in "turgurios"—one-room apartments opening on a courtyard or passageway. Another 11% were living in rented "jacales"—shacks made from scrap materials. The jacales had about 34 persons per toilet but most of the toilets were out of order and the jacale dwellers used the waste land around their shacks.

Altogether in Latin America an estimated 70% of existing urban housing units require rebuilding. In urban India alone, a shortage of nearly 5 million houses leaves 20 to 30 million people (equivalent to the combined population of New York and California) in need of proper housing.

According to one United Nations estimate, the increase in African, Asian, and Latin American urban households would mean a 133% step-up in urban construction 15 years from now. In Asia, urban construction would be 250% more; in Africa, 133% and in Latin America, almost 100% more.

### CONCLUSION

The housing problem in the underdeveloped areas has three dimensions: (1) The accumulated housing deficit and replacement of existing stock, (2) the critical situation in urban areas, and (3) the new housing required for population increase.

If, as the United Nations recommends, 30 years were taken as the target to meet the housing shortage, and the average life of a house taken as about 25 years, then annual construction needed for these two factors plus that required by population growth, would be nearly 22 million units in 1960. By 1975, annual construction needs would be almost 28 million units. Population increase alone would require over 45% of these units. (See table VI) The urban areas of Africa, Asia, and Latin America constituting less than 30% of the total population, would account for over half of the recommended construction.

TABLE VI

*Estimated annual housing needs in Africa, Asia, and Latin America,
1960 and 1975*

[In millions of dwelling units]

| | 1960 | 1975 | | 1960 | 1975 |
|---|---|---|---|---|---|
| Due to population increase: | | | To replace the stock:[1] | | |
| Africa | 0.84 | 1.50 | Africa | 1.03 | 1.03 |
| Asia | 5.30 | 9.40 | Asia | 7.10 | 7.10 |
| Latin America | 1.10 | 1.70 | Latin America | .90 | .90 |
| To eliminate the deficit or | | | Total new housing needed: | | |
| shortage in 30 years: | | | Africa | 2.60 | 3.26 |
| Africa | .73 | .73 | Asia | 17.20 | 21.30 |
| Asia | 4.80 | 4.80 | Latin America | 2.60 | 3.20 |
| Latin America | .60 | .60 | | | |
| | | | Total | 22.40 | 27.76 |

[1] Average life of a dwelling unit is assumed to be 30 years in urban and 20 years in rural areas. The 1975 figures do not take into account increments of stock between 1960 and 1975.
Source: United Nations, *World Housing Conditions and Estimated Requirements*, July 1962.

Unless population growth slows down and income levels rise rapidly, the housing situation in the underdeveloped areas is not likely to improve. Small-scale, low-income, public housing projects can hardly do more than keep a deplorable situation from getting worse. A United Nations report which reviews the social problems of urbanization in economically underdeveloped areas highlights these points:

"The housing problem cannot be solved simply by concentrating on construction of houses . . . the rapidity of city growth . . . can overwhelm even the most ambitious housing program. It has been reported that new construction for low-income groups sometimes encourages a large flow of (rural) migrants and, thus, diminishes the slum population not at all. . . .

The housing problem goes beyond the question of construction . . . because much of the population now living in the city slums is poorly adapted to urban life, economically, socially, and psychologically. These groups not only need an opportunity to move into better housing; they also lack . . . incomes permitting them to maintain these standards without depriving themselves of other necessities. If these conditions are not met, new housing is likely to deteriorate rapidly through lack of maintenance, and the occupants will smuggle in lodgers to supplement their incomes and, thus, reproduce the former overcrowding."[5]

The housing crisis is part of the economic and social crisis which is sweeping across the underdeveloped nations today. Checking rapid growth by bringing high birth rates into line with modern low death rates is a prerequisite to coming to grips with the problem. Growing recognition of this fact is encouraging.

<br>

## 12.

# THE AMERICAN FERTILITY CULT

### by Lincoln H. Day

The United States is currently experiencing a most rapid rate of population growth. If such a rate were sustained for 356 more years, our country would have the population density of New York City. Ninety-eight more years at the average growth rate of the last five would bring our number up to one billion—*over a third of the present population of the entire world*.

The apologists for unchecked population growth, whoever they are and whatever country they refer to, overlook limitations in the earth's capacity to provide. Raw materials and the amount of land suitable for settlement are not infinitely elastic, and they contract to the extent that we continue to raise our level of living in the ways we have been doing. If the arguments in favor of population increase continue to prevail— even in this country—we must inevitably be faced with a choice between quantity and quality: vast numbers of people living poorly at necessarily low levels of living, or fewer people, but those fewer living well. We cannot have it both ways. Those who condone our continued growth in numbers—whether they realize it or not—have decided in favor of quantity. The choice is remarkable.

The arguments in support of our current population increase are of three general types: (1) Economic; (2) Scientific; and (3) Social.

The "economic" argument is that population growth is necessary for the maintenance of our current level of economic prosperity, and a requisite for any long-range prosperity, as well.

"Your future is great in a growing America," reads a so-called public service advertisement in the New York subway. "Every day 11,000

Reprinted from Columbia University Forum, Summer 1960. Copyright 1960 by the Reader's Digest Association, Inc.

babies are born in America. This means new business, new jobs, new opportunities." And some weeks earlier the nation's most widely circulated weekly magazine had taken a similar tack with the cover title, "Kids: Built-in Recession Cure—How 4,000,000 a Year Make Millions in Business." Inside, it was "Rocketing Births: Business Bonanza."

Are such claims justified? Is economic prosperity in the United States a necessary result of population growth? Surely it was once. When a man's strength was an important source of energy and per capita consumption was at a low level, a growing population in a sparsely settled land could indeed be important in creating a high level of material living. More people meant more energy, a greater division of labor, and an expanding market for goods.

But today, the combination of increasing population and a generally rising level of living has revealed limitations in the supply of raw materials and increased the costs of developing them. All minerals and most of the sources of energy in current use are *non-renewable*. It has taken millions of years to create them. They represent capital. As we use them up we are using capital, not income. The fact that we have already had to resort to ores that are expensive to work and of relatively low grade is only one sign of approaching depletion. The predictions on copper, lead, tin, sulphur, and iron ore, among others, are that their real costs will increase in the near future (that is, their costs in hours of work and capital required per unit).

The outlook is no brighter for *renewable* resources. The size and growth rates of our forests already limit the use of wood and wood products, whose real prices have approximately doubled since 1900. And despite greater development and conservation of water resources, our continued growth in numbers, combined with our rising level of living, has placed steeply mounting demands upon them. As Robert and Leona Rienow have noted:

"More than a thousand cities and towns [in the United States] already have been forced to curtail their water service. Near Chicago, where artesian wells flowed under their own pressure a hundred years ago, new wells must go down 2,000 feet to reach the water table. Dallas is already pumping the salt-tainted Red River into its main, and New York faces the likelihood that eventually it will have to purify the polluted Hudson to slake its growing thirst. In Mississippi, wells are now 400 feet deeper, on the average, than they were only ten years ago. Denver, eager for new industry, has been turning away manufacturers whose production processes involve a heavy use of water."

With our growing population and our high level of living we are borrowing on the future—our own and that of our posterity. It is not that we will suddenly find ourselves without resources. Long before we completely exhaust them the resources that remain will have become so costly as to be unobtainable.

To advocate American population growth as a means to economic prosperity is to be not only domestically shortsighted, but also ignorant of the realities of world political and economic conditions. Already, we Americans, with but 6% of the world's population, consume half of the world's production of main minerals (iron, copper, lead, zinc); and we consume nearly twice as much commercial energy per person as Britain and eighty times as much as India. The imbalance between our numbers and our consumption of fossil fuels, metals, and so on highlights the fact that, important as the overpopulation—or threatened overpopulation— of much of the rest of the world may be, when it comes to depletion of the world's natural resources, it takes a lot of Asians or Africans or Latin Americans at *their* material levels of living to consume as much as one American at *his*. Any precise statistical comparison is impossible, yet it may not be far wrong to say that each year the average American consumes in natural resources as much as do twenty-five or thirty Indians. When we remember that because of a much greater life expectancy the American has more than twice as many years of consuming ahead of him, that bracing yearly addition of 4,000,000 American babies take on new meaning indeed.

We know that part of the new nationalism in Asia, Africa, and the Near East expresses the desire of other peoples to live more decently— this can only worsen the situation. Even without improvement in their levels of living, the rapid population increases in these countries will place ever-mounting demands on the world's resources. To the extent these peoples attain the higher levels to which they aspire, the supply of raw materials will be depleted just so much faster. That fraction of the world's population which lives in the United States cannot for long continue to consume 40 to 50% of the world's resources.

The support for our present rate of population growth which is supposedly drawn from "science" (for which read: science-and-technology) rests on the assumption that scientific development will somehow keep up with any population growth we may experience (or perpetrate). Like other forms of utopianism, such a belief must rest ultimately on faith, not reason. On the one hand we hear claims that interplanetary transportation will solve all shortages of land and raw materials, and, on the other, declarations that God will provide for His flock no matter how large it becomes. But even if minerals were found on the moon, the costs of transportation to and from the earth would surely prohibit their use; while to assume that God will provide is to overlook the more than a billion already in the world who are currently unprovided for by even minimum dietary standards—they starve.

Those who put their faith in Science are merely replacing one deity with another. Obviously any solution to the problem of population growth will depend on further work in such specialties as physiology, agriculture, and economics. But science and technology in turn depend on existing resources. Moreover, further development in these fields will require substantial expenditures for education, training, experimentation, and research. Yet, the greater the difficulties created by a growing population, the more we shall have to spend simply to meet such fundamental needs of that population as food, housing, primary education, transportation, and medical care. The larger our population, the more capital we must invest (and the less we will have available for the purchase of consumer goods) and the more we must produce—in short, the faster we must run, just to stay in the same place.

Our population difficulty (and many other difficulties) would be solved —according to the "social" argument in favor of population growth—if we could persuade *certain* segments of our society to have *larger* families. This view is often expressed by members of certain racial or religious groups whose preference for their own sort makes numerical increase seem desirable for its own sake: or who equate increases in size with increases in power. In more recent years this argument seems most convenient when one wishes to serve a specific bias: a preference for the college graduate, the higher income group, the occupants of professional and managerial positions. The notion appears widespread that the quality of our society would be improved to the extent that family size in these groups equalled or exceeded that of the low income groups, or of those with less schooling.

The assumption inderlying this view is, of course, either that the children of the former are inherently superior, or that their parents will offer them a superior environment. Those who have more of what the society values—material wealth, prestige, etc.—have always sought to justify their enviable position by boasts of innate or acquired virtue. Today, some support for the notion of upper-class superiority can be derived from a superficial reading of the results of various intelligence tests; for these show a rather consistent pattern of higher average group scores by the children of white collar and professional workers as against those of manual workers; by children of college-educated parents; by children from higher income families; by Whites as opposed to Negroes (although

northern Negroes score higher, on the average, than do southern Whites);
and by urban dwellers as against rural.

But these are only group averages. The degree of overlapping is considerable, and the extremes in each group approximate those of the
others. Moreover, there is the more fundamental question whether these
tests actually do measure intelligence. Aside from the well-founded uncertainty about just what intelligence is, various studies of these tests have
concluded that of great importance in any particular test result are such
matters as the number of years spent in school, prior experience with
tests, and motivation to do well—not to mention the ability to understand
the particular meaning attached to a given word or question used in the
test by the psychologist who wrote it (himself likely to have been recruited from the more privileged classes). In short, non-hereditary characteristics are important, if not decisive. If the children of the upper
classes have superior intellects, it has yet to be proved.

It is more plausible to say, as some do, that superior or not, the upper
classes of our society are better able to *provide* for their children. This is
not to claim that middle- or upper-class parents are better parents, but
simply that they are better *able* to provide, leaving aside the question
whether good provision is indeed made.

"You should have no more children than you can afford" is an admirable injunction. But does it follow that "couples who can afford them
should have more?" Does anyone really bear all the costs of supporting
his children? Perhaps the taxes paid by a few are substantial enough to
meet the monetary costs of schooling, public health measures, roads,
police protection, and the many other services a community must provide
for its citizens. But what of the *social* cost? What of the crowded schools,
the traffic, the vanishing countryside, the costs in time and peace of mind
that additional numbers entail? This is a question that concerns none of
the apologists for continued population increase. To quote the Roman
Catholic Bishops of the United States:

"United States Catholics do not wish to ignore or minimize the problem of population pressure, but they do deplore the studious omission
of adequate reference to the role of modern agriculture in food production. The 'population explosion' alarmists do not place in proper focus
the idea of increasing the acreage yield to meet the food demands of an
increasing population."

Man would appear to such apologists to be a strictly bread-and-po-
tatoes phenomenon: let him increase as long as he can be fed.

Assume for a moment that by some miracle the world's supplies of resources were rendered inexhaustible and that, by a second miracle, inter-

national inequities were adjusted to the satisfaction of all concerned. Would the population problem have been solved? What, for instance, about land area? The increasing shortage of space is probably for the majority of Americans the most obvious consequence of population growth. Witness the traffic jams which beset all our major cities and most of our smaller ones as well. In some places this blight has afflicted us so long that it is now an accepted part of urban life. But the traffic jam is spreading to places where no one could have expected it ten or fifteen years ago: Yellowstone National Park and the mountains west of Denver, for example.

And then consider the crowded beaches, parks, and recreation areas; the cities and towns that run together, connected by a gum of suburbia and "highway culture": a picnic or a walk in the open country within easy motoring distance of home has become a virtual impossibility for a near-majority of our citizens. After reporting that once-green country-side is being bulldozed under at the rate of some three thousand acres a day, William H. Whyte goes on to say, "It is not merely that the country-side is ever receding; in the great expansion of the metropolitan areas the subdivisions of one city are beginning to meet up with the subdivisions of another." Along the 600-mile strip of Atlantic seaboard from Maine to Virginia there are only two stretches—one of two miles and the other of seventeen miles—which are not parts of a metropolitan area. Like some dozen others scattered throughout the country, this area is in the process of becoming a strip city: 600 miles of Los Angeles on the Atlantic Coast!

Our national parks are the same. Visited by 7.4 million in 1940, their number of visitors had reached 19 million by 1955, more than double the number recommended by the Park Service. This is, of course, partly the result of higher levels of living—particularly the extension of paid vacations. But population increase *alone* would have brought the number of probable visitors up to the parks' capacity, had the level of living remained as it was in 1940. That levels of living have increased at the same time as population merely adds to the problem. It has now been proposed that certain roads in these parks be made one-way in order to handle the traffic!

The upper income groups may well pay higher taxes. But no group in our society can repay all of the social costs entailed by its excess reproduction—the rich probably least of all, for their style of life requires a much higher consumption of those very things upon which population increase —in whatever class—places a premium: raw materials and space.

If it is true that one must be born into a richer or better-schooled family in order to have the opportunity to develop his potentialities fully, an increase in family size among those segments of the population is hardly an adequate means to attain our ends. Must the right to bear children be distributed by the market mechanism? Would not a more efficient—and more democratic—approach be to raise the level of the less privileged?

Certainly the apologists for population growth are justified in claiming that much can be done with planning and scientific development to postpone eventual reckoning with the consequences of population increase. A different solution to the pressure of population upon resources—one not seriously proposed as yet—would be a decrease in the levels of living. But under even our present economic conditions fully one out of four Americans lives in poverty or close to it, so any such belt-tightening would seem neither practical nor ethical. Besides, as already indicated, lower levels of living are likely to occur anyway as real costs increase. Temporary relief could be achieved without necessarily reducing the general level of living if we transferred a sizable proportion of our productive energies away from material goods (especially those which require nonrenewable resources in their manufacture) and put them, instead, into education, social work, libraries, parole and probation systems, medical care, mental health facilities, music, art. Yet, continued growth in population makes more difficult the expansion of these services at the very time it makes them more necessary.

None of these arguments for continued population growth—singly or in concert—really faces up to the problem of such growth in a finite world. They are only palliatives, they are not cures. Some of the proposed courses of action could make life more enjoyable. Certain of them— better planned use of the land, for instance—are long overdue. But all are short-term measures at best.

Our population growth must be curbed or stopped in the very near future. But how? Any demographic change in a given area (the number of people, or their age or sex composition) occurs through the operation of only three variables: migration, death, and birth. The proportion of our current annual population increase due to migration (that is, due to an excess of immigrants over emigrants) is very small: only 12%. And, our death rate was already so low by the end of World War II that yearly declines since then have added relatively little to our growth in numbers.

The major share, over 85%, of our increase is due to an excess of births over deaths. From an all-time low of 18.4 in 1933 and again in 1936, our birth rate climbed to 26.6 in 1947 and has since then fluctuated around 25.0, a higher level than in any other Western country. Without trying to assess the numerous personal decisions which produce it, we can say that such a birth rate has *not* been due to an increase in the proportion of couples having large families, that is, six or more children. In fact, since World War II, the rate for sixth and higher-order births has continued to decline while that for fifth births has remained about the same. The increase comes, instead, from the larger proportion with three and four children and the smaller proportion with no children or with only one. It also comes from a decline in the proportion who never marry. More of us marry; a greater proportion have between two and four children; and a smaller proportion remain childless or with but one child. The result is a slightly larger average family size and a rapidly growing population.

Can we halt population growth before the depletion of resources and the filling up of land area so reduce our level of living that such a question must be answered by a return of the high death rates of non-industrialized countries? Can we, that is, halt it while we still have a high level of living and before we lose control over our demographic destiny?

Emigration is no solution, for without a concurrent decrease in population growth it would merely spread the problem to more countries. Moreover, all the habitable areas in the world have been peopled, while the rise of the nation-state has tended to reduce the amount of freedom given an individual in choice of national residence. At best, migration is only a temporary expedient.

From both a pragmatic and an ethical standpoint, the only alternative is a decrease in fertility. Because our death rate is low and the proportion who marry is high, our population could be maintained at its present size if each family had on the average only slightly more than two children. The couple with more than three is contributing to the population disaster I have sketched. It is, in this sense, *socially irresponsible*, the more so the more numerous its children. For in this country the knowledge of how to control fertility is well known and widely diffused. A variety of of means is available to us: late marriage, abstinence, abortion, *coitus interruptus*, contraception, sterilization. Aside from abortion, each is probably fairly acceptable to large numbers of people. Contraception appears the most widespread at the present time and probably presents the least psychological hazard. Sterilization may eventually become more common than it is now. But all means, so long as they are effective and do not endanger the well-being of the persons involved, must be considered.

The control of population by a check on fertility is the efficient way; it is the way most in keeping with our humanitarian and democratic values; and it represents the least social and ethical cost.

The best way for this control of fertility to come about is through the free decisions of individual parents. There can be no other way in a democratic society without serious loss to individual liberty. Let us hope that the current misuse of this most personal liberty by an unwittingly irresponsible portion of our citizenry can be halted before it jeopardizes any further the liberties of all of us.

# Resources and Population

❍ ❍ ❍

## 13.

## MAN AND HUNGER:
## THE PERSPECTIVES OF HISTORY

### by Arnold J. Toynbee

The Freedom from Hunger Campaign is one of three major educational campaigns on which the human race is engaged in our time. The other two are, of course, the campaign against war and the campaign against disease. War, pestilence, and famine have been the three traditional scourges of the human race. They have been Nature's brutal ways of keeping the human population of our planet within limits. Man, however, is unique among Nature's creatures on the face of this planet in his relation to Nature. Man is not condemned by *his* nature to be completely and permanently at Nature's mercy. He is not just Nature's passive product, instrument, plaything, and victim. To a greater extent than any other of his fellow living creatures, Man has the power to react against Nature. To some extent, Man can impose his own will on Nature. He can at least partially substitute for Nature's way a way of his own that he has chosen for himself. But he can have his own way only on one condition. If his own human, and humane, way is to prevail, it must be a way that, like Nature's brutal way, fulfills Nature's intractable ultimate requirements.

Man's choice is thus a choice between alternative means of obeying Nature's laws. For instance, Man can abolish premature human mortality caused by war, disease, and famine. We have already won a decisive victory over premature death through disease. We hope to win a still more complete victory over premature death through war. We are now waging the present campaign against premature death through famine— and, short of outright death, against the loss of strength and energy and happiness that undernutrition and malnutrition inflict. We intend to win this campaign too. Yet, if we were to win all these three campaigns and were to take no further action, our three victories would quickly turn into a major defeat on all three fronts. If we left it at that, we should not

Address delivered before the opening session of the World Food Congress of the Food and Agricultural Organization of the United Nations, Washington, D.C., June 4, 1963. Reprinted by kind permission.

have reckoned with the reproductive mechanism that Nature has implanted in our race, as well as in all the other races of living creatures.

Every species has the biological capacity to increase in numbers ad infinitum; and therefore its multiplication is bound to be checked sooner or later. The physical volume of our planet is limited, and the capacity of the planet's surface for producing food for living creatures is limited proportionately. Even if the human race were to succeed in breaking the bounds of its native planet, it would reach a limit to its food supply somewhere at some date, supposing that it succeeded in abolishing war and pestilence without taking any further steps.

We should then have regulated our human death rate without having regulated our human birth rate to match. We should still have left it to Nature to keep the growth of the Universe's human population within limits; and Nature would then limit this by re-imposing on Man her own brutal set of checks in the shape of famine, pestilence, and war. Therefore, if we are to defeat these three scourges, not just momentarily but definitively, once for all, we have to win a fourth victory. We have to conquer one of our most intimate and most deeply ingrained habits, traditions, and prejudices. We have voluntarily to regulate our birth rate to match the regulation of our death rate that we have already been achieving.

Unless and until we do regulate our birth rate voluntarily, the removal, or even the reduction, of any one of Nature's three methods of limitation will have the effect of increasing the danger of seeing our population growth limited by one or other of Nature's methods that we have not yet brought under control. This is evident today, now that we have succeeded in reducing, to a remarkable degree, the incidence of premature death through disease. We have still not yet got rid of premature death through war. Within the lifetime of people still alive, we have seen the world's population reduced by two world wars in which the slaughter has been on an unprecedented scale. Even since the end of the Second World War, local wars in Korea, Indo-China, Algeria, Cyprus, the Congo, and the Himalayas have been taking their toll of men in the prime of life. Yet, in spite of the continuance of war, the conquest of premature death through disease, thanks to the triumph of preventive medicine and public hygiene, has been enough, by itself, to set our race's population growth soaring at an unprecedented rate. Today mankind's future is at stake in a formidable race between population growth and famine.

It is true that, in our Freedom from Hunger Campaign, we have a mighty ally in Science. The application of science to food production happily promises, as we know, to increase our food supply vastly. But science cannot increase our food supply ad infinitum, and it is also powerless to distribute the product to the hungry mouths that need it. This cannot be done without political co-operation on a world-wide scale. So science, by itself, cannot ensure that Man shall win this campaign for freedom from hunger. Nor can science and politics ensure it together, supposing that politics were to mend its ways and were henceforth to do its utmost toward seconding science's efforts. In the long run the campaign cannot be won unless the planet's hundreds of millions of wives and husbands voluntarily decide to regulate the number of human births.

This is, I believe, one of the major challenges that confront mankind in our time. In at least one respect, it is a more difficult challenge to respond to than the challenge to abolish war. War could perhaps be abolished effectively by agreement among the small minority of the human race that has a monopoly of political authority. This minority is small, even in an increasingly democratic world; and it is likely, I believe, to remain a relatively small and manageable one, however democratic the World may eventually become. But the regulation of our race's birth rate requires voluntary and effective action by a majority of the planet's adult men and women. To educate our politicians may not be easy, but to educate the non political-minded mass of mankind is going to be a still more difficult task.

One way of trying to educate ourselves is to recall our past experience. Of course, we must not expect that past experience will provide us with a blue print for planning the future. Still, our experience of the past gives us the only light on the future that we have. We must therefore make the most of it that we can. I imagine that this was what the Director-General had in mind when he did me the honour of inviting me to deliver this address on the perspectives of history in which we have to look at our current problem of Man and Hunger.

By far the greater part of human history is shrouded in obscurity. Even our archaeologists and our palaeontologists, who have been doing such marvelous detective work in our time, have been able to reveal to us no more than a few glimpses of our race's more distant past. Here we are still largely in the realm of guesswork. Yet I suppose we can guess, with some confidence, that, since our ancestors first became human, most human beings have been hungry for most of the time. The toll that hunger must have taken from human happiness and human achievement is appalling to contemplate. Happily, this thought brings with it a converse thought. There must be a huge unrealised potential of human energy and creativity which would be released for the service of human welfare if the hunger that has been coeval with humanity were to be abolished by a definitive victory in our Freedom from Hunger Campaign.

We may also guess that the situation in which we find ourselves today has, in essence, existed since the beginning. The present race between the increase of population and the increase of food supply is not something entirely new. What is new is the present sharpness of the acceleration of the pace. The tempo of human life is now sharply accelerating in all fields of human activity. Yet even this acceleration is not something new. It has been gradually getting up speed since life made its first appearance. The faster the pace, the more conscious we are of the problem; that is the difference, and it is a fortunate one, because our consciousness of the problem stimulates us to grapple with the problem and to make a serious effort to solve it.

In the course of human history, Man has taken an increasingly active and positive line in his struggle to keep himself fed. He has passed over from passive food-gathering to active hunting and fishing; he has passed beyond that from feeding on plants and animals in their state of nature to the domestication of them and the deliberate planned breeding of them to satisfy his wants. Each of these technological revolutions has brought with it, as its reward, a sudden big increase in mankind's food supply. The present big increase through the application of modern science is only another term in this long series. Today we are hearing, with apprehension, the thundering tramp of our population increase threatening to overtake the mighty advance that science has been enabling our food supply to make.

This threat, on the part of unregulated reproductive Nature, to cancel the effects of human ingenuity and forethought in the technological field, is also not something new. The invention of hunting and fishing and the subsequent invention of agriculture were each, in turn, counterbalanced by increases in population which devoured the margin of food supply over numbers with which Man's technological prowess had promised to endow him. We have been godlike in our planned breeding of our domesticated plants and animals, but we have been rabbit-like in our unplanned breeding of ourselves. While we have triumphantly domesticated so many other species of living creature, we have improvidently left our own species in a state of nature in this vital matter of reproduction. We have continued to breed up to the limit with a lack of control that we have never dreamed of allowing to our domesticated animals and plants. Our self-imposed penalty has been to continue, with very few exceptions, to live in Nature's way—to live, that is, just, and only just, above the starvation line—in spite of our unique human achievement of creating a man-made abundance of food.

This behaviour of ours in our dealings with the problem of famine is disconcertingly perverse; and unfortunately we have shown the same perversity in our dealings with the problem of war. One of Nature's three brutal ways of keeping the members of any species of living creature within limits is to make the individual representatives of this species serve as a prey both for each other and for other species. Human beings, like the rest of Nature's creatures, have been exposed by Nature to this scourge, as one way of reducing their numbers. But, unlike other creatures, Man has the capacity to upset Nature's arrangements. Already, part way through the Palaeolithic Age, Man had released himself from the fate of being a prey for non-human forms of life on the face of this planet. He had established a decisive permanent ascendency over lions and tigers. The only fellow creatures of ours over which Man failed to establish his ascendency until our own times were bacteria. Man failed to master these because he remained unaware of their existence. As soon as he discovered the existence of bacteria, he was able to make them, too, into targets for human weapons; and, once discovered by Man, bacteria have proved hardly more capable of resisting human attack than lions and tigers and other big game that are visible to human eyes without the aid of a microscope. This recent partial conquest of the bacteria that used to prey on us with impunity is a major part of what we call the conquest of disease by preventive medicine.

Thus, part way through the Palaeolithic Age, Man had relieved himself of his original fate of being a prey for non-human creatures visible to the human eye. Apart from bacteria, the only living creatures that now still had the power to prey on human beings were other members of the human race.

In mastering the non-human forms of life, Man was dealing with creatures that, unlike himself, are not rational. These non-human adversaries of his could therefore be mastered by Man only through the use of brute force. They were not amenable to argument or persuasion. So, in his struggle with them, the only use that he could make of his reason was to forge, with it, artificial weapons that were immeasurably more potent than the natural weapons of his non-human opponents and competitors. As we know, the human reason, applied to the generation of overwhelming physical force, proved brilliantly successful; and this would have led one to expect, a priori, that human reason would be still more successful when used for dealing, not with an unreasonable creature, such as a tiger, but with a partially rational creature, namely Man himself. When the human reason had invented spears and bows and arrows for subduing tigers and lions, why could it not enable its human possessors to come to terms with each other without the use of force? In an encounter in which both parties were more or less rational human beings, how could they fail to see that it would be to their mutual advantage to refrain from using against each other the armed force that was the only recourse open to them in their struggle with lions and tigers? How could they fail to see that, as between human beings, rational agreement, opening the way for peaceful co-operation, was not only possible but was infinitely preferable to the use of organised violence?

In our relations with each other, we have, indeed, achieved peaceful co-operation within limits. We have created human society. But, so far, sociality has not been achieved over the whole field of the relations of human beings with each other. In some of our relations with each other we are still applying our reason, not to co-operating with each other, but to employing, against each other, the organised violence that is the only recourse open to us for dealing with non-human wild beasts.

Man is the most potent of all living creatures by virtue of his partial rationality; and, when Man applies his glimmer of reason to making weapons, he can invent artificial weapons that are far more deadly than any of the natural weapons that non-human nature has evolved. Thus Man has rescued himself from the fate of being food for tigers, but has subjected himself to the far more devastating fate of being food for cannon and for atomic weapons. This has been a most unprofitable exchange. The human race's prospects of survival were considerably better when we were defenceless against tigers than they are today, when we have become defenceless against ourselves.

I have dwelt on Man's self-inflicted scourge of war because this brings out the vein of perversity in human nature which has made human history so tragic a story up to date. This perversity in ourselves is our arch-enemy. We encounter it and have so far been worsted by it—in our dealings with all the problems with which we have to contend. This perversity is obviously the crucial obstacle to the abolition of war. Less obviously, perhaps, but no less truly, it is the crucial obstacle to the abolition of hunger.

By 'perversity', I mean an irrational and immoral resistance to acting in accordance with the light that is given to us human beings, alone among living creatures, by our distinctively human faculties of reason and conscience. By yielding to our perverse impulses we are playing into the hands of unregenerate Nature. We have to contend with unregenerate Nature in her external forms—such forms, I mean, as lions and tigers and floods and droughts. But we also have to contend with her in ourselves, where she shows herself in her ugliest form. Within each one of us, unregenerate Nature takes the form of the sub-human, inhuman element in human nature with which Man's reason and conscience have to carry on an unending inner struggle.

To play into Nature's hands unnecessarily is folly. It is also criminal. It is a kind of high treason committed against our own humanity, and this on one of the biggest issues with which mankind ever has been, or (perhaps) ever will be, confronted.

Let me state this issue again in terms of our Freedom from Hunger Campaign. The issue, here, surely is: Are we going to claim, or are we going to renounce, a human privilege that we can enjoy thanks to our possession of reason and conscience? Man, alone among living creatures, has the choice of regulating the size of his population voluntarily, by his own action; and, if once he allows himself to exercise this power that is in his hands, there can be no doubt, surely, about the principle on which he will act. Our aim will be the responsible aim, the moral aim, of doing our best to ensure that every human being whom we bring into the World shall have the best life that we can give to him or her. By 'best' I mean, of course, best in the spiritual sense, regarding physical welfare as being a means to spiritual welfare, and not as being an end in itself.

Maximum welfare, not maximum population, is our human objective. To breed up to the limit made sense for Man only in an age in which he was still a victim of the same maximum mortality that afflicted, and still afflicts, his undomesticated non-human fellow creatures. In an age in which Man has already gone far towards conquering disease and has perhaps come within sight of conquering war, to breed up to the maximum has become the surest way imaginable of undoing our victories over disease and over war. It would defeat us by delivering us into the hands of famine and inviting famine to bring war and pestilence back in its train.

Yet the greater part of the human race is still showing reluctance to regulate its birth rate. This unwillingness to deal rationally with the population problem is condemning mankind to continue to run its age-old race with hunger; and the reduction of the death rate, which we have now achieved, is making the race harder for us to win. The reduction of the death rate is, in itself, one of the finest achievements of the human reason. It ought to be an unmixed blessing; but, so long as it coexists with a persistent failure to regulate the birth rate to match, the reduction of the death rate threatens to turn into a curse instead of a blessing. It is making our race with famine harder to win; and this is the more serious because, in running this race, we are handicapped by the present inequality between the different sections of the human race in respect of this vital matter of food supply.

It has become a commonplace that the rich countries are growing richer while the poor are growing poorer. This is perhaps true of most of the various kinds of production in which wealth consists. It is certainly true of the production of food; and food is the basic form of wealth. A human being who is short of food will find that all other forms of wealth are valueless to him. This point was made, long ago, in the story of Midas' touch.

The technology that is the source of the rich countries' productivity is now generating, in these countries, a surplus of food production. The rich countries themselves cannot consume their own food surpluses; the poor countries, that have a shortage of home-grown food, cannot afford to buy from the rich countries the surpluses that these cannot use. Most of the countries that are now producing food surpluses are countries with a Western civilization, situated in the temperate zones. Tropical countries with a food surplus are exceptional. Thailand is the conspicuous exception that proves this rule.

This regional inequality in food production is not a new phenomenon. The earliest seats of civilization were regions in which food was produced in comparative abundance. Ancient 'Iraq, Ancient Egypt, and the river valleys of Ancient Peru are cases in point. Of course, even in these exceptionally productive regions, the production of food was abundant only by comparison with those other agricultural regions—and they were the majority—that produced no surplus at all. The surplus produced in the productive river valleys was still small when measured by the size of the population. It was enough only to relieve a tiny privileged minority from the common task of wringing the community's subsistence from a reluctant Nature. Even in these relatively favoured communities, the great majority of the population was still living hardly above starvation level after it had surrendered its slender margin of food-production, over and above its own bare needs for its own subsistence, in order to maintain the privileged few in a state of leisure.

A majority of the privileged minority no doubt abused their privilege by misusing the leisure that had been won for them by the toil of the majority of their fellow men and women. They spent the surplus on making war or in indulging in luxury and frivolity. Only a minority of the privileged minority made some return to society for the precious leisure which society had bestowed on them at so heavy a cost. Yet the fruitful use of leisure by a minority of a minority is the source of the civilization that has been achieved by part of the human race within the last five thousand years. All the progress of civilization, both spiritual and material, have been the work of a few people who have been released from the whole-time drudgery of running the race between population-increase and starvation.

This minimum amount of leisure, which has done so much for the human race during these last five thousand years, will be in danger of being wiped out if population continues to increase at its newly accelerated rate.

Yet, in our time, we cannot afford to lose the leisure that a food surplus makes possible. Far from being able to do without it, we need far more leisure than ever before, and therefore need a far larger margin of food production. In our time, we have to aim at nothing less than a modicum of leisure, not just for a minority, but for everybody. This is, first and foremost, a requirement of social justice. One of the odious features of civilization, up to date, has been the monopolization of its amenities by a privileged minority, when the surplus on which this minority has lived has been produced by the majority's hard labour. In our time there is also an imperative practical need to give everybody at least enough leisure to make it possible to discover whether he or she has any special gifts that would be of value to society. Ability is the only capital that mankind has ever had or ever will have, to offset our human physical weakness and nakedness; and today we cannot afford to leave any human being's ability undeveloped and unused. In a generation in which the population of the World is going to double or treble, technology and organization will be, more than ever, our life-lines; and organization and technology of the complexity that is going to be required will demand an ever larger supply of first-rate engineers, administrators, psychologists, researchers, inventors. This means that the proportion of the human race's man-hours that are spent on these non-food-producing services must be in a higher ratio than ever before to the man-hours spent on merely keeping body and soul together. But we shall not be able to achieve this necessary shift in the allocation of human activities unless we can release a much greater proportion of mankind's working time than in the past from the task of merely keeping mankind fed. This, in turn, means that we must aim at stabilising the planet's population at a figure that will allow a substantial part of our time and energy to be spent, not on keeping ourselves alive, but on making human life a more civilized affair than we have succeeded in making it so far.

It was, no doubt, the ability of a minority who had time to think, plan, and direct that originally made possible the reclamation of those river valleys that were the earliest seats of civilization. In those countries in the past, as in the temperate-zone countries today, the surplus of food was not a free gift of Nature. It was the reward of a conquest of Nature by Man. These river valleys, in their state of Nature, were covered with jungle and swamp that were inhospitable to human life. It took imagination and skill, as well as hard work, to break in these uninviting landscapes. It has been the same story in the valley of the River Po in Northern Italy, which has been broken in since the second century B.C., and in the green belt of North America, which has been reclaimed from the virgin forest only in the nineteenth and twentieth centuries of the present era. There have been few regions in which Nature has been propitious for food-production without having had to be broken in. The loess belt in Northern China and the blackearth belt in the Ukraine and in Western Siberia may be examples of this, but if so, they are exceptional cases.

If one examines the economic structure of ancient empires, one finds, in one case after another, that they depended on the surplus food production of some particular province of theirs. This productive region may have amounted, in area, to only a small fraction of the empire that it supported economically. But, without this local economic support, the empire would have collapsed, and in many cases it did collapse if and when it was deprived of this support through the loss of the key province. In the past, again, it was almost impossible for an empire to maintain a capital city, adequate to its political and administrative requirements, anywhere except in the immediate neighbourhood of a food-producing region that provided a surplus over and above the requirements of the local cultivators themselves.

Since the beginning of the history of civilization, statesmanship has been trying to find ways and means of conveying the surplus food of surplus-food-producing areas to areas with no food margin or with a food deficit. The ways and means have to be physical, in the first place. The surplus food has to be transported. In the second place they have to be economic or political or both. The surplus food has to be either bought or commandeered, if it is to reach the mouths that need it. To buy requires economic purchasing-power; to commandeer requires political and military power. A Chinese scholar, Ch'ao-Ting Chi, has written an illuminating history of China in terms of the relations between the political structure, the location of the capital city, and the location of the food-surplus-producing area from which the capital city has drawn its food-supply.

Without effective physical means of communication, a local food surplus is useless. It might as well not be produced if it cannot be transported from its place of origin, where it is superfluous, to places where it is needed. This has been one of the limiting factors in the territorial expansion of states. The obvious limiting factor here is an external one: namely, the military and political capacity of adjoining states to hold their own. But there is also an internal limiting factor in the territorial expansion of states: namely, the limit of their technological and administrative capacity to distribute the food surplus produced in one of their provinces to the remainder of their territory, or at any rate to their capital city. In China, for instance, there has been an alternation between periods in which this subcontinent has been divided up politically into a number of separate local states and periods in which it has been united politically in a single empire. The periods of political unity have been periods in which the problem of transferring food surpluses has been dealt with successfully.

In our present-day world this problem is acute; and here we have another disconcerting example of our human perversity. In our time, technology has solved, at last, the physical problem of transport. The 'annihilation of distance' has been a triumph of human skill that is comparable to the contemporary reduction of the death rate. We have stultified the reduction of the death rate by failing to regulate the birth rate to match. We are stultifying the 'annihilation of distance' by failing to unite into a single community the whole of mankind, as the whole of China has been united into a single state, and as the whole Mediterranean basin was united once, for a short time, in the Roman Empire.

In our age our revolutionary improvements in the means of communication are making unification on a literally world-wide scale possible at last, for the first time in human history. Yet we are depriving ourselves of the benefits of this technological triumph of ours by dividing up the surface of our planet into a larger and larger number of smaller and smaller states, each of which is, at least officially, sovereign and independent. At the same time we are increasing the economic barriers between states. In the past, the most serious hindrances to the international circulation of goods were customs duties. In our time we have reinforced this ancient man-made obstacle by inventing new and more effective obstacles, such as quotas for imports and the manipulation of currencies. The battle between increasing technological efficiency in the circulation of goods and increasing political obstruction to their circulation is not a new battle; its history can be traced right back to the dawn of history. What is perhaps new in our time is the intensity with which this old battle is now being fought.

This is a battle which mankind can no longer afford to leave undecided. We have to win it, because a victory in this field offers us our only chance of being able to keep hunger at bay during an interim period in which, at best, we are going to be pressed hard by the menace of famine. At best, it will take several generations to educate the majority of wives and husbands into voluntarily regulating the number of births. This change will necessarily take time because it involves a break with an immemorially old habit; and this habit, which now threatens mankind with disaster, still has prestige, because in the past it once made for our race's survival. During this interm period, we must look to the application of science to tide us over, and science may indeed be able to come to our rescue if it is not hamstrung by politics. Science will, however, be frustrated, as I have suggested already, if the surface of this planet continues to be divided up

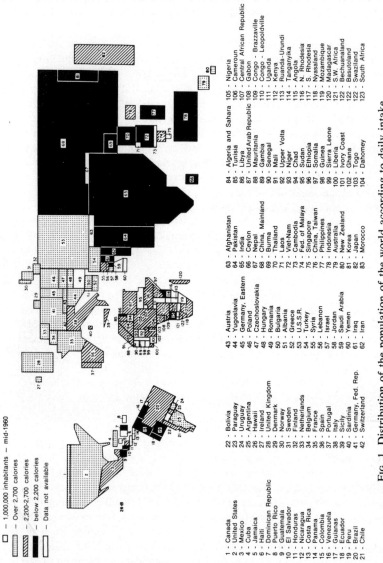

Fig. 1. Distribution of the population of the world according to daily intake

— 1,000,000 inhabitants — mid-1960
— Over 2,700 calories
— 2,200-2,700 calories
— below 2,200 calories
— Data not available

1 - Canada
2 - United States
3 - Mexico
4 - Cuba
5 - Jamaica
6 - Haiti
7 - Dominican Republic
8 - Puerto Rico
9 - Guatemala
10 - El Salvador
11 - Honduras
12 - Nicaragua
13 - Costa Rica
14 - Panama
15 - Colombia
16 - Venezuela
17 - Guianas
18 - Ecuador
19 - Peru
20 - Brazil
21 - Chile

22 - Bolivia
23 - Paraguay
24 - Uruguay
25 - Argentina
26 - Hawaii
27 - Ireland
28 - United Kingdom
29 - Denmark
30 - Norway
31 - Sweden
32 - Finland
33 - Netherlands
34 - Belgium
35 - France
36 - Spain
37 - Portugal
38 - Italy
39 - Sardinia
40 - Sicily
41 - Germany, Fed. Rep.
42 - Switzerland

43 - Austria
44 - Yugoslavia
45 - Germany, Eastern
46 - Poland
47 - Czechoslovakia
48 - Hungary
49 - Romania
50 - Bulgaria
51 - Albania
52 - Greece
53 - U.S.S.R.
54 - Turkey
55 - Syria
56 - Lebanon
57 - Israel
58 - Jordan
59 - Saudi Arabia
60 - Yemen
61 - Iraq
62 - Iran

63 - Afghanistan
64 - Pakistan
65 - India
66 - Ceylon
67 - Nepal
68 - China, Mainland
69 - Burma
70 - Thailand
71 - Laos
72 - Viet-Nam
73 - Cambodia
74 - Fed. of Malaya
75 - Singapore
76 - China, Taiwan
77 - Philippines
78 - Indonesia
79 - Australia
80 - New Zealand
81 - Korea
82 - Japan
83 - Morocco

84 - Algeria and Sahara
85 - Tunisia
86 - Libya
87 - United Arab Republic
88 - Mauritania
89 - Gambia
90 - Senegal
91 - Mali
92 - Upper Volta
93 - Niger
94 - Chad
95 - Sudan
96 - Ethiopia
97 - Somalia
98 - Guinea
99 - Sierra Leone
100 - Liberia
101 - Ivory Coast
102 - Ghana
103 - Togo
104 - Dahomey

105 - Nigeria
106 - Cameroun
107 - Central African Republic
108 - Gabon
109 - Congo - Brazzaville
110 - Congo - Leopoldville
111 - Uganda
112 - Kenya
113 - Ruanda-Urundi
114 - Tanganyika
115 - Angola
116 - N. Rhodesia
117 - S. Rhodesia
118 - Nyasaland
119 - Mozambique
120 - Madagascar
121 - S.W. Africa
122 - Bechuanaland
122 - Basutoland
122 - Swaziland
123 - South Africa

into the territories of more than a hundred sovereign independent states, each of which remains free to pursue a policy of its own about the production and distribution of food, however selfish and however short-sighted a state's food-policy may be.

Perhaps you have in your hands this FAO pamphlet called *Statistics of Hunger* which I am holding up at this moment. If you have it, please open it and look at the chart entitled "Food and Population" (Fig. 1), showing the distribution of the population of the World according to daily intake of calories. You will see that the lowest intake—a perilously low intake—is concentrated in Eastern Asia. And then look at the chart entitled "The Shape of Things to Come" (Fig. 2). You will see that the

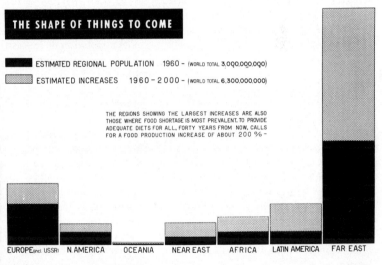

FIG. 2. Estimated population increases for various regions of the world, 1960-2000.

same region, Eastern Asia, in which the food shortage today is most acute, is also the region that is going to have by far the largest population-increase of any by the end of the present century. By the year 2000, Eastern Asia, by itself, is going to have a much larger population than the whole of the rest of the World put together. By A.D. 2000, the population of Eastern Asia is going to exceed the population of all the rest of the World by a figure that will be about equal to the estimated population, in A.D. 2000, of Europe, including the whole of the Soviet Union. The prospect opened up by a comparison of these two charts is sufficiently appalling, considered by itself, without taking any political factors into account. In the chart in this FAO pamphlet it is pointed out that the food situation, predicted for the year 2000, calls for a world food production increase of about 200 per cent, forty years from now, if adequate diets are to be provided for the whole population of the World at its estimated figure at that not very distant date.

Well, now, to get a realistic picture, we have to add the current political situation to the present and future food situation. You can see the political ingredient to the situation at a glance if you look again at Fig. 1. In this chart, the present political divisions of the World are displayed, and the size of countries is shown, not in terms of actual areas, but in proportion to population. Keep your eyes on that chart. You will see that, in terms of population, Eastern Asia already exceeds all the rest of the World put together, and this by a figure that is appreciably greater than the present figure for the population of the whole of North America. You will also see that about three-quarters of the huge population of Eastern Asia is accounted for by two countries only, namely India and China. The combined population of India and China is immense, and it is grievously underfed.

Now what have India and China been doing to solve the food problem? They have been diverting resources that they cannot spare from their imperatively urgent common task of increasing their food production. They have been diverting these resources to the wholly unproductive enterprise of fighting each other for the possession of strips of territory whose contribution to the World's food supply is, and always will be, infinitesimal. This is a tragedy. Chinese and Indian thoughts and efforts ought to be concentrated, not on making war, but on producing food. I do not apologize for singling out one pair of countries for your attention. This is not invidious, because India and China are not peculiar. They are a fair sample of the human race of which they constitute, together, so large a quota.

This is perhaps too gloomy a note to end on. The facts of human behaviour often seem to leave the human observer of human affairs no alternative to despair. When one has been almost driven to despair by the spectacle of folly and crime, it is a good thing to right the balance by reminding ourselves that, throughout the course of history, as far as we have a record of it, dancing on the edges of precipices has been one of mankind's favourite occupations. For human beings, this is, of course, a very dangerous game. Human feet are not nearly so well suited for this exercise as the feet of flies or lizards. Moreover, the danger has greatly increased as a result of the recent great increase in human power. Till lately, mankind was so feeble that it hardly had the strength to topple itself over the edge, however near to the edge it might be standing. Indeed, it is only since the invention of the atomic weapon in 1945 that race-suicide has come within sight of becoming feasible.

We have now exposed ourselves to the risk of committing mass suicide by fighting an atomic world war. Fortunately, an awareness of the revolutionary change, since 1945, in the nature of war seems to have spread quickly and widely and to have made quite a deep impression. Already a spirit of caution and self-restraint, which was conspicuously absent in the past, has made itself felt in the conduct of international relations. It is perhaps not foolishly optimistic to hope that, now that we are at the edge of the atomic precipice, we may forbear to advance any further and that we may even back away a little from the abyss. The peril of atomic mass suicide is dramatic. On the other hand, the size of mankind's stakes in the race between population growth and hunger is not so easily discernible. To appreciate it, one must be sufficiently at home with statistics and charts to be capable of having one's imagination stirred by them. The facts and diagrams in the FAO's Freedom from Hunger Campaign do appeal to the imagination. But I fancy that, till now, the effect has not been so great as the effect on our imagination of our knowledge of what an atomic war would mean. This is, no doubt, one of the reasons for our present campaign. The gravity and urgency of the problem of feeding the World's rapidly increasing population has to be brought home, not to the experts, who do not need educating, but to the masses, who do need this. For us human beings, the dangers to our survival are the most dangerous when we are unaware of them. They are the most dangerous of all when our blindness is at least partly wilful, as it so often is.

As soon as human beings face a danger, there is always some hope that they may bring their practical ability into play for overcoming it; and, since our practical ability is great, our chances are good, if only we allow our danger to jolt us out of our habitual perversity. This is why a campaign to educate ourselves in the problem of hunger is so important today.

If we are to master the problem of hunger, what have we to do? I see two principal points on our agenda. I have discussed both of them already; but, in concluding this talk, I will mention both of them again because, to my mind, they are fundamental. Both of them are educational projects, and both will take time and effort to carry out, because both will call upon human beings to break with habits that have become ingrained in us by long practice of them, and we tend to cling to ingrained habits irrationally.

The first piece of urgently necessary education is in the political field. We have to persuade ourselves to give to the interests of the human race as a whole a decisive priority over the interests of one's own particular section of it. Unless we can bring about this revolutionary redistribution of loyalties, we shall not be able to get the whole human race, over the whole surface of the planet, to administer itself as a single world-wide unit for the purpose of producing and distributing food; and, unless we can attain this political objective, we shall not be able to give science a chance to enable us to keep the World's population fed while our second piece of educational work is being carried out.

Our second educational task is to persuade wives and husbands voluntarily to regulate the birth rate to match the already achieved reduction of the death rate. This piece of sexual education seems likely to prove more difficult than the companion piece of political education, and this for two reasons. In the first place, a much larger number of people have to be educated before this campaign can produce practical results. In the second place, family affairs are a much more intimate side of human life than politics are. In asking people to change their habits in this field, one is running a greater risk of finding the way blocked by irrational prejudices. This piece of education will therefore take time; and, in order to find the time, we shall have to forge ahead with our piece of political education. Since this is the easier task of the two, we may hope to carry it out more quickly.

The existence and activities of FAO are an antidote to pessimism. I do not believe that the governments of the World's local states would have been capable of calling anything like FAO into existence in the times before 1914. The idea would hardly have occurred to them; and, if some unofficial human being had suggested it to them, many of them would have found it repugnant, because they would have seen in it a covert attack on local sovereignty. On this point, I fancy, the predicted growth of the World's population within the next forty years is going to have a radical effect, if what actually happens turns out to be anything like what has been forecast. By the time when the World's population has doubled or trebled, I believe that the World's hungry peoples are likely to compel their governments to thrust upon FAO a considerable part of the executive authority and responsibility, in regard to food, that today is still being jealously retained in the local governments' hands.

Meanwhile, FAO is actively preparing itself for its increasingly important future role. This is, I should guess, part of the significance of our present Freedom from Hunger Campaign.

14.

# FOOD SUPPLIES AND POPULATION

*by the Food and Agricultural Organization
of the United Nations*

World food supplies must be trebled by the turn of the century if the world population, which is expected to double and to exceed 6,000 million by then, is to have enough to eat. At present it is estimated that 300 to 500 million people out of 3,000 million in the world are underfed and that up to one half of the world population—perhaps even more— suffer from hunger or malnutrition.

It is against this grim background that the Freedom from Hunger Campaign launched by the Food and Agriculture Organization of the United Nations (FAO) needs to be viewed. The magnitude of the problem and the continuing inadequacy of food production in the "hungry regions" of the world present a challenge to all who think in terms of a better and a peaceful world. Such a world is impossible in the present circumstances.

A hungry man is a social liability. He cannot work effectively on an empty stomach; he cannot study and learn as he must to improve his conditions of life; he cannot think beyond his immediate needs, of which food is dominant; he cannot build up resistance to disease; and, in short, because he can be counted in millions, he retards not only the economic and social development of his country, but also the prosperity of the world.

This continuing problem can only be solved by the united efforts of all countries, with the brunt of the effort being borne by the hungry regions themselves. This global concept of the struggle is basic to the Freedom from Hunger Campaign.

Even before the Campaign was launched the existence of hunger in the world was an accepted fact. The only point at issue was the extent. Expert opinions differed widely, ranging from a few millions to two thirds of the world population. It is clear that there are many difficulties inherent in the case. These lie largely in assessing and interpreting how

Reprinted with kind permission from the FAO brochure *Six Billions to Feed* (Rome: Food and Agriculture Organization of the United Nations, 1962), pp. 3-4, 33-41.

much and what is available to eat, how much a person needs and how he or she actually does eat. A statstical study of the problem was recently made by Dr. P. V. Sukhatme, Director of Statistics Division, FAO. It confirmed that at least one third to one half of the world's people suffer from hunger or malnutrition.

Once the magnitude of hunger and malnutrition has been established, the next step is to assess how much more food is needed to overcome and correct the imbalance in diets within the foreseeable future. Food has to be increased in quantity, and more fruit, vegetables, and foods of animal origin are required to provide a balanced diet.

To ensure quantitative adequacy, the essential minimum increase should be computed to make up the shortage as measured by the gap between existing calorie supplies and national calorie requirements. Over a longer period, the goal will have to be set higher so as to make allowances for the unequal distribution of calories among the population and for the additional needs of a developing economy. As for quality, the aim is to set targets somewhere close to the level enjoyed by the developed countries in so far as conditions in the less developed countries will permit.

### CALORIE AND PROTEIN TARGETS

The poorest diets of the low-calorie countries are found in the Far East and African regions. For the Far East, the target for calorie supplies would range from a low and medium figure of 2,300 to a high and long-term target of 2,400 calories per person daily. The low target for animal protein intake would be 10 grams per person per day, rising to 15 grams as a medium target and 20 grams as a high target. In Africa, the low and high target would range from 2,400 to 2,450 calories per caput per day and for animal protein intake from 15 to 20 grams per caput per day.

The Near East and Latin America, excluding the River Plate countries, are the relatively better fed regions among the low-calorie countries. For the Near East and Latin America the calorie target would be the current supplies, which range from 2,400 to 2,500 calories per caput daily. The animal protein target for both countries would be 20 grams per caput daily. No target has been set for total proteins, except that in no case should they be less than at present.

Thus, as a general objective for the undernourished regions, the low targets mentioned seek only a modest increase of some 3 grams of animal proteins per caput per day, which may be expected to be achieved over, say, a 10-year period. For the medium target, a further increase of 4 to 5 grams is envisaged in the following 10 years, while the high target aims at an increase of a further 5 grams daily, to be achieved by the turn of the century. Thus, over the present levels, the high target represents an increase of some 12 grams daily. The total of 20 grams for the high target is less than one half of the level of 44 grams in the current diets of the developed countries.

In increasing food supplies over the short-term period, improvement in quality should be made simultaneously with an increase in quantity, as the most widespread and major deficiency in diets is in their quality. Should this not be done, and only quantity be increased, the current imbalance would grow worse. In the medium period, greater emphasis will have to be placed on quality, while the long-term target will aim for further increases in both the calorie and protein levels.

The nutritional targets proposed in the preceding paragraphs need to be translated in terms of food, and these will be governed by three conditions. First, that the increase in food supplies should be at a cost within reach of the ordinary consumer. This is very important, as hunger and poverty are closely related. The second condition is that, in computing the quantities of food groups, the existing dietary pattern of the people should not be changed substantially, at least in the immediate future. People are used to certain kinds of food and any major change might not be acceptable to them. And, third, all proposed increases should be possible to achieve—or better still, should be achieved—within a stipulated time.

The starting point in making these calculations would be to take the existing levels of supplies and determine how they could best be adjusted to satisfy the three basic conditions. For instance, the target for animal proteins in the Far East could be met by increasing the supplies of fish alone, as fish is the cheapest source of animal protein in this region. However, two factors—the possibility of increased catches and the dietary preferences of the Far Easterners with regard to fish—make it necessary to set an upper limit on the amount of fish to be provided. Similarly, the targets for calories and vegetable proteins could be achieved by increasing supplies of cereals and pulses alone. But the level of consumption of these products in the low-calorie countries is already disproportionate, and to increase it further would only exaggerate the imbalance in the diet. Appropriate upper limits, therefore, also need to be set for cereals and pulses.

On the other hand, a minimum target for fruit and vegetables, costly as they are, must be set above the present levels, so as to provide some of the essential minerals and vitamins which can be obtained only from these foods.

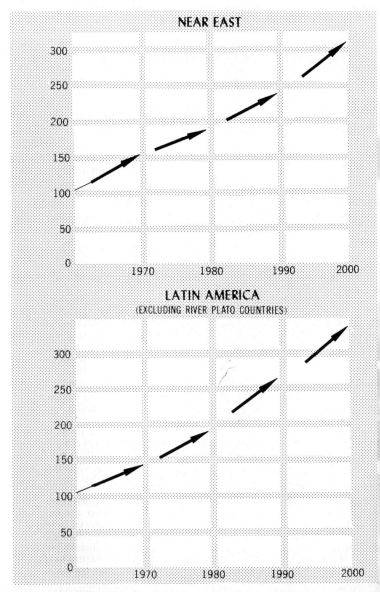

FIG. 1. Overall index of needs in total food supplies, 1970-2000 (available = 100).

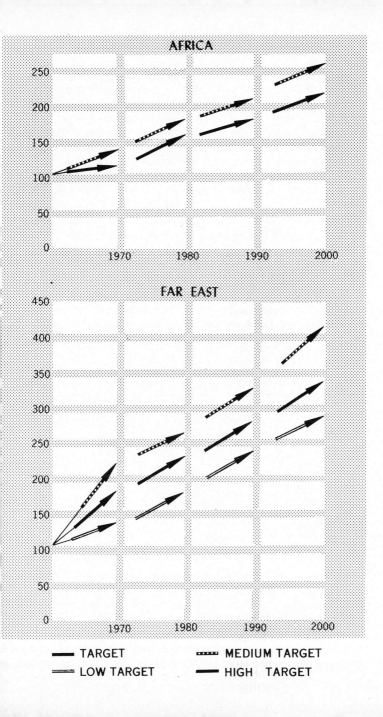

ESTIMATION OF FUTURE FOOD NEEDS

The increases in food supplies needed to achieve the proposed targets, on the basis of the three conditions mentioned above, have been estimated by FAO on the basis of the present world population. Population projections show that the present population of about 3,000 million will double by the year 2000, but the growth rate is uneven between regions. A regional breakdown shows that the populations of Europe, North America, Oceania and the River Plate countries of Latin America (Argentina, Uruguay and Paraguay) are expected to increase moderately, reaching 150% over the present number. This group of countries, however, already enjoys adequate levels of nutrition. But in the undernourished countries of the Far East, the Near East, Africa, and the rest of Latin America, the situation is worse. The population is expected to double in Africa, to treble in Latin America, and to increase by 250% in both the Near East and the Far East. This implies that, even without any improvement in the present level of nutrition, food supplies would have to be increased by 100% for Africa, 200% for Latin America (excluding the River Plate countries) and 150% for the Far East and the Near East by the year 2000.

OVER-ALL INDEX OF NEEDS IN TOTAL FOOD SUPPLIES, 1970-2000
(Available = 100)

|                                      | 1970 | 1980 | 1990 | 2000 |
|--------------------------------------|------|------|------|------|
| Far East:                            |      |      |      |      |
|   Low target               | 148  | 186  | 233  | 292  |
|   Medium target            | 175  | 219  | 274  | 343  |
|   High target              | 207  | 259  | 324  | 406  |
| Near East                            | 154  | 190  | 240  | 307  |
| Africa:                              |      |      |      |      |
|   Low target               | 128  | 155  | 189  | 230  |
|   High target              | 143  | 174  | 212  | 259  |
| Latin America                        |      |      |      |      |
| (excluding River Plate countries)    | 145  | 194  | 257  | 338  |

In other words, in order to meet future population needs alone, without any improvement in the present levels of nutrition, food supplies must be increased by about 150% in the low calorie countries and by about 120% in the world as a whole.

To achieve the low targets set out earlier for improved nutrition, the additional amount of food needed to provide for each increase of 100 million in the population of the Far East will comprise some 16 million

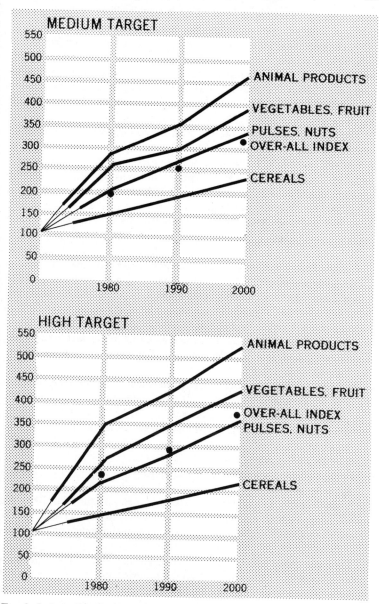

FIG. 2. Index of needs in total food supplies by selected major food groups (available = 100).

tons of cereals, 3 million tons of pulses, 7 million tons of fruit and vegetables, 3 million tons of meat, eggs and fish and 3 million tons of milk. In
terms of percentages, these figures would represent a 30% increase in cereals, 60% in pulses, 90% in fruit and vegetables and over 70% in animal
products. This works out roughly to an annual over-all increase in food
supplies of about 5% over the next 10 years, but because of population
growth it will only amount to about a 2% increase in per caput food
supplies.

The medium targets for the Far East would necessitate a decrease of
some 5% in the per caput level of cereal consumption and an increase of
some 50% in pulses; 100% in fruit and vegetables; 90% in meat, eggs
and fish; and 135% in milk. Interpreted in terms of future needs, the
medium target would call for some 33 million tons of plant products
(such as cereals, fruit, vegetables, etc.) in place of the 28 million now
available, and some 8 million tons of animal products in place of the 4
million now available, for every additional 100 million of the population.

It would appear, therefore, that the aim must be an over-all increase in
per caput food supplies of some 2% per annum for the Far East to
achieve the low target by 1970, the medium target by 1980 and the high
target before the turn of the present century. In terms of total needs this
means that over-all supplies would have to be increased by some 50% to
achieve the low target by 1970, by 120% to achieve the medium target
by 1980, and by 300% to achieve the high target in the year 2000. Thus,
four times the present supplies are needed by the year 2000 to achieve
the long-term target.

In order to meet the same target in the Near East, total supplies will
have to be increased 90% by 1980 and 200% by the year 2000. For
Africa, over-all supplies need to be increased by 75% by 1980 and 160%
by the turn of the century. The Latin-American region (excluding the
River Plate countries) requires an over-all increase of 90% by 1980
and 240% by the year 2000.

For the world as a whole, the total supplies needed by 1980 will require
an increase of some 45% in cereals, 95% in pulses, and 85% in animal
products in order to achieve the medium targets. By the year 2000, the
world food supplies will have to rise by some 110% in cereals, 200%
in pulses and 190% in animal products over and above the supplies available today.

Thus, the broad conclusion to be drawn is that, should the population
grow according to the United Nations forecast, the world's total food
supplies would have to be doubled by 1980 and trebled by the turn of
the century in order to provide a level of nutrition reasonably adequate
to the needs of all the world's peoples.

15.

# THE USE AND ABUSE
# OF LAND AND WATER

*by C. S. Christian*

Most biological species are subject to enforced population adjustments as food supplies and competition for them vary from place to place and time to time, but man is no longer prepared to accept this passive role. Ultimately some self-imposed control of his population increase will be essential, but the Freedom from Hunger Campaign is concerned with the practical means of feeding the human populations that already exist and those that will inevitably exist in the coming decades.

This World Food Congress is being held in the knowledge that at this very moment a large proportion of the world's population has an inadequate food supply and that the present rate of increase of the world population will surely aggravate this deficiency in many areas. This situation cannot be tolerated in the light of the emerging conscience of the modern world. Direct and positive steps are required to reduce this hunger that now exists and to limit the greater hunger that could face the next generations.

This Congress demonstrates man's confidence in his growing powers to influence his own environment and his own destiny and, furthermore, it demonstrates the increasing willingness of the peoples of the world to assist one another in circumstances of consequence to all the human race.

Man is dependent for his food supply almost **entirely on** the products of land and water and the plant and animal species of the earth. It is in the practical exploitation, development, conservation and improvement of these natural resources that man must seek the answer to hunger and rural poverty. Although many of the facets of modern civilization—in particular the complexities of finance, trade, and economics, transport and international relationships—will influence the time and speed with which different communities can achieve their aims, it is in the actual field practice of producing food from land and water by plants and animals

Paper read during the World Food Congress of the Food and Agriculture Organization of the United Nations, Washington, D.C., 4-8 June 1963.

ultimate solution lies. We must seek more efficient and more com-
use of these resources and the elimination of practices that reduce
their productivity or cause wastage.

Historical events have led to a concentration of communities of people
in certain defined areas where they are now committed to support themselves irrespective of the world distribution of natural resources. The size
and location of these historically determined areas bear no logical relationship to the present population density, or needs. Any readjustment
of these national boundaries on a grand scale is unlikely; so each community is faced with the necessity to use the resources it now possesses
to its best advantage.

It would be unrealistic to believe that all the people on this earth will
be equally well nourished but we must go as far towards this objective as
is humanly possible, and must be less than satisfied with anything less
than the impossible.

Each country presents a unique problem, with its own degree of population pressure and needs, its own kind and magnitude and deficiencies of
natural resources, its own stage of economic and social development. The
world problem of hunger, and the use of land and water to alleviate it, is
not one problem. It is a multitude of problems as numerous as the number of countries and the distinctive regions that comprise them.

The industrially well-developed countries can afford a high standard of
land and water use through high inputs such as irrigation developments,
fertilizers and machinery, and, because of advanced education systems,
by a high degree of practical application of advanced technical knowledge. For example, the amount of fertilizer used on arable land in Europe
is twelve times that used in Asia and Africa and, in 1960, the number of
tractors in Europe and North America was four times that of the rest of
the world. Favourable price arrangements for agricultural products are
made possible in industrial countries by the high average income. The
trend in such countries is to use land even more efficiently and to raise
yield per unit area still higher. As income derived from industrial exports
permits importations from food surplus producing areas, industrial countries, even those with dense populations, are not likely to face any critical
food problem in the near future even though the reserves of land awaiting
new development may be small.

Where industrially developed countries also possess substantial areas
still available for increasing cultivation, there are situations conducive to
the production of further surpluses of agricultural products for export. To
what extent these actual and potential surpluses can help solve the world
food problem, or to what extent they may inhibit the development of less
developed countries through market interactions and so actually aggra-

vate the problem, are major items requiring study. What major break-through can be made in this field in the light of all the political ramifications within and between countries remains to be seen.

Another group of countries includes those which are less developed industrially and have only moderate to low density populations, such as some countries in South America, Oceania and Africa. In the main, these have substantial areas available for further expansion of production and considerable scope for increasing yield per unit area. The application of known scientific methods could alleviate food deficiencies in most of these countries and provide surplus food for export. However, in this category there is a wide range of national earnings from the export of primary products, such as minerals, surplus food and industrial crop products, and also very different levels of production, standards of living, and technical application. Sociological, economic and technical problems involved in achieving expanded production will vary accordingly. Those countries which are economically poor and have low educational standards will find it particularly difficult to gain momentum without very substantial technical and material aid from outside. The rate of development of an expanded and more efficient agriculture in many of these countries will be acutely affected by world prices of food and industrial crop products and by their rate of accumulation of economic strength through industrialization.

In a separate category are the countries which also have limited industrial development but already have dense and rapidly increasing rural and urban populations with a low income per head, and limited areas for new cultivation. It is in this group of countries, which include many Asian countries, that the food problem is most acute and where it is likely to develop most seriously and be most difficult to overtake. Low input and less widely practised technical knowledge at present suppress the general level of food production per unit area. Human diets need to be supplemented in both calories and animal proteins. Vast importations would be necessary to offset total deficiencies and the finance and transport which would be required for this would seem to make this an impracticable solution. In these countries, the productivity of much of the land has declined as the result of long cultivation. The need to use land for the production of rural products for export because of the low level of other export earnings and the growing demand on land for industry, and for housing rapidly increasing new generations, imposes further limitations on food production potentials. In these countries, there is the three-fold problem of arresting the processes of land deterioration, of raising yields per unit area, and of bringing the remaining land, often poor land, into production. To provide the necessary capital, fertilizers, machinery and other inputs necessary to achieve these aims, a parallel economic development on a broad front is essential.

My point, before discussing land itself in more detail, is to emphasize first that, no matter what we know about advanced methods of land and water use, many economic and social factors have, and will continue to have, the major controlling influence on what can be applied. A knowledge of the advanced technologies is essential, but economic resources, as well as intellectual strength, are also essential if this knowledge is to be put to work.

LAND

Land is commonly spoken of as though it were a single variable, with good land at one end of the scale and poor land at the other. In reality, land is a complex of many interacting factors, all of which affect its production potential. It can be described as the combination of all features at and near the land surface which influence the welfare of mankind. Land must be considered as the whole vertical profile at a site on the land surface from the aerial environment down to the underlying geological horizons, and including the plant and animal populations, and past and present human activity associated with it. There are many features in this total profile, some easily observable like the soil and the vegetation, some measurable such as the rainfall and surface slope, but many not so readily observed or measured, such as the internal drainage and aeration features of the soil, the rate of chemical weathering and chemical migration in the soil, the level of microbiological activity, the variations in the microclimates, and the precise impact of former land use by man. The many features of this total profile vary from site to site and their many combinations and interactions result in a vast array of land types, each with its own potential and limitations for agriculture or forestry, each presenting its own specific barriers to the achievement of maximum plant or animal production. Rarely does one feature alone determine productivity. It is the combination of all that is important, and if we are to understand land we must think of it in terms of this complex rather than only of the individual components of it.

Primitive man was just another species adjusting himself to the world in which he lived, competing with other species for what it provided and making the best of it. Man's intelligence gave him certain advantages and he had the initiative to choose other species of value to him and to reproduce them in greater quantities and in locations where he most needed them. In doing so, he pushed many of them far beyond their natural habitats and, in order to favour their growth he learned to modify the natural environment and also to select certain varieties of the species better adapted to new conditions and better able to serve his particular purpose. Thus arose the practices of forest cutting and of cultivation of land to remove competition, of planting crops, of conserving water and irrigating land where water supply was inadequate, of clearing trees and shrubs to allow grass to grow, of domesticating animals and of improving plant production by adding manures and residues to the soil.

There emerged the many traditional practices of land use characteristic of different regions. Many of these were admirably suited to the conditions of the past when populations were so much smaller. Nomadic grazing made good use of pasture by following seasonal growth in different areas, shifting agriculture allowed encroaching weed species to be eliminated by regenerating forests and permitted land to slowly re-establish its fertility before it was cultivated again, irrigation and the addition of manure to soil increased yields and made crop growth possible in areas where crops would otherwise have failed.

Some of these practices are still essential parts of the socio-economic patterns of certain communities but, as populations have increased their pressure, the long continuation of some practices has disturbed many of the equilibria which were established in the land profile under more or less stable natural conditions. Man did not understand these complex changes, and, because their effects were slow to develop, they were not easily recognized. Time has shown that the inherent productivity of land may decline although the practices may have given temporary increased returns. Today the world is faced with large areas of land where the natural process of wind and water erosion has been accelerated and surface soil has been lost; where continued cultivation and the removal of nutrients in crop and animal products, particularly under monoculture, has led to a substantial reduction in soil fertility and deterioration of soil structure; where excessive or unwise irrigation, without adequate drainage, or irrigation of unsuitable types of land, has led to rising water tables, waterlogging and salting, to the point where crop production is no longer possible; where forests have been over-exploited and valuable species eliminated, and where the removal of forests has changed the hydrological regime of an area, affecting stream flow and underground water; where over-grazing or bad grassland management has caused the loss of better pasture species with their replacement by bare ground or by inedible or less nutritious competitors.

In the last few centuries, and particularly in the last few decades, science has learned a great deal about land and the causes of land deterioration. It is now possible to correct many of the faults of past practices and to design land use projects so that these need not recur. Unfortunately, this information is far from being universally applied and land is still deteriorating over vast areas. The challenge to rehabilitate despoiled lands and to prevent their extension is still as great a challenge as is the development of new lands, and the gains to be achieved in many countries where increased food production is most needed may be even greater than that to be obtained from new lands. Before disturbing traditional practices, however, planners should be sure that what they have to offer is, in fact, better and that communities are economically and sociologically capable of making the replacement.

Science has also learned a great deal about the individual factors and processes affecting plant and animal growth. Our knowledge is far from complete, but, by applying the approaches that are known and by experiment, many types of land which have low natural productivity can now be modified and their productivity raised far beyond the hopes of a century ago.

There are five groups of principles related to increasing crop yields. They are:

1. To correct deficiencies of the factors which directly influence the nutrition of the plant and to provide an optimum balance between them. The two main practical measures involved are (a) to provide irrigation or drainage in order to produce better water relationships, and (b) to apply, as fertilizers, the deficient plant nutrients, and to raise the total level of nutrients, in balance, to a point that the plant can make full use of the water available to it.

2. To control competing weed species and pests and diseases.

3. To develop varieties of crop species which are adapted to the climatic regime of the areas and which can make optimum use of both water and nutrient supplies.

4. To adopt land cultural practices which maintain land in a suitable physical condition, and land management practices which encourage an accumulation rather than a depletion of soil fertility—for example, by crop rotation, or mixed crop and animal husbandry or mixed grass-legume pastures.

5. To adopt modifications of mechanical procedures which permit more productive and economic operations, including such things as speed of cultivation in areas with a short growing season, precision of planting, better irrigation, fertilizer and pesticide application, efficiency and proper timing of harvesting, and better processing, storage and transport of the harvested product.

The kind of practices that are most beneficial will vary with the type of land and its history. With full application of the principles that have been established in the sciences of land, plant and animal production and forestry, the opportunities for increasing productivity are already available. The word "principles" is used deliberately because, although there usually are established practices available to accompany these principles, they relate mostly to the areas where the principles have been studied. There is a danger in transferring practices too freely from one area to another; broad principles can be expected to apply, but their application and limitations in new areas must be determined locally by field trial and investigation. This applies to the economic and social aspects of land use just as much as it does to the technical aspects. A good deal of very well-intentioned technical aid has been made less effective than it could have been because the complications of local conditions of climate, soil, and society were not recognized. To have technical information is necessary; to know where and when it applies is what makes it useful.

One overall principle must be stressed, with equal application to crop, pasture, animal, and forestry production. It is that maximum production is attainable only when all factors are satisfied. Irrigation without fertilization, or vice versa, or either without using a suitable crop variety, will not give maximum yields, nor is it likely to give the most economic returns. Often the combined effect of satisfying two or more factors is far greater than the sum of the separate effects, and economically very much sounder. The four ways in which increased crop yields are most universally obtained are the application of fertilizer, the use of irrigation or soil moisture conserving practices, the use of improved adapted plant varieties, and the control of pests and diseases. Even to adapt one of these principles to a new location requires a certain amount of experimentation and technical skill. To combine a number, possibly including other practices from the five groups of principles previously enunciated, requires a well organized experimental approach, and, in difficult circumstances, good research work. If developing nations are to raise the level of food production over wide areas and varying land types, it is important that they should build up their resources of technical personnel, and research and investigation facilities as rapidly as possible. Even with the most favourable rate of expansion, there would be an appreciable time lag before real effects on production were felt.

## The World Land Picture

On the average there are about 5 hectares, or 12.5 acres of land surface for each member of the world's human population at the present time.

Broadly speaking, 35-40% of the land surface is said to be virtually unavailable for agricultural use, because it is arid or cold, salty, or too mountainous, or because it has already been occupied by cities or roads, or is covered by inland waters. Of the remaining useful area, about 20 thousand millions acres, one-sixth is cultivated for crop production, one-third is described as meadow land or pasture of value for grazing domestic animals, and one-half is covered by forests and woodlands. The figures represent world proportions and they vary considerably from region to region. For example, in the three land regions with the densest population—Europe, Asia and Mainland China—the proportion of cultivated land exceeds 30%, but in all other major regions it is much lower and ranges from as low as 0.5% to only 17%.

The importance of irrigation is indicated by the fact that the densely populated countries—Mainland China, Taiwan and Japan—have approximately half of their total arable areas irrigated. The comparable figure for Asia is about 30%, and for the whole world about 15%.

In general, cultivated land produces more calories of human food per unit area than grazing or forest land, and irrigated land more than rainfed land. Both produce a wider variety of produce of value to industry.

To meet the food and other agricultural requirements of increasing populations in the relatively near future, there will certainly be pressure to increase the areas of land which are cultivated and irrigated, and particularly those which are used for cereals, in order to produce the basic calorie requirements of human diets. To provide better-balanced diets, however, increased emphasis must be placed on other food products, especially those richer in proteins, such as the pulses, milk, meat and egg products.

As the regions which are now most deficient in food, and the ones where future populations are likely to be the greatest, are mostly areas where rice is the main staple food, particular attention needs to be given to the increased production of this cereal, or to its replacement by some other acceptable food. For this reason, the activities of the International Rice Commission of FAO, and the International Rice Institute recently established in collaboration by the Government of the Philippines and the Ford and Rockefeller Foundations, have a particularly significant role to play in world food production developments.

The world's areas of cultivable land are gradually being encroached upon by urbanization and industrialization and in many areas this has already reached the point where deliberate control of the future use of land by planning authorities is essential to safeguard valuable arable lands.

FAO statistics indicate that, for each unit of land currently cultivated, there are about 2½ additional units suitable for cultivation. It is not clear just what categories of land are involved and a higher proportion certainly exists in difficult environments. However, the future expansions of cultivated areas must be largely at the expense of pasture and forest land, although there is also some scope in the reclamation of flooded and degraded areas and in the development of delta lands. At the present time, forest and pasture lands are not everywhere well used and some encroachment by cultivation will be permissible; but these assets are valuable in themselves and cannot be lightly destroyed.

For instance, where low protein diets occur, it would seem desirable that future food production programmes should include an increase rather than decrease in animal production and, where socially acceptable, meat production as well as milk products. The low efficiency with which animals convert plants into human food is an argument against feeding to animals food that could be used directly for human consumption, but grass eating animals have the advantage of being able to forage for their own food from crop residues and areas which are not used for cultivation. Although mechanization and modern agricultural science may eventually push the boundary of cultivated areas far beyond present limits, there will still remain areas of grasslands and woodlands, which would be unproductive unless used for animal production. Moreover, cattle and buffalo are important for draught purposes, especially in cultivated land areas, and are likely to be part of the agricultural scene for a long time to come. Through the return of dung, animals contribute to the maintenance of soil fertility and, in many areas, mixed animal, pasture and crop production has been found to be the most economical way to maintain productivity. Where dung is used for fuel, much of this soil fertility building is lost and it would be desirable, where feasible, to provide wood or other fuels or sources of heat to replace it.

Another aspect of animal production, of significance to soil fertility, is the trend to transport animal foodstuffs, rather than the animal product itself, and to produce the animal products nearer their urban markets. This is influenced by the part that plant products play in industrial processes and the usefulness of the by-products for animal production. Involved in this is the transfer of soil nutrients from one part of a country, or the world, to another and the need to ensure their replacement before exhaustion reduces the level of productivity.

The inevitable reduction of pasture areas by the extension of cultivation emphasizes the need to achieve higher levels of efficiency in the use and management of the remaining grazing lands which, apart from food, also produce the animal fibres so important for man's clothing and protection. Our knowledge of pasture improvement and utilization is less advanced in the tropical regions but the lag in application of knowledge is widespread in most regions. Grazing lands are often treated carelessly, as though they were inexhaustible, or expendable.

Forests are equally important for the welfare of man and wood products must continue to play an ever increasing part for building and construction purposes and for fuel, and as a source of new products and export incomes. Of comparable importance is the place that wood pulp must play. For instance, in the period 1956-58, the average consumption of pulp per head for newsprint in the Pacific area was over 25 times greater than that for Asia, and there were nearly as large disparities in other uses of pulp products. As educational and industrialization programmes proceed, this gap must gradually be narrowed. The demands for forest products are likely to increase at rates even greater than populations. The welfare of the developing nations requires that their potentialities for forest products and plantations should be developed and safeguarded. As with pastures, this will involve the intensification of improvement and management practices. At present, less than 20% of the world's accessible forests are subjected to any form of planned management and a very small proportion to advanced management practices.

It has been necessary to refer several times to the need for adequate fertilizer to obtain optimum crop production on both irrigated and un-irrigated land. Australian and New Zealand experience shows that this can apply equally well to pasture lands.

Fertilizer is one of the costly inputs that low income rural producers without credit or finance facilities cannot afford. Yet it has been estimated that the use of moderate amounts of fertilizers on existing cultivations in the food deficient regions could increase food production by at least 50%, and, combined with other practices, by 100%. In 1959/60, the world consumed 27 million tons of commercial fertilizer, FAO has estimated that, if half the food increase required by the end of the century is to be obtained as a result of fertilizer applications, the world consumption will need to rise to at least 100 million tons. Much of this increase will be required in the low income, densely populated regions. Unless this fertilizer is produced, and its purchase by farmers in these food deficient countries made possible, there is little hope of those countries achieving their production targets. Planners may very well have to judge whether fertilizer factories, or fertilizer finance schemes, should not come before costly irrigation, or new land settlement, schemes.

### WATER

So far we have referred to water mainly in its place in the land complex affecting plant production, but water has many roles to play, in domestic and urban uses, industry, power production, for livestock and irrigation, recreation, and as a source of food. Some of these roles are competitive and, where water is limited in quantity, decisions must be made about how it can be best used.

Were it possible to desalinate water at an acceptable cost, the oceans and seas could supply man's water needs for all times, but, in spite of progress in this field, it seems that present costs still restrict the available methods to special circumstances. Most predictions concerning the more extensive use of desalinated water for agriculture involve assumptions about technological improvements in the future which have yet to be substantiated. The scope for industrial or urban use is probably much greater, but it is likely, for a long time to come, that the source of fresh water for agriculture and food production will be the rain that falls on the land surfaces. We should be careful not to be carried away too readily by the visionaries who talk of irrigating inland deserts far removed from coastal areas, with desalinated sea water. The costs and difficulties of transporting water to such distant areas are likely to be equally as important as the problems of desalination itself.

The practical value of the great salt ocean and seas, apart from their place in the general recirculation of water vapour to the atmosphere, is mainly for transport, recreation, and in the food resources they provide.

The food harvested from the world's oceans and fresh-water sources constitutes only about 1.5% by value of the world's annual food production, although it is really more valuable than this because it is a source of animal protein. Certainly the potential resource is much greater and many countries have made rapid increases in their harvests in recent years. Some people consider the salt and fresh-water oceans and seas have a potential for fish and plant production even exceeding that of the land itself, and even as a source of fertilizer for crop production. This is a fascinating subject but too speculative to pursue here. Practical conclusions must await much more research. It is encouraging, however, to note the development of international co-operation in studying the oceans of the world, for marine resources can be over-exploited in specific areas just as easily as plant and animal populations on land. A knowledge of marine environments and the ecology of species is essential for sound harvesting controls as much as for harvest expansion.

The ultimate source of the world's fresh water required for agriculture, livestock, domestic, urban and industrial activities is rain. The average annual precipitation over all land surfaces is equivalent to about 26 inches of rainfall. Although this would be sufficient for a high standard of agriculture everywhere on suitable soils were it evenly distributed, there are in fact many deficient areas, and so the prospect of reliably increasing precipitation by artificial stimulation of raindrop formation is enticing. Unfortunately this is still a subject for argument and must be left as something for future assessment rather than as a practicability of the moment.

The world's fresh-water resources appear in three forms—

1. Fresh-water streams and lakes, replenished by run-off from the land surface.

2. Underground waters, not all of which are fresh, replenished by percolation from the land profile and from streams.

3. That part of rainfall which does not reach the first two, but which evaporates from the land surface or is transpired by plants.

The first two are transportable, in the sense that the water can be manipulated by engineering procedures such as pumping, damming, diversion, and distributed for use elsewhere. The last resource must be used where it falls.

The proportion of water in these two categories, transportable and non-transportable, varies considerably from place to place. In Australia, with an annual rainfall averaging about 18 inches, run-off has been estimated to average only 10% and water entering underground reservoirs considerably less. In this dry continent, only 15% to 20% of the water received as rain can be stored, or pumped, and redistributed.

In contrast, in the U.S.A., the average annual rainfall is nearly 30 inches. Run-off alone amounts to about 30% of this. In a continent of about the same size, about ten times more water is directly controllable by engineering procedures.

In smaller regions of high rainfall with land surface features conducive to high run-off, the figure may be of the order of 70% or 80% or more. Over much of the world surface, however, the greater part of the rain received is used or wasted where it falls and a relatively small proportion is available as transportable water.

It is this transportable water, however, that looms largest in the public eye. This is because it is controllable water, and there is growing competition for it from industry, domestic users, and farmers. Some of these uses are alternatives, some are conflicting, but there is also scope for complementary and multiple uses. Water used for power is usually available for re-use in other ways. In industrially advanced countries like France and the U.S.A., industry demands between 40% and 50% of the water at present consumed and domestic and urban users only 10%. In many rural countries a high proportion of the water conserved is used for irrigation.

The surface stream systems and the underground aquifers within individual river basins are usually closely interconnected and their uses need to be considered in conjunction. Any major interference in one part of the system can have a serious impact on the hydrological or land use features in other parts. Misuse of catchment lands and forests, excessive irrigation of upstream lands, the restriction of stream flow and of flooding by storage or diversion, the over-exploitation of underground water in some areas, and the pollution of water by industry will all have impacts on land and water use, and on the rights of land and water users elsewhere in the basin. For these reasons, and because of the need to plan the various competitive and multiple uses of water in relation to developing national needs, there is now general acceptance of the importance of planning the use of land, water and industrial resources of a river basin together. It is not always practicable to do this with the degree of precision that is desirable, because the essential hydrological, engineering and other data required are varied and extensive, and it is difficult to predict the extent of industrial and population growth and changes, and hence the nature of water demand many years ahead. Furthermore, developing nations do not always have the capital resources to proceed with the development of the water resources of a whole river basin at one time, nor will they always have the time to wait for a comprehensive plan to be completed. In order to have a more immediate effect on agricultural production and to keep within their capital resources, it may be necessary for countries to proceed with smaller schemes controlling only part of a drainage basin or even small local storages to serve a few or even single farms, especially in semi-arid areas.

Flexibility in planning must be maintained because new technologies and new needs emerging at each stage of development will introduce essential changes. Wise planning will more often follow a step by step approach, with an attempt to view each new water use project as part of the best overall plan that can be produced at the time. It should, however, include the continued accumulation of data to permit more precise planning at each stage.

As many river systems traverse several countries, the necessity for international negotiations and agreements may hold up major developments for a long time. Delays are caused by the difficulty of allocating benefits equitably in the future, and because the basic data for assessment and design are usually inadequate. That agreement can be achieved has already been demonstrated by the Indus River Agreement between India and Pakistan, the Rio Colorado Agreement between U.S.A. and Mexico, and by others.

The planning of water use in a whole river basin is a complex piece of work calling for the combined efforts of people in many technical fields. It is important that it should not be dominated by any special profession, whether this be engineering, forestry, agriculture, industry, economics, law, legislation, or administration.

In the context of this Conference, we are more directly interested in the use of transportable water resources for food production in the food deficient areas of the world.

The world's irrigation areas cover more than 300 million acres and it will probably be necessary to double this at least by the end of the century. There are not good data on the land and water resources available for increasing irrigation, but it would seem that this objective could certainly be achieved if required. In the past, many schemes have been less productive than they might have been because insufficient attention was given to the kind of land to be irrigated, the hydrological problems that could emerge, or the type of agriculture to be practised.

The greatest abuses of valuable irrigation water are its use in excessive quantities leading to wastage and waterlogging, or in inadequate quantities giving less than optimum production and often leading to land salting, its use on unsuitable land, and its use by farmers who, though well practised in other forms of land use, do not have sufficient knowledge or resources to make full and efficient use of their new environment.

In new projects, there should be equally thorough pre-planning investigation of land as of the engineering features, and drainage should be regarded as an essential part of the irrigation plan. To ensure that farmers can make efficient use of irrigation water, there should be a farm demonstration or extension programme to teach new landholders irrigation farm practices, a credit or finance scheme to enable them to purchase fertilizers, agricultural chemicals and equipment, a plant breeding seed production programme to ensure that plant varieties suitable to the high production conditions produced by irrigation are available, and an organized marketing scheme to dispose of the product. Many irrigation areas still suffer from deficiencies in these requirements, and it has already been stressed that the rehabilitation of misused land may frequently give more immediate and greater economic returns than the development of new areas.

Irrigation in arid regions produces dramatic results, but it has been found that supplementary irrigation in moderate rainfall conditions may make better use of water. Apart from selecting the type of land, careful consideration must also be given to the conditions under which irrigation water is used.

The development of further irrigation schemes will make important contributions to food production, but we should not lose sight of the fact that the greater proportion of the existing world's agriculture is practised with rainfall alone as the source of water, that is, water which must be used where and when it falls.

The amount of rainfall necessary for a satisfactory level of agricultural production varies widely between different environments and forms of production but over large areas where irrigation is not possible rainfall is insufficient for maximum growth, and water is the factor that sets the ultimate limit to production. It is important that this water be used well.

Taking an average annual rainfall of 20 inches (or 500 mm) as a rough basis for comparing regions, we find that about 15% of South America and Europe receive less than this, but in Africa and North America the proportion is about 50%, in Australia 60%, and Asia 70%. Irrigation water can be supplied to only a very small fraction of these areas.

Water deficient areas face three kinds of problems. The first is to impound, for controlled use, as much as possible of the intermittent, and, in lower rainfall areas, relatively small quantities of run-off. This will often mean many small storages and good designs are essential to avoid wastage. The second is to ensure that the crop varieties and methods used on cultivated land lead to the efficient use of water. Agricultural research programmes in semi-arid and arid areas should include more specific reference to the efficiency of water use by plants as a measure of their success. The third is to modify and manage the extensive plant communities on the extensive uncultivated areas, so that as much as possible of the rain which falls is channelled back to the atmosphere through plants useful to man or his animals, rather than through useless plants or by wasteful evaporation from inert surfaces. This can be achieved in part by pasture and forest improvement and management. Unfortunately, as rainfall decreases, the economic return per unit area also decreases, and with it the level of expenditure which is justifiable per unit area of land. In areas of very low rainfall, the emphasis swings from the development of a vegetation resource to the safe utilization of the natural resource in a way which is compatible with its conservation. Unfortunately, the vegetation of many of the drier regions of the world has been over-exploited to the extent that the level of production from the small amounts of rainfall received is now lower than from the original vegetation communities, and in many arid areas, uncontrolled exploitation is still aggravating the problem.

## Conclusions and Proposals

A review of land and water resources of the world leads to the conclusion that the total physical resources are ample to supply the food and other agricultural needs of the growing world population for the remainder of this century at least, and probably much longer. The challenge is to use these resources effectively in face of their unequal distribution in relation to population density and economic wealth. The available scientific knowledge is capable of meeting this challenge, but economic and political factors may continue to retard the full use of world resources and the free flow of products from one part of the world to another. The regions which are now most deficient in food are the ones where future populations are likely to be the greatest, and it would be unrealistic not to urge that each food deficient country should endeavour to solve its own food problems as far as possible from its own resources.

The application of science to increase production is not only the application of knowledge. It usually costs money and involves the use of greater quantities of material resources than those used for present levels of production. If standards of land and water use are to be raised quickly enough to match the increase in food requirements by the application of modern agricultural technology, it will be necessary somehow to concentrate greater economic resources than those which have ever been available in the countries largely dependent upon a rural economy.

Each country has its own variety of land and water resurces, suited to different forms of land use, its own range of plant and animal habitats with their specific problems. Each country is in a different stage of development and presents different economic, scientific, and sociological barriers to the increase in food production. Each has its own sociological, economic and cultural hopes and ambitions and these will, and should, influence the pathways by which it approaches national development.

A developing country will face the need to make decisions on the various possibilities for land and water development, and to make choices between the development of new areas, rehabilitation of old areas, and the establishment of supporting industries and services for agriculture and forestry.

We come to the question: how can the food deficient countries best be assisted in making these decisions and developing their own programs of land and water use?

We believe that the general principles of good land and water use are sufficiently well established to provide the appropriate scientific approach to most new situations but that the actual technological practices, based on these general principles must be selected and adapted to each new situation by trial, experiment, or research. We have recognized dangers that lie in assuming that scientific and technological practices can be transferred directly from one region to another and therefore see the need for each country to augment its scientific and technical resources so that it can make these adaptations.

Of the wide scope for direct technical assistance that this presents to helping nations, I believe that the form of aid with the likelihood of most permanent and continuing effect lies in helping countries to know themselves, to understand their own resources, problems, and possibilities, so that they themselves know what scientific, technical, and economic developments they need most urgently. If this can be achieved, developing countries will be in a position to establish their own order of priority of action, and to draw upon the mass of world scientific information and aid, selectively, according to the approaches that are most appropriate to meet their own particular array of problems.

International agencies and individual countries have already made considerable efforts in this general field, and countries have established various organizations for this purpose. In spite of this, it is doubtful if many countries, even advanced countries, have a sufficiently penetrating, comprehensive and co-ordinated understanding of their resources and what is involved in improving and developing them, to permit adequate overall resource planning; and in overall planning we must include socio-economic changes such as agrarian reforms, as well as project planning, and the advancement of science and education programmes.

Unfortunately, the departmentalization of government structures, and of sciences too, is not always conducive to the presentation of a balanced or complete picture. Often the difference in status or competence between departments or their officers leads to too much emphasis on one area, or on one field of science, at the expense of other possibilities which may be more worthy.

A knowledge of one type of resource indicates where its potentialities lie but it does not indicate whether that resource should be developed in one area in preference to others, or whether several resources or services might not best be developed conjointly.

Most countries could benefit from a more balanced and more co-ordinated approach to the assessment of their natural resources, even where development has already proceeded a long way. But food hungry nations cannot wait for long term, detailed programmes to be put into effect and completed.

Any attempt to survey all the characteristics of the resources of a country would be a colossal and time-consuming task and would produce a mass of detail which would be impossible to collate and interpret. What is required is a quicker, selective and progressive approach examining all resources objectively, sufficient at each stage for decision making, followed by more selective and intensive effort where and when it is most useful.

An approach which would appear to be ideal for adaptation to this purpose is what is referred to as the integrated approach to land survey and assessment, the term "land" being used in its comprehensive sense. Over the last fifteen years in Australia we have had considerable experience of this method in very extensive areas of underdeveloped and partially developed country ranging from arid to wet, tropical climates. We have learnt a good deal about its possibilities. These land resource surveys have been described elsewhere, and I will content myself with a few generalizations on how they could operate.

The surveys combine the use of aerial photographs with selected field studies. A relatively small group of scientists, each a specialist in a different field of resource study, works as a team in the field and laboratory, to understand, classify, and map areas of land, and to assess their broad development possibilities and problems. The approach is based on the concept of Land Systems (natural landscape patterns) and Land Units (the several distinctive land types which comprise and characterize these patterns), and aims at identifying those areas that can be considered together from the point of view of further research, or development, and those areas which must receive separate and different attention. The concepts can be applied at different scales and a preliminary reconnaissance survey can be made to select the more promising areas in which more intensive studies can be concentrated. The particular aspects of these areas deserving immediate examination are indicated and also the type of technical personnel and facilities needed to develop the work. Decisions on appropriate action can be made at each successive stage, leading to the progressive concentration of appropriate activity in each selected area, according to what the previous stage has shown to be most urgent. Science and technology of the right kind are brought to bear on the most urgent problems of each area as they are defined by survey, field trial, observation, experimentation, or pilot project. On the other hand, if circumstances require that immediate development of a certain kind proceeds, the broad framework of information provided by this approach will permit the development to be put into perspective and compared with other possibilities.

To assist countries to establish resource assessment programs, or to further develop those already in progress, help will be required in training the necessary personnel, and here I would like to make a suggestion. It seems to me that there is a place for an international center to train individuals, but more particularly to train teams of people, in the concepts, methods and techniques and operation of surveys, assessments, and preliminary use-planning of land and water resources and related services. In the first instance, such a Training Center might concentrate on primary survey and field assessment techniques for the newly emerging countries, but I visualize that the institute would itself evolve and would introduce more comprehensive training in the application of socio-economic and other special studies related to general resource use. It could hardly fail to develop as a center for information and objective advice to which countries could refer for help on the continually emerging technical problems related to resource planning, and it could become a channel through which the interchange of personnel might be arranged. As teams were trained, it would be helpful if arrangements could be made for the provision of material aid to enable them to operate in their own countries.

If such a scheme were adopted by FAO, or perhaps some of the great Foundations, it would assist countries to establish a sound basis for resource development, for unless outside economic aid is of a prodigious nature, the natural resources of a country must set the pattern for economic development and, in turn, define the paths along which science and technology should grow within the country in order to serve its essential practical requirements.

The Training Center could help fill a gap so often referred to by representatives of developing countries in terms of "wanting advice to know what they need." It could be complementary to, rather than conflict with, other international organizations concerned with the broader aspects of economic planning, or those providing economic or technical aid to approved projects, for it would help countries to be better prepared before making submissions to these other organizations. Development projects could be expected to emerge as obvious and logical consequences of thorough resource assessment.

The Center would provide postgraduate and specialized training, and would not attempt to duplicate the formal training of existing educational institutions. Expansion in these facilities will certainly be needed to provide the increasing number of trained presonnel required at various levels. Where such formal training is concerned with field practices of land and water use, which are so much influenced by local environmental and sociological conditions, it is extremely important that this training should be given in the atmosphere of these local environments. Too frequently, students who are trained overseas return to their countries with a need to completely readjust themselves to ecological conditions, and it is not surprising that many take a long time, or even fail, to do this.

To apply known science to the variety of agricultural production conditions in each country, there will be required increasing numbers of technically trained people who may not always be able to produce original ideas but who certainly must be thoroughly familiar with the circumstances to which the scientific principles and practices are to be adapted. It is important that, in the agricultural and animal production fields at least, more and more effort should be directed towards establishing basic training facilities within the developing countries themselves, or at least within regions, but this should in no way interfere with the overseas training of selected personnel for specialist activities which will always remain important.

There will be increasing need, too, for top level supervision or guidance of research and development projects. Until countries can themselves provide adequately trained and experienced senior personnel, they will need to continue to call on advisers from other sources. There are several observations that should be made about advisers. First, the expert advisers should be truly expert. This means that they must be not only capable people in their own fields but also knowledgeable in the application of their field in the particular region where they are advising. They must also be good advisers. These requirements are difficult to meet, but it is a responsibility of international agencies and contributing countries to ensure that their experts meet these qualifications as far as possible. A second generalization concerning expert advisers is that an endeavour should be made, wherever feasible, for them to operate with a trainee from the country they are aiding, so that when they leave there is an experienced individual left behind to continue the work. A measure of an adviser's success might well be how soon he can vacate the task, knowing that the country will be able to carry on without him. A third requirement is that advice should be continuous and consistent. Nothing is more disturbing to a project, and to the people of the country directly concerned, than to have discontinuity of expert advice; but what is even more disturbing is when successive experts on the same project approach it with different concepts. All may be equally good, but when local trainees are not experienced adherence to one method consistently is extremely important. For this reason, the practice of the adoption of individual projects in developing countries, by particular institutions in other countries, is to be commended and encouraged, for this procedure does offer scope for both continuous and consistent assistance.

Finally we might ask, from where will the incentive come for developing nations and their governments to do the most important things? I have often heard advisers who are attempting to give aid to a country comment that they doubt whether the recipient country is as genuinely enthusiastic about the activity as the adviser himself. One would expect that the growing nationalism of new countries and the vital need for production increases would provide this; but their needs, starting with the individual who is hungry or needy, must filter through the nation and finally be crystallized into action. There are many barriers in the way and many opportunities for good or bad decisions. I suggest that many of these barriers arise from uncertainties, from inadequate precise knowledge. I suggest that the greatest incentive to developing nations can arise from a confidence in their own knowledge of their potentialities, and how they themselves can achieve them. If the world gives them the means to know themselves, their resources, and how to use and preserve them, they will accept the challenge to ensure that these resources are developed soundly.

16.

# THE CONSTRUCTIVE USE
# OF WORLD RESOURCES

*by W. Taylor Thom, Jr.*

When the writer was asked to discuss the topic "the constructive use of world resources" he was, in fact, being asked whether and how an almost hopeless world situation can be converted into a hopeful one. This transformation can be made possible, provided that the resources of the human heart and spirit, as well as of the human mind and hand are urgently employed. For these resources can make it possible for us to "cultivate" (and thus enlarge, continuously) our essential mineral resources and supplies of other needed material substances. But even though we *do* learn *how* to make such resources inexhaustible through the employment of modern engineering science, we are confronted by time factors which render any discussion of "the constructive use of world resources" both a mockery and an exercise in futility—

*unless* the rates of human population increase can be, and are, properly, promptly and drastically controlled;

*unless* the rates-of-increase of "invisible-worker" or mechanical-robot populations can be, and are, properly and promptly controlled; and

*unless* economic integrations of certain natural regions are properly accomplished, in preparation for that global economic integration which is an indispensable prerequisite to the final creation of the kind of balanced, fair-exchange economy under which resources *can* be made inexhaustible.

Be it realized, however, that despite the pessimistic tone of what has just been said, the world situation is not hopeless, even though it obviously is desperate. For demonstrations already made have proven that human population increase can be controlled; that robot-worker populations can be controlled, if the public so insists, and that economic integrations of groups of "sovereign" states can be accomplished, with great benefit to all concerned. Above all, it has been established that where these three pre-conditions have been met, resources can be "cultivated" in such a fashion that the old economic Law of Diminishing Returns will cease to apply, and the new Law of Increasing Returns will take its place, thus transforming what once would have been exhaustible resources into inexhaustible ones.

That a Law of Increasing Returns can apply in the general mineral resources field (as in the domain of modern agriculture) is the result of a scientific and technological breakthrough made by the U.S. petroleum industry over 25 years ago, through the cooperative and competitive efforts of the industry's exploratory scientists, technologists, and engineers.

In referring to this breakthrough J. Edgar Pew, then Vice President of Sun Oil Company, said that the "Secret of the Widow's Cruse had been discovered."[1] Some years later, Eugene Holman, then President of Standard Oil Company of New Jersey, amplified this conclusion when he said that a wand had been found which could "reveal the invisible, transform the useless into the useful, waste into raw material of great value, exhaustible resources into inexhaustible resources."[2] It must be kept in mind, however, that before these conclusions can apply in full measure, the regional economic integrations now developing must be extended forward into a global economic integration. Only in this way can economic development progress in an orderly, balanced, secure and satisfactory fashion so as to make the Law of Increasing Returns properly operative with respect to material resource production.

Let us realize, then, that there are grounds for hope. And let us also remember that when people are determined and hopeful, they usually win. For under those conditions they are compelled to proceed in the spirit of that wartime slogan which said, "The difficult we do immediately, the impossible will take a little longer."

### Why World Resources Are of Transcendent Importance

Why the world's resources are of transcendent human importance, and why the constructive use of such resources is a matter of corresponding concern, is suggested by Figure 1. This diagram, which presents semi-quantitative data bearing upon the relationship between the world's population and resources, indicates quite clearly:

   *why* hunger and want now afflict such great numbers of people, in so many countries;

   *why* proper and effective controls over human population increase are urgently necessary;

*why* proper regulation of the rate of increase of "invisible worker" populations is necessary, especially in the United States; and

*why* regional (international) economic integrations are needed; in order that standards of living can be improved in all national areas, and especially those particularly afflicted by urgent present need.

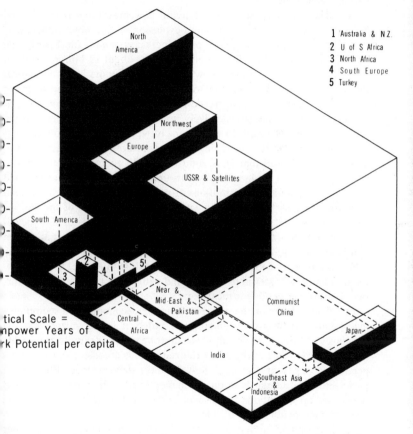

FIG. 1. Relative populations and per capita work potentials of particular nations and regions.

The surface areas of the several blocks represent the relative sizes of the populations of particular areas. The vertical heights of the several blocks represent per capita work potentials available for productive purposes. These are roughly indicative, therefore, of the average standards of living of the peoples in the specified areas. In this connection, the following can be noted:

(a) The rapid increases in human populations in the needy areas do now, or presumably soon will, more than cancel such increases of productivity as may be possible under fragmentary and unstable or chaotic national economies;

(b) The "affluent" standard of living now prevailing in the United States has resulted from a population explosion of "invisible" or mechanical-robot workers. This explosion has increased (and is increasing) the number of such workers from a base figure of about 11 billion robots in 1938[3] to a far greater number now. Thus as the automation of mass-production industries goes on, the robot population is beginning to make larger and larger numbers of would-be human wage-earners not only unemployed but, in fact, prospectively unemployable. For this reason the U. S. economy has begun to show signs of withering at its roots as is attested by the frantic advertising campaigns now in progress. Consequently, it is obvious that U. S. industry should give urgent attention to producing more of the inexpensive consumer goods items that are needed so urgently by hundreds of millions of people all over the world, instead of draining off for "affluent" use such a large proportion of the world's output of essential substances. Likewise the industrialists of the "developed" countries should all join in producing inexpensive tools and farm equipment and light industry machines of kinds that can be used for the self-development of the needier peoples—both with respect to food production and raw material processing and with respect to the manufacturing of consumer goods for local use;

(c) The stability of the world's whole socioeconomic and sociopolitical system will be greatly endangered unless it is recognized that the standards of living in the needy areas must be raised as rapidly as possible —(even while those in the industrialized nations are also rising)—in order that a parity of standards may be ultimately reached. For such a parity of living standards would permanently allay the threat of war and would set up conditions under which the world's resources will have been, in fact, made inexhaustible.

At this point some may ask, "Why are we interested in raising other people's standard of living?" To this key question there is a key answer. "We are (or should be) interested because if resources are used 'in the Service of Mankind,' the rendering of such service will ensure adequate and growing earnings incomes, at all levels, because such earnings can be scaled to give proper (incentive) recognition to quality and scale of performance; and because the earnings approach will enable the Law of Increasing Returns to apply."

*Methods for the Constructive Use of World Resources*

The methods which are especially appropriate to the constructive use of the world's material resources are those of (1) the scientist; (2) the technologist and inventor; (3) the engineer; and (4) the "engineering-scientist."

(1) The methods of the scientist need to be used because our problems need to be approached cooperatively in an objective, imaginative, and non-partisan way.

(2) The methods of technological research—invention and development—are needed because the workers in these fields discover ways of making established scientific facts and principles effectively useful.

(3) The methods of engineering are also essential because engineers seek to employ "that combination of Art and Science whereby creative imagination, natural resources, human capacities and intellectual and spiritual wisdom can be so integrated and supported as to make them all serve, constructively the needs and worthy purposes of Mankind."

(4) The methods and overall functional characteristics of engineering science should be given particular attention and particular employment.[4] For engineering science—"the science of operational systems"—has been called into being in order to bring into manageable and understandable forms those growing complexities which are more and more besetting policy-makers in industry and government and in university affairs. How important engineering science can actually be was demonstrated by the petroleum industry when it discovered "The Secret of the Widow's Cruse."[5]

*The Discovery of the Secret of the Miraculous Pitcher:* The Secret of the Miraculous Pitcher (or of the Widow's Cruse) was discovered prior to 1941, through the cooperative efforts of oil company exploration department scientists, technologists, and engineers. They discovered how to bring the natural but antithetical human inclinations toward scientific cooperation and toward competition into an effective and balanced alternation. The intellectual alternating current thereby generated has been used with such imagination and such skill that the scant oil reserves of the United States (as of 1922) have now become prospectively inexhaustible. This happy result was made possible because social, political, and legal conditions in the United States have been orderly and stable,—this in turn making it possible for operating oil companies to "cultivate" their reserves in much the same way that an intelligent and up-to-date farmer cultivates and uses the soil on his farm. An economic Law of Increasing Returns applies to this type of farming, for crop yields progressively increase as better and better seeds become available, and better and better methods of fertilization and cultivation become known. And so, too, has the Law of Increasing Returns become applicable to mineral-industry exploration and development which employs the same kind of enlightened and progressive operational methods.

*How Engineering Science made approaches which led to the discovery of the Secret of the Miraculous Pitcher:* Even though the scientific research approaches about to be described are well known to some, it would probably be helpful to many to know just how the "breakthrough" was made, by which material-resources reserves can become inexhaustible.

It was recognized in 1922 that the situation of the U. S. petroleum industry was precarious because of the small size of its proven and prospective oil reserves. Consequently, the scientists, technologists, and engineers of the industry (acting with encouragement of the industry's executives) undertook an active, cooperative scientific program of study, aimed at the collection of scientific facts, principles, and theories relating to oil origin and oil accumulation. These compilations were then analyzed deductively, with the establishment of a new crop of principles and guidance theories for use in future oilfield exploration. At this point, the natural cooperative impulses of the scientist gave way to those other normal, competitive human instincts such as induce athletes to compete in order to earn applause and recognition. And in this new phase, each individual or each exploratory staff sought to apply the new guidance principles and theories inductively, in ways which would, hopefully, lead to the discovery of new oilfields. According to that usual combination of skill and luck, a few competitors would make great discoveries, a greater number would make minor discoveries, and the majority would end up by drilling unproductive tests. However, in time, people would find out the reasons for the successes scored, whereupon the inductive and competitive activity would stabilize. And then, later on, the main activity would swing back again into a repetition of the cooperative and deductive compilation and analysis phase.

This balanced alternation between cooperative deductive efforts and competitive inductive efforts brought about, as it were, the generation of an extraordinarily useful intellectual alternating current, of a kind which can have enormous constructive effects in many areas of human activity.

### TEST-CASE PROJECTS FOR THE CONSTRUCTIVE USE
### OF WORLD RESOURCES

The paragraphs to follow will list a number of suggested test-case projects which are not only of major social and "human" importance but which also indicate how constructive use can be made of world resources. Since some of these projects have been described elsewhere in greater detail,[6] the following descriptions will be limited to tabloid statements:

*Project 1. Discovery or development of major sources of mineral wealth within the territories of needy nations,*[7] in order that these nations may have cash incomes that they can use for *self*-development. Nearly all such nations will, in time, be found to have such major sources of hidden or latent wealth. The critical point then, is to bring about these discoveries or developments quickly, before unsupportable population increases have induced economic and political chaos. Thus the efforts of the UN developmental agencies and of the World Bank should be given every encouragement. But needy "governments" should also realize that they should try to follow the example of other governments which have achieved financial independence, by employing the "poor landlord-rich sharecropper" tactic. By this means, the world's most experienced and effective exploratory and developmental concerns have been "hired" to do the needed exploration and development work, without cash cost to the country being explored, and with actual cash concession-rentals coming in, even during the preliminary survey period.

But, some will object, "those nations lacking known mineral wealth probably have none, or it would have been found by now." And for such pessimists, reference need only be made to Mr. Holman's conclusion, mentioned previously, and to the fact, for example, that an enormous natural gas field has recently been found in the northeastern (coastal) sector of The Netherlands, where people have been walking for centuries without a suspicion that immense wealth lay concealed beneath their feet. (See Project 11, below.)

*Project 2. Discovery and development of the capacities of individual citizens of all ages and of all stages of training.* This can be accomplished through "learn-while-earning" and "each one teach two" training systems,[8] which can best be carried forward by use of the apprenticeship technique at successive and progressive levels. The writers knows from personal experience that such a multiple-level apprenticeship training system not only awakens and greatly stimulates the natural aptitudes of the trainees involved, but also can hold the time, effort, and money-costs of the training operation to less than one third of what it would cost to get less satisfactory results under conventional "educational" procedures.[9] Conventional procedures tend to be dull and uninspiring because so many teachers are teaching "from the book," without reference to their own relevant *experience* (frequently nil) and without reference to the personal experience of the "students."

*Project 3. The development of planning capacity and experience among young people.* The development of the planning interest and planning capacity of young people is a matter of great moment. For it is very important that the imagination, enthusiasm, and legitimate self-interests of teenagers and adolescent citizens be focused upon the planning of community developments for the localities and regions within which they expect to live. Fortunately, there is a natural starting place for such training-for-planning. For nearly all lands have been, or are being, covered by air-photo mosaic compilations and by aero-topographic base maps made from such photographs. By using a simple and well-known method for producing cardboard-cutout relief models from such mosaics and maps, one can produce sectionized relief models at various scales, selecting the horizontal and vertical scales according to the purpose and according to the size of the area to be covered, whether a village, a nation, or a continent. Such models can be built, at very small cost, by pairs of 10-year-olds working under minimal supervision. Such work can be challenging because it excites general interest in the community and can lead to special praise for those who do well.

*Project 4. The Obliteration of Feudal, Latifundia and Clerical-Institutional Landlordism.* Great-estate landlordism is a hopeless roadblock in the path of progress for many ancient nations. Major incomes from discovered sources of mineral wealth would offer a fortunate solution for this problem. A nation having a large mineral-royalty income could dedicate a portion of that income to the servicing of bonds which would be used to purchase the big holdings at reasonable valuations, these bonds to bear interest (perhaps 2 per cent) and to be redeemable at the rate of 2 per cent per year over a 50-year period. Many land-owning families or groups would realize that such a plan would enable them to escape the losses that impending expropriations would otherwise bring. This kind of procedure could provide a just and honorable solution for a very thorny and explosive problem. Moreover, if such purchases were made, the lands so acquired by the government could go into a Public Domain, open to Homestead selection by farm families that were willing to earn farm homes for themselves.

*Project 5. The planning for road networks, for airports, and for the location of training centers and service centers.* Given a suitable scaled regional relief model, it is easily possible (subject to quick reconnaissance ground checks) to decide where farm-to-market roads should be roughed out; where main roads should be located; where dams should be built, where irrigation projects should be set up, etc.

On a similar but even larger scale, plans should be drawn for major river-diversion projects resulting in the southwestward diversion of one or many of the great Eurasian and North American rivers, which now carry enormous amounts of fresh water to the Arctic Ocean with very little benefit to anyone. Likewise, it is worth considering the possibility of using atomic power on a massive scale to pump large volumes of water across (or through) divides such as separate the Congo-Ubangi and Niger rivers from the dry-land areas to the north.

*Project 6. The utilization of ocean or sea water on a massive scale,* both by atomic-power pumpage of such water for direct irrigation of sand-flat or sand dune areas, and by a fractionation-separation or "refining" of sea water so that metals, minerals and chemicals could be won, in quantity, as by-products to the production of fresh water.

*Project 7. Increased storage of flood runoff waters in underground and near-surface sand-bodies and decreased use of surface reservoirs for such purposes.* As subsurface exploration has progressed, it has become clear that great volumes of fresh water can now be obtained not only from the lower parts of sand-bodies covering large parts of desert areas, but also from thick and widespread sand-sheets or channel-fill sands situated somewhat below the surface. Consequently, stored water supplies can be "cultivated" (a) by an active withdrawal of stored waters during times of need, coupled with (b) an active recharge of the underground reservoirs by injection of waters diverted from flood runoffs that would otherwise escape. By such a subsurface storage of flood freshets, great additional quantities of pure water could become available for use in arid or urban areas where water needs are great.

*Project 8. De-urbanization programs.* Active consideration should be given to the de-urbanization of the world's great cities as a hopeful alternation to "urban renewal." For in the long run, "urban renewal" will result in an acceleration and accentuation of the processes of slum creation and social decay within the heart areas of the world's great cities—cities which are largely anachronistic in this age of almost instant communication.

In place of a "megalopolis," it would be far better in every respect if multiple towns of moderate size were to be developed in rural settings and on a functional spacing arrangement, just as large corporations are decentralizing their offices and plants. This would, of course, excite utmost anguish among many large and very powerful vested-interest groups. But nevertheless, as even they will soon have to agree, such decentralization is indispensable. While urban renewal may seem applicable to reconstruction of obsolete buildings, it quite clearly cannot be applied to any effective social redevelopment or "renewal" of the increasing hordes of hopeless and jobless people, particularly adolescents, in big-city slum areas. This growth of slum populations seems to be a cancerous one, which needs to be dealt with promptly and imaginatively.

*Project 9. Air and water pollution studies.* Urgent studies should be made to determine how the atmosphere can be freed of smoke and fumes and other pollutants, and how streams and water supplies can be freed from pollution by pesticides, by detergents, and by untreated sewage. Air pollution problems are already critical in various smog areas, and water pollution is obviously becoming critical within the Mississippi River basin, where fish are dying in great numbers, presumably because of pesticides being washed in from farm areas. Water pollution is also beginning to afflict beaches and coastal fisheries in various areas.

Moreover, when one looks forward to what may happen when "urban sprawl" has been vastly extended as present human (and nonhuman) populations continue to proliferate, it seems most unwise to defer any longer a careful consideration of measures for pollution prevention. Otherwise a time may soon arrive when even a crash effort to abate pollution may come too late to ward off large-scale epidemics.

*Project 10. Regional agreements among certain nations for the construction of natural gas transmission pipelines,* to carry gas (now being flared in the oilfields around the Persian Gulf) either northwestward into Turkey and Southeastern and Central Europe or eastward into Pakistan and India. It was reported some years ago that engineering surveys had shown that the Persian Gulf-Central Europe pipeline was technologically and commercially feasible, if the group of nations concerned would consent to such a project. This would save the many, many millions of dollars worth of gas now being lost annually because it must now be burned in flares, for lack of a market outlet.

*Project 11. The development of a regional or international gas and oil compact,* covering off-shore areas with prospective gas and oil resources in the North Sea Basin and perhaps in the Baltic Sea Basin as well. It seems quite certain that the huge natural gas field now being developed along the northeastern coast of The Netherlands will extend seaward (i.e., northward) into international waters. It also appears certain that a great belt of oil accumulation may lie just north of the gas-producing area. Attempts undoubtedly will soon be made to develop this offshore gas and oil area. It seems important, therefore, that proper agreements be reached in advance concerning relative national interests in this connection, rather than allowing the matter to drift into a series of bitter and unnecessary disputes.

*Project 12. Youth-corps programs.* Current youth-corps activities, now being actively fostered by a number of nations, promise to be of enormous social advantage on a global basis. Those privileged to take part in such programs, particularly during and just after college training, should find it possible to gain a wealth of valid and realistic understanding of global problems, as well as insights into their possible solutions, that could not be acquired in any other way. In giving agricultural or handicrafts training, or other "each-one-teach-two" types of guidance, it seems certain that the perspectives gained on the cultural values, attitudes, and experiences of other peoples will be mutually useful to an almost unimaginable degree. This is especially true if there is a wider and continuing inter-regional circulation of young people who are energetically, intelli-

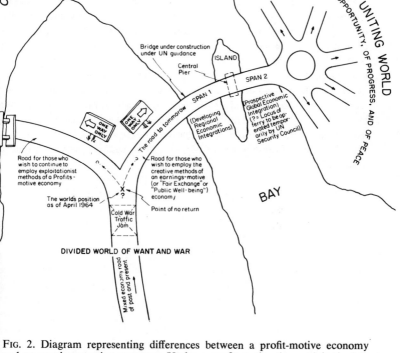

FIG. 2. Diagram representing differences between a profit-motive economy and an earnings-motive economy. Under a profit-motive (or exploitationist) economy, the "Law of Diminishing Returns" applies and resources are exploited, depleted and destroyed. Under an earnings-motive (or creative) economy a "Law of Increasing Returns" can be made to apply through a global employment of improving methods for resource discovery, development and use. (American Institute of Economy and Natural Resources, Inc., April, 1964.)

gently, and hopefully engaged in advancing human well-being and thus in advancing an effective means for the prevention of war.

## SUMMARY AND CONCLUSION

The writer's thoughts concerning the present world situation and the use of world resources are represented in Figure 2. The vanguard of the human race, advancing toward the future, has reached the "Point of No Return" at the fork in the road. A choice is now called for as to whether we shall continue to follow that old-style pattern of action which was developed in a divided world of international lawlessness and war, or whether we shall try to change to the cooperative-competitive course which can provide justifiable hopes for the future. The latter road can be made to take us across the projected two-span bridge and into a region where the new Law of Increasing Returns can operate. By contrast, the old way, if followed, will bring us all to a Dead End, as Malthus[10] prophesied many years ago.

Be it noted that the economic integration bridge is under construction, but not yet built, and be it noted that the bridge will be broken down if overloaded by too rapid an increase of human populations, or of robot-worker populations. Therefore, even though it seems probable that some terrible catastrophe lies ahead, should we not make all possible efforts to avert tragedy by showing how a creative and constructive use of human capacities, and of other world resources, can prevent war and can support a peaceful world?

*Part Two*

# IMPLICATIONS OF THE
# POPULATION EXPLOSION

❂ ❂ ❂ ❂

# Biological and Psychological Considerations

❦ ❦ ❦

## 17.

## CURRENT APPROACHES TO
## THE BIOLOGICAL CONTROL OF FERTILITY

*by Warren O. Nelson*

The urgent need for man to recognize the necessity for achieving an equilibrium with his environment, both physically and biologically, is by no means a recent consideration. Nor are methods for achieving these ends new; excellent procedures for the control of fertility have been available for many years. It might, therefore, appear unnecessary to call attention to the requirement for more and better methods of effective, safe, acceptable and economical methods for the control of fertility. Those of us who are biologists might simply accept the existing procedures and pass to others the task of promoting their acceptance. However, in spite of their availability, it is obvious that the conventional contraceptives have failed to gain general acceptance. Objections are founded on economic, religious or cultural grounds, or on the basis that available agents are too technical and sophisticated for mass employment. Unquestionably, an additional factor is a lack of proper motivation.

These reasons for non-acceptance are acknowledged, but the hope remains that new techniques, involving a physiologic approach, may receive greater acceptance—and use. Even the simplest physiologic method however, will fall short of deserved success if obstacles, including lack of motivation, are present. The problem of educating and motivating people remains, and efforts toward these ends are imperative if people are to be made aware of the pressing need for fertility control.

In devising methods for the physiologic regulation of fertility, those reproductive processes susceptible to interference must be considered. At least 8 major areas exist in both sexes where physiologic reproductive mechanisms are vulnerable.[1] Attention is being given to each of these by skillful investigators. Although studies are being made along many lines, in some instances, the possibility of practical application remains questionable. For the most part, this discussion will be confined to those physiologic procedures now used in man, or which show some promise of application in the relatively near future.

In the mammalian female, the reproductive process is a sequence of steps, each depending upon the successful fulfillment of the preceding one. In brief, these steps can be outlined as follows:

(1) production and release of the pituitary gonadotrophic hormones by way of hypothalamic mediation, (2) stimulation of egg and hormone production in the ovary by the gonadotrophic hormones, (3) ovulation and passage of the egg through the oviduct, (4) fertilization, (5) cleavage and early development of the fertilized egg during transport to the uterus, (6) entrance of the zygote into the uterus and formation of a blastocyst, (7) implantation of the blastocyst in the endometrium, and (8) maintenance of embryonic development.

The male, too, has a sequential progression of processes involved in reproduction. These are: (1) secretion and release of the pituitary gonadotrophic hormones, (2) production of spermatozoa and androgenic hormone by the testes under the influence of gonadotrophic hormones, (3) transport of sperm into and through the epididymis with concomitant physiologic maturation of spermatozoa, (4) passage of spermatozoa through the vas deferens to the ampulla, (5) suspension of sperm in the seminal plasma during ejaculation, (6) passage of sperm through the cervix, (7) ascent of sperm through the uterus and oviducts, and their capacitation, and (8) penetration of the ovum by a spermatozoon.

In both male and female it is possible to interfere with each step in the sequence of reproduction. Investigators in the field of reproduction are endeavoring to secure information enabling them to devise new methods for predictable regulation of one or another of the processes.

### Inhibition of Ovulation

Gonadal hormones, estrogens and androgens have, for many years, been known to inhibit secretion of the gonadotrophic hormones, and as a consequence, to interfere with ovulation. During the past 8 years increased attention to the need for methods of regulating fertility, has led to a study of the effects of many new synthetic compounds on the occurrence of ovulation. Compounds having chemical similarity to the endogenous ovarian hormones received special attention, this being particularly true for those found to be effective when administered orally.[2]

It is estimated that at least 1 and ½ million women in the United States alone are using one of these agents, Enovid, as their sole method of contraception. It is probable that as many more women are using some similar type of available preparation. Enovid contains the synthetic progestin, norethynodrel, plus a small amount of the 3-methyl ether of ethinyl estradiol, an orally effective estrogen. One 5 mg tablet taken daily for 20 days, beginning on the fifth day of the menstrual cycle, inhibits ovulation and the normal cycle by suppressing secretion of the pituitary gonadotrophic hormones. Since the ingredients in the compound possess intrinsic ovarian hormone-like activities, artificial menstrual cycles are established. These cycles are, generally speaking, more regular than the subjects' spontaneous cycles would have been. Some women complain of gastrointestinal disturbances resembling the "morning sickness" of pregnancy, or experience some degree of intermenstrual bleeding. These side effects as a rule, are of little consequence, and in most instances persist for no more than a month or two. If the dosage schedule is followed faithfully, this method can be regarded as absolutely effective. Enovid has been approved by the Food and Drug Administration for contraceptive use in doses of 10 mg and 5 mg per day and is now being considered at the 2½ mg level. Orthonovum, a related preparation, has also been approved for use in doses of 10 mg per day, and sanction for a 2 mg per day dose has been requested. These smaller doses are evidenced to be as effective as the higher ones and have the advantage of less cost to the consumer, as well as generally fewer side effects. However, concern exists on such matters as the ratio of progestin to estrin, incidence of breakthrough bleeding, and the possibility of non-physiological consequences which might result from their use. It is not clear as to exactly what these "non-physiological consequences" may be. Meanwhile, research on other synthetic progestins, usually in combination with estrogens, is being actively pursued. Some of the new preparations will undoubtedly be available in the relatively near future and may be superior to those currently available. At present, research is being directed toward substances which will cost less, have fewer side effects, and have a longer duration of activity. It would be highly desirable to have preparations which could be taken with less frequency than those now available, and efforts have been directed toward developing injectable substances with prolonged action. Preparations evolved thus far have been unsatisfactory because duration of activity has shown wide variation in different women. A solution for the problem may be achieved by proper exploration of a variety of doses and methods of preparation, so that a combination requiring administration only once every month or two can be secured. However, many women may very well question the acceptability of measures producing cycles of more than one month's duration.

In December, 1961 two women who had used Enovid as a contraceptive, died. These deaths focused attention toward the possibility that the drug may predispose women to thrombophlebitis, or to even more serious consequences. Other cases of thrombophlebitis and several additional deaths from pulmonary thrombosis have been reported to August 20, 1962. The total number of reported cases of both fatal and non-fatal thrombophlebitic and thrombotic diseases appears to have been no more than 100 of well over 1,500,000 women who have used Enovid, either for contraceptive or other purposes. So little is known of the casual incidence of thrombophlebitic disease and, more importantly, of fatal pulmonary thrombosis, that it is impossible to evaluate the extent of the problem. However, evidence collected from various sources suggests that the occurrence of these pathologic conditions in women using Enovid is no greater than that expected in the absence of any specific medication. At any rate, De Costa[3] has been unable to detect a definitive relationship between the use of Enovid and the occurrence of thrombophlebitis. Whether such a relationship actually exists, will continue to be a matter of great concern until a thorough study of all parameters of the problem has been made.

## Detection of Ovulation

Every investigator interested in the physiological reproduction is cognizant of the importance of accurate methods for detecting ovulation. Even one method provided for predicting ovulation would be extremely valuable in making the rhythm method of contraception more dependable and, therefore, more acceptable to many people. Conversely, the ability to predict ovulation would have important application to the solution of some cases of infertility. Procedures now available reveal the *occurrence* of ovulation, but obviously these are not applicable to the pertinent need. Claims have been made for a chemical method[4] and for two methods of detecting incipient ovulation by use of "test" papers applied to the cervix or vagina.[5] Although other investigators have been unable to confirm these observations, studies now in progress may lead to more reliable methods for predicting ovulation. Perhaps the most promising of these involves application of immunologic procedures for discovering changes in levels of the gonadotrophic hormones. At least three groups of investigators have shown, independently, that immunologic methods can be employed to detect pregnancy.[6] Since each of these procedures depends upon the presence of a gonadotrophic hormone (chorionic gonadotrophin) it is reasonable to anticipate that progressive refinement of techniques may eventually provide a method of foretelling ovulation.

### Antizygotic Agents

These are substances which inhibit development of the very early embryo. There is considerable evidence showing the early fertilized ovum to be vulnerable to a variety of adverse circumstances, both spontaneous and induced. Death of early zygotes almost certainly occurs spontaneously at least as frequently as one in four instances. The causes for this fetal wastage are numerous. In some instances they are evident, but usually they are unknown. It is not surprising, therefore, that the early embryo is susceptible to extraneous influences and that some chemical substances have noxious effects. The antizygotic effects of MER-25, 1–(p-2-diethyla-mino-ethoxyphenyl)-1-phenyl-2-p-anisylethanol, have been described[7] and a second compound, MRL-41, 1-(p-B-diethylamino-ethoxyphenyl)-1, 2-diphenyl-2-chloroethylene, was demonstrated to have even more potent activity.[8] It is noteworthy that each of these compounds has been shown not only to inhibit development of the early zygote, but also to induce ovulation in some women with long histories of anovulation.[9] Although these substances are known to be effective as oral contraceptive agents in animals, there is no more than indirect evidence to show that they have such activity in women. Clinical trials for this type of fertility control have their obvious problems, and before proper studies could be established, undesirable side effects emerged in the case of each compound. For MER-25 there was little reason to undertake serious clinical study in view of the fact that MRL-41 was found to have higher activity. When the latter compound was tested in animals over a long period of time, it was found to cause side effects which rendered its use unlikely.

A variety of substances apparently having the same antizygotic effect are now being synthesized and studied intensively. Such compounds include a series of 2, 3-diphenylindenes reported by Duncan and his colleagues at Upjohn Laboratories[10]. One of these (U-11555A), triethyla-mine 2-(p-[6-methoxy-2-(p-methoxyphenyl)-inden-3yl]-phenoxyl) hy-drochloride, has been studied extensively in our laboratory. We found it to have approximately the same order of effectiveness which we had observed in the case of MRL-41. When the drug was administered in a single dose to mated female rats on any one of the four days occupied in passage of the egg to the uterus, pregnancy was prevented in every case. In animals where treatment was delayed until the 5th day after ovulation and mating, no influence on gestation could be detected. This observation is precisely the same as that made in similar studies with MER-25 and MRL-41. Although it may be too early to dismiss U-11555A as a human contraceptive, side effects have been observed. The probability exists that this agent will be numbered as another compound with a promising beginning, but not able to survive the rigorous testing necessary before a new drug can be released for general clinical use.

Other compounds with even more exciting promises are under intensive study in my laboratory. These have shown high orders of activity in animals and have caused no side effects in man. Of those examined, two compounds synthesized in the Upjohn Laboratories, and one synthesized in the Ortho Research Foundation Laboratories have been particularly impressive. Each one when given at a very low dose in a single oral treatment, is effective in suppressing development of the cleaving ovum during its passage through the oviduct. Such observations lead us to expect preparations which will provide effective oral conception control *after* coitus.

### Antispermatogenic Agents

It has been known for about ten years that heterocyclic compounds of the nitrofuran and thiophene series[11] are capable of inhibiting spermatogenesis in animals by halting the process at the primary spermatocyte stage. This is a completely reversible phenomenon and does not involve the endocrine functions of either the testes or the anterior pituitary gland. Inhibition of sperm production by this procedure has a distinct advantage over the spermatogenic inhibition induced by compounds preventing ovulation in females. Although the latter drugs are exceptionally effective contraceptives in males, they cannot be regarded as acceptable, since they inhibit secretion of male sex hormones.[12]

The nitrofurans and thiophenes were not applied as contraceptives because the doses which were required for suppression of spermatogenesis also induced unpleasant side effects.[13] More recently a series of bis (dichloroacetyl) diamine compounds have been synthesized by the Sterling-Winthrop Laboratories. Although these compounds were evolved initially for their amebacidal activity, animal studies of the testes produced the same kind of effects that had been observed earlier for the nitrofurans and thiophenes.[14] Studies in humans demonstrated that spermatogenic inhibition could be achieved, and that the effect was reversible.[15] Sperm production returned to pretreatment levels about two months after treatment ceased. These observations, secured in two widely separated groups of prison inmates, were sufficiently encouraging to suggest clinical studies on the contraceptive effectiveness of these compounds. However, when the trials were made, an unexpected side effect became manifest almost immediately. Individuals ingesting the drugs experienced exaggerated responses to the peripheral effects of alcohol; although these effects were not serious, they were unpleasant enough to indicate that general acceptance of this form of contraception would be unlikely. Meanwhile, studies are under way in other laboratories, and are being continued by the Sterling-Winthrop Laboratories. Investigations have been directed toward development of compounds which will be effective antispermatogenic agents without possessing unpleasant side effects, and a number of preparations will probably be available for laboratory and clinical study. When one or more of these agents can be demonstrated to be effective, and to be without undesirable side effects, it will be exceedingly interesting to observe the degree of their acceptance as contraceptives by the human male.

Currently, the most promising of these is a group of dinitropyrroles prepared by the Ortho Research Foundation[16] Laboratories and investigated intensively in our laboratory. One of these, ORF-1616(1-[N, N-diethylcarbamylmethyl]-2, 4-dinitropyrrole), has been highly effective as an anti-spermatogenic in rats. A single oral dose induces, after exhaustion of sperm already formed, a period of infertility lasting four weeks. An infertile state has been maintained indefinitely by administering single doses at four week intervals. The process of spermatogenesis is halted at the primary spermatocyte state and recovers when treatment is finally withdrawn.[17]

### Immunologic Control of Reproduction

As early as 1899, reports appeared in the literature on the immunologic response of animals to injections of sperm or testicular extracts. Beginning with the pioneer studies of Landsteiner, Metchnikoff, and Metalnikoff, a large literature has gradually developed on the subject of immunoreproduction. Tyler[18] has recently reviewed both the earlier and more recent papers on this subject. During the past few years, interest in the possibility of controlling fertility by application of improved immunologic techniques has accelerated research on the subject, and some people optimistically believe that methods having human application will be found in the near future.

Perhaps the most advanced are those experiments concerned with active auto-immunization of the male with sperm or testes extracts. Although the concept that an animal is incapable of becoming immunized against components of its own tissues was generally accepted as a fundamental immunologic principle many years ago, it is now recognized that potential tissue antigens can assume antibody-inducing properties under certain circumstances. A report by Freund[19] on the induction of aspermatogenesis in guinea pigs by administration of homologous material combined with an adjuvant, created great interest and stimulated other investigators to undertake related studies. It is now known that in addition to impairment of spermatogenesis, concurrent manifestations of generalized immediate hypersensitivity, as well as delayed skin sensitivity to testicular extracts, are present in animals treated by the Freund procedure. However, the severity of testicular lesions do not always correlate quantitatively with the levels of circulating antibodies. This lack of correlation between serum antibody titer and histologic damage to the testes, and failure to induce aspermatogenesis by serum antibody transfer, has led to the conclusion that genital lesions are indicative of a delayed type of hypersensitivity due to a cell-bound antibody. Laurence & Perlbachs[20] have shown that aspermatogenic lesions from testes sensitive donors can be transferred to normal secondary recipients with mononuclear cells. The relationship between cell-bound antibody, humoral antibody and sequence of appearance of each type of immunological system is under investigation.

The testicular lesions resulting from this auto-immune phenomenon are limited to the germinal epithelium; the interstitial cells and other tissues of the reproductive tract are not damaged. Except for the granulomatous lesion stimulated by the adjuvant material at the site of injection, the procedure causes no adverse effects. Current experiments with adjuvant agents, other than the Freund type, have been designed to determine whether lesions of the testicles can be produced without causing local effects at the inoculation site.

Mancini of Buenos Aires has very recently secured results in human male volunteers duplicating those of the Freund procedures seen in animal experiments. While his observation suggests that the method may eventually be used to regulate fertility, additional studies are needed to assure that the testicular damage is controllable and reversible.

Weil and his associates[21] have been concerned with a somewhat different approach to the problem of sperm antigenicity. This report holds that antigenic substances which stimulate the formation of sperm agglutinins in man arise from the accessory sex organs, rather than the testes, and become associated with spermatozoa only secondarily. On the other hand, there is evidence which indicates that antigenic factors occur primary to the spermatozoa.[22]

These two concepts of sperm antigenicity actually may not be in conflict, but be concerned with different immunologic phenomena. In each case it is likely that application to fertility control is possible and may be achieved without causing serious testicular damage. Observations on the occurrence of sperm agglutinins in the serum of some infertile males[23] may be applicable in this regard. Testicular biopsies in such cases have usually revealed apparently normal spermatogenesis; sperm counts are frequently in the normal range, yet these men are infertile. Other instances of infertility are supposedly due to an antigen-antibody reaction in matings between blood type A fathers and type O mothers.[24]

Some avenues of approach to the immunologic control of reproduction have been centered upon efforts to understand the nature, and possible significance, of sperm antibodies detected in the body fluids of both men and women, induction in the female of antibodies to sperm by inoculation with spermatozoa,[25] immunization of the female against formation or survival of the placenta,[26] and interference with the activities of the sex hormones by the formation of antihormones.[27] It is reasonable to anticipate the development of several methods for the inhibition of fertility by inducing the formation of antibodies against one or another of the reproductive processes. In such cases, it would be possible for an occasional booster treatment to maintain an infertile state for any desired length of time. The possibilities are numerous and this area of investigation offers exceptional opportunities for the development of a new method of fertility regulation.

Another kind of immunologic research which has stimulated much interest is that concerned with the antigenic properties of pituitary gonadotrophins.[28] The possible application of such information includes control of fertility by neutralization of the action of gonadotrophic hormones, determination of ovulation time much more accurately than is presently feasible, and development of a simple test for pregnancy. At least three laboratories have now developed pregnancy tests based on immunologic principles. Although these are not yet as sensitive as available biologic methods, they have the advantage of being adaptable as office procedures and it is likely that greater sensitivity can be achieved.

### Intrauterine Devices

Although intrauterine devices are scarcely a physiologic method for fertility control, they have an exceptionally good record for contraceptive effectiveness. Existing evidence suggests that they represent an exciting possibility for use as a relatively cheap and acceptable procedure. A variety of devices are available, including several constructed from plastic material, and rings formed from silk worm gut, nylon thread, and stainless steel. Some of these can be inserted into the uterine lumen without dilation of the cervix. The record for effectiveness, and acceptability of each device appears to be surprisingly good. For many years, the medical profession has held that intrauterine devices are dangerous, but such conclusions appear to have been based upon subjective considerations rather than objective evidence. Publications by Ishihama,[29] Oppenheimer,[30] and Hall & Stone[31] suggest that further regard be given to this method of contraception. As a result, a conference of international scope on the use of intrauterine devices was organized and sponsored by the Population Council, on April 30—May 1, 1962. This meeting provided information encouraging enough to urge the undertaking of a vigorous study of the method for its efficacy, safety, acceptability, and mode of action. (A second international conference on intrauterine devices, held under the auspices of the Population Council on Oct. 2 and 3, 1964, reported highly encouraging progress.[32]—Ed.)

### Plant Extractives

During the last two decades a number of reports have suggested the presence of contraceptive substances in such plants as *Pisum sativum* and *Lithospermum ruderale*. Current evidence, however, is less hopeful, for there is no suggestion in any recent report that these plants, or, for that matter, any other plants are likely to yield substances having practical value in fertility regulation.

The Commonwealth Scientific and Industrial Research Organization of Australia has examined a variety of plants indigenous to Australia and New Guinea. Their studies indicate that a few of these may contain substances which do interfere with reproduction in rodents. This evidence, which has not yet been published, is more convincing than that offered for *Pisum sativum*, but thus far it is no more convincing than the evidence reported for *Lithospermum*. The possible existence of antifertility agents in plants cannot be denied, but available evidence for their presence is poor, and there is little to suggest their practical value. Perhaps the situation is one which should urge experienced plant chemists to recognize the challenge and apply their skills to the problem.

These remarks have been concerned with the status of research on physiological methods which are established as effective in the control of human fertility, or which have shown significant promise. Discussion of the subject well might be extended to include other areas of investigation less close to application, but of great interest to the subject of reproductive physiology. There is mounting evidence that attention to this field of investigation has increased progressively in recent years and that the importance of developing better methods of regulating fertility is beginning to be recognized in quarters where, until recently, the subject was studiously avoided.

(The author wishes to acknowledge the editorial assistance of Miss Joan H. Hoffman, B.A., American Medical Writers Association.)

18.

# THE PLACE OF STERILIZATION

*by Alan F. Guttmacher*

I should first like to address myself to the task of the difference between castration and sterilization. As clear-cut as the difference is to physicians, I find an appalling confusion among the minds of the laity. Castration is utterly different from sterilization. Castration is the removal of the sex glands—in the male, the removal of the testes; in the female, the removal of the ovaries. Sterilization, on the other hand, is not that at all. By modern surgical techniques one simply interrupts the passage of the sex cells, so that the two cells, sperm and egg, cannot meet to accomplish fertilization. In the female, a roadblock is established in the Fallopian tube by tying off and then excising a small portion of each tube. The sperm can progress upward only as far as the roadblock; the egg can only descend downward as far as the roadblock. Thus, there is absolutely no opportunity for the two to meet.

In the male the roadblock is created in the vas deferens, one on each side, the conduit leading from the testicle and thence finally to the penis. This roadblock prevents the sperm cells from making their egress, and therefore they are retained within the male and cannot be ejaculated.

Neither of these techniques in any way affects the sex physiology of the persons operated upon. Menstruation occurs as always; ejaculation in the male occurs without appreciable diminution of the amount of seminal fluid. So that, for all practical purposes, the male or female does not know, as far as their sex lives are concerned, that he or she has been sterilized, except for their inability to impregnate or be impregnated.

The sterilization techniques we use are relatively simple. In the male, in most parts of the world, except this country, the procedure is an ambulatory technique in the physician's office or the out-patient department of a hospital. In this country the male is usually hospitalized, given a general anesthetic, such as sodium pentothal, or a local anesthetic, and kept in the hospital for 24 hours after the operation. In some instances, male sterilization is an office procedure in this country.

Hospitalization is necessary for the female under all conditions; the procedure is performed under anesthesia and a five-day hospital post-operative convalescense is required. Currently most female sterilizations are done immediately following delivery. This has great advantages. Number one, the procedure is simpler since the uterus is high up in the abdomen and the midline, abdominal incision does not have to be as large to operate on the tubes. Number two, no additional hospital stay is imposed, because ordinarily, at least in this country, patients stay in the hospital about five days after childbirth.

Female sterilizations performed shortly after delivery are called puerperal sterilizations. Puerperal comes from the Latin "having borne a child," and therefore, it deals with that period immediately after childbirth. Ordinarily, the operation is done between one and 24 hours after delivery.

Why do we sterilize? What are the indications? First of all, eugenic; second, therapeutic; third, socio-economic; and fourth, population control.

The oldest indication for sterilization in this country is eugenic. We have twenty-eight states with laws governing such sterilizations in this country. These eugenic laws outline under what conditions we may sterilize within the law of the particular state. Enthusiasm for sterilization on eugenic grounds is constantly diminishing. As we know more and more about eugenics, we feel less confidence in our eugenic decisions. Many feel that one could virtually eliminate the eugenic group and very little loss would accrue.

The second group is therapeutic. This is largely confined to sterilization at cesarean section, because there is a feeling among women particularly and with doctors to a lesser extent, that two or three cesarean sections are enough. Actually, there is no mathematical limit for the number of cesarean sections. There is a famous woman who goes to the Woman's Hospital in New York every year and has an annual model by cesarean section. Last year I believe she had her eleventh and I look forward to reading tomorrow's paper for news about the twelfth. By common usage, cesarean sections are usually limited to two or three. There are many therapeutic reasons for female sterilization in addition to repeated cesarean section, such as organic disease of the heart, lungs, kidneys or other organs.

The third indication is socio-economic. This is an ill-defined group, some term it "sterilization for convenience." I do not like the latter appellation. I feel that there is ample reason, in this day of urban living, to limit the size of the family for socio-economic reasons. Such sterilizations are not uncommon in the United States. According to the very excellent study, *The Growth of the American Family*, which Freedman and others published in 1959, based on a survey conducted on 2,713 married white wives between the ages of nineteen and thirty-nine, 9% of American marriages are rendered infertile by sterilization of one or the other of the marital partners.

A new edition of *The Growth of the American Family* is now in preparation, but as yet unpublished. The depth interviews for the 1959 volume were conducted in 1955, those for the current edition five years later, 1960. The 1960 study shows a marital sterilization rate of 10%. Eight per cent of the wives had been rendered sterile through a surgical operation. In half the procedure had been performed only for the purpose of rendering the woman sterile and in half sterilization was not intended, but was simply the natural by-product of other gynecological surgery. Two per cent of the husbands in the 3000 couples had been sterilized by vasectomy in order to make them infertile. This was twice the male incidence of sterilization noted five years earlier.

In Puerto Rico, according to Stycos' study, of women between fifteen and forty-five, 20% have been sterilized for the sole purpose of ending their fertility. In North Carolina in 1958, according to a study recently published by Flowers & Donnelly, one woman in every forty-three had a puerperal sterilization.

I should like to call to the attention of interested readers a very valuable publication in this field, a selected bibliography of "Surgical Sterilization of Men and Women," which lists 403 articles dealing with the topic. It was written by Christopher Tietze and published by the National Committeee on Maternal Health, 2 East 103rd Street, New York City (29) in May, 1962. It is a splendid, unique contribution to this field which can be obtained by writing to the National Committee.

At my own institution, The Mount Sinai Hospital, because of the type of ward patient living in the slums who attends our clinics, we decided some years ago that it was only humane to carry out a socio-economic program of sterilization.

New York City is highly conservative in this matter, and in order not to be considered too radical, we imposed the necessity for the woman to have produced a sixth living child, to allow puerperal steriliziation, irrespective of her age or physical condition. This, of course, is wholly voluntary at the signed request of patient and husband. If the woman is thirty to thirty-five, we require the fifth living child; if she is thirty-five or more, the fourth living child. This is called the Law from Mount Sinai.

Be that as it may, I am sure that many of you would quarrel with me and say that we are being ridiculously conservative; others would say that we are being extraordinarily radical. On this basis we sterilize 9% of the patients who have had children on the ward service; and 0.3% of the patients on private service. You see there is some differentiation on the basis of the pocketbook; in this particular instance, the smaller the pocketbook, the larger the family and the better the chance to have one's sterilization request honored.

Actually, the private patient rarely qualifies on the basis of the number of children, because very few of our private patients have sufficient children to justify a parity, socio-economic puerperal sterilization.

Just a word about the legal situation in this country—it is in a tremendous muddle! Most of us do not know whether we are being legal or illegal when we carry out a sterilization without strict medical necessity, such as serious heart disease. There is a aphorism that physicians of this country who perform a sterilization operation simply to terminate fertility operate with good intentions and crossed fingers. Actually, in a state like New York, it would be useful if one of us were bold enough to request the state's attorney to arrest us after a socio-economic sterilization. Then, and only then, would we clarify the legality of socio-economic sterilization in New York State.

An extremely interesting legal development occurred in April, 1962, in the State of Virginia. Because of the legal ambiguity which existed concerning voluntary sterilization, their State legislature passed an unprecedented, liberal statute which was signed into law by the Governor. It provides that any couple may request sterilization of either marital partner and have it performed, provided that a thirty day notification is given, to permit a change of mind, and provided that two physicians recommend the operation. There is no reference to health, socio-economic situation or number of children.

Before leaving the topic of socio-economic sterilization, I should like to make mention of the important work being done by the Human Betterment Association of New York. This organization attempts to interpret human sterilization to both the lay and medical public. Furthermore, they maintain a national roster of physicians who will carry out socio-economic sterilizations. Patients may apply for advice and if unable to pay for the operation, the Association may arrange for it. If a Board of Physicians approve of the application, the Association frequently finances it.

The fourth indication, sterilization for the purposes of population control, is making slow progress throughout the world because today sterilization is a final, irrevocable procedure. We do not have reversible techniques. At Mount Sinai, thanks to the generosity of Mr. Hugh Moore, we are trying to develop some temporary reversible technique for the male, experimenting with male dogs, not humans. We are attempting to develop a removable clip technique for clamping the vas deferens.

There are similar developments in the female. Drs. Newman and Frick published in the April 1961 issue of the *American Journal of Obstetrics and Gynecology* some work they did on monkeys at Columbia Medical School on Dr. Howard Taylor's service. They placed clips on the fallopian tubes of monkeys by the abdominal route, hoping that when removed fertility would be restored. This is an incomplete study, as is our own.

A new development which is really a link between contraception and sterilization appears to be in progress. I am referring to the reintroduction of the intra-uterine ring first popularized by Gräfenberg almost thirty-five years ago. He dilated the cervix and inserted a silver ring within the uterine cavity, made in the form of a circular, silver spring, about the size of a quarter. While in position, the ring almost entirely eliminated pregnancy. To remove the ring, the cervix had to be dilated and the ring hooked and drawn forth. Objections to Gräfenberg's device were soon documented. The ring, being silver, corroded and often eroded through the uterine wall and was found in the peritoneal cavity, bladder or rectum. Furthermore, irregular bleeding with the ring in position was common and infections were not infrequent. Because of these serious objections, Gräfenberg's device fell into disuse.

Almost three years ago, Oppenheimer, from Israel, published a report on the use of nonmetallic rings made of twisted silkworm gut. This publication started a whole new era and there are several modifications now being tried all over the world. Some are made of polyethylene plastic, some from silkworm gut and others from nylon. It is too early to give them final assessment but preliminary studies show that they reduce the chances for impregnation tremendously and when withdrawn, pregnancy can be rapidly initiated. They cause cramps in some patients during the first few hours after insertion and occasionally staining during the first cycle. Profuse menses also have been reported. All of these rings are occasionally ejected, particularly during the process of menstruation. Some of the new rings, particularly the one made of nylon plastic, can be inserted through a catherer the size of a 3 Hegar without preliminary dilatation of the cervix and can be removed without cervical dilatation. There is also little evidence of infection to be imputed to these modern rings.

There is no question that if these rings prove as successful as it is now thought they are likely to be, they will remove in large measure the necessity for either male or female sterilization.

Where is sterilization being done for population control? The only two countries from which we have any extensive reports are Japan and India. I understand that in the eight-year period, between 1949 July and 1957 July, 258,235 sterilizations were done in Japan. That averages

33,000 a year. However, the number has increased gradually, so that in 1957, the last year for which I have figures, 44,380 sterilization procedures were performed in Japan.

In India, as reported by Ambassador Chagla, they did 41,000 sterilizations in 1960. I understand from Dr. Balfour that in the five-year period 1956 to 1960, 125,000 sterilizations in total were done. This is an also gradually increasing number; in 1959 there were 31,000 and in 1960, 41,000.

There are two more things I would like to say. In the first place, I think that the use of sterilization has been greatly impeded by separating it from contraception. I feel that one is permanent contraception, the other temporary contraception. The international Planned Parenthood Federation and the Planned Parenthood Federation of America by concentrating only on birth control methods, have put sterilization into discard; they have virtually pointed an accusatory finger at it. I am sure this is not conscious. It is unfortunate that many have to fragment their energies because many on the PPFA Board are also on the Human Betterment Board, and vice versa. The fact that there is this split weakens the position of sterilization particularly. This is also true on the international scene as well. It seems to me that the two groups should take cognizance of this in their future plans.

On the basis of Gregory Pincus' report, sterilization may not be necessary in the distant future; perhaps, after "x" number of years, the improvement in contraceptives may make sterilization unnecessary. To me this appears unlikely because for poorly motivated people sterilization is a much better technique than contraception.

I know this from practical experience at The Mount Sinai Hospital. A Puerto Rican woman living in the slums of New York who has four or five babies will rush as rapidly as possible to have her sixth baby at our Hospital so that sterilization can be done. They refuse to be bothered by birth control techniques. Therefore, I doubt that we can completely write off sterilization. It is likely to have a place, even after the ideal contraceptive is found.

19.

# THE PROBLEMS OF ABORTION:
# THE PERSONAL POPULATION EXPLOSION

*by Jerome M. Kummer, M.D.*

Psychiatrists do well to concern themselves with the impending avalanche of population explosion. The direct bearing that abortion has on population figures is all too apparent. In the United States alone, if we were to take the estimated one million abortions per year and calculate population curves predicated on these abortions *not* having been accomplished, the contrast to present curves would indeed be vivid. Then let us remember what a small part of the total world census we represent.

As psychiatrists we are interested in the significance of abortion on three main levels, as it relates to (1) the abortee, (2) society, and (3) a more specific segment of society, the medical profession.

Induced abortion can be traced back as far as recorded history. It has been found in all societies with almost no exceptions. The reasons for abortion have been legion, ranging from superstition and vanity on the one hand to very real physical and economic pressures on the other. It can be said that varying types and degrees of *relative population explosion* were among the most common reasons for abortion in primitive societies; lack of food and other essentials and the tremendous burden that rearing many children impose on primitive women have been described as primary motives toward abortion.

Devereux[1] is convinced that abortion is an absolutely universal phenomenon. The wide prevalence of this practice should lead one to consider the possibility that abortion, under certain circumstances, represents an instinctive drive. (Let it be emphasized that "instinct" is not being used in the psychoanalytic but rather the generic sense: "An organized and relatively complex mode of response, characteristic of a given species that has been phylogenetically adapted to a specific type of environmental situation."[2]

### ABORTION IN THE UNITED STATES

In the United States it appears that abortion is part of our social mores with society steadfastly refusing to acknowledge this to be so. The taboo that is discernible surrounding abortion is more concerned with talking about it rather than the actual act itself.[3] It is quite obvious that there is a direct derivation of attitudes concerning abortion from the prevailing attitudes toward sex in general. One might readily compare it with society's attitude toward masturbation; no one would deny its prevalence, nor could anyone deny the powerful silence that surrounds it.

The problem of criminal abortion is of enormous magnitude, both in terms of incidence and resultant mortality. Several studies[4] suggest that one out of every five pregnancies in the United States terminates in criminal abortion, or a total of more than one million per year, with a possibility of more than 5,000 deaths resulting therefrom.

The work of Gebhard *et al.*, of the Kinsey Institute, provided new and illuminating insights into many facets of illegal abortion. Although their sampling was not designed to be representative of our population, nevertheless it is possible to discern meaningful trends, mostly applicable to our urban women with relatively higher education.

Some of the highlights of the Kinsey group's study were: (1) One of every 3 to 4 women having live births had one or more abortions. (2) The higher the educational level, the greater the tendency to seek abortion. Thus white and negro unmarried women with a college education were found to have the highest abortion rate—well over 80% of all pregnancies. (3) Illegal abortion is more a problem of married women having several children, contrary to the popular notion that it mostly involves illegitimate pregnancy. The more pregnancies a woman has had, the more likely she is to seek abortion. This agrees with the findings of Kopp in her study which was done 25 years earlier (Fig. I). (4) A much higher rate of induced abortion in married women occurred at younger ages and in later life (Fig. 2).

To again refer to Fig. 1, the curve indicates a very substantial correlation between the number of pregnancies and the tendency to seek abortion. Are these women not seeking to avert a *personal population explosion;* where having another child at a given time represents an excessive strain on the individual's (and her family's) physical, emotional, intellectual, and economic resources?

The curve, midway between a "U" and a "J", seen in Figure 2, demonstrates an unreadiness to bear children early in life and, in later years, a rebellion—a refusal to go through child-rearing again, now that their families are grown. Both curves support my instinct theory—that any woman, with internal and external stresses accruing beyond a given level, will seek and secure abortion. Might these not be additional manifestations of the same natural defenses brought out in some of my earlier papers?

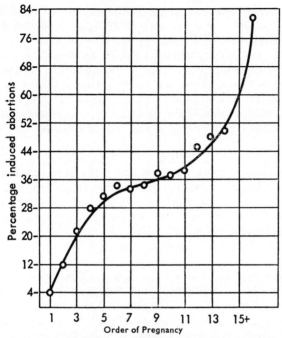

Fig. 1. Percentage of pregnancies terminating in induced abortion according to order of pregnancy (after Kopp, M.E., *Birth Control in Practice,* 1934).

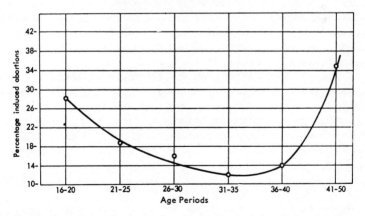

Fig. 2. Percentage of pregnancies terminating in induced abortion for women currently or previously married at age of abortion (from Gebhard et al., *Pregnancy, Birth and Abortion,* 1958).

The substantial incidence of psychiatric illness precipitated by pregnancy and childbirth, as contrasted with the negligible incidence of post-abortion psychiatric illness (discussed in more detail further on), led me to postulate that abortion provides relief and protection for women susceptible to disabling psychiatric illness. Far from being the precipitator of psychiatric illness, as was so generally assumed, abortion appears to be a defense against such illness.

Is the markedly lowered fertility rate among schizophrenics and manic-depressives not a manifestation of their natural defenses?[5]

### OTHER COUNTRIES

Of the major contemporary nations, only Japan freely permits abortion as a method of birth control, designed to stem the force of their already felt population explosion. The Soviet Union and her satellites, although they now have very relaxed rules concerning abortion, have never acknowledged population control as their purpose.

While we hear more talk these days about population explosion, one might wonder if we do not encounter a resistance similar to that seen against preparing ourselves for the dangers of thermonuclear war or any other disaster. Contemplating such horrible spectres is too threatening to our individual and collective egos, and we defend against this in a variety of ways, mostly through rationalization and denial. Japan, as an isolated example of an industrialized nation in the throes of population eruption, was forced into concrete action. Legalizing abortion rapidly cut their birth rate in half. One cannot infer that this is a necessary or desirable solution for our country or other western nations. Moral and religious standards in Japan were (and are) such that legalized abortion did not encounter much opposition. Obviously the situation is vastly different in western countries; our social standards cause us to look in other directions for answers to this problem.

It might be helpful at this point to dispel certain popular notions concerning laws on abortion in the Scandinavian countries. Abortion is *not* freely available; they have very strict laws and very methodical procedures for carrying them out. Briefly stated, their laws and procedures are roughly comparable to our practices in this country (but not with our laws!), with one notable exception. They give fuller recognition to socio-medical factors, such as their "worn-out mother" syndrome.

### POST-ABORTION PSYCHIATRIC ILLNESS

Although frequent mention of psychiatric illness following abortion is found in American medical literature, up to this time there has been no statistical documentation of such sequelae. As I reported in an earlier paper,[6] a preliminary survey among a group of American psychiatrists revealed that post-abortion psychiatric illness occurred either very rarely or, for the most part, not at all. Surveying foreign literature and communications with psychiatrists in other countries, particularly those in which more liberal attitudes prevailed, tended to confirm the extreme rarity of post-abortion illness.

Gebhard and his co-workers were able to show that induced abortion did not result in the ill effects that had been so generally assumed by others. Statistically their material gave no evidence of any resultant sterility or damage to capacity for achieving orgasm. Other physical and psychological after-effects appeared less frequently than had been previously supposed.

If the ill effects of induced abortion have been so grossly exaggerated, we must ask ourselves why. Might the answer be that this was part of the means of enforcing the taboo?

### MEDICAL ATTITUDES AND PRACTICES

Current medical attitudes and practices, in connection with abortion, add up to a series of contradictions. While an extremely small percentage of physicians are believed to be engaged in performing illegal abortions, a good many refer patients to illegal abortionists indirectly, and some directly, even in writing. While the majority of physicians have a reasonably tolerant attitude toward this practice, most of them scrupulously avoid even discussing abortion with their patients. This undoubtedly results in many troubled women having no one but the criminal abortionist to whom they may turn for advice and relief. "Society," according to one well-known physician-abortionist, ". . . abandons the woman in her greatest need."[7]

### LEGAL STATUS

This contradiction is further reflected in our society as a whole and more specifically in our legal institutions. Although criminal abortion is labeled a felony, the abortees are almost never prosecuted and for professional abortionists the rate of prosecution is low and the rate of conviction even lower.[8] It is apparent that morals, religion and the criminal law offer little restraint when it comes to abortion, leading Taussig to remark that he knew "of no other instance in history in which there has been such frank and universal disregard for criminal law."[9]

Most therapeutic abortions in this country are in violation of state laws. Guttmacher[10] stated unequivocally "that the abortion laws in the United States make hypocrites of all of us." More than 90% of the therapeutic abortions done at New York's Mount Sinai Hospital did not fall strictly within statutory requirements "to preserve the life of the mother." Hospital authorities and physicians vary widely in their interpretation of the laws and their willingness to place themselves in jeopardy of prosecution. In a recent survey of California hospitals 18 out of 24 replied that therapeutic abortions were performed knowingly in violation of the law.[11]

### RECOMMENDED LEGAL CHANGES

The medical and law-enforcement professions are in need of laws which can provide clear guideposts for therapeutic abortions. Until very recently nothing was done toward modernizing these laws. The American Law Institute, in its 1959 Model Penal Code, proposed a Therapeutic Abortion Statute, which has promise of giving us our long-needed guideposts.

Mr. Zad Leavy, Former Deputy Los Angeles County District Attorney, and I have made the following recommendations for a therapeutic abortion act.[12] While these are similar to the Model Penal Code, significant differences exist. Therapeutic abortions should be allowed for the following reasons:

*Eugenic*—mental deficiency in the parents or the likelihood that a congenital disease or malfunction will be present in the child.

*Medical*—where terminating the pregnancy is necessary to preserve the life or the physical or mental health of the mother.

*Humanitarian*—where pregnancy results from forcible rape, incest or moral irresponsibility of the female (because of youth or mental incompetence).

### CONTROLS

Certain controls are recommended which would broaden the base of responsibility and reduce the possibility of abuses. For the medical and eugenic categories it is suggested that the laws permit licensed hospitals to regulate the performance of therapeutic abortions through a qualified committee of staff physicians, composed of at least two obstetricians, one internist, one psychiatrist, and a fifth person. Such committees have been functioning well for some time in most leading hospitals.

Under the humanitarian category, where the decision must be based upon a finding of fact as to the mother's claim of forcible rape or incest, provision should be made for the courts to order an abortion if the facts appear to substantiate the claim. Such a finding of fact is considered to be more within the framework of the courts than within the confines of sound medical judgment.

California has a bill pending, patterned after the Model Penal Code. Although there is excellent support for this bill from the 1960 and 1962 Los Angeles County Grand Juries, organized medicine and other groups, the extremely well-organized opposition, namely the Roman Catholic Church, makes passage in the near future improbable.

It is believed that the harshness of existing laws concerning therapeutic abortion together with the confusion surrounding processing of abortion recommendations help to swell the already large number of illegal abortions. No one is under the illusion that modifying our existing laws will eliminate abortions done illegally. As long as there are any restrictions at all, women with unwanted pregnancies who are determined to abort will find illegal abortionists. This is, however, no reason for abandoning all attempts to prevent widespread termination of pregnancy by unskilled hands.

### PREVENTIVE MEASURES

Nor is one under the illusion that modifying these laws is the most important step. Preventive measures are certainly called for; the most significant are:

*Consultation Centers*—similar to those in Sweden, where women with unwanted pregnancies may go for counseling by competent professionals. With experienced counseling many women find that they can and want to go to term, others may qualify for therapeutic interruptions, and still others can have the possibilities of adoption explored. Those who are still intent on illegal abortion can be educated about the dangers and the necessity for early treatment afterward.

*Research* toward developing of the "ideal" contraceptive.

*Education of the public* must include sex instruction for children at levels understandable to them. For adults the sex instruction should be more comprehensive, including information on planned parenthood, birth control and abortion.

### PROBLEM AREAS

The problem areas, which must be explored and resolved include:

I. *The drive toward abortion—among* the multiplicity of factors, are we dealing with an instinctive drive?

II. *Psychiatric sequelae of induced abortion*—if these and physical after-effects have been so grossly exaggerated, was it a means of perpetuating the taboo?

III. *Social forces and attitudes:* Is society in fact protecting the mother's welfare by maintaining stringent laws which drive her to illegal abortion?

IV. *Therapeutic abortion laws:* qualified physicians cannot operate honestly within the framework of current abortion laws: the legal threat of prosecution hangs over their heads, when in reality the community has no intention of punishing medical practitioners acting in good faith.

The forces in our society opposing abortion, namely religious and legal institutions, are well-known and quite obvious. What is also obvious is that these social forces have not accomplished their stated goals, maintaining morality and preventing abortion. Instead we are confronted with a sea of heartache and confusion and an estimated 5,000 deaths per year from illegal abortions. Is it not time that we took a long, hard, critical look at these forces in an effort to better understand them and to determine if indeed they are in the best interests of the individual and society?

The problems of abortion are of utmost complexity, requiring study and remedy on many levels from a variety of disciplines. My experience with this enigma has led me to believe that significant strides can be made by utilizing methods borrowed from psychotherapeutic theory and techniques in isolating, identifying, and helping the patient (in this case *society*) deal with the problem.

# Eugenic and Genetic Considerations

❍ ❍ ❍

20.

# THE PROTECTION AND IMPROVEMENT
# OF MAN'S GENETIC INHERITANCE

*by Frederick Osborn*

This chapter is concerned with problem of genetic inheritance. It will not attempt to cover the problem of social inheritance, although these twin aspects of population quality are not easily separated.

There is convincing evidence from both psychological and medical genetics studies that variations in genetic factors have a part in determining individual variations in intelligence and personality as well as in susceptibility to disease and many serious abnormalities. Revealing studies have been made on identical twins reared at home or reared apart, on siblings, on adopted children reared in homes or in institutions, and on random pairs. When the environment is closely similar and the heredity varied, there are large individual differences which can only be explained by differences in the heredity. When the heredity is held constant and the environment varied there are differences which must be accounted for by the differences in the environment. We will not attempt an analysis of these studies in the brief space of this chapter. Their findings are quoted because, if there were no scientific basis for believing that individual differences were influenced by variations in heredity, it would be useless to discuss the "improvement" of our genetic inheritance.

Individual differences range from differences in intelligence and emotional balance to physical differences ranging from vigorous good health to disabling defects. The extreme range of defects are the easiest to study; they are easiest to measure, and if they run in family lines they are most easily located. Further, they are of particular interest to a large professional group, the whole medical profession. For these reasons the first individual differences to be studied from a genetic point of view have been departures from the normal in the form of defective development, extreme susceptibility to disease, and mental defects arising from constitutional causes. Large scale interest in this field developed among doctors after the second world war, and greatly hastened the pace of investigation.

As a result of these studies we have come to realize that genes that cause defects are not limited to those families afflicted, but that many such genes are spread widely through the population. We have learned that the genetic consequences of artificial radiation, of life-saving influences in medicine, and of new migration and marriage patterns are reflected in an accumulation of deleterious genes over and above the subtle equilibrium previously established by natural forces. Methods are being devised to detect the individuals who are carriers of genes that cause defects as well as to treat some of the defects at an early age. Increasing medical knowledge and increasing public interest have led to the establishment of heredity counseling centers, and to a new recognition of the importance of heredity in human affairs.

It is generally accepted that genes that make for defect originate in so-called "mutations" which occasionally take place in one or another of the many thousands of genes which are present in pairs in every human cell. Usually the mutated gene is a recessive, that is, it does not have its harmful effect unless the other gene in the pair has the same characteristics. The chances of two such genes meeting as a pair depend on the number of such genes distributed throughout the inter-marrying population. Thus if one person in a hundred carries a particular deleterious gene, the chances of his mating with a person with a similar gene are one in ten thousand. This may seem like a small chance, but in a large population such as that of the United States it may mean a great number of defective persons.

With every increase in the proportion of people who are carriers of a particular defective gene, there is an even greater increase in the likelihood of a mating in which two such genes will be paired in the same fertilized cell. When this happens, there will be a defect. If the defect is lethal, the two deleterious genes will be taken out of circulation. If the defect is minor, but of a sort to make marriage or reproduction less likely, the genes are to that extent less likely to survive. Thus at some point nature establishes a balance in which, for every new deleterious gene brought into circulation, a similar gene is lost from circulation. The human race carries a considerable load of defect. Geneticists believe that most people carry at least a few deleterious genes,—some geneticists put the average as high as eight,—and at least 2% of the babies born into this world will carry all their lives some major or minor genetic defect. We get along just the same, but if the load became much heavier it might seriously threaten our future.

Most scientists are afraid that the proportion of carriers of deleterious genes may be increasing now quite rapidly—though the results in the form of a great increase in defect will not be apparent for several generations. Exposure to X-rays and to fall-out from atomic explosions is thought to be increasing the mutation rate, while at the other end, where failure to reproduce takes genes out of circulation, medical science is carrying an increasing number of people with some kind of defect through a period of successful childbearing. Diabetics for instance formerly died early, and the genes for diabetes were lost with them. After a cure was found in insulin, they survived and led useful lives, but were not generally able to have children. Now means have been found for enabling them to have children, and the safe delivery of the children of diabetic mothers is a commonplace in all our hospitals. The deleterious genes remain in circulation, and the proportion of diabetics is undoubtedly increasing from generation to generation. Of course we can get along with a lot more diabetics, and with good medical care they can live happily and bear diabetic children of their own. But there is a limit beyond which this process cannot be carried, and if we consider not diabetes alone, but all the other ills to which the human race is genetically heir, that limit is not far away. The fear of the scientists is that the accumulation of deleterious genes may creep up on us unaware, and after a few generations burst out in an uncontrollable explosion of defect.

Evidently the doctors and the public health authorities have a new and heavy responsibility. It cannot be carried out without an increase in public understanding. The current evidence from established heredity clinics indicates that couples will run a considerable chance of defective children rather than remain childless. It is the practice in heredity clinics to give the couples who come to the clinic for advice the whole picture on their heredity so far as it can be determined by a study of their family histories and their own condition, and if possible to give them an estimate of the chances of their having an unsound child. When a husband and wife each carry a recessive deleterious gene similar to one carried by the other, the chances of their having a defective child are one in four, with two children carriers of a single gene, but themselves without defect, and the fourth child being neither a carrier nor defective. Couples in such a position, knowing that they have one chance in four of having a seriously defective child, and that two out of four of their children are likely to be carriers, still frequently take a chance that things will turn out all right. Heredity clinics have been a great help to many anxious couples, but from a eugenic point of view it is hard as yet to assess their value. Perhaps a better education of the public in genetic matters will have the necessary effect. But we cannot rule out the possibility that any serious reduction in deleterious genes will not be possible by voluntary means alone. It would probably take a grave and terrible increase in the proportion of people born with crippling genetic defects to bring about acceptance of compulsory limitation of childbearing by carriers.

There is at least one dreadful form of insanity which comes on in middle age as a result of a mutated dominant gene. Because the gene is dominant, half the children of a couple, one of whom is going to be afflicted will develop the insanity. It is probably possible to detect the carriers. The disease could be wiped out in a generation, and the untold suffering of tens of thousands of people forever avoided. But no serious consideration is being given to such a possibility.

There is one consolation for our present neglect of genetic deterioration. Knowledge in this field is advancing rapidly. Each year an increasing number of defects are being defined, the type of hereditary transmission understood, and in many cases means found for spotting carriers. By the time the public and the public health authorities are ready to attack the dreadful scourge of genetic defects as in the past they have attacked cholera and yellow fever, the science of medical genetics should be ready with knowledge sufficient to make the attack successful.

Arbitrary methods may some day be necessary to control the growing incidence of genetic defect. But there is little chance of the public accepting such an impairment of everyone's "right to have children" unless there is a far better understanding of human genetics than we have at present and a better appreciation of the responsibilities of parenthood.

Quite a different situation exists with respect to intelligence and personality. There is a genetic base to individual variations in these traits as there is in variations in health and defect. But there is no need to consider abritrary controls for improving the genetic base for intelligence and personality. A great improvement could undoubtedly be made without in any way infringing on anyone's "right" to have children. Very slight changes in our social institutions and in the psychological factors which influence the size of individual families would probably tip the balance of births in a direction favorable to genetic improvement. Most of these changes are already being demanded by people who want to improve the environment in which children are brought up, quite apart from any genetic factors.

The fact is that no one knows whether in the United States today the genetic base is improving or deteriorating. In the early days in this country, when the death rate was particularly high for the people least able to fend for themselves, there was probably a trend towards the survival of the more vigorous and able stocks. A generation ago, when the death rate had gotten to be very low for almost all of our people, there were large differentials in the birth rates of different social and economic classes. The more educated people were having the fewest children. Many scientists took this as an indication that the genetic base for intelligence was on the decline. Others held that there was not much evidence for believing that the more educated people of the country on the whole had any better hereditary qualities than the less educated. Both sides agreed that the differences between couples within each social class were much greater than the average differences between social classes, and that nothing was known about the quality of the individual couples who were having the most children in each of the social classes. Today, over 95% of the children born alive live beyond their 30th year, and with the spread of birth control social class differences in size of family are much diminished. There is little evidence that any great changes are going on in genetic quality.

But there is room for great improvement. On this everyone is agreed. We know that genetic quality affects achievement. If we could raise the genetic quality of the lowest 20% in our population to a level above the present average, we would be making a tremendous contribution to the improvement of American life. There are many present trends which could be exploited to make such an improvement possible. The most important of these trends is the continuing spread of birth control.

Recent studies indicate that most American married women use some form of birth control to prevent or postpone further births after they have had two or three children. Even among Catholics, 85% of fecund Catholic wives age 35-39 use some form of birth control including of course the rhythm method approved by the Church. The spread of birth control has been an important factor toward equalizing the birth rates of different socio-economic classes. Its use and effectiveness is constantly increasing. If, as scientists expect, means are soon found for preventing conception by some form of immunization, or by taking an inexpensive and occasional pill, there should be great opportunity for reducing the number of unwanted children born in this country.

There are good grounds for believing that unwanted children are on the average less well endowed genetically than the average for the country as a whole. Such a statement brings a howl of protest from a great number of believers in the American ideal of equality, but it is time they should face the situation with a little sense of reality. To take an extreme example, the number of illegitimate children born in this country is quite high, in some areas or groups as much as 10 or more per cent of total births. It is fair to say that most illegitimate children are unwanted. It must also be recognized that people who have illegitimate children have on the whole somewhat less socially valuable traits of character than do people whose children are born in wedlock. To some extent at least, perhaps to a considerable extent, genetic as well as environmental influences have operated to make these people behave differently from their neighbors. Eliminating illegitimate births would reduce the survival of whatever genetic factors are involved and thus tend to reduce the proportion of people at the lower levels of personal responsibility. (It would at the same time reduce the proportion of children brought up in an inferior environment, as would most other changes which would improve the genetic inheritance.)

Illegitimate births are not the only unwanted births today. Many unwanted children are born to married couples. When they are unwanted because there are already enough children in the family they are not a genetic handicap, though they may pose an environmental problem in their bringing up. But when children are born to couples who do not want them because they are not ready for the responsibility of children, or do not want the responsibility, or can't take care of them, we may suspect that the parents have on the average somewhat less vigor and competence than their neighbors, and that this difference has to some degree a genetic base. Here again we may hope that the increased use of family limitation may be to genetic advantage.

Of course we have no guarantee that better methods of birth control will produce these results. They will only be effective if our people are so informed, and so influenced by a strong public opinion, and so situated in their economic life, that all these forces will operate to reduce illegitimate and other births which are not positively wanted by both members of the couples involved. In this country none of these forces have been so directed. Great numbers of young or ignorant people have only the haziest notion of what methods of birth control are effective and how they should be used; social workers are seldom much motivated to instruct on birth control, indeed many would lose their jobs if they did; under present economic arrangements, mothers with illegitimate children and others with large families of unwanted children are usually paid children's allowances which increase with each child, and the fathers of illegitimate children are seldom found and required to pay for their upbringing. Surely different attitudes and methods could be found without diminishing the care we properly want to give to children who are brought into the world through no fault of their own.

The fear has been expressed that such general access to birth control would on the one hand lower our moral standards, and on the other hand so reduce the number of births that the race would soon die out. Neither fear is justified by recent experience. Access to birth control has undoubtedly shown up a lot of people with low moral standards, but the much larger proportion of responsible people who are now raising children have a birth rate well above that of a generation ago. There is no reason we should encourage people with low moral standards to reproduce, which is just what we are doing in far too many cases. We should save our encouragements to reproduction for those who are most likely not only to bring up their children well, but are also able to give them a good genetic endowment.

Besides the trend to birth control there are many other trends which properly understood could be turned to genetic advantage. There are trends towards an increasing social and job mobility and the elimination of fixed hereditary classes, and a trend towards giving everyone a chance at the best education he is capable of absorbing. These are all trends towards sorting people out according to their genetic qualities and putting each into the kind of life and work for which they are genetically most fitted, whether as artists, business men, ministers, mechanics, lawyers or manual laborers. These changes are important for the effects they may have on the mating of like with like. Many studies have shown that there is a natural tendency for men and women to marry people who are like themselves in physical appearance, coloring, intelligence, tastes, interests and social background. Of course there are many exceptions, and people notice them and find it hard to believe the story told by the statistical studies, that like tends to marry like. There is another notable fact about marriage. People only marry people they have actually met.

Not long ago people moved about much less than they do today; they were forced to marry the people they met on the neighboring farms or in their immediate locality. They did not have much chance to meet and marry people who were like themselves in their genetic qualities, though their social background was likely to be similar. Today the situation is very different. People move about a great deal, not only from place to place, but also from one social group, work group, and educational level group, until they are likely to find themselves among people who are like themselves far more than was the case a generation ago. By this, and by the fact they have a larger circle of acquaintance than in the past, assortative mating is undoubtedly on the increase. We should encourage it and take advantage of it. By changing the distribution of genes assortative mating makes for a greater number of people with particular and special qualities. An increase in assortative mating would increase genetic diversification in the process of adapting to the diverse elements of our society. One could expect a greater variety of specialized talents.

But there is another aspect of assortative mating. In association with selection it can rapidly change gene frequencies. This means that if certain genetic types of people had fewer children than the average, the proportion of such people would diminish from one generation to another. They would be selected against, and the frequency of their type of gene in the population would diminish. On the other hand, if certain other types had more children than the average, their type would increase from one generation to another, and the frequency of their type of gene would increase.

Thus while assortative mating should be encouraged because it will make for a greater variety of specialized talents, society should at the same time try to provide conditions which would tend to influence the birth rate of different kinds of people in different ways; means should be found to encourage larger families among couples who are above the average of achievement in their particular activity, and at the same time conditions should be such that those couples who are less successful would tend to have smaller than average families. The influences which could be brought to bear range all the way from the climate of public opinion to the use of economic measures such as larger income tax deductions for children through the whole period of their education.

The search for means of getting such a discriminating selection of births has only just begun. Studies by students of population on the social, psychological and economic factors which affect size of family have provided a number of leads as to the conditions under which people want to have more or less children. Much further research is needed to find out what particular conditions would make for the kind of birth selection which is needed, but the problems are not impossible of solution. The needed changes will be the more easily accepted because they will also tend to improve the environment in which children are brought up, and so can be urged for other than genetic reasons. If they can be made effective, we could reasonably hope for not only a greater variety of talents, but a constantly higher level in those qualities which have a common tendency towards achievement in all environments.

The protection and even the improvement of our genetic inheritance should not prove a difficult task compared to many other social advances man has already made. The obstacles are ignorance and misunderstanding. The education of public opinion is the first necessary step towards a resumption of the slow but rewarding process of evolution by which man made his long upward climb.

21.

# BETTER GENES FOR TOMORROW

### *by Hermann J. Muller*

#### PERILS OF OUR PROGRESS

Man of today is the "heir of all the ages," both in regard to the marvelous and fearful culture that he has built up for himself, and the incredibly capable genetic organization, conferred by biological evolution, that has made it possible for him to fashion this culture. Yet we know that we have attained no utopia, and that our perils and problems have enormously increased in consequence of the increase in our potentialities. Most of these perils arise from the short-sighted use of our transcendent modern science and techniques for the intended benefit of restricted portions of humanity, but in opposition to the benefit of humanity in general, and for the intended benefit of people of the present-day world, but at the expense of those who will come after us.

This unbalanced situation is of course most glaringly illustrated in the application of modern technology to the development of weapons of mass destruction. It is similarly evident in our present unparalleled successes in the despoliation of our natural resources. Readers of these pages will also have come to recognize, as a third major peril, that twentieth-century medical and industrial techniques, combined with ancient ideologies, are promoting a population growth so widespread and rapid as to be degrading human living over ever greater areas, and to be threatening both the material and mental basis of culture in the world in general.

It is not so widely realized that our triumphs of medical and industrial technology, through the very same practices as those by which they foster overpopulation, are conducting an ever more effective assault upon that inner source of all human potentialities—our genetic constitution. For the forces that are unleashing the population explosion are undiscriminating. They work by defeating the operations of the natural selection that prevailed through ages past. These were the processes whereby those individuals who were especially heavily loaded with defective genes tended to survive in smaller numbers than the rest and to leave fewer offspring while, conversely, those endowed with genes especially helpful for the species tended to survive and multiply more abundantly.

Today, as has been pointed out in the preceding article by Osborn, the vast majority of persons born, even when subnormal, are enabled to reach maturity. Moreover, under modern conditions, foresight, conscience, and competence seem to express themselves rather by successful restraint in reproduction than by abundance of offspring. In this connection it is to be noted that detrimental mutations continue to arise in each generation anew, at such a rate that something like 20% of persons receive some newly arisen mutant gene, and that such genes, once arisen, tend to be handed on down through an indefinite succession of generations. They tend to continue until the lines of descent that carry them die out as a result of their own incapacity. Thus it is evident that under modern conditions, so long as this dying out is seriously interfered with, human populations must become ever more defective in their genetic constitution, until at long last even the most sophisticated techniques available could no longer suffice to save men from their biological corruptions.

It follows that, if the social system should for centuries manage to withstand the strain caused by the persistence of these practices, people would again find themselves dying before maturity, or failing to reproduce, in consequence of their innate infirmities, at just as high a rate—one or more in five—as that which they had suffered from in primitive times. And these human failures would be but a token of the many more who just managed to drag out their existence. On the other hand, if civilization should then break down, the miserable, decrepit remnants of men, denied its support, would perish under the, to them, intolerable rigors of primitive life.

Yet it is not a foregone conclusion that the epitaph "*Sic transit gloria*" will be applicable to the unprecedented enterprise of mankind. It is becoming increasingly recognized that, in dealing with global politics and ideologies, the tools of dispassionate analysis and creative imagination, working in the service of humanity at large and powered by modern science and technology, can and must find ways to turn our perils to our profit. To succeed in this men must learn to advance in increasing cooperation, and to utilize their newly-won nuclear furies, potent chemicals, and sophisticated computers in conquests over natural difficulties, instead of over each other. So too in matters of reproduction: today's dilemmas, raised by the shortsighted applications of science, can and must be met by the development of more far-seeing science, and of techniques founded upon it, that are used in behalf of mankind everywhere, and with due regard to the future. Moreover, these same practices will, as we shall see, redound powerfully to the benefit of the individual participants. However, in this situation just as in international relations, deep-seated changes in attitudes, based on a more scientific and ethical insight into human values and needs, will be necessary to allow the implementation of the required reforms.

The mainspring of these reforms will be found not in fear but in hope. It would be pitiful and shameful if we, the proud "Lords of Creation," were to limit ourselves, in the genetic field, to the task of merely mending our fences, and holding our own in a constant struggle against decay. No, the same means that best enable us to defend ourselves against genetic deterioration can also serve, when applied with greater intensity, to *advance* our genetic position significantly. Moreover, we have no more reached any limit in the possibilities of our genetic advancement than in those of our cultural advancement. Herewith the genetic situation is lifted out of the realm of dire foreboding, and dangers to be gloomily warded off, into that of inspiring opportunities, inviting our zealous efforts.

### MISCONCEPTIONS TO BE AVOIDED

In seeking ways of resisting deterioration and effecting actual improvement in the human genetic constitution we must recognize, first of all, that every person, and every group of people, represents an inextricable complex of both heredity and environment. In the development of psychological characteristics the human being is especially plastic, being influenced drastically in personality, mentality, and capabilities by his cultural environment.

Despite the potency of the environmental forces, differences in the genes have also been proved to play an enormous role in the causation of the differences found between individuals with similar cultural and physical backgrounds. But when peoples of radically different circumstances are compared, such as those living under primitive conditions versus those under modern industrialism, or underprivileged or pariah groups, on the one hand, versus first-class citizens of the same country, on the other hand, the environmental disparities are so overriding that whatever differences in the genetic basis of psychological traits may or may not exist between them are entirely obscured. Doubtless differences do exist between peoples, or races, in the frequencies of genes affecting psychological characters, as they certainly do for some physical characters, but we cannot by present means judge what they are. However, the ease with which individuals and groups born and brought up in a culture alien to that of their parents take to and succeed in the adopted ways indicates that these "racial" genetic differences, whatever they may be, must be comparatively unimportant. Certainly they must be much smaller than the genetic differences, in regard to the same characters, that are prevalent among *individuals* of any one comparatively homogeneous population.

As for the more conspicuous physical differences between peoples, as in their pigmentation, facial and hair form, and body build, and in some associated physiological traits, such as tolerances to differing temperatures, altitudes and foods, it has become evident that these consistent diversities have evolved in adaptation to the different climates and other natural conditions of life to which the respective peoples had been subjected over thousands of years. However, the modern techniques which are spreading throughout the world are proving so effective in aiding men against the diverse difficulties which had sundered them that these special adaptations are rapidly losing the advantages they afforded in their given domains. Thus, except for extraordinary situations, such as enormous altitudes, groups of practically any ethnic type can today survive successfully in any region habitable by another type. This consideration, and also those discussed in the preceding paragraph, illustrate how hollow are the pretensions of the racists, in claiming a genetic basis for their delusions of superiority.

Similar considerations apply to the arguments of the so-called "social Darwinists," who maintain that classes of lower economic and social status are genetically inferior and should therefore reproduce less than those of higher status. No reasonable person can deny that the modern extension of educational and other opportunities, as well as better living conditions, to economically less favored groups, has served to uncover among them surprising resources of native mental ability, moral fiber, and physical vigor. Moreover, it is notorious that until comparatively recent times the more "cultured" families of any population—those of the nobles, well-to-do burghers, and city-dwellers generally—tended gradually to die out and to become replaced from the ranks of rising rural workers and craftsmen. The celibate priesthood alone contributed a strong influence of this kind. Yet the supply of able persons did not seem to become reduced in the process. Doubtless there was some filtering of better talent, selectively, into the socially higher ranks, but the natural selection occurring within the masses must during most of this long period have been enough to largely compensate for any such drain.

Despite powerful counter-currents, the economic, social, and educational forces of the modern world are, fortunately, moving it in the direction of ever more meaningful human rights, and of the more potent democracy needed to maintain those rights. Under these circumstances, the institution of discriminatory conditions against social or ethnic minorities is increasingly felt to be abhorrent, while their institution against majorities is entirely anachronistic. Similarly, special privileges for favored classes are passing away, along with the other relics of ancient aristocracies. All this is essential for the removal of brakes on progress. This being the case, it is evident that any attempt to intentionally manipulate the social system, so as to make child-bearing or child-rearing harder or easier for one ethnic group, or for one social or occupational class, than for another, would meet with deserved defeat and obloquy.

The really important genetic inequalities of man are those between individuals, and they are commonly much greater than the differences, in the same genetic respects, between the averages of different social or ethnic groups. It is these individual differences, therefore, that must be dealt with in any policy for genetic conservation or advance, and in judging these differences every effort must be made to discount differences referable to social and ethnic groupings and backgrounds. Most important of all in this connection, procedures intended to promote genetic well-being should be thoroughly democratic in their mode of application. That is, they should involve entirely voluntary decisions, arrived at freely by those participating in the undertakings. At the same time, the choices should represent reasonable judgments, actuated by a soundly based set of values. How is this paradoxical seeming combination of conditions to be arrived at?

### ADVANTAGES OF THE POSITIVE APPROACH

It is generally recognized that free democratic government, if its operation is to be salutary, requires well-grounded popular education. Similarly, if genetic betterment is to be conducted in a democratic manner toward wholesome objectives it is essential for the public in general to be led to understand and appreciate the principles of evolution and genetics, especially in relation to themselves and to humanity in general. Without such education they cannot gain a due perspective on the past and on the mighty possibilities of the future. The outlook thus engendered will help to imbue people with a sense of responsibility to later generations, along with a feeling of fulfillment in cases in which they themselves are able to be active agents in the great advance of mankind.

Such basic education will make people more receptive to the advice of the specialists of heredity clinics, concerning the likelihood of the children of given parents, in given unions, being genetically well or ill endowed in diverse particulars. Already there are a number of such clinics performing useful functions, and it is to be hoped that this method will become increasingly influential. It should be realized, however, that it suffers from certain limitations. Thus, one of the principal aims of this work must be to influence the choice of partners in such ways as to minimize the production of children who *manifest* a defect, and to maximize the *concatenation* of valuable traits. This work is very valuable in itself, but it has no direct effect on the task of major genetic importance: the influencing of gene frequencies in the population at large in desirable directions.

Such an influence is, to be sure, brought to bear when given persons are warned that they have definite genetic defects and are thus discouraged from having children. However, these cases are usually concerned with rare abnormalities of specific types. Let it not be forgotten that practically everyone really carries a fair number of less noticeable yet significant defects in more or less hidden form, along with some genes of especially favorable kinds. What would be ideally suited for substantial progress in this situation would be a rate of reproduction graded according to an over-all estimation of each person's genetic composition. This is in fact the feat that natural selection did accomplish with man in the long run in ages past, by assessing each individual on the basis of his achievements, even though environmental inequalities caused numberless errors to be committed by this method. However, the day when similar ratings could be made for people in general by geneticists is neither in sight nor around the corner.

In fact, no single science or discipline could competently weigh all these factors, in relation to the present and possible future conditions of life. Moreover, a clinician or a committee who attempted to give advice along these lines would probably be regarded with skepticism and often with resentment by the person or couple in question. Realizing the "subjectivity" of the judgment arrived at, they would tend to substitute their own subjective appraisals of themselves. But, on the whole, there is no appraisal so faulty as self-appraisal. Thus we should have come full circle back to the present reproductive disorder in which wishful and egotistical thinking, hand in hand with lack of thinking, lead the way in the race to procreate, while forethought, conscience, and humility drag behind.

Nevertheless, no real impasse is involved here. For there is in any large population a fair number of persons whose attainments and performance are clearly extraordinary, demonstrating a combination of high abilities, all-round fitness, and, in some of these cases, unusual humanity of disposition. One must of course beware of the biases about people that arise during their heydays. However, at longer range from them in time and space, truer estimates of the merits of their lives emerge among specialists in the same lines of activity as the persons had engaged in, and can thus become available to the interested public. The next question is, how could these comparatively objective means of judgment serve in the implementation of genetic betterment?

There is in any present population a considerable proportion of couples —from 2 to 8%, according to age—who would like to have children but who are unable to because of the sterility of the male partner. An increasing number of these—perhaps more than 10,000 per year at present in the United States, according to Guttmacher (1961)—are utilizing the procedure termed "AID," that is, artificially controlled insemination by a physician, with semen from a donor selected by him but unknown to them, and they are thereby enabled to have children. Follow-up studies show that, in general, this method has been highly successful, as judged both by the happiness of the couple's subsequent married life, and by the well-being of the resulting children. How much more, then, would these couples have welcomed the opportunity to have children by controlled insemination, if they had to begin with been well grounded in genetics, evolution, and the problems of society, and if in addition they had been enabled to utilize the procedure in such a way as to make a significant contribution to human progress!

They could have made such a contribution if they themselves had been given an opportunity to participate in the selection of the germinal material, from among banks of it derived from persons judged, in the perspective of time, to have been of outstanding worth. Technically, this procedure would even now be entirely feasible. For the method of preserving the germ cells of a man for an indefinite period without deterioration, in a deeply frozen condition, is already well established, thanks to a long succession of researches (Montegazza 1866, Jahnel 1938, Shettles 1940, Hoagland & Pincus 1942, Hoagland 1943, Polge *et al.* 1949, Sherman & Bunge 1953, Bunge & Sherman 1953, Bunge, Keittel & Sherman 1954). The culmination of these is represented by recent work by Sherman (1963), partly parallelled by that of a Japanese group (Iizuka & Sawada 1958, Sawada 1959, Nakajima *et al.* 1962), which have put the techniques of processing and preservation on a thoroughly practical basis.

In fact, banks of frozen human germ cells are at present in existence in a number of places. However, no attempt has yet been made to provide these germinal reserves with material from outstanding sources. This being the case, even the couples resorting to this form of "pre-adoption" (to use Julian Huxley's term) still have no ground for departing from the accepted pattern of secrecy for such cases. So too, the all-important matter of the choice of the germinal material still rests with the clinician alone, and only he is aware of what choice was made. It is then maneuvered to have the official record of parentage made under the direction of another physician, from whom knowledge of the procedure used was purposely withheld, so that the *de facto* adopting father—the social father—becomes falsely registered as the genetic father.

In such cases the subterfuges employed, although sordid, were justified because they enabled the participants to practice a new and higher ethics than that of the past, an ethics made possible by the more advanced techniques and knowledge of the present. In another generation, however, considerable sections of society will feel scandalized at the backwardness of the mores and legal attitudes that occasioned such indirections and resulted in such inadequacies, for persons who were putting forth their best efforts in the interests of the whole population. With the building up, in the future, of ever richer stores of valuable germinal material, worthy couples denied by sterility from having children possessing the husband's own genes would feel cheated by man even more than by nature if they were also deterred, by society, from rendering it the supreme service of bringing a part of its precious biological resources to fruition.

Moreover, such couples would consider it a triple humiliation if, while permitted to devote themselves to such an undertaking, they nevertheless had to accept these conditions: (1) that they were to have no voice in the choosing of their child's paternal heritage, (2) that they were to be kept in ignorance concerning this choice, and (3) that they would force themselves, their child, and the public to live a lie concerning its origin. Conversely, the thousands of sterile couples who today practise pre-adoption would be joined by many more when the opportunity was opened to them to participate in the choice of their children's heritage and when, with the spreading of the practice, it became widely recognized as a notable social service, and therewith cast off its blight of secrecy.

But even today, despite the arbitrariness and furtiveness now characterizing pre-adoption, the practice is being taken up increasingly not only by sterile couples but also by some who could have reproduced in the ordinary way. The fertile couples resorting to it are oftenest cases in which the husband would have been likely to transmit to the children a serious hereditary defect. Besides these, there are couples utilizing the method in whom some hereditary incompatibility, as for instance in blood groups, exists between husband and wife, that would threaten the wellbeing of their children. Finally, some men and women are already to be found among us who, though by no means ill-endowed, are idealistic enough to prefer for a child of theirs a biological heritage of even more promise than their own genes would be likely to provide. As yet, such couples are thwarted by lack of the required facilities for exercising germinal choice. However, this lack is not primarily based in difficulties of a biological kind.

Thus a nucleus is already on hand which might in the course of time develop into a much more considerable enterprise, one that eventually became more than adequate to counteract any tendencies to genetic deterioration and to institute in their stead substantial genetic advancement in varied directions. Requisite for such an undertaking would be not only extensive, long-treasured stores of germinal material, representing natural faculties and predispositions of very varied types, but also ample records concerning the lives and characteristics of the persons from whom the material had been derived, and records concerning their close relatives, including of course their progeny. Couples who thought of assuming the grave responsibility of utilizing such material, and who satisfied requirements of competence to do so, should be assisted, in coming to their decisions, by advice from diverse counsellors. These should include geneticists, physicians, psychologists, and specialists in the activities that had been pursued by the prospective donor, as well as persons with an unusually well-rounded understanding of the general problems of man and society. Preferably, at least twenty years should have elapsed since the death of the donors considered. This is a provision which it would gradually become more practicable to follow as the supplies of germinal material increased, and as research disclosed ways of rendering smaller amounts of it effective.

Among the advantages of this type of positive approach to genetic betterment is the very fact that because of the difficulties raised by the mores prevalent today, it will for a considerable time to come be taken up by a comparatively small minority. For these will consist in unusually large measure of persons of independent mind, imaginative but rational in their thinking, deeply motivated ethically, and strongly oriented socially: in a word, practical idealists. Thus the standards adopted in the choosing of germinal material by these persons will tend to be exceptionally high; they will be inclined to take earnestly into account the records and counsel available to them, and, in general, to give especially serious consideration to the making of their choices. In this way a wholesome precedent will be set, and a new set of attitudes and mores, pertinent to the procedure of germinal choice, will take shape. In consequence, the larger numbers who later take up the practice will find these attitudes already established and, after the fashion of followers everywhere, they will tend to conform to the patterns already marked out for them.

This manner of origination and growth of the practice of germinal choice must result in the generation by it, in its early stages, of a clearly exemplary lot of children. These living object lessons will constitute the most persuasive argument to others, and will thereby lead to ever firmer acceptance and greater prevalence of the practice. At the same time, progress will gradually be made in regard to other matters underlying the making of effective choices. For one thing, the available stores of germinal material will be considerably added to. Secondly, the techniques concerned with reproduction, including germ cell processing and cultivation, will be improved, perhaps radically. Thirdly, the methods of forming genetic judgments and of getting data for them will become more advanced. Fourthly, the public will become better educated and motivated with regard to genetics and evolution in general, and with regard to human needs, means and goals in particular. Fifthly, the whole field of evolutionary possibilities, values, and directions will be subjected to ever more searching investigation, criticism, and creative thinking. In all these connections, moreover, the fact should not be lost sight of that whatever increment the practice of germinal choice may produce in the number of persons at the uppermost levels of understanding and of social propensities—and some tangible increment of these kinds should appear even in the early stages—this increment will, by a process of positive feedback, exert an influence in better promoting all the advances previously mentioned. Thus the process will be self-increasing.

## THE TRANSITION IN MOTIVATIONS

However, so deep-seated a change in human outlook and conduct as that here discussed must inevitably be confronted by powerfully psychological obstacles. These will take the form both of habits of mind that are ingrained in the individuals and appear to them as self-evidently right, and of social institutions, including legal and religious forms, that support, sanction, and sanctify the individuals' feelings and convictions. Nevertheless, we know, from the differences found in the attitudes and practices of different peoples and also from the drastic changes in such respects that have occurred before our eyes within a few decades, under the impact of recent economic, political, scientific and technical revolutions, that even changes of the magnitude here in question lie well within the range of plasticity of the individual and of society.

The central psychological obstacle in the present situation is the attitude of individual genetic proprietorship, or pride of so-called "blood." Its artificiality is evident in the desire of a man, and also of his wife, to have a child who will hand down his name, that is, a son, although in genetic fact his daughters inherit some 5% more of his genes. Of course in primitive societies that did not realize that the father played a role in conception no such feeling of *genetic* proprietorship of the male could exist. In fact, even in some not-so-primitive societies, such as those of Eskimos or Polynesians or Ethiopians to whom the role of the male in conception is known, there is nevertheless no strong feeling of *genetic* proprietorship attached by him to his children. Thus it is often felt an honor, by husband as well as by wife, if she has a child by some distinguished visitor, and the child is as well loved and cared for as the ones whom she has conceived by her husband. The same genuine attachment is seen to spring up, even in our own society, for children who have been adopted early, when they were really wanted by the couple.

It is clear that the natural attachment for one's children results from the experiences of close association with them, of nurturing and sustaining them, and of being loved, trusted, and played with by them in return. Natural selection has provided us with the predisposition of having these feelings aroused in us in these ways, since this arrangement was of survival value for the species. But of course we are also equipped by nature with egotistic emotions, leading to vanity. Consequently, once we know of the existence of biological inheritance or genes we may become inclined to rate our own genes and our own idiosyncracies above those of others. Thus also we tend to see in our genetic descendants an extension of ourselves, such that their progress reflects credit on us, and their survival is our survival.

However, a more realistic consideration of the situation will show our own particular genetic combination to be, in the long view, very ephemeral, usually much more so than the ways of thought and feeling that we transmit culturally in our families. It will usually show, in addition, that we have about as much to be ashamed of in ourselves genetically as to be proud of. It will reveal us as being one small even though potentially significant mote in the whole human assemblage, a mote constitutionally inclined to overestimate itself. This greater realism will lead us to see that we can lead much more meaningful lives if, instead of insisting that just exactly our own genetic peculiarities be handed down, we exert ourselves to leave humanity better and stronger than we found it, either culturally or genetically or both, by whatever means we can most effectively accomplish this. By this course, moreover, we will actually do more to bring about the continuance, with enhancement, of what is best within ourselves, and we will thus partake in greater measure in humanity's continuance.

For we are, potentially at least, beings who can reason and who can create with our minds and hands, and for whom it is natural to use these means to further the well-being and promote the advancement of our species. It is this potentiality which is most characteristically human in us, and most valuable. We can be truest to our own natures and we can achieve the best grounded self-respect if our efforts in these directions have been significant. In relation to the question here confronting us, this means that—to paraphrase what my friend Calvin Kline has said—we should feel prouder of what we have consciously produced by means of our head, hands and heart than of what we have automatically produced by means of our own reproductive system. And let us hope that later generations also will judge us rather by the progress that we have thereby implemented for them by means of our conscious strivings, including those of germinal choice, than by the foibles that our own personal genes may happen to give expression to among them in ages to come. That is, our truest genetic contribution to posterity would consist of our brain children, those fathered by our deliberate germinal choices. It is in successors of this kind, therefore, that we could, on genetic grounds, take the most justifiable pride.

Similarly, in regard to the legacy of a cultural sort that we bequeath to posterity, our truest individual projection into the future in cultural respects resides in the persons of those in whom, through the rearing and education they received from us, our spirits have become imbued. If at the same time these persons represented our germinal choices we would achieve a form of survival more genuine than that prevalent today. All these considerations show how essential it is, for the couples undertaking pre-adoption, that the privilege of choosing the germinal material be vested in them. It is mainly this aspect of the matter that raises the process into an act of creation on their part, and this act far transcends in its creativeness that of ordinary reproduction. Herein lies one of the principal inducements and sources of strength for the new morality of reproduction as compared with the old. In this way human freedom and human rights are extended into a new dimension.

The pathway to germinal choice that we have discussed is the most direct one. But, just as has happened in the case of other techniques that raised radically new possibilities, multiple pathways are opened that all lead in essentially the same direction, out of the mores of the past. Thus, the new possibility of readily storing germ cells in a deeply frozen condition offers an obvious means of germinal protection for the increasing number of persons who are subject to exposure to influences damaging to their genetic material or to their capability of reproduction. Among such influences are irradiation, such as might be received in high-altitude or space flights, in work with sources of radiation, or in war. Mutagenic chemicals constitute another considerable group. Even against bodily injuries that resulted in sterilization or in death itself such storage might be desired by some couples as a germinal insurance. In these ways the stores could be considerably augmented, and later generations might find some of this material of exceptional value.

A similar situation is likely to arise through the utilization of germcell storage as a complement to vasectomy, by the increasing numbers of men who would use such sterilization as the most effective and convenient means of birth control, provided only that they could be sure it was not irrevocable. Thereby the stores of germinal material might become vastly increased, by the contributions of persons who had also paid the costs of this service. And except in special cases, in which the donors had disapproved, some of this material also might later be made use of by others.

All this, by making a far wider range of choice available in the future, would be conducive to greater utilization of the stores by the population in general. Ideally, everyone for whom it was possible would come to adopt the insurance of having some of his germinal material subjected to long-term storage. Among the reserves thus accumulated there would inevitably be not a few, the value of which had not been recognized in their own time, but which became more adequately appreciated and utilized subsequently. Ultimately, then, the choices would not be limited by the decisions of a few individuals or groups who had controlled the acquisition of the stores. In this way the procedure would develop a broad and thoroughly democratic basis, and proceeding from this basis, with the aid of relevant records and counsel, each couple would strive for what in their considered judgment was the best.

## QUO VADIMUS?

Although such judgments must strive to be rational they must certainly be value judgments at the same time, as our intentional use of the word "best" in the preceding sentence implied. But there is no real contradiction here. For it is the function of all rationality to work out ways of gaining our ends, that is, of more effectively pursuing and promoting our values. Moreover, since different values of ours sometimes run counter to one another, it must be a part of this operation to try by rational means to coordinate values, sometimes reconciling them, sometimes subordinating one to another, sometimes working out more basic values, the pursuit of which is more inclusive and results in greater all-round, long-term fulfillment.

Of course human nature is intrinsically many-sided, in that for a wholesome personality diverse psychological needs must all be met, as for instance love of a number of kinds, including a feeling of oneness with one's fellows and even with nature, esthetic excitement of varied types, joy in work and accomplishment, curiosity, hope, and zest in diverse bodily feelings. All these, and much more, must have an opportunity for fulfillment if the spirit is not to suffer, in some direction, from a deprivation that, becoming ever more gnawing, tends to eat out the heart of the whole. We have been shaped to have all these needs, and therefore these values, because our efforts to meet them result, on the whole, in the enhancement of our strength in ways that serve the survival and advancement of the species. Moreover, the values are in the main so balanced and adjusted that in conflicts between them those take precedence the pursuit of which result in longer-range fulfillment for us or at least for our fellows. In static societies folk mores and codes, themselves worked out through long experience, often aid in charting the course through such situations. But individual reasoning is also indispensible in gauging the possible effects of different choices. And in societies that are undergoing change, as a result of the introduction of techniques, knowledge, or points of view new to them, the old codes may fail and individual reasoning must assume more responsibility.

At any rate, if reason shows that the individual's actions in pursuit of certain more immediate desires are such as to be conducive to his earlier death, or to his misery in the future, the reasonable individual will if at all possible sacrifice the present for the future, although on rare occasions his fortitude or self-control may be sufficient and intense pain or some unbearable deprivation or overriding emotion may cause him to act against his own interests. Similarly, he will, if he has a socially oriented upbringing, tend to identify his interests with those of his fellows, or of the species, in consequence both of his native fellow-feeling and of his realization that this constitutes his greater self. He will therefore make similar sacrifices for his community, his group, or his species, subject to the limitation that when personal deprivations are carried too far the returns become too greatly diminished, both for him in a personal, psychological sense and in regard to his effectiveness in serving others.

All this, then, shows that the multiple values of humanity, while real, are subordinate to the value represented by service to the community in general. They occupy this subordinate position not only as a result of biological natural selection but also, in a more decided way, in the codes of almost any community, and, finally, in the judgment of the rational individual who is at the same time socially minded.

It is not surprising, in view of all this, that despite the enormous differences in the traditions, religions, and social customs of different human groups, the more prevalent groups have developed very much the same set of basic ethical values, and that, on the whole, these serve the more general aim of promoting the welfare of the group. Moreover, any such set of values, concerned with the pursuit of psychological and material objectives, also has implications regarding the relative esteem in which different traits of character, mentality and disposition are held. For the more approved traits will be those more conducive to the pursuit of the recognized ethical values; hence they too must be such as to promote the well-being of the family and group to which the individual belongs. It follows that throughout most of the world, and in cultures of varied kinds, especially high approval has been given to the types of character that are strong in genuine fellow-feeling, love, sympathy, benevolence, and integrity, and that accordingly find expression in what we call the Golden Rule. Likewise highly approved in most societies are wisdom and mental capability in general, including competence in expression and in workmanship. Occupying high places also are fortitude, stability, joy of life, and perceptivity.

This whole combination of faculties, working together, which we may epitomize by the term "cooperatively acting intelligence" or "intelligent cooperation," is the combination, unique in man, which has enabled him alone to engage in social evolution. thereby developing civilization and finally science, and giving him unprecedented ascendancy among all living things. It would have been strange if man had not realized that these were the faculties of supreme importance for him and had not exalted them accordingly in his cultural codes and institutions. Yet during the historic period the emphasis on these traits has often been so vehement, even so desperate, as to disclose that men in general still fall pretty far short in these respects, as compared with the models held before them in parable, precept, and fable. This is only to be expected, for these qualities are needed even more, under conditions of modern civilization, than we usually have them, yet the processes of natural selection that developed their genetic basis have been slackening. Unquestionably the human race would be better off if men in general had the native endowments, in regard to these faculties, possessed by those individuals already among them who have them in highest degree.

That people have a basic realization of these shortcomings is shown by their repeated and often pathetic strivings to do better in these regards and also by the prevalence of feelings of guilt regarding their own nature. Surely the great majority of them would jump at the chance if they could somehow come closer to their own ideals of the good, the wise, and the capable. Similarly, they would eagerly seize such an opportunity for their children, unless they were held back by the grip of ancient tradition.

We should not deny that, barring world catastrophe, social reforms and improvements in upbringing will enable people in the future to attain much higher levels of feeling, understanding, and performance than those of today, even without changes in their genetic endowment. Perhaps too, some day (and some of my biologist friends think it will be soon), advances in the control of physiological and developmental processes will be of powerful aid for the same purposes. However, the higher the native capacities are, the more potent will the influence of an improved environment be in enabling the individual to attain to greater heights. Let us, then, do the best we can for later generations by the means that we have already gained.

It is nevertheless true that different existing cultures, despite their basic agreements, place somewhat different emphases upon the different faculties mentioned. However, this tendency toward diversity is rather to be welcomed than deplored, especially in a time like ours, in which we are aware of only the general direction of the light. Likewise, the special preferences that different groups, families, and individuals have for particular abilities and predispositions (e.g. volubility versus reserve), like their preferences for different bodily characteristics, will be serviceable in enriching the factual basis for later judgments, the future range of choice, and the potential versatility, available to people of coming generations, provided only that the clearly basic values noted above, those common to mankind in general, have also been striven for.

Beyond this, however, it should also be recognized that large groups in all present societies are still relatively undeveloped ethically. Some follow ancient patterns of thought that included no idea of progress and allowed little or no opportunity for decison-making regarding matters of principle. One of the traits of character they would value most is rigorous conformity and adherence to archaic modes of thought and behavior. Others, such as some teenage delinquents, acknowledge practically no standards or ideals except for the fads they avidly follow, the appeal of which is superficial and escapist. Again, there are great numbers uncritical enough to allow themselves to be duped and stampeded by paranoid demagogues and dictators. How can these powerful trends be reconciled with any salutary democratic form of germinal choice?

Our previous discussion has stressed the essential role of sound education in the principles of evolution and genetics, especially as they apply to man, in lifting people to a higher sense of their responsibility toward future generations, and in making them more conscious of the unique combination of faculties that lies at the root of mankind's greatness, but that is still in sore need of enhancement for meeting the ever more difficult problems of modern civilization. It is of course the people who have been deeply reached by this education, who will tend to feel stirred at the prospect of participating in the promotion of human progress. Just this group will also have an especially well crystallized awareness of the basic human values to be striven for, and their main objective will in fact be the furtherance of these values themselves. Moreover, being a vanguard group, one courageously challenging traditional mores, they will be unusually predisposed to recognize the major importance, for sustained progress, of those components of character and intellect that make for creativity, honesty in thinking, moral courage, and venturesomeness— attributes that tended to be inadequately appreciated throughout the long periods when the culture of mankind was nearly static. In this way the ground will be laid for genetic progress in the direction most needed by a democratic society.

The precedent thus set will be reinforced as the children thus engendered, reaching maturity, are seen to enjoy, on the whole, unusually favorable endowments. Moreover, during the same period, a very much larger section of the public is likely to have acquired a point of view much like that which had actuated the pioneers in germinal choice. For it is to be anticipated that in progressive countries—again, barring global catastrophe—there will have been a further extension, deepening, and integration of education, bringing to nearly everyone a realization of the evolutionary basis of the world and man, together with an awareness of both the grave dangers and the stirring possibilities ahead of us. At the same time, the social advances are likely to have been such as to lead to an increasing conviction that democratic methods must be used, and developed further, for meeting the great challenges confronting mankind. Thus the time will have come when the example that had been provided by the pioneers of germinal choice will be far better appreciated, and will be followed, in its selection of aims as well as in its methods, by a considerable and growing portion of the population.

Any powerful tool can be misused, but that is all the more reason why, if it falls into good hands, it should be used, and used well, for otherwise it will be left only for those who would misuse it. Certainly a Hitler or a Mussolini might be able to establish among his people a vicious form of controlled reproduction—controlled by him, and perhaps producing a few mimics of himself and many docile slaves. Most likely this attempt would after a while defeat itself, but it could in the meantime do untold harm. However, such an undertaking would bear no more relation to that of germinal choice than the use of an ax in killing a man bears to its use in building a house. In both cases, it would be equally senseless to prohibit all use of the instrument in order to prevent its misuse. On the contrary, a people who had engaged in actual germinal choice would be especially likely to resent the interference of a dictator, to be appalled at his aims, and to join in overthrowing him.

Signs of paranoid tendencies are among the expressions of unsound mentality that persons engaged in germinal choice for the purpose of enhancing basic human values would be especially alerted to, and likely to recognize and detest. Obviously, paranoids, as well as exhibitionists and "four flushers" generally, would try to put themselves forward for multiple propagation. But that is a main reason why records, counsel, and a period of serious deliberation are advisable, before any choice is decided upon. Similarly, both members of the couple should have passed the age (at least 21) before which flippancy and irresponsibility are too prevalent.

However, the feature of the method that would do the most to prevent the making of mistakes of the kind in question lies in the requirement that, after enough time has passed to make such a rule possible, only germinal material that has been preserved for at least twenty years after the decease of the donor be put to use. During this period any natural children of a prospective donor, having grown up, may have added a little to the data available for genetic judgments concerning him. But the main function of such a "cooling-off" interval is that it will provide time for the specious pretensions of the megalomaniac, and charlatan, the empty charmer, the unscrupulous schemer, the "big brass," and the eminent "stuffed shirt" to have become recognizable for the shams they really were. Conversely, solid worth will be likely to have withstood much better the attritions of storm and tide, and to have become more clearly manifest.

The above discussion has concerned itself almost entirely with psychological traits, because these are the ones in which progress is most important for our species. However, as will be almost universally agreed, a worthy mind and a wholesome character can develop and function more effectively, and can attain deeper, more all-around fulfillment, if harbored in a sound body. To be sure, concessions can be condoned in regard to some less essential attributes when these are far overshadowed by outstanding worth in more important respects. Yet on the whole the salient bodily benefits will also be sought for. Among the more significant of these are a high degree of physical command over one's person, general health and vigor, and delayed senescense.

On the other hand, the conspicuous differences in physical characteristics of form and coloration which engage to much popular attention at present represent in large degree matters of "taste." Disputation concerning these would be not merely foolish but even dangerous. Any given people, within the course of only a few centuries, is likely to change its own ideal of figures and features. This is readily seen on comparison of the portraits made in the same country in two different periods, for in these portraits the eminent personages of the day are shown with their features subtly warped, into closer conformity than they really were with the then popular ideal type. Thus the American heroes of 1776 tended to be shown with prominent or aquiline noses, whereas the "arrow-collar 100%" Americans of 150 years later were represented with short straight noses. Meanwhile, cosmetics can engage in almost as much remodelling as the artists. So we may, in a neutralist spirit, leave such fads to run their courses, if they must, and may remember that the counter currents in different places and times will tend to balance one another, and to maintain a kaleidoscopic variety of superficial multiformity that will continue to lend spice to personal associations.

## WHY PROGRESS?

Whenever a new way of life, challenging to the old mores, presents itself, all sort of arguments, often mutually contradictory, are thought up, in the attempt to prove that the old ways are better. Thus in the ancient Roman world, in the period when its own malpractices were leading toward its disintegration, most priests and rulers found the doctrines of Christian charity, of the brotherhood of man, and of the non-divinity of the emperor, most reprehensible and subversive, and put up what they thought a strong case against such heresies. Not long afterwards, however, these alleged aberrations became generally accepted throughout the same region, albeit usually in a rather perverted form that allowed major concessions to the predatory practices of those in positions for perpetrating them. But as time has gone on increasing numbers have realized that ours would be a much happier world if these professed principles were to be further incorporated into the structure of society and more wholeheartedly followed in individual living.

The advances in democracy and in the acceptance of human rights, continued over a dozen centuries but with much greater momentum recently, have shown that it is in fact possible for life to be lived much more humanely than was commonly the case in imperial Rome, especially when the technical and economic reforms associated both as cause and effect with these changes in outlook are included in the picture. The enormous benefits, both material and psychological, have been obvious. Unquestionably humanity can travel much further along this road, especially if more attention is paid to making the upbringing of children and also the conditions of life and work of adults more wholesome, freer from unnecessary repressions, and provided with greater scope for work that is appreciated and companionship that is reciprocated.

However, even this is only part of the story. For although those cynics may be decadent who see the element of tragedy as necessarily the most significant thread in all human life, and who maintain that under almost every human mask there lurks a demon of ingrowing desperation, nevertheless it must in common honesty be admitted that the tragic conflicts that take place within most normal individuals are not all caused by faulty upbringing and avoidable evils in the social system. They are in no small measure also the result of the fact that some of our urges, natural to primitive man, such as those which express themselves in combat, must be curbed to a degree uncomfortable to us, to allow the functioning of civilized society, while, conversely, some of our other impulses, such as those expressed in civilized amenities toward persons in competition with us, may be so inadequate as to be replaced by a guilt-ridden and frustrating hypocrisy.

Thus, men grievously need the Golden Rule, but the Golden Rule grievously needs men in whose very nature it is more deeply rooted than in ours. These men would not require the wills of saints, for their way of life would be normal to them. They would take it for granted, and could live full wholesome lives, joyously carrying out the ever greater enterprises made possible for their strengthened individual initiative, working hand in hand in free alliance with their enhanced cooperative functionings. At the same time their personal relations would be warmer and more genuine, so that they could enjoy more of the love that gives itself away. Along with this, less forcing would be required of them in extending their feelings of kinship to those more remote from their contacts.

We do not argue that any personality can be free from inner conflicts. For almost all acts of life in a complex world call for the organization of one's urges and the consequent subordination of some to others. However, a nature in which there was a stronger genetic basis for the positive affections, led by love, and a lesser basis for the negative ones, which reach their acme in hate, would find itself much less wracked and strained in bending its efforts so as best to serve society than would a nature having the genetic basis of the man of today, which is surely the same as that of the man of the stone age. Moreover, in a society in which more individuals were similarly endowed in this respect, an individual more nearly in accord with this ideal would find ampler and deeper reciprocation. Thus the sacrifices involved in the pursuit of "the good" would be minimized both from without and from within the individual.

At this point a digression may be made in order to clear up possible misconceptions regarding the degreee of certainty involved in genetic selection for traits of the kind in question. Few persons acquainted with genetic principles would any longer dispute the important role played by differences in genes in causing persons to differ markedly in respect to the strength of the affective traits here under discussion, as well as in regard to emotional propensities in general. Such genetically based differences are of course more readily demonstrated in studies of psychologically less advanced animals, as in comparisons between different breeds of dogs, since here the relevant environmental factors can be better equalized, and the genetic differences are more uniform. These studies have shown the existence of very marked differences in such respects, while of course these differences are even greater between different species, some being far more socially disposed than others. There is no reason to question the existence of similar differences in man.

Nevertheless, as we have previously pointed out, ethnic and social groups cannot be compared genetically in regard to these traits, because of the large and more or less consistent differences in their cultural backgrounds. Moreover, since these backgrounds also differ markedly from one individual to another within the same group, the genetic differences even between the individuals of the group are commonly obscured and overlaid by the environmental ones. Yet, as in the case of all traits that are strongly influenced in their development by both hereditary and environmental factors, we can be reasonably sure that individuals who are clearly outstanding in some such respect do have a marked genetic basis for it, as well as an environmental basis. Consequently, intentionally practised selection that is based on the character as it is actually expressed will exert considerable genetic influence in the given direction, just as natural selection does.

In this connection it should be distinctly understood that one can hardly ever be sure, in advance, of the result of any given conception. This is not only because we cannot know the degree of influence of the environment on the parents and the offspring in the given case, but also because the random play of genetic segregation and recombination prevents the prediction of just what will be inherited. But, for all that, there will be a trend, and the trend will be strong enough to allow highly significant genetic results to be obtained in just one generation of selection. That this must be the case is evident from the fact that, genetically, the child stands *on the average* half way between his two parents. To couples engaging in germinal choice the individual uncertainties involved will be made clear. Those who decide for it will be the ones who accept these uncertainties and hold them to be, for them, outweighed by the propitious individual possibilities, and by the promise inherent in the over-all trend.

The same kind of considerations apply to selection for psychological traits concerned with any aspects of intelligence. This is because the intelligence of an individual, like his emotional make-up, is the resultant of a highly organized biological system, the development of which depends on many different genes and also on many features of the individual's environment, especially his cultural environment and his experiences generally. In fact, since intelligence actually consists in the ability to adjust and readjust, according to previous as well as present experiences, it is in a sense the most subject to modification by the environment of all the individual's functions. Accordingly, we may readily be led to wrong conclusions regarding the relative mental capabilities of groups, as well as of individuals, as a result of their having had very different cultural opportunities to develop in one or another mental direction.

And yet, it is also clear that, between individuals of any one human group, enormous genetic differences in mental capability also exist, ranging them all the way from hopeless idiots to persons who, given only an average chance, will be likely to make a highly meritorious contribution of some kind, that involves really creative thinking. Persons of the latter type, moreover, are far more aided in their mental development by a given amount of improvement in their environmentally based conditions and opportunities than are those of average native ability. Here again, then, those who have become genuinely outstanding are sure to represent not only a favourable environment but also a very fortunate genetic endowment. Moreover, evidence exists that some relatively rare individual genes have decided effects of this kind, giving relatively sharp segregation within families. Among these there are some concerned with rather specialized types of mental ability and others very generalized in their effects.

The same kind of case exists for the conclusion that man under modern civilization would be better off if the genetic basis of his mentality were to be raised, so as to be comparable with that of the most intelligent persons now living, as for our previous conclusion that he would greatly benefit by the raising of the genetic basis of his affective social proclivities. One of the greatest bugbears of our present-day youth consists of the painful efforts they expend in trying to glimpse—or to *evade* glimpsing—a pitiful few of the highlights of the modern view of the world they live in, of human relations, and of the activities of mankind. This is the view that natural and social scientists, along with engineers and other specialists in techniques, have succeeded in winning for them. By no means all of this inadequacy of our youth arises from faulty methods in bringing up and educating them. Yet it is of practical importance for the people in general to have a sound grasp of many of these matters that have thus far eluded them, if their country and their world is to be run democratically, in their own (and therefore in mankind's) true interests. For the knowledge does exist, in bits, and it is being used—or abused— by persons of partial vision, and of insular allegiances, in ways that could lead to disaster, rather than to the increasing triumphs of humanity that all-around understanding, coupled with social motivation, would achieve. Thus, it is imperative that the people's voice in matters of general policy, and also in more special matters, be an intelligent voice, and today this has as one of its major requirements a scientific understanding.

Aside from these more directly practical considerations, we should not overlook the enormous enrichment of life that a more adequate view of the world and man, as disclosed by modern science, can bring to those participating heartily in this breath-taking experience. For those to whom it comes readily, and even for those who find it laborious but possible and worth-while, there is an enormous exhilaration in mastering the principles underlying the workings and structure of the natural world, and also of the uses to which they may be put by man, in following the paths by which these principles were discovered, and in contemplating the grand panoramas as well as the vignettes of existence as already perceived. There is additional stimulation for those who press the quest further, for the greater extension of our vision.

All this is in a sense a human birthright, and those who would confine it to a tiny aristocracy of intellect, as it is confined today, are guilty of the same kind of snobbery as were those who believed in hiding "higher studies" from the masses by expressing them only in Latin. Yet today, for most of humanity, much of this knowledge, most of the thought processes involved, are inescapably locked up in what to them must remain an unreadable Latin. It is the right of the man of the future to gain the transcendent view to which his eyes of today cannot penetrate. It is the duty of the people of our own times to help in making this possible for our successors, by taking the steps that would endow men with the invaluable gift of ready understanding.

But still we meet objectors who complain that man should not be too intelligent for his circumstances. A nation of intellectuals, they say, is unhappy in a world where the majority must be hewers of wood and drawers of water. This is truly a short-sighted view, the view of the slave-owner. It ignores the fact, attested to by history, that the more men's eyes are opened and the greater social and technical freedoms they win, the more do they themselves find ways to reduce their routine labor. The more do they devise means of operating on a higher level, utilizing calculations, machines, psychology, medicine, social science, so as to allow them ever greater scope for more engrossing enterprises, deeper quests, nobler constructions, farther ranging adventures. Man not merely discovers world beyond world, he also creates them. But to do so he must advance within himself. And it would be shameful to deny these opportunities to men in general.

Finally, let us consider the objection that man in any given period cannot foretell what his situation and requirements will be in later generations and that therefore by trying to remold himself according to his present lights and values he may be actually unfitting himself for the future (see for instance Dubos, 1962). For with changes in culture and unforeseeable improvements in knowledge and techniques, it is said, present needs are likely no longer to apply, and some present evils, as we now regard them, may even turn out to be advantages or virtues. So, for example (if we may put words into the mouths of our critics), an earlier generation, using such methods, might have tried to make us parsimonious rather than generous in our ways, dogged rather than flexible, submissive rather than independent of mind, content to get along with little rather than eager to create much. It should be admitted that there are plenty among us who hold such an attitude still, although they are surely not the ones who will lead the way in germinal choice.

In brief, these objectors are defendants of a biological *status quo* or *laisser faire* policy, on the ground (or is it an excuse?) that we are *not progressive enough,* being too short-sighted to know what will be good for us. Can these critics really believe that the persons of unusual moral courage, progressive spirit, and eagerness to serve mankind, who will pioneer in germinal choice, and likewise those who in a more enlightened age will follow in the path thus laid down, will fail to recognize the fundamental human values stressed in our earlier discussion? Or do they really believe that people in general already have in sufficient degree the faculties which make for willing cooperation, that they have quite enough native keenness of intellect, and a bountiful supply of those subsidiary attributes, such as perceptivity, curiosity, expressivity, that render these primary faculties more effective? Do they think that it would be dangerous to have most men as socially motivated, or as able intellectually, as they themselves are? Or would they regard it as a pity and a danger if most men actually excelled them in these respects?

Surely the fundamental values here sought do not represent the short-sighted choices of today or yesterday alone. An enhancement of the faculties by which they are pursued would never make men less suited for "the good life," or for further progressive evolution—quite the contrary. It is these faculties, primarily, which render man so adaptable, and it is because we already have them in some measure that we can recognize their worth and contrive to gain them in greater measure. If in any future culture the possession of these faculties would become a hindrance or if a lesser development of them would tend to make men more comfortable or more numerous, then that culture would be a decadent one. In that case it would become the first job of man's cooperatively acting intelligence to alter his culture, in such wise as again to promote the forward march of his understanding and of his community of feeling.

Aside from these primary objectives in germinal choice, there would as we have said previously, be room for manifold divergencies in details. Thus, there might even be minor groups striving in such different directions as boisterousness versus reticence, intense drive versus meditative calm, or versatility versus single-mindedness. There would also be those who strove to emphasize some special gift or proclivity, such as a musical bent, love of bodily effort, unusual kinesthetic sensibility, high retentiveness, etc., etc. But all this kind of division of aim in regard to these lesser propensities would serve to increase the wealth of faculties of the future population. And that population would then be better alerted for considering such problems, and provided with a better basis for assessing the consequences of the varied choices.

There is of course no such thing as the "ideal man," or the ideal organism, and persons (e.g. Dobzhansky, 1962, Dubos, 1962) who charge the advocates of germinal choice with fostering such a goal have either failed to read or failed to grasp the ideas involved. This by no means signifies that "ideals" in a more general sense form no part of the picture, for ideals in the sense of values, and directions in which to strive, are of course of the essence of the matter. But there can, for the person aware of the courses and principles of evolution, be no final, perfect end, certainly not man as he is today, either biologically or culturally. Neither could we regard as near "the end" a population patterned after the persons of greatest mind, heart, and spirit who have ever lived. However, a population possessed of such qualities, if also balanced by a good infusion of the hardihood, humility, and common sense of the "common man," would nevertheless represent a considerable step in a progressive direction.

Where we would proceed from there is a matter we need not worry about now. It would be arrogant and absurd to think that we could at present do better in seeing ahead of such a stage than could the people who had already arrived at it. Let us be glad that the way does indeed seem to be open ended, but let us not take that idea as an excuse for not moving forward where we can in fact see the direction of advance. The greatest contribution that we, as paltry individuals, can make is to aid in getting us to the next step. And as the advance continues, it can become surer, more purposeful, and more effective, and the making of it will constitute the highest expression of human freedom.

# Public Health Considerations

❍ ❍ ❍

22.

## PUBLIC HEALTH IN AN
## OVERPOPULATED WORLD

*by John E. Gordon and Hazel Elkington*

The startlingly rapid growth of world population brings two-fold demands on the public health profession.[1] First, the health needs of existing numbers of people have to be met: numbers already are so great, and increasing to such extent, as to exceed facilities and the capacity of available trained health workers. This is a technical and administrative problem, appreciated by the profession, costly in terms of time and money. Secondly public health must assume its share of responsibility for creating public awareness of a population problem that is both world-wide and local; and take action to find a solution.

The two obligations have equal significance. Both warrant attention, but the second is the root of the problem. The potential development of public health is inhibited not so much by lack of progress in enlarging its capacities and improving its methods as in dilution of services by the increased numbers of people requiring them. The central difficulty is of populations constantly outgrowing facilities.

### PEOPLE AND RESOURCES

Economic and social progress depends on continuously adapting people to resources and resources to people.[2] Much of the benefit from agricultural and industrial expansion is being dissipated in taking care of growing numbers of people. Modern methods of production will result in an increasing supply of goods and services. Given time and relatively stable numbers, economic use of resources and technological inventions yet to come will increase the rate at which living standards rise. Together with education and industrialization these are the broad long-term forces tending toward a solution of the population problem.

Public health has a powerful potential influence on the future turn of events. Anti-malarial measures have already opened up huge fertile areas in India, Ceylon and Java for cultivation of food. On the other hand, some major breakthrough in medical science could well result in a means for prevention or cure of any one of the five leading causes of death, and consequently in many more lives being prolonged. Conversely, a disease occasionally becomes resistant to known therapy: antibiotics are already losing their effectiveness against some infectious agents. Or again, a now benign disease may take a virulent form, as influenza has done repeatedly in the past.

The current situation permits no temporizing. Increases in population continue to exceed expansion of resources: and ultimately, unless means are found to create a satisfactory balance, the result will be a lower standard of living for all and, at the worst, social unrest, disease and famine. With the momentum now under way in population growth, all agencies of society are of necessity involved in the search for a solution.

The factors responsible for increased numbers of people are manifold.[3] Man in the beginning was equipped with sexual drives and capacities designed for a primitive and dangerous environment. Those were the days when less than half of children born survived to adult age. Meanwhile the social, biological and even the physical environment has changed. In earlier days modification of the environment came slowly, because the means to change fundamental conditions were poor. Modern technology has played an important part but no more than medical science. The concern of public health with improved environmental sanitation, the provision of pure and adequate water supplies, the prevention and control of communicable diseases through immunization, insecticides and antibiotics, and the mounting attention to nutritional disorders, have been the major factors in achieving dramatically lower death rates.

Advances in life expectancy that took a century to accomplish in Western nations are now being made in a decade or two in some of today's pre-industrial societies. In Ceylon, for example, life expectancy rose from 32 years in 1921 to 60 years by 1954. The death rate dropped from 19.8 per 1000 population in 1946 to 12.3 in 1949 following institution of malaria control.[4] In the Bursa province of Turkey at a time when rice cultivation was practiced, malaria was endemic and the death rate about 28. In 1941 mosquito breeding was attacked through prohibiting rice culture and malaria control methods were applied on a wide scale. By 1947 the death rate had fallen to 10.

Death rates tend to decline universally while birth rates generally remain high. In repeated instances the lost balance between births and deaths has resulted in the substitution of one health problem for another, a population problem for a specific disease.[5]

The population problem affects most aspects of human welfare. The health professions have no more obligation than any other discipline to search for a solution, yet some of the necessary action and research is peculiarly within the competence of medical practitioners, administrators and investigators.

The problems of more people, different kinds of people and national interdependence require that public health expand its traditional concern with the control of deaths to include control of births. In Europe, population growth has been halted from time to time by plague, famine and war. During the 18th and 19th centuries, vast numbers of people emigrated to the New Worlds.[6] Then came limitation of births by means available and suitable to the particular people concerned. Roman Catholic France evolved a pattern of population control along lines that differ materially from those of Roman Catholic Ireland or Protestant England. Today there are no new world frontiers with emigration a ready solution: therefore a selective reduction in births would appear to be the only answer.

Of known birth control measures, no one procedure is suited to all cultures, but at least one is available for any particular society. Methods include mechanical means such as the condom, diaphragm and douche: chemical jellies, creams and foam tablets: and, taking advantage of physiological processes, the rhythm method or safe period. A variety of steroid compounds have been developed as effective contraceptives in pill form, but to date the cost is prohibitive for people of low-income countries and the compound must be taken every day for 20 days between menstrual periods, a further disadvantage. Much research is in progress toward an improved oral contraceptive of longer action, and economically within the means of needy families. In the meantime, other proved and inexpensive methods are available, perhaps not wholly ideal but within a range of effectiveness sufficient for a practical control of conception.

Population control measures have been known and practiced in varying degree in all cultures throughout recorded history. Primitive methods now largely discounted for moral or ethical reasons have ranged from infanticide to abortion and senilicide. Unhappily, the practice of abortion persists and is currently a serious health problem in many countries in spite of religious, medical and commonly legal sanctions against it. More than one million induced abortions per year are reported in Japan, or roughly one for every live birth. Induced abortion was legalized in Japan in 1948. In European countries the incidence of illegal abortions per thousand live births is estimated to range from 300 in Czechoslovakia to over 1000 in Hungary. In Chile, the estimate is of 500 per 1000 and the practice is seemingly widespread throughout Latin America. In Turkey, the high incidence with resulting detriment to the health of mothers and children is considered almost as urgent a problem as that of tuberculosis. Abortions are frequent in the United States. According to the Kinsey report, 22% of married white females had had at least one induced abortion by the time they were 45 years of age. By 40 years of age, 25% of single white females had become pregnant and between 88 and 95% of these extramarital conceptions were resolved by abortion. The prevalence of abortion suggests a demand by the public for some form of birth control. It is a major method of birth control for millions of people. The alternative is family planning by contraception, or sterilization.

Sterilization is practiced extensively in Puerto Rico and performed at many public hospitals for a minimal fee. Hill, Stycos & Back reported that sterilizations in public and private hospitals corresponded to 17.8% of total hospital deliveries for 1949, and as many as one fifth of all wives had had what is locally termed "the operation." Sterilization is practiced increasingly in other countries, including India, Japan and Pakistan. While less objectionable than abortion, no such drastic and irreversible method of birth control is believed universally suited to the common need. As with abortion, a more reasonable substitute is seemingly family planning by contraception.

Birth control by whatever means is a concept foreign to many societies. The cultural obstacles blocking the rapid adoption of contraceptive practices often appear insuperable. Birth control cannot be forced on a people, nor should it be withheld from those who want it. To be widely acceptable, methods must conform to religious and cultural patterns, be simple, cheap, efficient, safe, reversible, and with no side effects. No one method meets all these requirements, but within varying degrees of efficiency and acceptability suitable methods exist and more become available. The main difficulty lies in getting people to use them.

The ultimate responsibility for limiting family size rests with the individual couple. Deaths within a population have declined largely by reason of medical progress implemented in its practical applications by government and society: the individual has had secondary responsibility. The control of births presents the opposite situation and is the harder task. Motivation is a vital consideration. The demonstration that five children are no longer necessary to assure that three live to become adults is a strong incentive. More survivors also provide visual evidence of the difficulties of providing proper education and material advantages.

## PUBLIC HEALTH AND POPULATION CONTROL

The approach of the individual and of society to birth control may be said to have been based thus far on principles of curative rather than preventive medicine.[7] People commonly resort to birth control when family size exceeds material resources. Their aim is to remedy or ameliorate a situation already developed. The more logical first step would appear to be adoption of the principles of prevention, to encourage spacing of births throughout childbearing age by inculcating in the newly married the advantages in health and welfare to be derived from using logic and reasoning in planning their families. Experimental evidence has shown spacing of births to be beneficial to the health of mothers and children: the optimum interval in a series of observations was three years between births. Evidence accumulates that shorter intervals result in higher morbidity and mortality, both of mothers and infants. Economically, the advantages of spacing are obvious: for example, the strain of putting three children through college at the same time, when one at a time could be financed. There is the basic obligation to provide for the physical and cultural needs of all living children before more are brought into the world. Planned spacing accomplishes a relative limitation of numbers.

The advantages of the preventive approach to family planning become evident when the desired number of children has been achieved. After couples have been accustomed to spacing their children, methods are familiar and experience has been acquired when the need so generally arises for limitation of size of family. While the active interest of individual families is essential for the success of any national program for population control, society also has an obligation.

With the world as it is today, every country would be wise to make a careful survey of its population to determine whether or not a problem of overpopulation exists, and if so to formulate a considered population policy. Some will find the remedy in inducing their people to cooperate, through educational campaigns on population control adequately supported by a defined public policy. In Western countries population control has come from individual conviction, but this is a slow process. In some parts of the world there is need for direct initiation of effort by government, and many have instituted programs for family planning under pressure of population increase. In some countries the government extends moral and financial support to voluntary organizations, in others the government itself has instituted programs.

In Japan a family planning program is administered centrally by the Ministry of Health and Welfare through the Maternal and Child Health

Section of the Children's Bureau.[8] Magazines, newspapers, radio, movies, lantern slides, all means of publicity are used and have exerted a noticeable effect on popular attitudes. Some large companies in business and industry include family planning services as part of welfare measures for their employees. The birth rate in Japan declined from 34.3 in 1947 to 17.5 in 1959, halved in little over a decade. The decline was achieved mainly through induced abortion, which developed to such extent as to become a matter of concern to the Japanese Government. According to the 6th of the two-year surveys conducted by the Population Problems Research Council of the Mainichi Newspapers in April 1961, 40% of women reported at least one abortion. Currently about 40,000 midwives have been licensed as family planning instructors, to work towards the substitution of conception control for abortion and sterilization: a reported 42.5% of wives in Japan under 50 years of age now use contraception.

In India the highest priority is given to family planning in the 3rd 5-Year Plan which began in April 1961. Operations center in the Ministry of Health, and birth control clinics are a feature of larger urban health departments. In rural districts family planning and public health activities are associated. A variety of contraceptive methods is offered, including rhythm. Sterilization is not generally used, although in Madras City a sterilization program was initiated in 1958. Men are paid 15 rupees ($3) and women 25 rupees ($5) to undergo the operation. The program was extended to the state of Madras 18 months later. The state of Maharashtra started a similar campaign in December, 1959.

A Family Planning Scheme, 1960-65, estimated to cost 6 million dollars was approved by the Pakistani cabinet in October, 1960. By November, 1961, there were 641 family planning centers in the country. A total of 530 doctors, 450 health visitors and nurses, and 5000 village aid workers had had training in the principles and methods of birth control directed towards staffing these centers and incorporating them in the public health work of the country. Male sterilization by vasectomy has been approved and is performed in government hospitals. The use of oral contraceptives is under consideration.

Other countries have organized similar services. In Barbados, government subsidized birth control clinics first opened in May, 1955. Hongkong has a government subsidized program carried out as part of the social welfare and public health activities of the colony. Korea has budgeted about $400,000 for expenditure on family planning in 1962, the emphasis to be on public education. A training program for doctors, nurses, midwives and community leaders began in November, 1961.

Progress in population control is limited among other things by lack of understanding of the processes of fertility. Population research to date has been predominantly demographic, social and economic, with secondary emphasis on biologic aspects. Many basic questions remain unanswered relating to menstruation, ovulation, conception, sterility and the diseases and physiologic states which modify fertility. Preoccupation with contraception should not cloud the opposite problem of helping women who want children but have difficulty in conceiving.

Many clinical trials of contraceptive measures have been made under the controlled conditions of hospital or outpatient clinic. The need is for more field trials in general populations, such as those of Koya[9] in rural Japan. The objective there was to determine how many people could be induced to take up contraception, how conscientiously they would follow the program, and finally to assess the effect of the program on population numbers as judged by birth rates. Some 1161 families in three rural villages were observed, beginning in 1950. Originally they were offered 8 different contraceptive methods: the condom proved the most popular, with diaphragm and jelly and the safe period (rhythm method) next in order. After 7 years, 75% of families were using some contraceptive measure. Birth rates were 26.7 per 1000 population before the program started: they dropped to 13.6 after 7 years, exceeding the decline in the country as a whole but achieved in this case mainly through use of contraception instead of abortion. In a coal mining village annual rates for abortions decreased from 16.2 to 8.4 per thousand population, while age adjusted birth rates declined from 27.6 to 13.9 per thousand.

Observations in a rural population of India, at Ramanagaram, Mysore state, and in a suburban population of New Delhi, beginning in 1952 and ending after 18 months, constitute the only field investigation concerned wholly with the rhythm method of contraception.[10] Data are available from other sources, but under conditions where rhythm was employed secondarily to some other agent or as one of several methods used. The studies suggest that the method is not the best for use in a general population. Some persons have difficulty because of menstrual irregularities: a high grade intelligence and motivation are required for its success. In this study relatively few took the trouble to learn its proper use and as a field trial the results were negative.

A study in 23 rural villages near Lucknow, India, by Baljit Singh has been in force since 1952. Materials and instruction on contraception by foam tablet, oil and sponge, and rhythm techniques were provided to a population of 8000 persons. Acceptance was greatest for foam tablets, but for all methods did not exceed one-third of eligible women. From the results obtained the conclusion is justified that the rhythm method is not suited to the Indian culture. The remaining two methods were rarely used.

The India-Harvard-Ludhiana study of population dynamics began in the autumn of 1953 in the Ludhiana district of the Punjab, northern India, and ended in July, 1960.[11] The aim was to determine whether contraception would be accepted and if so to evaluate its effectiveness. One village of 1087 people was observed in an exploratory study to determine choice of method. Five procedures were offered: rhythm, coitus interruptus, contraceptive paste and pad, salt solution and pad, foam tablets. Most people chose foam tablets. Subsequently this contraceptive method was the main reliance in the principal study, begun in 1956 and continued for 4 years. Although the initial enthusiasm was commendable, actual use according to directions over an appreciable time was at a low level, such that no measurable impact on birth rates was demonstrated. After 2½ years, 17% of all couples where the wife was 15 to 44 years old were using foam tablets. Another 8% were using the rhythm method or abstinence. The population of the villages remained close to stable, despite a high birth rate and a relatively low death rate, but the result came about through migration to other localities, primarily cities. With people as they are and with existing knowledge of the social and biological factors influencing birth rates, the fundamental impression was that control of population numbers is not to be had by a crash program centered in a few years of effort. The attempt to alter social habits is most successful when introduced slowly, discreetly and with a sensitive regard for local attitudes. Generalities do not suffice. Control measures must be fitted to the individual situation.

## OPERATIONAL ORGANIZATION

An independent agency of government could be developed to organize and implement effective programs for family planning, but seemingly it is more practical and less exhaustive of time and money to take advantage of existing organizations. The official organization for public health is an agency of society well fitted to undertake the practical work of a program for birth control. Trained staffs are accustomed to meeting people in their homes, they have technical methods of inquiry applicable to family planning, and an extensive experience in education of the public. This applies solely to operational procedures: the belief has been stated earlier that the cooperation and effort of all disciplines is needed in the general endeavor. Education of the public to an awareness of the problem, the derivation of facts upon which to work, the cultivation of public opinion must engage the activities of all agencies of society, including public health, each in its particular sphere.

Venereal disease, alcoholism and mental illness are among the accepted responsibilities of official public health agencies, with emphasis on the health aspects. All have an important social component, along with problems of morals, ethics, and religious beliefs. When mental health came to be recognized as a medical problem, an independent department of mental health was created in many places. Now the tendency is to recognize mental and physical disabilities as being closely allied, with much to be gained by unified effort. There would appear much advantage in recognizing that control of births is similarly a health problem, to be integrated with other public health procedures.

The American Public Health Association includes a concern with population dynamics among its established policies, stating forcefully that:

1. Public health organizations at all levels of government should give increased attention to the impact of population change on health.

2. Scientific research should be greatly expanded on (a) all aspects of human fertility; and (b) the interplay of biological, psychological and socio-economic factors influencing population change.

3. Public and private programs concerned with population growth and family size should be integral parts of the health program and should include medical advice and services which are acceptable to the individuals concerned.

4. Full freedom should be extended to all population groups for the selection and use of such methods for the regulation of family size as are consistent with the creed and mores of the individuals concerned.

Some state and local health departments in North America are fostering increasing numbers of family planning programs. A logical place for these activities is in the division of maternal and child health.

A growing number of schools of medicine and public health, particularly graduate schools, are giving attention to population dynamics, but so far minimally. The health professions are too little aware that the population problem is one of the major health hazards in the world today, and that they have an obligation to contribute within their capabilities to amelioration of the broad social problems involved. Some aspects are entirely within their interests and responsibilities. They have an important function in influencing governmental decisions and the conduct of operations, if the public welfare is to be safeguarded.

Education of the public in so intimate a matter as contraception is a formidable task. There is no universal approach. Interest must be stimulated within the framework of established cultural concepts. The demand so created can then be satisfied by provision of methods, materials and advice. Without direction, information on control of conception tends to spread by hidden routes and not always reliably. Urbanization, education and other social changes favor more rapid spread of ideas because people get together more, read more and talk more. With exposure to mass media, ideas and social customs tend to became more uniform. A public health approach to birth control brings discussion into the open and provides for direct communication between experts and the public on preferences, needs and the practicability of procedures. Ideally, the target should be the adolescent, so that when the time comes for marriage the idea of planned and responsible parenthood is firmly implanted. Practically, and under present conditions, the place to start is with the mother after the birth of the first baby.

## SUMMARY

The solution to the population problem is to increase production of material resources and to limit numbers of births. The latter is clearly to be recognized among health problems. Being in large part responsible for population growth through success in lowering death rates, public health has a moral obligation to aid in achieving an ecologic balance between man and his environment. It has the facilities for an active part in research, services and education directed toward lowering birth rates. Public health centers exist. More must be provided and traditional services expanded to include a control of births as well as deaths.

# Cultural Considerations

❦ ❦ ❦

23.

## POPULATION, SPACE, AND HUMAN CULTURE

*by Henry B. van Loon*

We, like all other forms of life, must maintain a working relationship with our environment. But while this relationship is still fairly simple and direct for all other organisms, ours is now maintained through each other, as a group, and through the patterns of behavior and the values of that group. This has given us a freedom of movement and expression that no other creature has, but, at the same time, it has also made us responsible for our own well-being. We must, therefore, seek to know ourselves and the world around us as best we can if we would insure the brightest possible future for mankind.

Space is both a measure and a function of our environment, and a resource in itself. For the lower forms of life, its values are quite tangible and easily measured; for us, on the other hand, because our relationship with our environment is no longer direct, but through our culture, it has come to have intangible ones as well. It is our appreciation of these intangible values and how they may best be implemented that determines whether and at what rate we, as a civilization, advance.

The direct and tangible relationships between ourselves and our environment have been well studied; the intangible ones have not. We can approximate how much food we shall probably have, how much coal, how much iron, by the year 2000. We can figure how much room each one of us shall have, depending on our numbers. We know very little, however, of the effect of space or lack of it on our cultural development. We do not know whether or not there is a point in the decline of per capita space and resources beyond which the cultural growth of a nation is arrested, and whether or not we are anywhere near such a point.

About a hundred years ago, von Liebig wrote,[1]

"A nation arises and develops in proportion to the fertility of its land. With the exhaustion of the land, culture and morals disappear. However,

Reprinted from a symposium, Population Control, Vol. 25, No. 3 (Summer 1960), by permission from "Law and Contemporary Problems," published by the Duke University, 1960.

the intellectual properties of the nation do not vanish; it is our consolation that they merely change their dwelling places."

This statement not only poses a fundamental question, but also hints broadly at the answer. The question, of course, is: Why does disruption of the landscape bring about a cultural decline? The hinted answer is: The development by man of a cultural relationship with his environment has brought about a physico-psychological relationship between environment and culture within his civilization that may not be too different from the psycho-somatic interrelationships that exist within the individual. The human being whose continued existence is no longer dependent on his ability to maintain rapport with his environment through change in his individual characteristics—form and function—has simply passed these requirements on to his state, nation, or civilization.

We would be deluding ourselves, furthermore, were we to think that von Liebig's thesis is rendered obsolete because of our industrial development. Industry is simply an extension of the process that began with agriculture—a capacity to exploit resources. Fertility of land has the same significance for an agricultural society, to all intents and purposes, as have total resources for an industrial one. If we substitute environment for fertility of land, von Liebig's statement immediately is brought up to date. The plain facts are that culture and environment are so intimately linked that the quality of an environment has as direct an effect on the quality of a culture as a culture, through its values, has on the space and resources of a civilization.

The relationship between primitive man and his environment could very simply be expressed: A region could support as many people as its resources times its space could feed. The relationship between us and our environment is somewhat more complicated, however, and has been expressed formulaically by Dr. Paul B. Sears, Chairman of the Yale University Conservation Program, as $\frac{(Rs)}{(P)} f(C) = 0$, in which $R$ is resources, $s$ is space, $P$ is people, and $C$ is their culture. All of these factors are variable, of course, but space, the subscript of resources, is variable not only in tangible, but in intangible ways as well. It can have endless values to us because of the cultural approach to environment that we have developed; and conversely, the continuation of our culture depends on the fullest exploitation of our space's aesthetic as well as material potential. It behooves us to study the implications of this in some detail.

### SPECIFICS OF THE CASE

It is not yet 200 years since the Constitution of the United States was written and adopted. This new departure in governmental philosophy and form brought about an unprecedented degree of freedom in human-environmental relations. What is more, this occurred in a brand new land and just as man was getting hold of a new source of power—namely, steam. The consequent outburst of energy, both physical and mental, that took place was phenomenal. Free minds and strong bodies sustained by a new and fertile soil moved without hindrance in all directions, using whatever was needed of space and resources, and there was spawned such a collection of "tinkers and geniuses," as Edmund Fuller called them,[2] as had never before been seen. Few countries since Greece in its heyday have boasted as many men of genius of all kinds—in relation to its population, of course—as did ours in the early 1800's.

In a scant 150 years, however, we have converted our country from a storehouse of raw wealth and space to what may well become a slum-ridden, have-not nation; from a land of men to one of members. The signs of the conditions for social stratification and decline are everywhere evident—the disease is already well advanced in our culture. But to be more specific as to what we may do to save ourselves from going the way of other civilizations, let us review the actual state of our space and resources and see, if we can, where we now stand. It is, of course, impossible to make direct comparisons with the past or with other present-day countries with anything approaching scientific accuracy, but some valid analogies and comparisons can certainly be drawn.

On a world-wide basis, population rose 30% from 1900 to 1940, while the production of food increased only 10 to 12%. Since 1940, world population has risen at an even faster rate than before; world food production, however, actually declined during the war and did not regain its prewar level until 1952, since which time, it has continued to increase, but not by any means at the same rate as has population.[3] Meanwhile, we have been proceeding on the assumption that because we have a "food surplus," our larder has no limits. Actually, of course, it has. Our present surplus is largely the result of a politically useful schema by which we pay "farmers" to take the capital out of our soil, which our grand-children should have and deposit it to their personal accounts. This cannot go on indefinitely, and it will not.

In the late 1930's, when we were seriously worried about our future, our Government made a most exhaustive study to determine the total number of acres that might be profitably used for farming and came up with just under 500,000,000 acres. At that time, we were already using some 300,000,000 acres (we had been using almost 360,000,000 in 1930).[4] Since then, by concentrating on the best land only, using much more fertilizer, cutting down on our exports and what we feed to horses and mules, we have managed to take care of our much larger population (177,399,000 in 1959 as compared with 122,755,046 in 1930) with only about about 420,000,000 acres. It has been estimated that by 1975, our population may be 225,000,000 and that to feed those people would require about 550,000,000 acres, under present productive levels. By increasing the annual amount of fertilizer from 5,500,000 tons used in the 1953-55 period to 10,600,000 tons and by applying this fertilizer to 48% of the acreage used instead of 30%, however, we could reduce the acreage to about 430,000,000.[5]

All of this looks quite promising; but this kind of performance cannot go on indefinitely. After certain levels of production are reached, the response of the land to more fertilizer appears to be negligible. Production thereafter depends more and more on intensive cultivation. Thus, although Japan uses twice as much fertilizer as Europe and five times as much as we do, it has not been able appreciably to increase production per acre since 1935.[6]

Meanwhile, we are steadily increasing not only our total, but our per capita needs for other resources of all kinds: for sources of energy, for metals, and for other materials that are all very finite in amount. While the demand for food increases more or less arithmetically with population, the demand for all other resources appears to increase geometrically. In short, however we regard our resources, all indications are that somewhere within the next twenty or thirty years, and in some respects possibly sooner, our larder, which has seemed so inexhaustible, will turn out to be like any other barrel. Yet, ours has only recently been tapped.

In any practical sense, living space on the planet Earth is finite in amount, too. True, the thrifty Dutch continue to reclaim land from the shallow margins of the North Sea, but only fast enough to make up for fertile land lost to roads and urban use. True, also, tall apartments continue to multiply and grow taller on an expensive piece of rock called Manhattan Island, but even this ingenious scheme has its limits. By and large, therefore, we shall have to make do with the existing land surface for the foreseeable future.

For the wisest and most effective use of that surface, we shall require help from many sources, not least from science. Yet, ironically, it is the applications of science that threaten us with a crisis in our relation to the space on which we live. For science has, through lowering our death rate while our birth rate remains high, brought about an unprecedented increase in human numbers. Moreover, in raising our material level of living, science has vastly increased our demands upon raw materials. And while it has probably lessened the amount of space required to provide each of us with food, it has made necessary great new highways, factories, and other greedy consumers of space. Finally, at the same time that pressure upon space has thus been steadily growing, the utilities, conveniencies, and diversions made possible by science are monopolizing our time and attention; the elaborate rituals of modern civilized life are divorcing us more and more from contact with the world of nature of which we are—inescapably—a part.

Even the word space itself begins to connote to us only outer, astronomical space. The result is a kind of mass hypnosis, a fascination with celestial form-sheets and planetary scoreboards. This may be, as we are assured by some specialists, essential to our physical survival as a nation, or it may not be. There are some cogent reasons, however, aside from expense, for thinking that the dangers may outweigh the insurance. Be this as it may, this new emphasis upon the promises of outer space deflects our concern from the more immediate kind of space problem that involves our daily lives. When we become more concerned over Soviet priority in reaching the moon than in guiding the design and location of highways and suburbs, one wonders what will be left to arouse our patriotism. As a distinguished American once said, "A man may die in defence of his home, but not his boarding-house."[7]

The present land area of the fifty states of this country is 3,552,226 square miles (land area only); its population, 177,319,000. This same area in 1900 contained 75,994,575 people. The number of acres per capita, accordingly, has fallen during this period of time from 22.4 to 12.2. This is still a generous allowance compared with Japan, where the corresponding figure is just under one. But at our present rate of population increase, it is estimated that we shall have only about seven acres per capita in the year 2000, while in less than a lifetime of seventy years, we shall be little better off than the Japanese are today—and unless we match their skill and energy in exploiting our resources, we shall be a great deal worse off.

How much is too many people? This depends upon way of life and the values that are considered most important. Bands of hunters and fishermen may require several square miles per capita, besides wide buffer zones to protect them against outside interference. A simple farming people can get along with a few acres per capita, provided they are not dependent upon the rain that falls elsewhere and do not need anything from outside. A highly industrialized state, such as Ohio, can accommodate 9,000,000 persons in a space that was once crowded by fewer than 20,000 Indians.

But these instances are deceptive. The hunters and simple farmers may require wide buffer zones, such as "the dark and bloody ground" or the Egyptian desert, to give them sure protection against constant raids. And it is seldom that any economy above the primitive level is self-contained

—it must have access to acres beyond that of its immediate occupation. Thus, of the scant million who work in Manhattan Island, 370,000 do not even live there, but commute, while the 14,049,000 who live in the Metropolitan New York area survive by virtue of the production and activity of our whole continent and lands beyond the seas.[8] To regard familiar urban densities as the universal norm for the entire habitable earth is not simply an error, therefore; it is a cruel injustice.

Several circumstances make the issue more than academic. One is a prevalent mood induced by the industrial revolution and noted long ago by Ortega y Gassett. This is a feeling never before entertained by sane mankind—that effortless abundance is the normal order of nature. As the efficiency of mass production increases, it becomes steadily more difficult to counter this idea, although unlimited mass production hastens the depletion of essential capital in the form of raw materials.

This suggests a further difficulty in the logical planning of space and numbers. The sheer and steady increase of population in a finite space offers superb opportunities for gain to those in a position of advantage. Slum properties are notoriously profitable in relation to investment and maintenance. William H. Whyte, Jr. has shown how much of the wealth of the United States has come from increased value attributable not to effort, but to the sheer momentum of increasing numbers in a space that remains unchanged.[9] This, of course, was the basis of Henry George's "single tax." This notion, that society, not the individual, should benefit by increased values not attributable to individual enterprise, has been laughed away repeatedly, only to bob up with remarkable persistence in serious discussions.

Beyond the mood of optimism and the temptation for profit is a profound biological fact. Man has become the dominant organism on earth not only because of his manipulative skill and highly developed central nervous system, but equally because of his powerful reproductive instinct. In this field of experience, powerful subconscious drive is reinforced and intensified by many aspects of consciousness. The slightest knowledge of cultural history, or even its current documentation in magazine advertising, shows this to be true. We conveniently forget that the strength of this impulse results in the advent of countless human beings whose arrival was by no means consciously invoked and whose welcome, to say the least, is dubious. Meanwhile, we have gone all out to insure the survival of as many for as long a time as possible—thus reducing the death rate, while dealing furtively and ineffectively, if at all, with the birth rate.

Again, our very attitude towards space is confused and ambivalent. Nor is this attitude unique, for the same is true as regards other resources —say, the forest and water. The forest is a source of materials and intangible values—and at the same time, our rival for space. Water is necessary for survival—yet, a convenient dumping ground for toxic wastes. Similarly, we require space for living, work, and recreation—but have gone to extraordinary lengths to annihilate it by rapid transit and communication. Thus, we both love and hate space—an inconceivably bad formula for any rational approach to intelligent planning.

PLANNING FOR THE FUTURE

Keeping in mind that both our continually growing pressure upon space and our relative disregard of its importance are ascribable to deep-seated aspects of human nature, what, in a technological sense, is involved in space-planning?

Any planning we may want to do for the future must, of course, be predicated on a thorough understanding of the conditions to be met and the objectives to be attained. It is obvious that we face an inexorable decline in our total resources, no matter what new ones we may find. It is obvious, too, that we shall increase the rate at which we use them for some time at least, especially those that are most available. There will also be a continuing shortage of food on a world-wide basis until the rate of population increase is brought under some kind of control. Lastly, our space, that 10% or so of the surface of the globe that is fit for human habitation, has been most badly used and has deteriorated. Thus, in our formula, both resources as a whole and space in its tangible form have been reduced so markedly that any chance of maintaining a balance in the future will depend on how soundly we plot our course, how fully we take advantage of those values that are intangible.

Now, for our objectives. Obviously, we want to survive. But are we willing to settle for physical survival alone—or, rather, can we? Can we take it for granted that so long as we can keep ourselves, as a species, alive, we shall automatically continue to evolve and be able to cope with life's demands for improvement and change as they come along? Shall we not be taking a truly great chance if we decide to take no responsibility for our continued cultural growth but rather leave it to nature? Is it not possible that having once taken on the responsibility for our own evolution to a fair extent, we may already be beyond what might be called a point of no return; that we may already be so far along that road that any failure to take the responsibility for our continued growth, to develop the right cultural values, to use the space we have left correctly, physically as well as aesthetically, may bring to an end our freedom from the control of physical, adaptive evolution?

Our cultural evolution has enabled us to increase in numbers. Thus, it has greatly increased our chances of bringing forth the minds that could move our culture onward. But—and this is the key to the whole problem—cultural gains have always been made in those countries that have had the resources; and always when the ratio of men to resources has become too high the intellectual properties of the country have vanished, as von Liebig wrote, to reappear somewhere else. Now there are no new lands to which our intellectual properties can go if we spoil the ones we have. Our continued cultural evolution, our lives as men, thus depends on how we exploit our environment.

Specifically, we should begin now on the following two-part program: planning for the immediate future, and planning for the years beyond. Part one should be a continuation of the investigation into the tangible values of our environment, or space. Part two should be an investigation of the intangible values and an attempt to integrate them with the tangible values, so that we can learn how to make the most of our environment's aesthetic potential, in order to compensate for the loss of space and resources that we must inevitably face.

From the point of view of its use to us, the value of our space—our land—is declining rather rapidly, although increasing in cost, for two very definite reasons: the one, because we are not yet taking the trouble to find out the ultimate best use or uses of each piece of land before doing something with it; the other, because we must use more and more machinery and can thus use only those lands or resources that can be handled by it. This is true whether we are speaking of farms, coal mines, or land for subdivision. In almost every case, the machine now largely determines what we do and where; and this is becoming the rule in almost every country as it, too, is forced to use more and more machinery.

There is a definite need, then, to extend the principle of multiple-use planning, as understood by foresters and conservationists, to land-use management as a whole, and to then integrate with this work a thorough understanding of the conditions that have been introduced in resource development and land-use by our increasing reliance on machinery and the growing interdependence of our economy. This does not mean that we should try to set out in detail how each piece of property is to be used; that would lead precisely to the kind of regimentation we must avoid. But it does mean that we should begin to develop means by which to arrive at fairly good estimates of the various possible values to us of any particular lands or regions, and an order of priority for those values.* With these, we can then set up the guidelines within which free enterprise can operate without the risk that one man's work will spoil another's. This is now being done, of course, in a small way through zoning in our com-

* Editor's note: This is now being realized by the "International Biological Programme" of the International Union of Biological Sciences.

munities; it is being done in a larger way by our valley authorities. The principle must, however, be extended and combined with the conditions set by our technology to bring about an understanding of how our land— our space—should be managed best to meet our present-day needs.

*     *

At the same time, we know almost nothing of the intangible values of our environment—of space—or their effects on us as individuals and as a group. The effects of space, of form and color, on man have been known for centuries by our master builders or architects: the lines of columns in the Egyptian temple to overawe the populace, the peace and sanctuary of a Gothic chapel, and so on. But we know very little of why these things are so; and because we have not been able to give these effects a statistical measure, the public, which is apt to think that statistics and truth are synonymous, is very reluctant to admit their existence or validity.

Yet, this subject must be mastered, just as we had to develop and bring together the body of knowledge that is now known as the science of psychology. The presently intangible values of our environment can have as profound effects on us and on our culture as do the physical, tangible ones. We must know them, have some measure of them, and be able to use them in order to keep the "$R_s$" (resource-space) factor in our formula as high as possible, and for as long as we can.

This brings us to the last and most important point: the place of the legislator and the lawyer in the whole scheme of our cultural life process. Our laws are, in some ways, much older than our present culture. They are an extension, in part, of the controls and rights we felt instinctively when our relationship to the world around us was still physical; the conventionalization, for the rest, of those concepts as to how we should live together that we have worked out for ourselves. The speed and security with which our culture can move ahead will depend largely on how well we are able to judge the moral rightness and cultural worth of the course that our scientists say we should follow. It is in this that our lawyers must help us, for our culture can be no better than the concepts on which it is based; and those concepts can do no good until they are translated into workable arrangements for our daily use. The scientist and the lawyer must work together closely in the interest of mankind; the scientist to give us facts, the lawyer to help us make them useful.

There is a need now to establish some organization, or group, of scientists and lawyers to begin to draw together all that we know on the whole subject of our cultural relationship to our environment. This group should not be large; it might well be patterned on the one brought together by President Hoover some years ago to study the social trends of the nation.[10] It should not try to carry out research itself; it should rather act as a steering committee and clearing house for information, working through regional organizations to gather information on our resources, space, and needs, advising on research, and bringing together and making useful all work now being done by others that could increase our knowledge of our interrelationship with our environment. In this way, we may be able to learn to establish a successful working arrangement with our environment within the time we can afford. After all, another 2500 human beings moved in to share our living space while you were reading this.

## 24.

## THE WRITER IN
## AN OVERPOPULATED WORLD

### *by F. L. Lucas*

> It is useless to go to bed to save light, if the result is twins.     *—Chinese Proverb*
>
> 'Tis heavy odds
> Against the gods
> When they will match with myrmidons,
> With spawning, spawning myrmidons.
> Our turn today! We take command.
> Jove gives the globe into the hand
> Of myrmidons, of myrmidons.
>     *—Emerson (after Béranger)*
>
> We shall see finally appear the miracle of an animal society, a complete and definitive ant-heap.
>     *—Valéry*

In a facetious moment, Sheridan the dramatist is said to have observed that if all the fleas in his bed had been of one mind, they could have pushed him out of it. But fleas are seldom of one mind. So with creative writers. By temperament they tend to be individualists, anarchists, heretics—the last kind of creatures to agree. To make them even seem to think alike has taxed the ingenuity even of propaganda ministries and police states. When the Russian Soviets were young, they dreamed hopefully of literature turned out by teams. But the results proved unrewarding.

Therefore, with a world problem like population, though one can talk usefully of the viewpoint, say, of the Roman Church—for the Roman Church is organized to hold views both dogmatic and unanimous—little seems gained by discussing the viewpoint, as a class, of writers. Collect a dozen writers at random and you may collect two dozen opinions. In general, they cannot endure organization; they die of it. Therefore, it may be of more use to consider, first, how overpopulation may affect writers at large, whatever their views; and secondly what, if anything, the individual writer can *do*.

The root of the evil seems grimly simple. Nature's way is to balance extravagant fertility with extravagant mortality. But now, for the human race, medical science has abruptly changed all that. In many countries it has cut death rates by more than half. And, not surprisingly, the result has proved a nasty surprise. Half dam the Mississippi and you get a deluge. Consequently, whereas it took perhaps the first seventeen centuries of our era to double mankind, mankind is now doubling in a generation. The 2½ billion of 1950 may be 5 billion by 1990. And the rate of growth itself still grows.

Within one lifetime humanity has acquired unprecedented power both to produce men and to destroy them. Babies have become a still worse menace than bombs. The bombs may never explode, but the population is exploding all the time, and no one knows how to stop it.

There are, of course, scientific optimists who are left undisturbed by this human avalanche. They could feed, they say, not merely our present 3 billion, but even 50 billion. It is simply a matter of developing enough nuclear energy, enough new techniques of getting food from factories, proteins from grasses or water-weed, plankton and fresh water from the oceans, sugar from sawdust, and similar luxuries. Naturally, the habitable earth would have to be largely urbanized or suburbanized. But why not? Eventually, of course, as even these optimists admit, all the joyous procreation would have to slow down, or our posterity would be sitting in one another's laps. But this slowing down, they hope, will somehow happen of itself, without any iniquitous interference with the fundamental human right to drag any number of little unborn wretches from the peace of insentience into an overcrowded world. Men can be punished for taking life, even their own (which might be thought their own affair); but they must on no account be helped to avoid inflicting it on others.

For ages, while warring states sought strength in brute numbers, even the most improvident parenthood was counted a virtue. Mussolini, Hitler, Stalin still gave it official benedictions. And today well-meaning philanthropists continue to encourage it throughout the earth. Men are slow to see that, in the modern world, improvident parenthood has become a crime. (It deepens the grim paradox of our plight that while the science of medicine automatically *increases* the numbers of the world's workers, the science of automation will simultaneously *decrease* the numbers needed.)

Of life's values in this future world-termitary the scientific optimists hardly speak; they are concerned only with making it possible. But creative writers of any value must be concerned about values. And, wildly though they may differ about other values, they must surely agree in valuing literature. What, then, of literature in a world urbanized, con-urbanized, suburbanized from New York to Buenos Aires, from Calais to Kamchatka?

Writers might find there bigger publics and fatter royalties. Yet some will suspect that human quantity endangers human quality. Artists have often been solitaries—men who impressed their fellows by being different, aloof, inflexibly themselves. Characters like Michelangelo, Milton, Rousseau, Wordsworth, Ibsen, Tolstoy, were nowise inclined, like good Leninists, to "lose themselves in the mass"; and they would have won no approval from the type of employer or bureaucrat who likes good organization-men.

> *Alone* the sun arises, and *alone*
> Spring the great streams.
>
> Thy soul was like a star, and dwelt *apart*.

Similarly, it is strange how often great art has sprung, not from multitudinous nations, but from small communities whose members need not feel themselves insignificant drops in a human ocean. It was in tiny city-states, small as our country-towns, that Greek literature flowered— "leaving great verse unto *a little clan.*" Plato held that the fullest and most perfect life would be found in an independent city with not more than 5,000 male citizens; Aristotle wanted still fewer. With its first giant-city, Alexandria, Greek art was already in decline, though Greek science, for a while, still progressed. So with Rome. Few of her lasting writers came from the dense streets of the Eternal City; they were largely provincials. So with saga Iceland. So with the Italian cities of Middle Age and Renaissance. Elizabethan England had perhaps less than a tenth of the present population, yet of our Niagara of books, how many will live as long as some of theirs? In Ireland, wrote Synge half a century ago, "for a few years more, we have a popular imagination that is fiery, and magnificent, and tender; so that those of us who wish to write start with a chance that is not given to writers in places where the springtime of the local life has been forgotten, and the harvest is a memory only, and the straw has been turned into bricks."

In short, for the spirit, character, and imagination on which literature depends, vast populations seem to me a vast evil. I am passionately convinced of the truth in what was written by another Irishman, Desmond MacCarthy, one of the few minds I have known that were not merely clever, but also wise: "We shall never have a civilization of which we can be proud, never a State which we can each feel is a greater self, until the newspapers can report, with pardonable exaggeration, as a most significant event, that 'a vast concourse of over 500 people assembled to support the policy of the Government.' "

It is easy, of course, to retort that modern writers have often written in great capitals. And it is true that Paris has long battened on the vitality of the French provinces; that London lights have long attracted, moth-like, whole swarms of gifted country boys. Inevitably. For in the density and pressure of metropolitan life, the writer can find a more intoxicating stimulus, more dramatic human struggles to observe and paint, bigger audiences, richer prizes of wealth, luxury, and fame. Lichfield could not have given Johnson what London gave; Lamb would not have exchanged Fleet Ditch for all the streams of Westmorland; Balzac, full of the peasant energy of his Touraine, needed Paris as a field for his Napoleonic ambition; and Mme de Staël preferred the Rue du Bac to all the glories of the Alps or the Bay of Naples.

Yet the price of living in vast human conglomerations can be heavy. Hardy has well summed up London as "that hot-plate of humanity on which we first sing, then simmer, then boil, then dry away to dust." Even Milton's angels, entering the infernal capital of Pandemonium, shrank to pygmy size.

All civilized life, with its psychological stresses, is a kind of cage; and great cities are cages double-barred. In the past there was still plenty of unspoilt country on which to draw, and to which to return, for fresh vigor. But now the beauty and freedom of wild Nature yearly dwindle before the profligate proliferation of mankind. Much of the English countryside, and most of its coast, have already been befouled. In the Highlands, brae and glen grow bestridden by electric pylons, till the wry jest runs that "Scotland has become Pole-land." Wordsworth would have shrunk horrified from a Tintern Abbey besieged with rows of motor-coaches; through his own Grasmere hoot hordes of cars, almost climbing on one another's backs, while his lakes are swilled by the greedy throats of Manchester, and from his fell-tops one sees smoking the Satanic chimneys of nuclear power. It is fast becoming the same everywhere. Athens has grown hideous; Greece and the Alps are desecrated with tarmac and trippers. Every week blithe journalists chant to millions the praises of some spot they have found "still unspoilt," so that it may, as quickly as possible, be spoilt in its turn.

And all this may be a mere foretaste of a time when most of the earth's landscapes will be enmeshed in spider webs of wire; its skies thick with flying objects, like flies above carrion; its forests felled for futile newspapers; its roads blocked with a mass-produced humanity in mass-produced cars, crawling in queues to the accompaniment of mass-produced music; its wild life exterminated to make room for more men and still more men, as if man were the one good thing of which there can never be too much.

This fool's progress was already denounced by writers of the nineteenth century. It was denounced by Ruskin when he wrote, of the new railway at Buxton:

The valley is gone, and the gods with it; and now every fool in Buxton can be at Bakewell in half an hour, and every fool in Bakewell at Buxton; which you think is a lucrative process of exchange, you fools everywhere!

It was more calmly mocked by the irony of Arnold:

Your middle-class man thinks it the highest pitch of development of civilization when his letters are carried ten times a day from Islington to Camberwell and from Camberwell to Islington, and if railway trains run to and fro between them every quarter of an hour. He thinks it nothing that the trains only carry him from an illiberal, dismal life at Islington to an illiberal, dismal life at Camberwell.

And far away in Russia, a like protest was uttered by one who combined with the passionate imagination of an artist the dispassionate vision of science—Anton Chekhov. For Dr. Astrov in *Uncle Vanya* is the clear mouthpiece of Dr. Chekhov himself, as he laments the spoilation of the Russian land:

The forests of Russia are groaning under the axe. Millions of trees are being destroyed; the homes of birds and animals laid waste; the rivers dwindling and drying up; lovely landscapes vanishing for ever . . . We are confronted with the degradation of our country brought on by the fierce struggle for existence of the human race. It is the result of the ignorance and senselessness of striving, shivering humanity that, to save its children, snatches at whatever can warm it and quiet its hunger.

One need not carry misanthropy so far as Lawrence of Arabia with his wish for an ending of the human race by birth-control within fifty years, and its replacement by "some cleaner mammal—I suppose it must be a mammal?" But some may sincerely wish that half mankind could be painlessly changed, like nymphs in Ovid, into trees; in which arboreal state many of them would be both less unhappy and more beautiful, and often a good deal more use.

If, then, it is asked how the literary writer is affected by man's crazy increase, the answer seems that he is affected doubly. As a human being, he shares the general risk that he and his posterity in the coming century may have to face growing scarcities and ruthless racial pressures—particularly from Asia; and as a lover of literature he may feel far from happy about its prospects in an ant-heap world, crowded into sprawling hideousness, prosaic and Philistine, defaced and debased.

Here, of course, he can only guess. At any period, few things remain as utterly unpredictable as the arts. Literature might triumph even over the challenge of this new mass-age (though that seems improbable optimism); or, again, it might dwindle away to nothing but popular journalism, radio, and technical manuals. The writers of the nineteenth century were as outstanding as its scientists; but it would be bold to claim as much for the writers of the twentieth. Some will feel that the literary history of the last eighty years is already of darker augury—that literature has already reflected the present trend of the world by growing more vulgarized, more decadent, more demented, more preoccupied with depicting in fiction and drama the lives of rats, rabbits, and robots, tarts and toads.

Be that as it may, what, in this population crisis, can the writer *do*? It might, no doubt, be exhilarating to reply, "Writers of the world, unite!"; to preach a eugenic crusade; to intone a demographic *Marseillaise*. But it is wiser, I think, frankly to face the difficulties.

First, propaganda now seldom makes good literature; and literature seldom makes good propaganda. True, one may cite as instances of effective propaganda that is also lasting literature, the Bible, or Donne's *Sermons,* or Bunyan's *Pilgrim's Progress*. But these perhaps belong to an earlier phase of civilization when prophets, priests, or poets could more effectively dictate to audiences more swayed than now by the imaginative word. Today the world has grown more complex, more scientific, more prosaic. Burke may have helped to arrest revolution in Europe; Tom Paine, to hasten it in America; *Uncle Tom's Cabin* to hasten the freeing of the slave. But who reads them now—even (apart from a few purple passages) Burke himself? Such writers perhaps furthered the march of history, but they are now abandoned to the historian. The most influential writer of the nineteenth century was probably Karl Marx, but even the Marxists would hardly claim him as an artist. Rather his work was a kind of science—a rather dubious blend of economics and sociology.

Again, good writers are seldom good propagandists. Literary readers have grown to dislike books with a "message"; and readers in general tend to distrust literary writers as lacking knowledge or judgment in practical matters. Not without reason. For artists are often feelers rather than thinkers; intuitive rather than rational; emotional rather than wise.

This accusation is as old as Plato's *Ion* and *Republic*. "Do not listen to him!" cried the exasperated patron of Lulli, as the great musician talked twaddle at table; "He has no common sense, he is all genius." In literature and art there have been many Lullis. Look, for instance, at Victor Hugo, perhaps the greatest of French poets; but at many of his ideas, it is better not to look. So with Lamartine, as unfortunate in politics as Woodrow Wilson; so with Tolstoy, unsurpassed among Russians for imaginative power, and yet largely fantastic in his ideals. One begins to understand Frederick the Great's remark that the worst punishment he could inflict on a province would be to sentence it to be governed by men of letters.

It can be objected that Voltaire and Rousseau were not only gifted writers but also markedly effective in preparing the French Revolution. Yet the Revolution would have horrified them; that was not what they really wanted. Shelley might talk of poets as the unacknowledged legislators of the world; but in the century and a half since he said it, how much have creative writers really affected practical events? What came, for instance, of all the thunders of Carlyle? Only perhaps a rather sinister foreshadowing of Fascist and Nazi. Ruskin lamented that the practical result of his efforts had been to fill England with debased Gothic. All his eloquence had little effect in staying the ravages of Philistine and Vandal.

In our time results seem produced not so much by individual writers as by organizations. The modern mind appears to work most effectively through bodies—bodies with hundreds or thousands of members. I hate this conclusion. I abominate organizations. I share Ibsen's ironic laughter whenever he read "A committee has been appointed." But that, I am afraid, is how something—sometimes—now gets done.

"Ah, but Ibsen!" you may cry. "Great writer, yet great propagandist as well. *A Doll's House, Ghosts* . . ." But, firstly, Ibsen denied preaching; and he preached less than some suppose. Secondly, his later, greater, more living work preached less and less. Thirdly, the things he stood for —women's freedom, frankness about sex—were coming anyway. Shaw, again, *was* an avowed propagandist. But, with all his wit and verve, what did he effect? He amused; he did not inspire. Much more real results came from the Fabian Society. So in our day Huxley's *Brave New World*, or Orwell's *1984*, may have made a stir among intellectuals. But what are intellectuals? Flies on the world's coach.

Suppose one is a poet. One wishes to draw one's pen against man's mad multiplication. Can one hope to produce anything more telling than the bitter, ironic brevity of Hardy's *Mad Judy*? When Judy (who, oddly enough, is descended from certain barbarians in Herodotus) heard of a birth in the village, she would sigh and weep.

> She was crazed, we knew, and we
> Humoured her infirmity.
>
> When the daughters and the sons
> Gathered them to wed,
> And we like-intending ones
> Danced till dawn was red,
> She would rock and mutter, "More
> Comers to this stony shore!"

But when an infant was released from life, Judy would sing happily again beside her fire.

> What she liked we let her do,
> Judy was insane, we knew.

Or suppose one is a novelist. One feels it a duty to denounce reckless parenthood. Is one likely to invent a more unforgettably horrible example than Hardy's *Jude the Obscure*, where the eldest boy hangs the younger children, then himself, with that pitiful last scribble, "Done because we are too menny." Yet one may doubt whether *Jude* or *Judy* has lessened the world's births by even a single dozen.

Changes of magnitude in the modern world, I am reluctantly driven to conclude, are no longer produced by literary works, but, very largely, by the iron pressure of events on human idiocy and indolence; by the fanaticism that such pressures produce; by organization; by the crudest forms of propaganda. So Hitler rose from the dragon's teeth of Versailles and the misery of a world slump. He triumphed, not by that unreadable book *Mein Kampf*, but by fanaticism, organization, and a hysterical rhetoric that could bawl millions into equal hysteria. So with the triumphs of communism. The same factors were present—populations under grinding pressure; an absolutely unscrupulous fanaticism; an iron organization. But little of all this was achieved by literature.

A gloomy view? But I am trying to strike an honest balance between defeatist gloom and a falsely facile optimism. To sum up, were I asked by a writer what he could do against the population peril, I should answer, with all due hesitancy:

"You *can* write novels or plays about it. But they may prove, being so purposeful, not very good novels or plays. They may neither increase your repute nor lessen the birth rate. You may, no doubt, do rather more by journalism or radio. But in the main this problem seems to me the field of scientists, of statesmen (if any), and of organizations. (Of such organization, even if only on a very small scale, this very book is itself an example.) However this does not mean that the individual writer can, or should, do nothing. He can at least help to keep ideas in the air."

Consider what often happens in human crises. A danger looms on the far horizon. A few far-sighted Cassandras cry their warnings. No one listens. For men are largely too lazy, lethargic, and engrossed in their private trivialties, to do anything about general problems, until not doing anything grows acutely uncomfortable. But the danger deepens. More and more individuals begin to feel its actual effects on their own backs or bellies. They are driven to that form of activity they so profoundly detest—thought. They begin to recall, at last what the Cassandras had said. And then—sometimes too late, sometimes at the eleventh hour—counter-measures are finally taken.

So it was with the danger from Hitler. So with Japan. Before the war the militarist government of Japan, after the fashion of their kind, encouraged philoprogenitiveness with all the virulence in their power. Then came defeat, with the threat of famine and ruin. Today Japan is the one country that has dealt effectively with an excessive birth rate. But even here—so terrible is the time lag in such things—the population is not expected for thirty years to reach its final peak, and a dangerously high peak, at that.

But this success in population planning could not have happened if ideas about it had not been already, for decades, in the air. The writer too can at least help to keep them there—by persistent iteration, by talking of population, alluding in his writings to population, becoming, if necessary, a bore about population, just as Cato, on whatever topic he addressed the Roman Senate, remorselessly ended 'But I think Carthage should be destroyed.' It was. Tolstoy's harping on non-resistance showed little effect in his own time and country; but it happened to influence Gandhi; and Gandhi did find a situation, and build up an organization, that led Tolstoy's idea to a practical triumph.

But let us have no great expectations. This process is appallingly slow and precarious. Thoughts are like wind-blown seeds. Millions perish for one that germinates. But, if there are enough of them, some take root. Somewhere, in the end, a forest may grow.

Further, the imaginative writer has still certain advantages over the now dominant scientist. He may be more sensitive to values; he may be better at dreams. So let us dream of a world with finer values than ours, a world, for example, with a carefully selected aristocracy of human beings, served by a proletariat of machines; a world restored to a happier balance between man's civilization and wild Nature's beauty; a world where giving life would be a grave responsibility, not a feckless and reckless orgy.

Of course one sickens of the seeming futility of such efforts. For six years I wrote against Hitlerism, with no visible result except being called a busybody and troublemaker by those of my countrymen who would give anything for a quiet life; and being put on the Gestapo's list for arrest when England should be theirs in 1940. I have written on population—letters to the press, articles, part of a book; but the critics kept cautiously to the less alarming topics in the book, or evaded the whole issue by kindly praising my style. Charming, but not very helpful. But even if nothing comes of it, it is something at least to have done what one could.

Under Louis XI of France a condemned prisoner was reprieved for a year on his undertaking within that time to teach the King's ass to speak. "Fool!" said his friends, "you know it is impossible." "Ah, but in a year the King may die, or I may die, or the ass may die—or the ass *may* speak." So here. The prospects are not rosy. Some of my scientific friends regard the problem as hopeless in its immensity. Yet something may result from patient persistence. It is a question, now, not of making an ass speak, but of making billions of asses listen. But who knows? In the end they might.

# Part Three

## ACTION PROGRAMS

◐ ◐ ◐ ◐

● ● ●

## 25.

# THE PROBLEM OF NEW PROBLEMS

*by Brock Chisholm*

In the new era of human social development which began roughly six-teen years ago, after the Second World War, many new problems have appeared. Most of the very important ones stem from man's, or some men's, tremendously increased ability to kill and destroy, or his also greatly increased ability to save and prolong life. The scientific and en-gineering development of the ability to split and to fuse atoms and the great advances in public health and medical fields have been the chief initiators of these changes.

Since long before the dawn of history man's survival has been by groups in competition to the death with other groups. During some thou-sands of years certain feeling, thinking and behaviour patterns, associated with survival, have become firmly established. Exclusive loyalty to the survival group, whether family, clan, tribe, city, state, principality, king-dom, empire or nation, has been a demand of the highest priority affect-ing almost all human beings. As a crime, treason has ranked above even murder in most cultures; murder is often legalized, as in war or execu-tion, while treason never is. The ancient system of survival depended on the ability of the survival group to defend itself against attack and/or to attack other groups successfully, that is, to win wars. To win wars re-quired the largest possible number of fighting men, exclusive loyalty, the best weapons, unquestioning obedience to authority even at the cost of life, adequate supplies of food and material, and high morale. The obliga-tion to provide all these has been taught each generation, very force-fully, by the development of strong moral attitudes through myths, sys-tems of heroes, biased history, medals and awards, and public acclaim. In almost all cultures any questioning of these values or of the methods by which they were supported was, and is, strongly discouraged by governmental and private action.

Under these circumstances of built-in conservatism in the field of inter-human and inter-societal relationships, adequate adjustment to new cir-cumstances faces strong barriers. When tension arises between survival groups—in recent centuries usually either nations or groups of nations—a highly emotional state of anxiety is produced. In such a state there is a

Summary of address before Twenty-third American Assembly. Arden House, Harri-man, New York, May 2, 1963.

tendency for emotion to take precedence over intellectual function. Conscience, the early-learned system of values to which every person has been exposed in childhood, is mobilised and strong feelings about what is "right" or "good" are felt and expressed. Almost all of us have learned in childhood that when we feel threatened the right and good and effective thing to do is to increase our ability to kill to the greatest possible degree and then to threaten any potential enemy into submission. This has been our standard, admirable and effective pattern throughout history; it is sometimes called "negotiation from strength." Unfortunately for the continued use of this old pattern, the conditions have changed. As soon as the potentiality for destruction became absolute, or nearly so, any increase in power became meaningless. With the weapons now available in the world, nuclear, biological, chemical and conventional, we are capable of killing everyone, including ourselves, at least three or four times over, yet many people earnestly believe that if we can just arrange to be able to kill everyone, including ourselves, say ten times over instead of only three or four times, in some way we would be more secure and less frightened. This is obviously insane thinking, based on emotional reaction and not on intellectual process.

The same situation obtains in relation to our present rapid increase in population. To our ancestors, growth of the survival group was "good"; it increased power and security at every stage of social development. It is now a threat to the whole human species, but we have no tradition of concern about threats to the species; the occasion had not arisen until just recently, long after the systems of values into which we were born were incorporated into our personalities as "conscience values." To have plenty of children has been admirable in practically all cultures and at all times, both for national defence and to provide social security for parents. Only intellectual conviction, which commonly has been subjected to censorship and control by conscience, tells us that large families have become a threat to all of us. Thus, by all sorts of distortions of reasoning, most of us still avoid the painful implications of our present population situation.

Associated with the population problem is the world's present food situation. The problem is not only that a large proportion of the world's people suffer from lack of adequate food; that has always been true. The important change is in the fact that, while resignation to hunger or starvation was normal wherever there were frequent shortages of food, that resignation has disappeared or is rapidly disappearing from the world. No longer will any people peacefully die of starvation, or even suffer severely from malnutrition. They all know now that it is not necessary, that the human race is quite capable of feeding adequately all its people. We are not doing it because we don't care enough; we have no tradition of concern for such distant threats. Our consciences do not make us uncomfortable enough to drive us to the trouble and expense of organizing food production and distribution on a world basis. The hungry people are not within our concept of our survival group.

It seems that the common factors in these three great world problems, security, population and food, are that they are all threats to the whole human race and that they are associated with new situations not amenable to control by the methods learned from our parents or ancestors. They demand new solutions which require feeling and thinking independently of the accident of our birth into this or that community or group. We do not have social or political institutions which were designed for the solution of world problems, except for a few developed recently such as the United Nations and its specialized agencies, and these are so beset with controls exercised for the benefit of individual nations or groups of nations that it is very difficult for them to deal with world threats. Each nation tends to break down all problems into what is good for "us," at whatever cost to anyone else, the traditional survival group attitude, ignoring the fact that the survival group has now become the human race itself.

Recently a few people in some countries have begun to try to think as members of the human race and beyond the limitations of exclusive national loyalties, but they still meet strong criticism from their own "loyal" compatriots. Still no government has set up a department or institution to recognize and advise on dealing with new threats to the human species, while many governments try to use the United Nations to enhance their own prestige and power or to gain economic or political advantage. In the presence of universal threat we are fumbling badly because few people have developed emotionally and socially to a level of maturity appropriate to a world where security and welfare have become indivisible and where we shall survive as members of the human race or not at all. Out-breeding, out-gunning or out-producing other groups can no longer be counted on to provide security, prosperity or peace, or even survival.

26.

POPULATION COMMISSION, TWELFTH SESSION,
ITEM 4 OF THE PROVISIONAL AGENDA

# UNITED NATIONS GENERAL ASSEMBLY RESOLUTION ON POPULATION GROWTH AND ECONOMIC DEVELOPMENT

*Note by the Secretary-General*

1. At the sixteenth session of the General Assembly (1961), a draft resolution on "Population Growth and Economic Development" was introduced, and allocated to the Second Committee. The Second Committee was not able to consider it for lack of time, and the Assembly decided that the item should be placed on the agenda of the next session.

2. A draft resolution relevant to this item was introduced at the seventeenth session with the following sponsors: Ceylon, Denmark, Ghana, Greece, Nepal, Norway, Pakistan, Sweden, Tunisia, Turkey, Uganda and the United Arab Republic. It was considered by the Second Committee at its 866th-869th and 874th-875th meetings. After some amendments, the draft resolution was approved by a roll-call vote of 43 to 14, with 42 abstentions. The draft resolution as approved by the Committee was presented to the General Assembly at its 1197th plenary meeting on 18 December 1962.[1] The Assembly decided by a roll-call vote that it should be considered as an important item requiring a two-thirds majority vote. A vote was first taken on the latter part of operative paragraph 6 in the draft, stating: "and that the United Nations give technical assistance, as requested by Governments, for national projects and programmes dealing with the problems of population." This part was rejected by a roll-call vote of 34 to 34, with 32 abstentions. The remainder of the draft resolution was then adopted by 69 votes to none, with 27 abstentions. The resolution in its final form[2] is attached as an annex.

General Assembly Resolution adopted 18 December 1962*

POPULATION GROWTH AND ECONOMIC DEVELOPMENT

*The General Assembly,*

*Considering* that rapid economic and social progress in the developing

* General Assembly resolution 1838 (XVII).

countries is dependent not least upon the ability of these countries to provide their peoples with education, a fair standard of living and the possibility for productive work,

*Considering further* that economic development and population growth are closely interrelated,

*Recognizing* that the health and welfare of the family is of paramount importance, not only for obvious humanitarian reasons, but also with regard to economic development and social progress, and that the health and welfare of the family require special attention in areas with a relatively high rate of population growth,

*Recognizing further* that it is the responsibility of each Government to decide its own policies and devise its own programmes of action for dealing with the problems of population and economic and social progress,

*Reminding* States Members of the United Nations and of the specialized agencies that according to recent census results the effective population increase during the last decade has been particularly high in many low-income less developed countries,

*Reminding* Member States that in formulating their economic and social policies it is useful to take into account the latest relevant facts on the interrelationship of population growth and economic and social development and that the forthcoming World Population Conference and the Asian Population Conference might throw new light on the importance of this problem, especially for the developing countries,

*Recalling* its resolution 1217 (XII) of 14 December 1957, in which the General Assembly, *inter alia*, invites Member States, particularly the developing countries, to follow as closely as possible the interrelationships existing between economic and population changes, and requests the Secretary-General to ensure the co-ordination of the activities of the United Nations in the demographic and economic fields,

*Recalling* Economic and Social Council resolution 820 (XXXI) which contains provisions aiming at intensified efforts to ensure international co-operation in the evaluation, analysis and utilization of population census results and related data, particularly in the less developed countries, and which requests the Secretary-General to explore the possibilities of increasing the amount of technical assistance funds for assistance to Governments requesting it in preparing permanent programmes of demographic research,

*Recognizing* that further studies and research are necessary to fill the gaps in our knowledge about the causes and consequences of demographic trends, particularly in the less developed countries,

*Recognizing* that removals of large national groups to other countries may give rise to ethnical, political, emotional and economic difficulties,

1. *Notes with appreciation* the report of the Secretary-General, entitled "The United Nations Development Decade proposals for action" which, *inter alia*, refers to the interrelationship between population growth and economic and social development;

2. *Expresses its appreciation* of the work on population problems which has up to now been carried out under the guidance of the Population Commission of the Economic and Social Council;

3. *Requests* the Secretary-General to conduct an inquiry among the Governments of States Members of the United Nations and of the specialized agencies concerning the particular problems confronting them as a result of the reciprocal action of economic development and population changes;

4. *Recommends* that the Economic and Social Council in co-operation with the specialized agencies, the regional economic commissions and the Population Commission, and taking into account the results of the inquiry referred to in paragraph 3 above, intensify its studies and research on the interrelationship of population growth and economic and social development, with particular reference to the needs of the developing countries for investment in health and educational facilities within the framework of their general development programmes;

5. *Further recommends* that the Economic and Social Council report on its findings to the General Assembly not later than at its nineteenth session;

6. *Endorses* the view of the Population Commission[3] that the United Nations should encourage and assist Governments, especially those of the less developed countries, in obtaining basic data and carrying out essential studies of the demographic aspects, as well as other aspects, of their economic and social development problems;

7. *Recommends* that the second World Population Conference pay special attention to the interrelationships of population growth with economic and social development, particularly in countries that are less developed, and that efforts be made to obtain the fullest possible participation in the Conference by experts from such countries.

27.

# THE POLITICS OF POPULATION:
# A BLUEPRINT FOR INTERNATIONAL
# COOPERATION

*by Richard N. Gardner*

December 18, 1962 marked a turning point in the recognition by the international community of the world population problem.

On that day the United Nations General Assembly concluded the first debate in its history devoted entirely to the subject of population. It adopted, with 69 affirmative votes (including that of the United States), 27 abstentions, and not a single negative vote, a major resolution calling for an intensified program of international cooperation in the population field.

Except for the members of the Soviet bloc, all of whom abstained, countries of every major political, economic, cultural, religious, and geographic identification were among those voting in the affirmative. In the presence of an issue of such incalculable importance to the future of mankind, the many divisions which are so characteristic of debates on most international problems dissolved, giving way to a broad consensus on the importance of the population problem.

It may be useful to consider in some detail the significance of these recent developments in the United Nations. Specifically, there are at least four questions that come to mind:

Why was the population problem on the agenda of the United Nations?

What exactly did the United Nations decide to do about it?

What did the United Nations debate reveal about international attitudes to this question?

What program of international cooperation in population should we be seeking in the future?

I

The short answer to why population was on the agenda of the United Nations at the 17th General Assembly was that the Government of

Address before the Twenty-Third American Assembly on "The Population Dilemma" at Arden House, Harriman, New York, Saturday, May 4, 1963 at 8 P.M. D.S.T.

Sweden, supported by a number of other countries, decided to put it there. But obviously this is not a satisfactory answer. Ten years earlier, a full scale debate in the United Nations devoted entirely to the population question would have been unthinkable. The wide support that developed in the interim for the inscription of an item on the population question and for a Resolution calling for action to deal with it reflected a growing international appreciation of the significance of the population question for the future of mankind.

Until very recently, at least, Western thought has been characterized by an optimistic faith in the inevitability of progress. Despite two terrible wars, a great depression, and the revolutionary ferment which is currently shaking our civilization, many of us still cling to the assumption that the fate of man on earth is destined to improve as time goes on.

This confident assumption is somewhat undermined by the realization that despite all the progress of science and technology in recent years there are more people living in misery and deprivation today than there were at the turn of the century. Of course, there are also more people enjoying adequate living standards. But the increase of the underprivileged has probably exceeded the increase of everyone else. Whether such a development can be considered progress is, to say the least, an open question.

To be sure, some people cite as evidence of progress the upward trend of aggregate statistics. But progress cannot be measured merely by increases in gross national product.

The object of economic development is the welfare and dignity of the individual human being. We must concern ourselves, not with aggregate statistics, but with the progress made in assuring each person a full and satisfactory life—adequate levels of personal consumption, including food and housing, health and education, and also satisfaction of those political, cultural, and spiritual needs that are fundamental to all men.

If the condition of the individual, and not gross statistics, is to be the measure of our progress, then it is absolutely essential that we be concerned with population trends. So long as we are concerned with the quality of life we have no choice but to be concerned with the quantity of life.

There are today some three billion people in the world. It required hundreds of thousand of years, from the beginning of life on earth to the beginning of this century, to reach one and a half billion. Within the last 60 years we have doubled that number. According to United Nations estimates we will double that number again to six billion by the end of this century.

It is obvious from these statistics that the world's population is not merely growing in *absolute numbers*. The *rate* of population growth has increased at an extraordinary pace. The annual growth rate has doubled from 1% in 1945—itself an unprecedented high in world history—to 2% today. It is expected to go even higher. But even if the present rate of growth of world population is maintained at its present level, the numbers we have to contemplate are staggering.

Whether the growth of world population continues at its present rate, whether a reduction in that rate is brought about by increases in the death rate or decreases in the birth rate, and whether, to reduce the birth rate, measures are found which are consistent with the economic, cultural, ethical, and religious circumstances of individual countries—these are all questions of paramount importance.

It was considerations such as these which led to the inscription of the population item at the 17th General Assembly. But the inscription of this item did not reflect just a generalized concern with the population problem; it reflected a particular concern for the dilemma facing the less developed countries.

The nature of this dilemma can be succinctly stated. For reasons which are well known, the rate of population growth tends to be higher in the less developed countries than in the developed countries—about 70% higher on the average. In many less developed countries the rate of population growth exceeds 3% a year.

About 80% of the one-half billion growth in the world population in the last decade took place in the less developed areas. In the years ahead the highest rates of growth are likely to continue to be in these areas. It is estimated, for example, that, if present rates of growth were to continue, between now and the year 2000 the population of North America would grow from 200 to 300 million, while the population of South and Middle America would grow from some 200 to 600 million.

It is bad enough that less developed countries tend to have a faster rate of population growth than developed countries. But the problem is compounded further by the fact that the less developed countries are less able to cope with the consequences of rapid population growth.

The problem for developed countries is to increase already high per capita income levels and to devote increasing portions of already large national savings to services such as medical care, health, and housing. But less developed countries whose economy is at the subsistence level may be able to save little or nothing at existing income levels for improvement in social infrastructure.

It is all many of the developing countries can do to enlarge the total economic product as fast as the added people. Yet they have not merely to provide additional facilities for increased population but to create new and adequate facilities for the existing population as well.

For newly developing countries the problem of population growth is not, as some people think, the problem of avoiding starvation or finding standing room. It is the problem of finding sufficient savings after current consumption needs are met to assure a tolerable rate of progress toward modernization and higher standards of living based on self-sustaining economic growth.

In some of the world's poorest areas population increase is outpacing the increase in gross national product. As a result there are no resources available for capital formation and no increases in living standards. The prospect is for more and more people to have less and less income.

Just a year and a half ago the United Nations General Assembly set as its goal for the United Nations Development Decade the achievement by 1970 of an annual growth rate of 5% a year in aggregate national income in each of the developing countries. The achievement of this goal will require enormous efforts.

It has been estimated that in the decade of the 1950's the developing countries over-all had a growth rate of 3% a year and a population growth of 2% a year, with annual per capita increases of income of 1% a year. Making the generally accepted assumption of a capital-output ratio of 3:1, these countries will have to increase their savings and investment from 9 to 15% of gross national product in order to achieve the goals of the Development Decade. This is obviously a formidable task at present levels of population growth.

Assuming that the goals of the Development Decade are achieved, prospective increases in population will greatly dilute the impact of over-all increases in income on individual levels of welfare. For example, gradual progress toward the 5% annual growth goal during the Development Decade would by the end of this decade increase a $100 per capita income to $123 in a country with a 2% rate of population growth and $111 in a country with a 3% rate of population growth.

Obviously there is much that we do not know about the relationship of population growth to economic and social development. But from an examination of these and other facts one conclusion seems inescapable —that in certain less developed countries it may be virtually impossible at the present time, even with maximum external assistance and maximum self-help, to bring about a rate of economic growth which will provide the rate of improvement in individual living standards which the country seeks to attain and which, more fundamentally, is essential to the proper exercise of the individual's human faculties.

In the light of these hard realities it was scarcely surprising that a large part of the impetus to discuss the population problem in the United Nations came from the less developed countries themselves. In recent years, a growing number of these countries have adopted population policies of one sort or another—policies in accord with their particular economic, social, cultural and religious circumstances.

In July 1962, shortly before the opening of the 17th General Assembly, the Cairo Conference of Developing Countries, including countries from Asia, Africa and Latin America, unanimously adopted a Declaration which contained the following significant statement:

"Countries that suffer from the pressure of population on resources available should accelerate their rate of economic development, and in the meantime take appropriate legitimate measures to deal with their population problems."

It was against this background of a growing concern that the United Nations General Assembly began its historic debate on the population problem.

II

While the Resolution on "Population Growth and Economic Development" was the first of its kind ever passed by the General Assembly, the United Nations has not previously been inactive in the population field. In the 17 years of its existence the United Nations has

—Established a population unit in the Secretariat (now the Population Branch of the Bureau of Social Affairs),

—Created the Population Commission, a group of government representatives meeting once every two years,

—Held a World Population Conference under U.N. auspices in 1954.

—Encouraged Regional Economic Commissions located in the less developed areas—the Economic Commission for Asia and the Far East, the Economic Commission for Latin America, and the Economic Commission for Africa—to become increasingly active in the population field.

—And organized Regional Demographic Research and Training Centers in Bombay, Santiago and Cairo, to provide advisory services to countries of these regions.

Through activities such as these, the United Nations has been making a major contribution to an understanding of the population problem:

In the field of *information*, it has encouraged and assisted member governments to obtain factual information on the size, composition, and trends of their populations and the interrelation between population growth and economic and social development.

In the field of *training*, it has helped develop a whole range of skills in the demographic field— in census taking, population projections, and economic analysis.

In the field of *discussion*, it has promoted a full and responsible exchange of ideas on all aspects of the population problem.

These contributions of the United Nations should not be underestimated. When the Population Commission met for the first time in 1947, demographic statistics, including census and vital statistics were so incomplete that it would scarcely have been possible to speak knowledgeably of *world* population trends or *world* population problems. It is easy to overlook the fact that if it were not for the devoted labors of the population and statistical sections of the U.N. Secretariat, both operating under the guidance of the Population and Statistical Commissions, we would even now not be able to discern the outlines of the *world* population problem or the problems of most major regions.

Sixteen years of slow, careful accumulation of basic factual information helped lay the groundwork for enlightened consideration of the economic and social implications of population trends.

Building on this solid record of achievement, the General Assembly resolution on "Population Growth and Economic Development" was designed to increase the level of U.N. involvement in the population field. The resolution called for action under five main heads:

*First*, the Secretary-General was requested to conduct an "inquiry" among member states "concerning the particular problems confronting them as a result of the reciprocal action of economic development and population changes."

This inquiry will help focus the attention of responsible officials in all countries on the implications of population trends for economic and social planning, open up channels of communication between policy makers and local demographic experts, and encourage governments without competent experts of their own to seek outside assistance. Such assistance will be available not only from the United Nations but from various foreign governments and private institutions—in the case of the United States, from such agencies as AID, the U.S. Census Bureau, the Ford Foundation, and the Population Council.

*Second*, the Economic and Social Council of the United Nations was asked, in cooperation with the Specialized Agencies, Regional Economic Commissions and the Population Commission, to "intensify its studies and research on the interrelationship of population growth and economic and social development with particular reference to the needs of the developing countries for investment in health and educational facilities . . ."

The intensification of studies and research called for under this section will involve not only a substantial increase in the program of work of the population section at U.N. Headquarters, the demographic staffs of the Regional Economic Commissions, and the Regional Demographic Research and Training Centers, but also correlative studies in the educational and health fields conducted in cooperation with UNESCO and the World Health Organization.

*Third*, the Economic and Social Council was directed to report its findings with respect to all of the foregoing to the General Assembly not later than at the Assembly's 19th session in 1964.

*Fourth*, United Nations agencies were asked to encourage and assist governments, especially of the less developed countries. "In obtaining basic data and carrying out essential studies of the demographic aspects as well as other aspects of their economic and social development problems."

*Fifth*, the World Population Conference scheduled for 1965 was requested to "pay special attention to the inter-relationships of population growth with economic and social development particularly in countries that are less developed . . ."

As noted earlier, the Resolution containing these five action paragraphs was approved overwhelmingly with no negative votes. A good deal of controversy developed, however, over another section not included in the Resolution as finally adopted which read:

". . . and that the United Nations give technical assistance as requested by governments for national projects and programs dealing with the problems of population."

This section was widely interpreted as calling for United Nations technical assistance in the actual implementation of family planning programs. It was approved by a narrow margin in Committee but in the Plenary, where a two-thirds majority is required on important questions, it failed of adoption by a vote of 34 in favor, 34 against, with 32 abstentions.

As a practical matter, the defeat of this paragraph did not alter the authority already possessed by the United Nations as a result of previous resolutions of the General Assembly and of the Economic and Social Council to grant technical assistance upon request to member nations.

The momentum generated by the General Assembly resolution was maintained at subsequent meetings of the United Nations which have taken place in the last few months.

A resolution on Intensification of Demographic Studies, Research and Training introduced by the United States in association with Japan and the United Arab Republic was unanimously adopted by the Population Commission in February and the Economic and Social Council in April. This resolution spelled out some of the practical implications of the

General Assembly resolution and contained other important provisions as well.

Among other things, the resolution

—Invited the Regional Economic Commissions to intensify their demographic work;

—Requested the U.N. to accelerate preparation of technical manuals for use in demographic work, hasten revision of certain basic demographic publications, and study the use of electronic computers in the analysis of demographic data;

—Requested adequate budgetary provision for this and other work,

—And urged the developed countries to "consider the value to the developing countries" of initiating or expanding research on the interrelationship between population trends and economic and social development, research related to population such as on health and education, training of experts in the less developed countries in demography and statistics, and providing technical assistance to the developing countries in census taking, vital statistics and utilizing demographic data in social and economic planning.

Since the passage of the General Assembly resolution the U.N. Secretariat has also begun work on the inquiry to member governments.

This inquiry will take the form of a questionnaire which will be sent to each member of the United Nations or of the Specialized Agencies.

When the answers to this questionnaire are compiled and analyzed and laid before the General Assembly in 1964, the United Nations will have before it the most comprehensive information yet assembled on the attitudes and policies of government on the population problem.

### III

The debate in the General Assembly which preceded the passage of the resolution on "Population Growth and Economic Development" provided a striking illustration of the unique value of the United Nations as an international forum. It was an enlightening experience for all of us who had the privilege to participate on behalf of our respective Governments. It is tempting to describe this fascinating debate in detail, but time will permit only a brief (and inevitably oversimplified) summary of the principal viewpoints which emerged.

The *first* viewpoint was represented by the Government of Sweden and the other sponsors of the resolution—Ceylon, Denmark, Ghana, Greece, Nepal, Norway, Pakistan, Tunisia, Turkey, Uganda and United Arab Republic. These supporters of the resolution argued that population growth posed grave problems for economic and social development and that urgent action was required to deal with it. They advocated a major increase in United Nations activity in the population field—including technical assistance in the field of family planning. Beyond the cosponsors of the resolution support for this viewpoint was expressed by most Moslem countries, some countries of Asia (e.g., India, Thailand, Malaya and Japan) and some countries of Africa. This viewpoint found only scattered support in Latin America.

A *second* viewpoint was put forward by Argentina and Ireland, with support from a few other countries, principally in Latin America. These countries questioned the existence of a population problem, challenged the right of the United Nations to discuss it, and were particularly outspoken in opposing a U.N. program in family planning financed from technical assistance funds to which they were contributing.

A *third* viewpoint was expressed by a substantial number of countries including France and other countries of continental Europe, some French African countries and some Latin American countries. These countries conceded the existence of population problems in some areas but argued that action by the United Nations should be deferred pending further study. This group opposed the controversial technical assistance section and took the initiative in introducing the proposal for an inquiry on member countries' population problems.

A *fourth* viewpoint was that expressed by the members of the Soviet bloc. During the General Assembly debate, the Soviet Union and some of its satellites expounded the traditional Communist position that Western discussions of the population problem were based on "neo-Malthusian fallacies" and that population problems ceased to exist under Communism.

This Communist line was poorly received by the Assembly. At least one representative of a less developed country chided the Soviets for favoring planning in all sectors of economic life except the human sector —the one most important in its implications for economic and social growth.

The negative Soviet statement in the population debate was followed by a significant shift in the Communist line. When it came time to vote, the Soviet bloc did not oppose, but merely abstained, on the General Assembly resolution.

What is even more surprising, the Soviet representative at the recent meeting of the Economic and Social Council commended the United Nations for its work in the population field, agreed that population growth is an urgent problem for less developed countries, and announced the willingness of the Soviet Union to provide technical assistance in the demographic field.

This change in the Soviet position on population in the United Nations follows reports of increasing resort in recent years to birth control and abortion within the Soviet Union and some other bloc countries and of Khrushchev's personal interest in a recent publication stressing the economic dangers of over-population.

The recent discussions at the United Nations may signal a new era of Soviet propaganda on the subject of population. Whether because of internal problems, or a desire to cultivate the favor of less developed countries, or both, the Soviet Union now appears ready to exercise leadership in action programs in the population field.

As for the United States, our position in the United Nations debate is already known. We made a strong statement underlining the importance of the population problem, the need for more knowledge about it, and the necessity for each country to determine its own population policy in accordance with its economic, social, cultural and religious circumstances.

More specifically, we expressed support for the resolution on "Population Growth and Economic Development" in its original form, which included the controversial section on technical assistance. We abstained, however, in the separate vote on this paragraph for two reasons:

—First, because it was superfluous, neither adding nor subtracting from the authority already possessed by the United Nations to grant technical assistance upon request to member nations;

—Second, because of our belief that, in the light of the views expressed in the General Assembly debate, United Nations activity should emphasize those three areas in which there was broad agreement among the members, namely, information, training and discussion in population problems.

I shall have more to say about this second consideration in a moment.

IV

What conclusions can we draw from the United Nations debates on the population problem? What forms of international cooperation should we be seeking on this subject in the years ahead?

I believe we can identify an emerging consensus on the subject of population. My review of the recent United Nations debate has emphasized the differences between the member countries. Yet this debate—just as recent discussions within our own country—also revealed a large measure of common ground.

To begin with, the desire for increased knowledge about population trends, particularly in relation to economic and social development, is now nearly universal. We have passed, almost without noticing it, from a period in which the major uncertainty concerned the existence of the world population problem, to a period in which the major uncertainty is what can and should be done about it.

Moreover, even in the matter of what should be done about the population problem, it is possible to see:

—That there is no significant body of responsible opinion among people of any major religious, ethical or ideological persuasion which advocates totally unplanned or unregulated fertility, although there are sincere differences of opinion about the means which are morally permissible and the effectiveness of the means which are available.

—That there is virtually universal agreement on both ethical and practical grounds, that decisions about responsible parenthood can be made only by individual parents themselves in the light of their responsibilities to their children and their society, and to the moral values which govern alike parents, children and societies.

The time has come to develop out of this consensus a blueprint for international cooperation which takes account of the politics as well as the economics of the population problem.

The fundamental concept in such a blueprint should be the principle of free choice.

Despite the growing consensus on the matters already mentioned, differences continue to exist between religious groups on specific methods of family planning. When it comes to implementation of population policy, the views of all groups should be respected. Participation in programs of family planning should be contingent upon the agreement of the country concerned.

As we noted in the Assembly, the United Nations already has authority to grant technical assistance in the population field upon request to member governments. From a practical point of view, however, it is unnecessary to earmark United Nations funds for those particular activities in the population field on which members are seriously divided. The potential resources of the United Nations both in terms of funds and personnel for the implementation of family planning programs are minuscule compared to the resources in member countries. In the pluralistic society of the free world there is a wide variety of sources of assistance from governments, foundations, universities, and even private business firms as well as international organizations.

All of these have something to contribute in the field of population. All can make more substantial contributions in the future than has been done in the past. What we need is an international division of labor, taking account of the comparative advantage, from the political as well as the economic and technical point of view, of the different sources of potential assistance.

The following is a rough blueprint of a program of international co-operation which the United States will be supporting in the months ahead with respect to the key elements of the population problem:

## 1. *Information and Analysis*

There is, as noted earlier, a need for more demographic information and analysis, particularly on the interrelation between population growth and economic and social development. Since there is universal agreement on this need, all governments and international organizations, as well as private institutions, can play a significant role.

The United States will continue to support the expansion of United Nations activities in the demographic field. Moreover, the Agency for International Development will respond to requests for assistance from developing countries in preparing, executing and analyzing population censuses, and in utilizing demographic data and analyses in social and economic planning. It will do this both by making United States advisers available and by training experts from the developing countries themselves.

## 2. *Medical Research*

There seems to be widespread agreement on the need for more knowledge about the basic life processes which govern child bearing. As President Kennedy pointed out in a press conference, we need to know more about the whole reproduction cycle, and this information should be made more available to the world so that everyone can make his own judgment.

Paradoxical as it may seem, we need more knowledge on how to overcome both involuntary childlessness and involuntary parenthood through measures which are consistent with different religious, cultural, and economic circumstances. We need particularly a great deal more study of human fertility and reproduction.

We support studies to this end through our own National Institutes of Health. Moreover, we favor the conduct of such studies through the United Nations, specifically through the medical research program of the World Health Organization.

## 3. *Health and Social Services*

The major obstacle to the implementation of family planning policies in the less developed countries is the lack of a network of health and social services to implement policy at the village level. The development of such an institutional infrastructure is desirable for its own sake as well as for the implementation of family planning policies. It commands wide spread endorsement and should be the object of intensified efforts by governments and private institutions as well as by United Nations agencies.

### 4. *The Implementation of Family Planning Programs*

This is the only area in which major disagreements exist and may continue to exist for the foreseeable future. Countries seeking help in the implementation of family planning programs should have access to the whole variety of sources of assistance available throughout the world.

While the United States will not advocate any specific family planning policy to any other country, we can help other countries, upon request, to find potential sources of information and assistance on ways and means of dealing with population problems. The provision of materials for this purpose can best be done by those governments whose citizens are not divided on this question, by private foundations, and by business firms.

The implementation of this blueprint in the years ahead will require flexibility and imagination. The further challenge is to devise programs of action founded on the principle of free choice which make sense in political as well as in technical and economic terms.

28.

# THE ASIAN POPULATION CONFERENCE

*by Annabelle Desmond*

The first Asian Population Conference was held in New Delhi, India, December 10-20, 1963. Sponsored by the United Nations Economic Commission for Asia and the Far East (ECAFE) and the United Nations Social Affairs Department, it was the first conference of governments ever held with a mandate to make recommendations for population policies. Delegates represented 15 Asian countries, the United Nations and its specialized agencies, and a number of Western governments, including the United States. In addition, there were observers representing private organizations such as foundations and church groups.

This article consists of excerpts reprinted with permission from the April 1964 issue of Population Bulletin, which is published eight times a year by the Population Reference Bureau, 1755 Massachusetts Ave., N.W., Washington, D. C. 20036.

The Conference's recommendations reflect the thoughtful consideration which was given to the many problems created by rapid population
growth in the ECAFE region. The recommendations cover in depth the
following broad areas: national population policies; international cooperation; questions of economic and social policy and planning relevant to
population problems; and development of demographic statistics, population projections, and analysis.

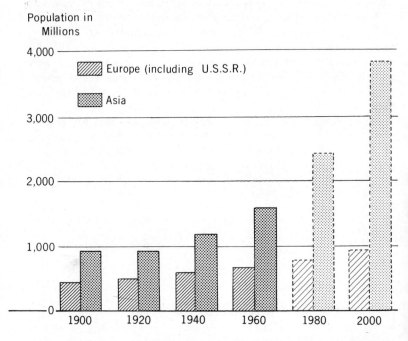

FIG. 1. Population growth in Europe and Asia, 1900-2000. Asia's population
is growing more than twice as fast as Europe's. If present growth rates continue to 2000, Europe's population will remain below the billion mark while
Asia's will soar to almost 4 billion.

Among the questions of economic and social policy and planning
relevant to population problems, specific recommendations were proposed relating to agriculture and food supply, health programs, social
welfare problems, educational programs, problems of economic growth,
policies designed to promote fuller utilization of human resources, programs relating to fertility and family planning, and policies and programs
relating to urbanization, internal migration and population distribution.

The recommendations relating to health programs and fertility and family planning are quoted in their entirety:

*Health Programmes.* Although death rates have been reduced drastically during the last few years in most of the ECAFE region, the public health facilities available in many countries are still only elementary. In the face of the high levels of infant mortality, high proportions of deaths from communicable diseases, high death rates from intestinal diseases attributable mainly to the lack of environmental sanitation and safe water supply, and high death rates of females in the reproductive ages, the need for further development of health programmes is apparent. This, as well as economic and social development aimed to improve the levels of living of the population, is adversely affected by the rapid growth of population.

Nevertheless, substantial and rapid reductions in mortality have been achieved by improving medical and health services in many areas of the region, and where, as in most ECAFE countries, there is an absence of corresponding reductions in fertility, the result has been increasing rates of population growth. A similar trend is also imminent in the remaining areas of the region where mortality is still relatively high. It is recognized that improvement in health, as in other components of the level of living, may be jeopardized or at least retarded by too-rapid population growth.

The Conference therefore recommends:

(a) Research on the changing health needs occasioned by current and prospective demographic trends, as well as the demographic consequences of health programmes, should be intensified at the national level.

(b) In addition to national efforts, international agencies should direct more attention to the study and evaluation of demographic aspects of health problems in the ECAFE region.

(c) As an aid to expansion of study and research in this field, national data on mortality and morbidity must be improved; and at least until adequate facilities render this unnecessary, consideration should be given to the use of temporary measures such as nomenclatures and classifications of diseases for non-medical personnel.

(d) In countries where it is found desirable and feasible to promote measures for the moderation of fertility as a means of promoting family welfare and health, such measures should be an integral part when planning or extending health services.

The Conference recognizes that health needs are served not only by medical, but also by other social and economic programmes and activities, and that the consequences to health arising from social and economic changes are very considerable. It therefore considers important the integration of health programmes into overall development plans for each nation, and emphasizes the need for long-term programming of training of personnel and provision of utilities, facilities and services, taking into account the changing needs in the future, so that the long-term as well as short-term returns from investments in health may be maximized.

*Programmes Relating to Fertility and Family Planning.* In view of the rapid rates of population growth, several governments in the region, including those of India, Pakistan and the Republic of Korea, have made family planning a national policy. Some other governments in the region are assisting voluntary organizations in family planning work. Still others have expressed concern with respect to the consequences of high birth rates for mothers' health and family welfare as well as national social and economic development.

The Conference notes that the Asian countries which have made family planning a part of national policy are handicapped in their efforts to make this policy effective by lack of experience and pertinent knowledge. It observes that each government is developing its programme to suit national needs in keeping with the cultural values of different sections of the population. With a view to accelerating progress in achieving the goals of family planning programmes, the Conference recommends that governments which have undertaken such programmes or are contemplating such action should pool their knowledge and experience with respect to communication of ideas on family planning and adoption of family planning methods.

The recognition given to the policies of governments, and the suggestion that countries with action programs discuss their mutual experiences, represent an immense advance over previous years when conferences considered the problems of population growth but never dared mention the basic need to attack high birth rates. However, one might ask whether the recommendation to pool "knowledge and experience with respect to communication of ideas on family planning and adoption of family planning methods" is not a timid approach to the basic solution—lower birth rates—in view of the lateness of the hour in Asia's population crisis.

Some of the ECAFE nations have adopted population policies to control growth and others are moving in that direction. (A review of population policies in individual countries is given in *Population Bulletin*, April 1964, pp. 44-45.) In India, Korea, and Pakistan, government programs to control population growth are in operation. In Ceylon, Hong Kong, Taiwan, and Singapore, the governments support voluntary, non-official family-planning programs. In Japan and Taiwan, this service is offered in the health centers. In Thailand, the government has begun to examine its population problem and is considering a program to limit growth. None of these programs, however, is adequate to the need. Some of them are experimental, restricted only to a single or a few areas.

The time has come for the governments of these and other countries to give their population problems a priority equal to that given economic development. Governments should mobilize all resources for action programs which will speed acceptance of the small family pattern. Unless this miracle of social revolution can be accomplished within the next few decades, governments might be faced with economic, political, and social chaos. In that event, death rates would rise to check population growth.

## *The Conference Resolution*

The Conference recognized that each country in the ECAFE region has its own population problems, and that no single population policy would be suitable for all "in view of the differences among countries in size, density and rate of growth of population, natural resources and other conditions of the economy, and characteristics of national culture." This parallels the view of the United Nations General Assembly that each government must decide its own policy. However, the Conference resolution stresses the urgency for the governments of the ECAFE region to adopt national population policies and to initiate programs to implement those policies. The resolution also calls for international cooperation, through the United Nations, to provide national governments with the necessary technical assistance for experimentation and action in all aspects of the population problem, including family welfare planning programs. The resolution is reprinted in full:

*Recognizing* that the problems of population and social and economic development are inter-related and that the acceleration of social and economic progress is, in its turn, of great importance to the removal of obstacles created by high rates of population growth:

I. National Policy and Action

*Considering*:

(a) that the rapid growth of population in many countries of the ECAFE region is impeding their economic and social development and threatening the success of their efforts to reach satisfactory levels of living within a tolerable length of time;

(b) that the high proportion of young children in the population which results from a high birth rate is an impediment to progress especially in the educational field;

(c) that rapid growth of population in the countryside increases pressure on the land while any consequent acceleration in migration creates additional problems of social and economic adjustment;

*Invites* the governments of States, members of the Economic Commission for Asia and the Far East:

(a) to take account of the urgency of adopting a positive population policy relating to their individual needs and to the general needs of the region;

(b) to take account of the recommendations of this Conference relating to national population policies in the formulation and execution of their general policies and plans for social and economic development.

II. International Co-operation

*Further noting* that the efforts to find satisfactory and effective solutions for population problems are hampered in many countries in the region by lack of facilities and funds, of technical assistance, and of comprehensive and reliable demographic statistics, and by insufficient development of demographic and socio-biological research and shortage of personnel with appropriate training and experience;

*Recalling* the recommendations of the General Assembly in its resolution 1838 (XVII) of 18 December 1962 favouring intensified research on inter-relationships of population growth and social and economic development with particular reference to the developing countries, and of the Economic and Social Council in its resolution of April 1963 inviting regional economic commissions to examine possibilities of intensifying their work in the demographic field;

*Requests* the Executive Secretary to take note of the recommendations of this Conference, with a view to:

(a) facilitating direct exchange of information at the department level among governments within the region on all aspects of population and social and economic growth;

(b) expanding the scope of technical assistance available to governments in the region, upon their request, for data collection, research, experimentation and action in all aspects of population problems, including family welfare planning programmes, through regional advisory services, development and strengthening of regional, sub-regional and national training and research institutions, study tours, fellowships, and meetings of technical groups;

(c) expanding the services of the ECAFE secretariat in the field of population;

*Strongly requests* the Economic Commission for Asia and the Far East to give its full support to the recommendations of this Conference.

## Action Needed Now

Conspicuous by its absence in this discussion of public health and population growth is the United Nations World Health Organization (WHO), which should be an important catalyst in bringing knowledge relating to health and welfare to all of the world's people. In 1952, the government of India requested technical aid from WHO in dealing with its population problem. This resulted in a proposal made by Norway that an expert committee be appointed to examine the health aspects of the population question. The ensuing debate on the proposal almost tore WHO asunder. The delegate from Ireland made a statement implying that the organization might lose members if it became involved in birth control. Delegates from Belgium and Italy supported this position. On the population problem, WHO's voice has hardly been audible since that unfortunate dispute.

In the interim, world population has increased by more than half a billion. World opinion concerning the problem has changed radically. In view of this, WHO's inaction can only be interpreted as anachronistic. Today, it is the economic and social agencies of the United Nations which are moving ahead on the population front. But there are clear, well-defined functions for WHO since strengthening health services in member countries is a basic objective.

WHO could meet the new challenge to public health by working to break down two major barriers which now block the transfer of health and welfare knowledge to the people in the developing countries. Health facilities and services must be greatly expanded in areas where they now exist; and they must be extended to areas with no health services. Multitudes of Asians must be trained to transmit health education, including family welfare planning, to millions of their compatriots.

Family size should be a matter of individual decision. Today there is an urgent necessity to transfer this message of freedom and hope to all of the world's people. This enormous task should be given the highest priority by the governments of all countries. It should concern all United Nations agencies, not only those working to stimulate economic development. It is a task which is central to the objectives of WHO, the United Nations International Childrens Emergency Fund (UNICEF), and the United Nations Educational Scientific and Cultural Organization (UNESCO).

All of these organizations support programs which defer death. Now that low birth rates are essential for the health and welfare of the world's people, they must accept the challenge of balanced health programs by supporting action which reduces rapid population growth.

Improved statistical services, study tours, fellowships, and meetings of technical groups—all of these are important, and their long-term practical value is not to be denied. However, one point cannot be too strongly stressed: If emphasis on these activities is allowed to blur the urgent need to get ahead with a direct attack on dangerously high birth rates, this would invite delay and equivocation. This danger is illustrated in the repeated statements made by spokesmen for the U. S. Government, emphasizing official participation through AID programs to improve censuses in the underdeveloped countries.

Such programs obviously should continue. But they should not be allowed to dilute the central problem of balancing birth rates with modern death rates. Such an attack on high birth rates extends very far beyond the purely technical and demographic aspects. Though the two areas of activity are related, they can and should be dealt with independently and simultaneously. The population crisis would be no nearer a solution if a complete census of the entire population of the earth were possible tomorrow, or in 1980. To pretend otherwise is to invite disaster.

29.

# PLANNED PARENTHOOD—
# WORLD POPULATION REPORT

*By Alan F. Guttmacher*

"Reverence for Life," the theme of the Planned Parenthood-World Population organization for 1964, expresses with simple eloquence the essence of the family planning movement. Planned Parenthood applies the Reverence for Life concept by placing the creation of life under the discipline of man's ethical principles and intellect—through conception control. The aim of Planned Parenthood is to assure each new infant the birthright of a warm welcome in a loving home, by enabling parents to have the number of children they want, when they want them. Today hundreds of thousands, perhaps millions, share with us the conviction that the greatest threat to collective peace and stability, and individual happiness and dignity, is the heedless, unplanned multiplication of the world's most precious commodity—people.

This report covers the activities of Planned Parenthood in the United States during the year 1963, carried forward by local family planning organizations in nearly forty states, and by the national headquarters of Planned Parenthood—World Population (PP-WP). In 1963, more Americans than ever before requested and received fertility control services from Planned Parenthood Affiliates. Meanwhile, family planning has grown swiftly as a global answer to help curb the population crisis—with PP-WP as a mainstay of its leadership and support.

Deputy Assistant Secretary of State Richard N. Gardner heralded 1963 as "the year of the big breakthrough on population." He, of course, was assessing the situation in terms of the change in official United States policy. This change was high-lighted in April of that year by the late President Kennedy's forthright endorsement of efforts to learn "more about the whole reproductive cycle" so that this knowledge can "be made more available to the world." It was reflected in a published acknowledgment by former President Eisenhower that his opposition in

This article consists of excerpts from the Planned Parenthood-World Population Annual Report for 1963, by Alan F. Guttmacher, M.D., President. It was published by the Planned Parenthood Federation of America, Inc., 515 Madison Avenue, New York, New York.

1959 to government action on population was carried "too far." Expressing the urgency of discovering "realistic" ways to cope with the population explosion, the former President called for mobilization of scientific research on this problem and asserted that the U.S. "should tell [other] nations how population growth threatens them and what can be done about it."

The shift from acceptance in theory to positive action was foreshadowed by developments in four major areas:

1. The continued evolution of official U.S. policy, marked by public support for action programs from leaders of both parties and the adoption by Congress of its first legislation in the field.

2. Assumption of responsibility for family planning by an increasing number of tax-supported health and welfare agencies.

3. The deepening of discussions between non-Catholics and Catholics aimed at solutions which respect the conscientious convictions of all faiths.

4. The continued burgeoning of service programs offered at the 249 family planning centers run by PP-WP's 106 Affiliates across the country. The number of birth control patients at our Centers increased by one-quarter during 1963, while the number of patients choosing oral contraception jumped more than 60 percent.

Since nearly seven out of every ten of our patient-families have net incomes below $4,000 a year, these unprecedented gains bear witness to the eager acceptance of sympathetic and authoritative family planning guidance by low-income families.

The extraordinary climate that was clearly evident during 1963, together with the refocusing of the nation's attention at year's end on the manifold problems of low-income Americans, offered many new opportunities for constructive leadership and service by PP-WP and its Affiliates. To meet these challenges adequately, Planned Parenthood took steps to create in 1964 a nationwide campaign structure capable of attracting funds sufficient to support urgently needed expansion programs —locally, nationally and internationally.

## U. S. POLICY

President Kennedy's statement was the first by any President to endorse action on the population problem. His words were followed by the government's contribution of $500,000 to the World Health Organization for studies in human reproduction, and by the creation of a major new research division of the National Institutes of Health—the National Institute of Child Health and Human Development.

The new policy also stimulated increasing activity by agencies concerned with foreign aid. Almost immediately following the President's remarks, the State Department and the Agency for International Development distributed to Embassies and Missions overseas a statement affirming U.S. willingness to "help other countries, upon request, to find potential sources of information and assistance on ways and means of dealing with population problems." The direction of U.S. policy became further evident in December when Congress authorized, in the new foreign aid bill, the use of assistance funds for "research into the problems of population growth." Significantly, this provision, authored by Sen. William Fulbright (D-Ark), was adopted unanimously by the Senate Foreign Relations Committee.

Nor was this the only indication of Congressional concern, for during the year Sens. Joseph Clark (D-Pa) and Ernest Gruening (D-Alaska) took the floor to deliver major addresses on the subject of population. Later, the Pennsylvania Senator underscored the new climate of political feasibility by advising his colleagues that he had received no serious criticism from his constituents. This prompted Sen. Clark to observe that "the atmosphere had changed completely in the past year or two."

The population problem figured in the hearings of several Congressional Committees—the House Subcommittee on Immigration and Naturalization, the Senate Committee on Banking, and the Senate Committee on Labor's Sub-Committee on Employment and Manpower, which heard testimony by PP-WP Chairman Donald B. Straus urging that efforts to cope with unemployment should include research into the impact of rapid U.S. population growth on joblessness.

The nation's most distinguished scientific body, the quasi-governmental National Academy of Sciences, in a comprehensive report issued in April 1963, added its powerful voice to those supporting massive expansion of biological and social research on population, as well as training programs for family planning administrators. "Other than the search for lasting peace," the report stated, "no other problem is more urgent."

The growing consensus that positive action is now needed was indicated by the sweeping call for constructive measures by federal, state and local governments which emanated from the 23rd American Assembly held at Arden House. Eighty leading educators, business executives, scientists of many disciplines and religious leaders from all three major faiths attended the three-day Assembly which examined the population dilemma. Your president was there, and many Planned Parenthood leaders participated in the subsequent regional Assemblies which took similar stands.

## THE EMERGING PATTERN OF PUBLIC RESPONSIBILITY

National developments were paralleled at state, county and city levels by the emergence of a clearly discernible, though still nascent, pattern of assumption of responsibility for family planning services by tax-supported institutions. In this process, PP-WP and its Affiliates played a significant role, serving as catalyst, consultant, conscience and not infrequently, cooperating agency.

Of greatest significance, perhaps, was Congressional approval of a $25,000 appropriation to provide birth control services and supplies in Health Department maternity clinics of the District of Columbia. The District's appropriation bill also authorized the Welfare Department to spend $30,000 for similar services for relief recipients. Credit for the evolution of this program, which began operation on April 1, 1964, is due largely to PP-WP's Washington Affiliate.

Elsewhere, there were unmistakable signs that tax-supported health and welfare departments and public hospitals are at last *beginning* to remedy the long-standing discriminatory medical practice which has virtually restricted effective family planning to those able to employ the services of a private physician. To be sure, there is wide variation in these initial programs, which range from simple referrals and information to state- and county-sponsored and financed services and supplies. But by the year's end, one could point to 21 states and the nation's capital in which at least some beginnings have been made toward the integration of family planning in publicly financed medical and welfare programs.

There is room here only to sketch a few highlights. In Illinois, the protracted battle over birth control for welfare recipients resulted in an interim compromise, restricting the state-financed service to married relief clients, while a legislative commission considers future public policy. In Maryland, some form of family planning is now offered in health departments in 11 out of 23 counties. In California, the number of city or county health agencies offering varying programs has increased to 21. In Kansas, repeal of a restrictive state law has paved the way for initiation of services in county clinics. In Tennessee, the policy-making Public Health Council endorsed birth control as part of medical care and instructed the State Health Department to launch a pilot project. In Oregon, the State Board of Social Welfare approved referrals to PP-WP's new Portland Affiliate, while in Dallas, our Affiliate's mobile unit functioned at well-baby clinics operated by the County Health Department, offering free contraceptive services to thousands of indigent mothers.

And a prolonged campaign reached its partial objective in January of this year when welfare officials in both New York State and New York

City adopted policies authorizing referrals for birth control of married couples on relief—and reimbursement for the cost of service and supplies.

In addition to developments in the new areas, there was a qualitative change in programs offered in several of the seven Southeastern states which for two decades have authorized birth control services through their health departments. Projects offering oral contraceptives to women on relief were initiated in Dade County, Florida; Florence County, South Carolina; and Johnston County, North Carolina, following the un-questioned success of a welfare clinic of this kind launched in 1960 in Mecklenburg County, North Carolina. Oral pills are, also being pre-scribed extensively by the Mississippi Health Department. In Alabama, where 64 of 67 counties offer some form of birth control, the State Health Department joined with the Planned Parenthood League of Ala-bama and the University of Chicago's Community and Family Study Center in a project designed to increase family planning services in health clinics. In Florida, with PP-WP Consultant Robert Browning serving as coordinator, 14 counties agreed on a plan designed to provide continuity of health services, including family planning, to agricultural workers in the East Coast migrant stream.

In this context, it is not surprising that requests from public agencies to both National headquarters and Affiliates for guidance and assistance in-creased noticeably. A possible prototype for the orientation of public health personnel was developed in the convening of two all-day training institutes in family planning, sponsored jointly by the North Carolina State Health Department and PP-WP under a grant from the Mary Reynolds Babcock Foundation. Utilizing Federation staff and health department officials from several states as participants, the sessions in Winston-Salem and Raleigh were attended by more than 200 physicians and nurses representing 58 of the state's 100 counties, as well as official observers from Georgia, Mississippi and Tennessee.

Enhanced interest in this aspect of our program was evidenced by the reception given to a major new Federation publication, *Birth Control Services in Tax-Supported Hospitals, Health Departments and Welfare Agencies,* which assembled the views of 15 experts who participated in recent PP-WP symposia. Two printings, totalling 20,000 copies, have been necessary to fill requests for the booklet from professional workers.

## ACTIVITIES OF PROFESSIONAL GROUPS

In consonance with these trends in the public agencies, several impor-tant professional groups stepped up their activities in the family plan-ning field. The American College of Obstetricians and Gynecologists for the first time approved a resolution urging that birth control methods, consistent with religious convictions, be made available to all groups, and at the same time recommended expansion of research on all aspects of human fertility. The American Medical Association, which approved birth control as long ago as 1937, established a new Committee on Human Reproduction charged with considering problems pertaining to family planning and related areas.

The American Public Health Association, which formally endorsed family planning as an integral part of preventive medicine in 1959, established a Program Area Committee on Population and Public Health, thus recognizing the field as a major object of APHA concern. To implement the recommendations contained in its report referred to earlier, the National Academy of Sciences created a continuing committee on population. Government-sponsored birth control programs for indigent families also received a strong endorsement in September from the president of the National Medical Association, the organization of Negro physicians.

Intensified professional interest was further indicated by the numerous requests for members of the Federation staff to lecture before medical schools, schools of public health, medical societies and specialists' groups. Similarly, PP-WP participated in a seminar on family planning during the conference of the National Citizens Committee for the World Health Organization.

## THE DIALOGUE

Underlying these significant national events was an outpouring of forceful and friendly discussion between Catholics and non-Catholics, as well as among Catholics themselves, on the problems of global population growth, responsible parenthood and fertility control. A strong stimulant to this creative ferment was Dr. John Rock's book, *The Time Has Come,* in which the eminent Catholic physician clearly detailed the substantial agreemeent among the faiths on the objective of responsible parenthood and vigorously called for a major mobilization of scientific talent to discover family planning techniques acceptable to all religious groups. While many Catholic spokesmen disagreed with his argument that the oral progestational agents are acceptable within Church doctrine, there was support for his plea for research as the key to the solution of remaining religious differences over permissible methods of family limitation. For example, Cardinal Cushing of Boston voiced his dissent on the oral pills but nevertheless found "much that is good" in Dr. Rock's book and described his appeal for a concentrated research effort as "eloquent and much needed."

Catholic leaders placed increasing emphasis on the Church's doctrine of responsible parenthood. This was exemplified by Cardinal Ritter of St. Louis who said that "there is an erroneous idea that Catholic couples should have as many children as God will give them. God bless them if they desire it, but there's no such Church law." The widening area of interfaith agreement was underscored by the simultaneous publication in a national Catholic weekly, *Ave Maria,* and a Protestant periodical, *Christian Century,* of three cogent articles urging action on the population problem by the Rev. John A. O'Brien of the University of Notre Dame. Opportunities also multiplied for the frank exchange of views between Catholic spokesmen and Planned Parenthood spokesmen.

The newly established Center for Population Research at Georgetown University is engaged in research on menstrual periodicity in the hope that ways will be found to anticipate ovulation by some fixed observable changes, thus helping to perfect the church-approved rhythm technique. Coincidentally, an increasing number of Catholic hospitals (in several cases with Planned Parenthood cooperation) opened clinics offering the rhythm method. Among leading European Catholics, there were similarly extensive explorations of the new avenues of approach to the population problem, particularly in the context of the Ecumenical Council.

A comprehensive synthesis, published by the *New York Times* in a series of four major articles, brought these developments to public attention and documented the existence of national and international trends which may open the way for joint action by Catholics and non-Catholics. In all this, informed observers saw the beginnings of a historic transformation. *Science,* the journal of the American Association for the Advancement of Science, commented:

> Feelings are still tender from the prolonged and nasty controversy that surrounded anything associated with birth control, and, since cooperation and peace are essential and highly prized, no one is trumpeting victory. But it is probably safe to say 1963 was the year when the efforts of population planning organizations and the enormity of the population problem overwhelmed long-established and tenaciously held ideological positions, and opened the way for beginning substantial efforts toward turning down the world's population curve.

### The International Picture

The stepped-up pace of activities at home in 1963 was more than matched overseas as governmental and voluntary groups in many nations developed their programs. In these efforts the International Planned Parenthood Federation, with member groups in 35 countries, played an increasingly significant role. PP-WP leaders actively participated in shaping the IPPF program. Furthermore, America's financial contribution to the world organization was increased by nearly 40 percent.

The IPPF's Seventh World Conference, held in Singapore in February 1963, drew more than 350 delegates from 38 nations and was clearly the most impressive meeting of the international birth control movement to date. Especially noteworthy was the fact that an unprecedented number of health ministers and other government officials participated, and there could be little doubt that the conference served as a stimulus to action on family planning by many governments, particularly in Asia.

The training of family planning personnel in the Southeast Asia Region will be greatly facilitated by the opening during 1964 of the IPPF Asian Training Center in Singapore. Land for this center was contributed by the Singapore government and most of the necessary funds for the building were raised in 1963.

There were significant developments in other countries also. In Korea, where the government has appropriated $300,000 annually for family planning, the Planned Parenthood Federation of Korea, with IPPF assistance, has been requested to train clinicians and help extend the program to rural areas. In Thailand, the Council of Ministers approved a program and, as a preliminary to the initiation of services, asked the IPPF to send two Health Ministry physicians on a world-wide trip to study the operation of birth control programs. The International also provided field personnel to work with men in Ceylon. In Pakistan, IPPF conducted a survey to evaluate the feasibility of utilizing village midwives in family planning education.

In a similar manner, IPPF programs have expanded substantially in Africa, the Near East and other areas with rapid rates of population growth. Funds contributed in the U.S. are being utilized to establish adequate regional headquarters, employ a professional staff and build a strong program. The acquisition by the International of a suitable headquarters building in London was another noteworthy development during 1963. To give world-wide medical leadership in the family planning field, the Medical Committee of IPPF was reorganized during the year, and I am honored to serve as chairman of this body.

Of special significance to Americans are the many new and exciting developments in the family planning field in Latin America, an area which has some of the highest rates of population growth in the world. With the active cooperation of the IPPF's Western Hemisphere Region, to which PP-WP belongs, a number of countries took important steps forward during 1963. In addition to Chile, which opened several clinics in government hospitals two years ago, family planning organizations were formed in at least seven other countries, five of which—Brazil, Honduras, Mexico, Uruguay and Venezuela—now have some clinical facilities for the first time.

The United States again played host in 1963 to the two-week Second Family Planning Seminar for Latin American Leaders, which was attended by physicians, public health officers and other specialists from ten of the eleven South American republics. This has proved to be an extremely valuable vehicle for the orientation of foreign leaders in the philosophy and methodology of fertility control. The sessions coincided with our Annual Meeting and many of the Latin American delegates were interested participants in both meetings. The seminar was ably presided over by Dr. Aquiles J. Sobrero, Director of the Margaret Sanger Research Bureau, himself a Latin American physician. Discussion leaders included many distinguished U. S. professors and government officials.

30.

# THE INITIATION OF CONTRACEPTIVE SERVICES

*by Clarence J. Gamble*

After the discovery of each new means of promoting health there is a long slow process of public education required before its benefits are generally available. Jenner's discovery of vaccination with cowpox made deaths from smallpox unnecessary, yet thousands continued to die of it. Needless deaths from diphtheria occurred long after the antitoxin was known, and they still happen. So, too, it has been with the health benefits of contraception.

For the spread of new health measures the fundamental requirement is public education. The discoverer and his early followers must tell the world of what is available, and for the greatest effectiveness this should be done as rapidly and extensively as possible. With birth control this was not easy. It was so inextricably connected with sex that the repression of public discussion in this field closed many customary educational channels. Margaret Sanger's public meetings to tell families that babies could be spaced were raided by police, and her publications were denied the use of the mails on the grounds that they were obscene. Nonetheless she continued her educational program for decades and is still continuing it.

In addition she provided birth control services for the families of the poor. Her Brownsville, N. Y. clinic was closed by the police in 1916, but in 1923 she, with the help of Dr. Hannah Stone, opened the permanent clinic in New York now known as the Margaret Sanger Research Bureau.

In 1929, the National Committee on Maternal Health under Dr. Robert L. Dickinson, which had been carrying on laboratory researches in the field of contraception, decided to test methods of making pregnancy spacing available in other cities. Miss Louise Bryant, a social worker, was engaged, and Cincinnati, Ohio, was chosen as the first city in which she should work. Because of its newness and the sexual taboo progress was slow. She found, however that leading citizens were interested in providing this health service for their fellow citizens. With her encouragement they formed the Maternal Health Committee of Cincinnati, and helped leading physicians to open a clinic in the Cincinnati City Hospital.

To assist those in other cities to do likewise, a medical social worker was added to the Committee's staff. Following the pattern of Mrs. Sanger in New York and of others in Chicago, Cincinnati, Cleveland and Philadephia, she found health-minded leaders to form committees and open contraceptive clinics under the supervision of physicians in cities in Michigan, Ohio, Indiana, Iowa, Missouri, Kansas and Nebraska. The larger cities were chosen, with the hope that they would subsequently encourage similar activity in their smaller neighbors.

The Third International Conference on Planned Parenthood at Bombay in 1952 brought out the fact that while the United States, the United Kingdom, and India had national Planned Parenthood or Family Planning Associations to spread contraceptive services, local centers of clinical instruction were few in other countries. The National Committee on Maternal Health, therefore, using the experience gained in cities in the United States, undertook to accelerate the formation of such groups by local leaders. In 1958 this work of the Committee and the staff which had been engaged in it were taken over by the Pathfinder Fund.

Beginning in 1952 the author and his son, Richard Gamble, made two trips to Asia; Mrs. Margaret Roots, a social worker from Canada, worked in Asia; Miss Edith Gates, health educator, travelled in the Near East, Africa, and South America; Mrs. Edna McKinnon, former field worker in planned parenthood organizations in the United States, assisted in the Malay States, Indonesia, and Nepal; and Miss Ruth Martin, a registered nurse, visited Africa and South America. Help has been given with the formation of Associations and clinical services in 43 cities in Africa, Asia,

Europe, and the Near East and South America. In 19 countries the staff has helped in the formation of national organizations, 9 of which have become (by 1963) members of the International Planned Parenthood Federation.

From the experience in these countries the following conclusions have been drawn.

1. The best progress in providing contraceptive services is made if a group of local leaders can be found with the interest and energy to form an association for the purpose. Even when such services are provided through governmental or other channels, an association has value in continuing education regarding the value and availability of family planning.

2. Though it was helpful to have preliminary contacts and correspondence, when available, these were found not to be necessary. Talks were readily arranged with leading physicians and nurses, and through them community leaders could be discovered and interested in helping their fellow citizens.

3. A field worker in travelling continually learns what methods of organization and of clinical services are proving to be most successful in the various countries visited. She* can, therefore, offer newly forming associations a wide choice of procedures, enabling them to choose those most suitable to the habits and conditions of their country.

Local leaders, visiting cities in which elaborate clinical equipment and procedures have been developed have sometimes been given the feeling that only these can be effective, and are discouraged and the progress of their groups retarded by the fact that these cannot be duplicated at home.

4. Educational procedures, lectures, discussions, newspaper articles and radio talks, should be planned and local persons guided and encouraged in arranging them. The worker's arrival can be used as a basis for a news item which can often carry the theme that family planning does not require the sacrifice of married life. If clinical services are available they can be mentioned with the street address and the hours when they are open.

5. Printed leaflets telling of the advantages of pregnancy spacing and giving clinic address and hours can be printed in local languages by the local group with the worker's guidance, and using suggestions from samples of leaflets found successful elsewhere. Posters adapted to the customs of the country are also valuable.

6. The greatest element in arousing and continuing local interest was

* There are situations in which, and persons with whom men are needed to present the values of contraception; for others, women are appropriate. In most cases, however, the personality, interest and ability of the representative are more important than the sex. In the experience of the Committee and the Pathfinder Fund the field representatives, most of them women, have shown these qualities to a high degree.

found to be the desire of those working with the association to provide health and happiness for their own neighbors. The form in which this is done varies greatly. In some places, in the early stages, it may be reference to the office of an experienced physician. In others it may be the provision by the Association of services in a government clinic, or the persuasion of government physicians to give the needed instructions. Or it may be by visits to houses by social workers, health workers, or volunteers to give supplies and instructions as directed by the Association's supervising physician. Each family served becomes an educational center through neighborly discussion. Each is an addition to the force of public opinion, with its bearing on future governmental or familiar decisions.

7. Because of the newness of family planning, and the fact that its sexual roots still make it a controversial subject in some communities, the raising of money in the early stages of a family planning committee is extremely difficult. For this reason the provision of the costs of initial activity for lecture halls, printing, room-rent, supplies, and part time or full time workers, has been found in many places to give valuable returns. It may in some places require several years for a newly formed Association to secure adequate local financial support.

8. While much help can be secured from a citizen of the country where the work is being done, the field worker does not need to be a native of the country where the establishment of new family planning services is being attempted. In the early stages of the introduction of such services no local person will have had the necessary experience, and much time and expense would be required to train one. To expand the work from the largest city to others it is valuable to discover and train a suitable local person, but local customs often make this difficult. In some multiracial countries such a person may be able to work only with those of her own race.

9. The most successful family planning associations have been those in which all sections of the community have been included. In some countries in Asia different races or languages have met in this way, and in many African countries the Africans, Asians, and Europeans have worked together. Clinics open to all races were encouraged wherever they were acceptable to local custom.

10. While it might seem that a person from an adjacent country would know local customs better than one from the other side of the globe, this often is not the case. Local jealousies between countries, some of them war-engendered, often make a person from a neighbor-country unacceptable. The very fact that the worker comes from a distance may assure her a better hearing. Fortunately English is so widely understood,

especially in medical circles, that the Pathfinder Fund representatives have met with little language difficulty in talking with community leaders.

11. A physician has advantages in some aspects of the work. It is difficult, however, to find a satisfactory physician who is free to travel continuously. With a worker who is not a doctor local physicians do not have the feeling that someone is coming to teach them what they believe they already know. She can quote physicians in other countries and show reprints of their articles. Pathfinder's non-physician workers have been asked to address Medical Associations in many countries, and their talks have been well received. (Talks have also been given in a mosque and a cathedral.)

12. Associations are apt to become less active with the lapse of time after a worker's visit. Members of the Committee may move away, or go on long-leave, or lose their initial interest. It has been found that a visit at least once a year has been welcomed by the Associations and has proven effective in encouraging them to further steps and to expansion into nearby communities.

13. Periodic reminders of the Associations' objectives have been found helpful in maintaining the interest of those already adherents of the movement and in expanding interest among others. Subscriptions to the Family Planning News and to Round the World News of Population and Birth Control have been used for this purpose. Lists have been prepared, usually of 30 or more in each community, of Association members, leading physicians, city officials and other community leaders to whom these bulletins have been sent. The frequent reminder that the new public health measure is being used in many countries is valuable, and the educational techniques described are often found helpful by the local group. The total value of the mailing to the unconvinced is, perhaps, greater than that to those already Association members.

Some active Associations ask for copies of each issue in bulk to mail from their office, a procedure which makes easier the keeping up-to-date of the mailing list.

14. The argument that family planning is needed to protect a nation from the dangers of a constantly growing population was found to appeal to the more intelligent and educated citizens, but except in India and Japan did not seem to be understood by most people. Far more effective than the population explosion was the argument based on the health and economic condition of the family, that children born at spaced and chosen intervals could be given healthier surroundings and a better upbringing.

15. While interest in and provision of contraceptive instruction will

eventually spread to all countries, experience showed that the process was greatly accelerated by the ability of the field workers to tell community leaders what other nations had done, and to explain the methods by which the new health service had been provided.

16. The numerous centers for the expansion of family planning services which have followed visits of the field representatives of the National Committee on Maternal Health and the Pathfinder Fund have made the program seem an effective procedure. While the numbers of families instructed have not yet been large they have been increasing.

Moreover the Family Planning Associations are reaching beyond their own cities and aiding in the establishment of new associations and new services. The program is helping to bring nearer the day when the ability to space their children will be available to every family.

# 31.

# FINAL REPORT ON
## "THE POPULATION DILEMMA"

### *By The American Assembly*

Never before in history have the security and welfare of mankind been so indivisible. Never before has man acquired the capability of achieving his own extinction. These circumstances require him to marshall his intelligence, control his emotions, and rise above his traditional thought and action in an unprecedented way. Failure to do so may threaten not only his prosperity, security and peace, but also his survival.

Among the serious threats to welfare and security, and therefore to peace, is the accelerating rate of world population growth. The less tangible but very real injury to personal development and the maintenance of family life must also be of concern. Rapid population increase and its accompaniments are obstructing economic development, and thereby contributing to frustration, social unrest and political instability in many areas of the globe.

At the close of their discussions the participants in the Twenty-third American Assembly of Arden House, Harriman, New York, May 2-5, 1963, on The Population Dilemma, reviewed as a group the following statement. Although there was general agreement on the final report, it is not the practice of The American Assembly for participants to affix their signatures, and it should not be assumed that every participant necessarily subscribes to every recommendation included in the statement.

Rapid population growth contributes to difficult and complex problems in the United States.

The Twenty-third American Assembly believes that:

A. Present and prospective world rates of population growth cannot be maintained indefinitely. Such growth contributes substantially to the perpetuation of low levels of living for two-thirds of mankind, and creates difficult problems of adjustment in the economically advanced nations.

B. World birth rates must be reduced in view of the reductions in death rates already achieved.

C. Reduction of family size would produce important gains for many families as well as for entire nations. Unrestricted fertility tends to damage the health of the mother, impairs family life and restricts opportunity for adequately rearing and educating children.

The time has come for vigorous and coordinated action to alert mankind to the need for a reduced rate of population growth and to develop multilateral and bilateral programs to assist nations which desire to reduce their fertility.

### I. WORLD PROBLEMS

A high birth rate obstructs the economic development of low income countries in a number of ways. It diverts resources and hampers economic growth in the less developed economies and makes it necessary to provide for a larger population rather than for a higher level of living. It contributes to imbalance in rural-urban and regional population distribution. It generates an age structure with large numbers of young dependents in relation to workers. It impairs efforts to improve the quality of a population by restricting per capita expenditures for improving health, raising educational levels, and teaching new occupational skills. It reduces natural resources per capita.

Reducing the birth rate and thereby lowering the rate of population increase is of course not the complete solution to the improvement of economic conditions in the less developed areas. It is a major element but other factors—social and economic—are also involved. These include capital investment, technology, diversification of the economy, distribution of income, occupational skills, entrepreneurship, and attitudes and institutions favorable to innovation and social reform. The expansion of international trade and investment would also contribute to economic advance. More effective utilization of natural resources is required; in the short run world resources are sufficient to permit rising levels of living.

International migration can help many persons and temporarily ease some population pressures. It cannot, however, solve the world's major population problems.

## Recommendations

The United Nations and the Specialized Agencies should:

1. Expand activities in the field of population.

They have significantly improved population data and research. They should now undertake more comprehensive and intensive population research, particularly on the interrelationships of population, economics and social change, and develop more effective programs for the dissemination of its findings.

2. Expand and strengthen the population staff and the regional population training and research centers.

This would enable the agencies better to assist nations to comprehend their own problems and formulate appropriate solutions.

3. Provide direct aid to countries wishing assistance in family planning programs.

The World Health Organization and other international agencies should recognize the consequences of their great achievements in reducing death rates; they should assist nations in dealing with the resultant population growth.

4. Encourage and support, especially through the WHO, biological and medical research in human reproduction.

5. Strive to contribute to the growing world consciousness of the implications of population growth through appropriate revisions of and additions to youth and adult educational materials prepared for world distribution by UNESCO.

### II. THE POSITION OF THE UNITED STATES
#### ON WORLD POPULATION PROBLEMS

The "Statement of United States Policy" to the 17th General Assembly of the United Nations represents an important step forward. It offers the assistance of the United States to nations, upon request, "to find potential sources of information and assistance on ways and means of dealing with population problems."

This policy should explicitly recognize that:

(1) Population growth in all countries affects the destinies of the world's people. It is an international problem of concern to all. (2) Parents everywhere should be free to decide how many children they should have. (3) Sustained progress in economic well-being requires the reduction of population increase.

## Recommendations

In view of the relation of population to economic and social development, and the need for bilateral as well as multilateral programs of technical assistance, it is recommended that:

1. Since the ultimate objective of foreign aid is to improve living conditions, the United States give consideration to the way in which developmental plans are affected by population trends.

2. The United States extend assistance to developing nations, at their request, for the investigation of population problems and in support of programs to promote the voluntary regulation of fertility.

3. Administrative means be established by the federal government for disseminating knowledge about population problems and methods of regulating family size.

Such action is needed to implement the statement by President Kennedy of April 24, 1963, that the government could support increased research in fertility and human reproduction, and make the results more available to the world so that everyone could make his own judgment.

### III. DOMESTIC POPULATION POLICY

There must be a greater concern by our national, state and local governments with our own population problems.

The postwar resurgence in population growth coupled with the growth of metropolitan areas has created complex problems not only at the state and local levels but also on a regional and national basis.

Rapid population growth has undoubtedly contributed to additional effective demand and thus to increased economic growth. Although there are no insuperable economic difficulties in the short run, we see increasing dangers in the continuation of the present rate of growth that would double the population every forty years with the prospect of constricted social opportunities and progressive crowding.

Accelerated population growth has already intensified problems of urban congestion, education and transportation, and contributed to pollution of air and water and crowding of outdoor recreational facilities. It has required federal, state and local governments to provide new and expanded public facilities and services with consequent increased taxation. Furthermore, the wave in young workers now entering the labor force constitutes a serious challenge to our economy which is already confronted by readjustment to the advent of automation. These challenges will require special attention.

*Recommendations*

The American Assembly therefore recommends:

1. Intensified investigation of our population trends and problems—including their long-range as well as their short-term implications.

2. Accelerated research through the United States Public Health Service and private agencies, on the biological and medical aspects of human reproduction so that a variety of improved methods of fertility control are developed.

3. Assumption of responsibility by the federal, state and local governments for making available information concerning the regulation of fertility and providing services to needy mothers compatible with the religious and ethical beliefs of the individual recipient.

Freedom of decision regarding family size is a basic human right which in practice is now effectively withheld from a portion of the American people. This discrimination would be eliminated by making fully available to all adults through public and private agencies information and service regarding the various methods of family planning which accord with the ethical and religious convictions of those involved.

4. The cultivation with the assistance of schools, religious organizations and other cultural media, of a sense of responsibility concerning marriage and parenthood, including the responsibility of bringing into the world only those children whom parents are prepared adequately to care for and educate.

5. Recognition that the United States is an economic and social unit, to the end that all of our citizens, no matter what their area of origin or race, are adequately prepared for full participation in the life of any part of the nation.

Since the end of the war, millions of persons have moved to urban parts of the United States. Many are ill-prepared for life in the areas to which they moved. In consequence, problems of accommodation are severe for the migrants and for the communities to which they come.

6. Our immigration policy should be in accord with the following principles:

a. selection among applicants without discrimination by race or country or origin

b. total immigration should not exceed the present level except in emergencies

c. exclusion of persons who do not meet established personal standards such as those relating to literacy and health save under extraordinary circumstances

d. consideration of (1) special skills, abilities and employment opportunities, and (2) kinship to persons already present in this country

7. The acceleration of economic growth and increased employment opportunities in view of the current levels of unemployment and the impending increase in the labor force.

8. More research on the resources of the United States and other parts of the world with attention to the lessening of waste and protection of the claims of oncoming generations. (In this connection attention is called to the recent report of the National Academy of Sciences-National Research Council on *Natural Resources*.)

9. Appointment by The President of the United States of a Commission to inform, after investigation, the government and the American people of the nature of population problems at home and abroad with respect to: implications for all aspects of American life, and relevance to our efforts, in cooperation with international agencies, to promote economic and social progress throughout the world.

\* \*

The vast majority of the people of the world, including a large proportion of the people of the United States, do not yet recognize the full implications of present population trends. The Twenty-third American Assembly cannot emphasize too strongly that time is running out for the formulation and implementation of world and national population policy.

To continue to ignore world and United States population problems is to ignore the welfare and security of all peoples. We must not remain complacent in the face of a major threat to world peace and survival.

# *Appendix*

❤ ❤ ❤

## VOLUNTARY ORGANIZATIONS AND RESEARCH PROGRAMS

Private groups are tackling the population problem in a variety of ways, depending upon their particular interests and their resources. It is our aim here to provide a reliable cross-section of those groups with major programs in the field of population, as well as a few with related interests. The organizations are arranged in five categories: (1) action programs; (2) information programs; (3) foundations; (4) professional societies; and (5) other groups.

The information on voluntary organizations is followed by a list of university research programs dealing with various aspects of the population problem. These include population study centers, medical schools, and schools of public health.

### ACTION PROGRAMS

#### *Planned Parenthood-World Population*

Interest in the economic consequences of the population explosion is only one aspect of the total program of Planned Parenthood-World Population. Organized a half century ago, the Planned Parenthood Federation of America, Inc. merged in 1961 with the World Population Emergency Campaign. The merger served to emphasize the interest and concern of both groups in the population problem in the United States and abroad.

Basic objective of the group is: "To make available to all the peoples of the world the most effective and acceptable scientific means of voluntary conception control, and to encourage them to use them, so that responsible parenthood will become a universal reality." The organization presses for expansion of federal support for research in fertility control; marshals support from business leaders, distinguished citizens, organizations, and communities for intensified public action in this field; and helps to secure the integration of birth control services in state health and welfare programs. The national headquarters conducts an extensive public

This appendix consists of excerpts reprinted by permission from the January-February 1964 "Focus on World's Population" issue of INTERCOM, a world affairs handbook published six times a year by the Foreign Policy Association, 345 East 46 Street, New York, New York 10017. Copies of the issue on this and other subjects are available at $1 each from the Foreign Policy Association.

information program through press, magazines, radio and television, speakers, and publications.

Some 120 affiliates in 33 states and the District of Columbia operate medically supervised clinics which offer instruction in a variety of family planning techniques. Orientation sessions on family planning programs are provided by both national headquarters and affiliates for physicians, public officials and citizens from foreign countries. In the past year, these visitors have come from Indonesia, Japan, Kenya, Nepal, Pakistan, Turkey, and the United Arab Republic. In addition, the national group contributes financially to the International Planned Parenthood Federation (see below) for its work in many areas of the world.

Among the non-technical publications issued by the organization are the following:

*Planned Parenthood News.* Three times a year. Subscription: 50 cents; 20 cents per copy. Newsletter of developments in family planning.

*The Economic Consequences of the Population Explosion.* With a foreword by John Gunther. 1963. 36 pp. 50 cents. Report of conference held in October 1962.

*Population and Human Progress,* Christian Herter. 1963. 14 pp. 15 cents.

*The New Crusade,* William H. Draper, Jr. 1963. 18 pp. 15 cents.

*Reverence for Life.* National and international needs in population control. 16 pp. 35 cents.

*The Population Crisis vs. Peace and Prosperity.* Declaration by American Nobel Laureates and Business Leaders. 1962. 7 pp. 5 cents.

*Annual Report.* 1962. 31 pp. 15 cents.

*Population and Our Shrinking World,* Ambassador Adlai E. Stevenson. 1963. 15 pp. 15 cents.

*Reprints:* "Birth Control: The Problem We Fear to Face," William H. Draper, Jr. (*Look*); "Catholics and Birth Control," George Barrett (*New York Times*); "Population Growth" (*Journal of the American Medical Association*); "Birth Control: A Sensitive Subject Too Long Neglected" (*The Johns Hopkins Magazine*); "Some Unpleasant Facts About Population Pressures" (*America*).

For a complete list of publications, write to Planned Parenthood-World Population, 515 Madison Ave., New York 22, N.Y.

### International Planned Parenthood Federation

Launched in 1952 at a meeting in New Delhi, the International Planned Parenthood Federation (IPPF) has 35 national organization members in 35 countries and territories. These are currently organized into five regions: Europe, Near East and Africa; Indian Ocean; Southeast Asia and Oceania; Western Pacific; Western Hemisphere.

The formation of family planning associations in all countries is a major concern of IPPF; also the training of physicians, nurses, health visitors, and social workers in practical administration of family planning services; and the encouragement of research into human reproductive processes and into biological methods of controlling fertility.

An international conference held in Singapore in February 1963 was attended by representatives from 40 different countries. (Report of the conference, titled "Changing Patterns of Fertility," will be available shortly for about $6. Reports of previous conferences are also available.) Regional conferences have been held in West Berlin, Jamaica, Netherlands, Barbados, Pakistan, Poland, and Puerto Rico. The latest Western Hemisphere Conference was held in Puerto Rico in April 1964.

*Around the World News of Population and Birth Control.* Monthly newsletter. Annual subscription: $2. (Canada and U.S.)

International headquarters are located at 64 Sloane St., London, S.W. 1, England. Address of the Western Hemisphere headquarters is 51 East 42 St., New York 17, N.Y.

## INFORMATION PROGRAMS

### *Population Reference Bureau*

The primary aim of the Population Reference Bureau is to alert the people of the world to the mounting crisis created by rapid population growth. Founded in 1929, the Bureau is a nonprofit educational membership organization which "provides the educational link between research and action on the population problem."

The basic belief of the Bureau is "that people will take corrective action to control births when they understand that too rapid growth dilutes living levels." To create this understanding, the Bureau's educational program presents complex demographic information in simple, factual, noncontroversial terms. The program includes publishing educational materials on a regular basis; maintaining an international clearinghouse for demographic information, interpretation and reference assistance; providing schools and colleges with low-cost teaching materials through a bulk-purchase plan; cooperating closely with other national organizations; and providing mass media with factual information.

The Bureau's Latin American Program, launched in 1961, extends distribution of selected educational materials, with summaries in Spanish and Portuguese, to the region of the world where population growth is greatest. These are provided on a year-round basis to newspapers, technical and scholarly journals, universities and selected individuals in Latin America.

Among the many materials published by and available from the Bureau are the following:

*Population Bulletin.* Eight issues a year. $3 per year. Single issue 50 cents. Each issue is devoted to a country, region or major aspect of the population story. Recent issues were devoted to: "Population Growth and Immigration Policy" (3 issues: Western Hemisphere, Asia, United States); "World Population—1963"; "China: A Demographic Crisis"; "The Population Problem: Toward a Solution"; "U.S.A. Population Changes 1950-1960."

*Population Profiles.* 10 cents each. Brief reports supplementing the *Bulletin* discuss demographic trends and problems and are accompanied by graphs and tables. Recent topics are: "The American Family: A Composite Picture," "The New Africa," "Marriage and the American Woman," "Central America—World's Fastest Growing Region."

*World Data Sheets.* A yearly, world-wide review (127 countries), on one sheet, of present populations, annual rates of increase, birth and death rates, life expectancy and illiteracy.

*Clipsheets.* Brief items, some with graphs, of interesting population facts.

*Classroom Charts.* 18″ x 24″ charts. 75 cents each. "A Thousand Years of World Population Growth" (pie charts); "Population Growth in the Americas, 1960-2000" (maps indicating population growth); "World's Ten Largest Nations" (bar graph); "Speed-up in Population Growth" (from stone age to modern times).

Annual dues for Associate Members are $5 (teachers $3 and for Contributing Members, $25. Members receive all Bureau publications. Further information about the Bureau, a free publications list and information about a special bulk-purchase plan for schools and colleges may be obtained by writing to the Bureau's headquarters at 1775 Massachusetts Avenue, N.W., Washington, D.C. 20036.

### Hugh Moore Fund

Major activity of the Hugh Moore Fund, a privately endowed foundation established in 1944, is a broad public information campaign to call to the attention of the American public the dangers inherent in the "population explosion."

To accomplish its purpose, it has awarded grants to support similar efforts of such groups as the International Planned Parenthood Federation, Population Reference Bureau, Human Betterment Association. It also initiated the World Population Emergency Campaign (now merged with the Planned Parenthood Federation). The Fund also awards occasional technical and scientific research grants.

In 1962, the Fund organized a Population Policy Panel to "mobilize public interest with a view to stimulating research and education proportionate to the magnitude and importance of the population problem." The Panel's program includes the placement of ads in newspapers throughout the country.

Publications of the Fund include:

*News Items.* 4 pp., published irregularly by the Population Policy Panel, single copies free; request placement on mailing list.

*The Population Bomb.* 22 pp. Single copies and limited quantities free. Discusses the dangers of overpopulation, the role of governments, cultural and religious attitudes, and the U.S. role in this area.

*The Population Explosion and Your Taxes,* Marriner S. Eccles (8 pp., single copies free).

*Business Profits and the Population Explosion,* Adolph W. Schmidt (11 pp., single copies free).

*The Population Bomb: Is Voluntary Human Sterilization the Answer?* 18 pp. Single copies and limited quantities free.

*Organizations and Institutions Working in the Field of Population.* Free. List of education, action, scientific and research groups.

*Publications on World Population Problems.* List of some twenty-seven books and pamphlets.

Reprints: "Population Explosion Nullifies Foreign Aid" (Advertisement); "Birth Control Must Go With Foreign Aid" (*Reader's Digest*); "Catholics and Birth Control," George Barrett (*New York Times*); "Population and Responsibility" (*Commonweal*); "The Population Question" (Excerpt from Draper Report); "What Women Can Do for Peace," John Fischer (*Harper's*).

Offices of the Fund are located at 51 East 42 St., New York 17, N.Y.

## FOUNDATIONS

### *Ford Foundation*

In announcing intensified Ford Foundation support of activities in the population field in July 1963, Henry T. Heald, the president of the Foundation, noted: "In the effort to integrate population practices and policies with programs for human betterment, individuals, governments, and private organizations have a role to play. . . . The Ford Foundation, which has long assisted educational, agricultural, and other development efforts of countries in Asia, Africa and Latin America, regards its present efforts to help meet the population challenge as appropriate and essential in a field where time is of the essence, even though eventually other agencies, private and public, must provide far greater support."

As part of its accelerated activities, the Foundation recently announced the establishment of a separate Population Program to encourage projects dealing with population programs which 1) support research and training in reproductive biology in the United States and abroad, 2) attract talented young scientists to the field, and 3) acquaint scientists generally with its challenges.

At the same time, the Foundation also announced grants and other actions for research, training, and experimental programs on the problems of population growth. Awards were made to private and government agencies, universities, and scientific laboratories in the United States, Britain, India, and Tunisia. Some of these included:

A $5 million program of assistance to India for an intensive family-planning program in selected districts.

A $475,000 grant to the Population Reference Bureau for distribution of information on population problems.

A $200,000 grant to the Government of Tunisia for an experimental program in family planning by the Ministry of Health.

A $700,000 grant to the University of Chicago for research and training on demography and the administration of family-planning programs.

The awards by the Ford Foundation brought to $24.2 million the total of Foundation support since 1952. Of this total, $22.1 million has been committed since 1959, and $11 million of it in 1963.

More than half of the total amount awarded by the Ford Foundation has been in the area of reproductive biology—the recruitment of scientists, training programs, and research. The remainder has been for work in the fields of demography and family planning.

*The Uses of Talent,* Henry T. Heald. 1963. 8 pp. Single copies free. Speech by the president of the Ford Foundation discusses the dynamics of population growth and its relation to economic and social development.

Offices of the Ford Foundation are at 477 Madison Ave., New York 22, N.Y.

## Milbank Memorial Fund

Since 1928 the Fund has undertaken research and provided a limited number of grants in the field of demography. The research has included cooperative projects with the Census Bureau, other governmental agencies, universities and other foundations. The Fund has also conducted, sponsored and participated in research on fertility and the social and psychological factors affecting fertility.

Its activities in the field of demography include the maintenance of a small staff engaged in research, publication of the *Milbank Memorial Fund Quarterly* ($2 per year), and the sponsorship of conferences in demography. The conferences are mainly of a technical nature. Proceedings are published. (See *Population Trends in Eastern Europe, the U.S.S.R. and Mainland China,* 1960. 336 pp. $2.)

The Fund also provides support to a limited number of demographers at the advanced graduate level, as well as an annual fellowship given to the Office of Population Research at Princeton University whose general programs also receive modest support from the Fund.

The Fund undertakes no public education in the field of population programs, holds no policy views on population and family planning, and all of its activities and publications are of a strictly technical nature. The fund is located at 40 Wall St., New York 5, N.Y.

### The Population Council

The Population Council is a foundation established in 1952 to advance knowledge in the broad field of population by fostering research, training and technical consultation and assistance in the social and biological sciences.

The Council makes grants to support the training of demographers in U.S. universities. It also supports the UN Regional Demographic Centers in Bombay, Cairo, and Santiago, as well as population projects in specific countries and domestic universities such as Harvard, Cornell, and Princeton. It has sponsored topical conferences and supplied needed books.

On invitation by foreign governments, the Council sends consultative missions to advise about the formulation of actual programs of population control. It trains technical personnel, helps to establish the necessary training and research institutions and laboratories, and helps in the procurement of initial equipment and supplies needed for training and experiment. In cooperation with American and foreign universities, it sends teams to work with local personnel to seek, by field experiments, more efficient ways of spreading the practice of population control. Finally, through conferences, publications, and staff visits, it endeavors to keep workers engaged in such experiments in touch with the technical problems of similar groups elsewhere in the world. The Council already is deeply involved in Pakistan and Taiwan.

The Council supports both basic and applied research in the physiology of reproduction. Much of this takes place at its own laboratories at the

Rockefeller Institute in New York City. Beyond that, the Council supports complementary research in universities and hospitals and other research institutions within the U.S. and increasingly in other countries.

The continuing fellowship program was one of the Council's earliest ventures. Fellowships are given to potential leaders in both the demographic and medical-biological fields, particularly to those from countries in which appropriately trained people are lacking. In 1963 alone, 81 fellowships were granted.

Offices of the Population Council are located at 230 Park Ave., New York 17, N.Y.

### Rockefeller Brothers Fund

The Rockefeller Brothers Fund has directed its attention not only to the increasingly recognized problems of continued population growth but also to the positive aspects of the subject of population viewed as human resources. Questions relating to the quality, development and preservation of resources, both human and natural, cannot, in the Fund's view, be considered in isolation, but rather must be brought into balance and considered together under the broader heading of conservation.

Activities under the Fund's program include support of a number of undertakings in the field of population. With regard to this area of interest, the Fund has awarded more than $2 million in grants since its establishment in 1940. Of this amount, some $1.7 million has been awarded to the Population Council, $254,000 to the Planned Parenthood Federation of America, and $55,500 to the Population Reference Bureau.

The Fund is located at 30 Rockefeller Plaza, New York 20, N.Y.

### Rockefeller Foundation

In outlining the Foundation's plans for the future on the occasion of its fiftieth anniversary, the Trustees stated in September, 1963: "In the belief that an urgent need exists to stabilize world population and thus prevent the eventual condemnation of millions of future citizens to lives of underprivilege, misery, and hopelessness, the Foundation expects to expand its support of critical research and of action programs in population dynamics and population stabilization."

For more than a decade, the Rockefeller Foundation has had the subject of population as one of its primary interests. Believing that in the building of viable societies, the problems of economic development are intimately related to those of population stabilization, the Foundation has made a number of grants for research and study to: Office of Population Research, Princeton University; Scripps Foundation for Research in Population Problems, Miami University, Oxford, Ohio; Population Research and Training Center, University of Chicago; Population Investigation Committee, London School of Economics.

The Foundation has also given financial support to the Population Council's fellowship program to train population specialists from Asian, African, and Latin American countries where population problems exist or may be foreseen.

In addition to these grants, the Foundation has given financial grants and awards for a number of demographic and family planning studies overseas. For example, it recently awarded $14,000 to support a pilot study in family planning in Santiago, Chile, to be administered jointly by Harvard University's School of Public Health and the University of Chile's Faculty of Medicine.

Since initiating its program concerning population, the Foundation has awarded some $7 million in grants. Of this sum, more than $5 million has been given for the support of demographic studies and training programs, and $2 million for physiological research.

*Plans for the Future,* a statement by the Trustees of the Rockefeller Foundation (September 20, 1963, 9 pp., free), outlines the interest of the Foundation in five areas, including that of population.

Headquarters of the Foundation are at 111 West 50 St., New York 20, N.Y.

## PROFESSIONAL SOCIETIES

### Population Association of America

A major activity of this professional association of U.S. demographers is the convening of an annual meeting for presentation and discussion of technical papers on population problems. Secretary-Treasurer of the Association is Paul C. Glick, Population Division, Bureau of the Census, Washington 25, D.C.

*Population Index.* Official publication of the Association published jointly with the Office of Population Research, Princeton University. Quarterly. $5 per year. Order from Office of Population Research, Princeton University, Princeton, N. J. Annotated international bibliography of publications on population, short articles and current statistics.

*Demography.* Tentative title of a new annual journal of PAA, the first volume of which is now in preparation. It will contain about 25 articles, most of them presented as papers at the 1963 annual meeting.

### International Union for the Scientific Study of Population

A professional association of demographers with membership in some 57 countries, the Union's principal function is to facilitate the exchange of information among its members. The Union cooperates with other organizations in the sponsorship of conferences and is currently cooperating with the UN and six of the Specialized Agencies in organizing the 1965 World Population Conference.

The Union recently compiled for the UN an international multilingual dictionary of demography and conducted a survey on teaching of demography in various countries of the world at the request of UNESCO.

The Union publishes *La Demographe,* a bulletin issued irregularly, about twice a year, $1. It includes text in English and French, presenting activities of the Union and various questions of general interest to demographers.

The Union is located at 29 Quai de Branly, Paris 7ème, France.

## OTHER GROUPS

In addition to the groups described above, there are others that carry on related activities or provide financial support to organizations working in the field. A few are briefly described below.

### American Eugenics Society

The Society was founded in 1926 "to further knowledge of the biological and socio-cultural factors affecting human populations." It publishes the *Eugenics Quarterly* in March, June, September and December (subscription: $7). Address of the Society is 230 Park Ave., New York 17, N.Y.

### Brush Foundation

Founded by a Cleveland industrialist, the Foundation contributes "toward the betterment of human stock and toward the regulation of the increase of population." During the last ten years, the efforts of the Foundation have been concentrated in two fields: support of field work in family planning in the less developed countries, and research on human reproduction. Its total support in these areas has amounted to more than $300,000, some $200,000 of which has been for field work of the International Planned Parenthood Federation and for local organizations in Thailand, Philippines, Ceylon, Korea, and Taiwan. The Foundation has also awarded grants to the Western Reserve University Medical School for research in the reproductive process. The Foundation's address is 2027 Cornell Rd., Cleveland 6, Ohio.

### Conservation Foundation

The Foundation sees world population as one of the major pressures on the earth's natural resources. While primarily concerned with the better use of natural resources, a concern about population goes into all of its efforts and a full-time Consultant on Population Pressures in Relation to Resources is on the Foundation staff. In 1961 the Foundation invited a number of eminent writers to present their views on the impact of population pressures on the various fields in which they specialize. The essays appear in the book, *Our Crowded Planet,* ed. Fairfield Osborn (Doubleday and Co., 1962). The Foundation also aided in the production of a film, *House of Man* (20 min. Color. For information on rental, write Encyclopaedia Britannica Films, 1150 Wilmette Ave., Wilmette, Ill.) The Foundation is located at 30 East 40 St., New York 16, N.Y.

### National Committee on Maternal Health

The basic objective of the NCMH is to "assemble materials and to prepare objective reports . . . concerning the various methods of controlling human fertility." To promote this objective, the Committee collects and evaluates information gathered by scholars throughout the world on all methods of fertility control; it provides technical assistance to, and cooperates with, organizations and individuals in the planning and execution of clinical studies. Offices are at 2 East 103 St., New York 29, N.Y.

### The Pathfinder Fund

The greater part of the Fund's activities are in the field of medical family planning. Organized in 1958, it makes grants to a variety of scientific and charitable organizations within the United States and carries on its own work through field workers and researchers in scientific fields. It has assisted with the formation of family planning associations and has given advice and assistance to groups within a number of countries in Asia, Africa and South America. It publishes *Family Planning News* (*Worldwide Notes on Family Planning*) twice a year (subscription: free), and occasionally issues other publications. Address of the Fund is 73 Adams St., Milton 87, Mass.

### University Research

### Population Study Centers

A number of university centers have been especially created to conduct programs of training and/or research on demographic questions. They are briefly described below.

*Brown University, Center for Aging Research,* Providence 12, Rhode Island. Sponsored by a grant from the National Institutes of Health, the Center is conducting a study of persons approaching old age in order to evaluate the demographic, social, and health changes associated with the aging process. In addition, the Department of Sociology offers a variety of graduate training courses in demography.

*University of Chicago, Population Research and Training Center,* 935 East 60 St., Chicago 37, Illinois. Conducts demographic research and training program for students seeking advanced degrees as well as for those not working towards a degree. The University's Community and Family Study Center works in the area of mass communications and motivational research with reference to family planning.

*Cornell University, International Population Program,* Department of Sociology, Ithaca, New York. Created in 1962 to offer a research and training program in social demography. Research is currently focused on Latin America where, in cooperation with the UN Demographic Training and Research Center (CELADE), researchers are interviewing women to determine demographic characteristics and implications for family planning.

*Georgetown University, Center for Population Research,* Washington 7, D.C. Established in 1963, the Center conducts research in demography and the physiological aspects of reproduction with a grant from the Ford Foundation. Future plans for the new Center include research on other topics and training of students.

*George Washington University, Population Research Project,* Washington 6, D.C. Prepares and publishes series of booklets, such as "Population Growth and International Migration" and "Population Problems in the Development of India and South Central Asia."

*Harvard University School of Public Health, Center for Population Studies,* Cambridge, Mass. Still in planning stages, the Center will "be concerned with developing new knowledge through research, with the practical application of knowledge among population groups, and with the teaching of graduate students to prepare them for careers in the population field." (The School of Public Health's Department of Demography and Human Ecology has done extensive research, and also field work in India, on the population problem.)

*Miami University, Scripps Foundation for Research in Population Problems,* Oxford, Ohio. Established in 1922 by the late E. W. Scripps, the Foundation also receives assistance from the Rockefeller Foundation and other organizations. Conducts research relating to world problems and to population study in the United States. Although not a training or teaching organization, the Foundation employs some graduate and undergraduate students on research projects.

*University of Michigan, Population Studies Center,* 527 East Liberty St., Ann Arbor, Mich. Organized in 1961, the Center conducts research and training activities in fields of population and human ecology. Descriptive brochure and list of staff publications are available.

*University of Pennsylvania, Population Studies Center,* Philadelphia 4, Pa. Provides graduate student training under a Ford Foundation grant and conducts research under grants from the Federal Government, foundations and the University.

*Princeton University, Office of Population Research,* 5 Ivy Lane, Princeton, N. J. Since 1936 has conducted research programs on the development of methodology in demography and the relationship of population growth to economic development. Also has program providing training in demography primarily for visiting students and fellows largely from developing areas. Operates under grants from Rockefeller Foundation, Milbank Memorial Fund, and the Population Council, which is currently supporting a study in African demography. List of publications by staff members available.

*University of Texas, Population Research Center,* 217 Archway, Austin 5, Texas. Organized in 1960 as an integral part of the Department of Sociology, the Center provides advanced training in demography and human ecology and conducts research projects. In addition to using Texas as a field of research, the Center in 1963 began an internationally-oriented research program focused on the demographic problems of underdeveloped countries as seen in Latin America.

*University of Washington, Office of Population Research,* Seattle 5, Washington. Conducts basic research in demography and ecology with emphasis on the problems of the Pacific Northwest; provides information and consultative services to public and private agencies and individual citizens; and conducts a graduate and undergraduate training program.

*University of Wisconsin, Center for Demography and Ecology,* Madison 6, Wisconsin. An autonomous research and training center within the Department of Sociology, the new Center is expected to conduct a graduate training program under a grant from the National Institutes of Health.

In addition to the centers described above, many other universities conduct research and training programs as part of the work of their regular departments. Among these the most notable are sociology and economic departments and, where they exist, schools of public health.

### Medical Schools and Schools of Public Health

A number of schools of medicine are engaged in research in reproductive biology, and in addition the twelve schools of public health in the United States are actively engaged in research and the teaching of demography. The list of medical schools follows, including a parenthetical note where a school of public health exists in the same university.

Bowman Gray School of Medicine; University of California, Los

Angeles (also School of Public Health); University of California, San Francisco (also School of Public Health in Berkeley); University of Chicago; University of Colorado; Columbia University (also School of Public Health); Cornell University; Dartmouth College; Emory University; University of Florida; Harvard Medical School (also School of Public Health); University of Illinois; Indiana University; Jefferson Medical College of Philadelphia; Johns Hopkins University (also School of Public Health); University of Kansas; Loyola University Stritch School of Medicine; University of Maryland; Medical College of South Carolina; Medical College of Virginia; University of Miami; University of Michigan (also School of Public Health); New York University; State University of New York; University of Oregon; University of Pittsburgh (also School of Public Health); St. Louis University; Seton Hall University; Stanford University; University of Tennessee; Vanderbilt University; Washington University; University of Washington; Wayne State University; Western Reserve University; University of Wisconsin; Yale University (also School of Public Health).

Four other schools of public health, not mentioned above, are: Universities of Minnesota, North Carolina, Puerto Rico and Tulane.

# NOTES

## 2. *Geography and the World's Population*

1. M. K. Bennett, "A World Map of Foodcrop Climates," *Food Research Institute Studies,* Stanford University, I, November, 1960, 285-295.

2. One notable exception is in parts of South America where enormous land holdings are in the hands of the few and hence are held out of full settlement; a second is in Inner Asia, where pastoral peoples, unwilling to farm, hold lands capable of agricultural settlement. Under the Communists, however, this system is breaking down in Mongolia, Turkestan, and elsewhere. It is expected, too, that latifundia will begin to give way in Latin America in the near future. The third exception is the Rainy Tropics.

3. There are two schools of thought regarding the tropical rain forest as a home for man. The devotees of one school are highly optimistic (they are known as the "Cornucopia boys"). The other school is extremely pessimistic. Reputable scholars line up on both sides. No one knows positively whether the future is bright or dismal.

4. This statement is a generalization and hence not applicable to many areas within the climatic realm. But insofar as broad generalizations are justifiable and reasonably accurate, the concept holds.

5. Douglas H. K. Lee, *Climate and Economic Development in the Tropics* (New York: Harper and Brothers, 1957), pp. 157-158.

6. C. Langdon White, "Industrialization: Panacea for Underdeveloped Nations?" *Yearbook, Association of Pacific Coast Geographers,* 17, 1955, 3-20.

7. Elmer W. Pehrson, "Minerals in National and International Affairs," Chapter II in *Economics of the Mineral Industries* (New York: American Institute of Mining, Metallurgical and Petroleum Engineers, 1959), p. 512.

## 5. *Problems of Fertility Control in Underdeveloped Areas*

1. The very insularity of the demographer has in some ways produced salutary results not unlike those produced among artists working in a highly limited medium. In addition to milking with great imagination every drop of significance out of unimaginative date, demographers have been impelled to make various sorts of assumptions about human attitudes and behavior which, although often unrealistic, have allowed the development of very elegant and useful mathematical models.

2. Prediction is usually less hazardous in other branches of the social sciences. The predictions are often not quantified, as is necessarily the case in demography; or there is little danger that adequate data will be collected to test the accuracy of the prediction. The extensiveness, pervasiveness, and regularity of crude population data foster both caution and constant re-examination of assumptions on the part of demographers, no small advantages in the social sciences.

3. Japan seems to be an exception, but the case may be unusual for a number of reasons including the abortion program, the long period of industrialization, and traditional attitudes favoring family limitation.

4. Recent studies in the United States show that the completed family size of Catholics is about the same as that of non-Catholics, but that Church-approved methods (rhythm and delayed marriage) are more characteristic of Catholics, especially the better educated ones. It may be that as Catholics become more sophisticated and better educated, they become more accessible to Church teaching. In Latin America, where educational levels have been low and the number of priests few, relative to population, it is probable that Church influence will increase with economic development. There are already signs of religious revivalism in a number of countries, an additional argument against the assumption that education and economic progress will automatically bring fertility declines.

5. *News of Population and Birth Control* (London, February 1955).

6. *The Sixth International Conference on Planned Parenthood* (London: International Planned Parenthood Federation, 1959), p. 10.

7. S. Radhakrishnan, *Third International Conference on Planned Parenthood* (Bombay: Family Planning Association of India, 1952), p. 12.

8. K. C. K. E. Raja, "Family Planning in Public Health Programs," *Third International Conference on Planned Parenthood*, p. 64.

9. R. M. Pierce and G. Rountree, "Birth Control in Britain, Part II," *Population Studies*, XV, No. 2.

10. M. C. Balfour, "Family Planning in Asia," *Population Studies*, XV, No. 2.

11. Leo F. Schnore, "Social Problems in the Underdeveloped Areas: An Ecological View," *Social Problems*, VIII (Winter 1961), p. 187.

12. In some countries there is a growing tendency to rely on demographers for shaping such programs. While a gesture in the right direction, this is basically an error. The traditionally trained demographer has little more to offer in this field than has an actuary to programmatic solutions of problems of mortality and morbidity.

13. *Family Planning in Japan* (Tokyo: Asia Family Planning Association, 1961).

14. The Japanese have been made to feel defensive and apologetic about their abortion program, which is probably the only case in the world to date of a successful mass program of fertility control.

## 6. *Demographic Dimensions of World Politics*

1. *Determinants and Consequences of Population Trends* (New York: United Nations, 1953), Chap. 2.

2. See the objection to this phrase in "Statement by Roman Catholic Bishops of U.S. on Birth Control," *New York Times*, Nov. 26, 1959.

3. H. Brown, *The Challenge of Man's Future* (New York: Viking, 1954).

4. *The Future Growth of World Population* (New York: United Nations, 1958).

5. This fact was ignored by Roman Catholic bishops (see *New York Times*, Nov. 26, 1959) and by the Pope (see "Pope Denounces Birth Limitation," *New York Times*, Dec. 15, 1959).

6. The impracticability of colonizing other planets is considered by G. Hardin, *J. Heredity*, 50 (1959), 2.

7. *Determinants and Consequences of Population Trends*, p. 23.

8. W. H. Leonard, *Sci. Monthly*, 85 (1957), 113.

9. "National and Per Capita Income of 70 Countries in 1949," *U. N. Statist. Papers*, Ser. E, No. 1 (New York: United Nations, 1950). The calculations were made by using United Nations per capita income figures for each continent, applied to revised United Nations estimates of 1950 population of

continents, to obtain revised aggregate income by continent and for the world, as shown in Table I. A new world per capita figure of $223 was obtained, as compared with the published figure of $230.

10. For the Communist position see F. Lorimer, "Population Policies and Politics in the Communist World," in *Population and World Politics,* P. M. Hauser, ed. (Glencoe, Ill: Free Press, 1958); for the Catholic position see "Pope Denounces Birth Limitation," *New York Times,* Dec. 15, 1959; for the Socialist position, see J. D. Bernal, "Population Growth is No Threat for a Free Society," *Natl. Guardian,* Dec. 7, 1959 (extract from J. D. Bernal, *Science in History*).

11. W. S. Woytinsky and E. S. Woytinsky. *World Population and Production* (New York: Twentieth Century Fund, 1953); S. Kuznets, "Regional Economic Trends and Levels of Living," in *Population and World Politics,* P. M. Hauser, ed. (Glencoe, Ill: Free Press, 1958).

12. *Report on International Definition and Measurement of Standards and Levels of Living* (New York: United Nations, 1954).

13. Note the different definitions of area in Tables I and II. In Table II, which gives population projections to 1975 and 2000, "Northern America" includes only North America north of the Rio Grande; "Latin America" includes South America, Central America, and North America south of the Rio Grande. For the rough comparisons made, no adjustment of the data was necessary. See *The Future Growth of World Population* (New York: United Nations, 1958).

14. Calculations were based on revised data, as explained in (9). For Latin America the calculations were based on a comparison of estimated aggregate income for "Latin America" in 1950, per capita income for "South America" being used.

15. The "population problem" differs for areas with different ratios of population to resources; for example, see "Political and Economic Planning," in *World Population and Resources* (Fairlawn, N.J.: Essential Books, 1955).

16. P. M. Hauser, "World and Urbanization in Relation to Economic Development and Social Change," in *Urbanization in Asia and Far East* (Calcutta: UNESCO, 1957), p. 57, based on work of K. Davis and H. Hertz.

17. ———, "Implications of Population Trends for Regional and Urban Planning in Asia," UNESCO Working Paper No. 2, U.N. Seminar on Regional Planning (Tokyo, Japan, 1958).

18. ———, ed., *Urbanization in Latin America* (New York: UNESCO, in press); P. M. Hauser, "World and Urbanization . . .," *op. cit.*

19. "The Population of South Asia (Including Ceylon and China: Taiwan) 1950-1980," *U. N. Rept. No. 3 on Future Population Estimates by Sex and Age* (New York: United Nations, 1958); *The Future Growth of World Population* (New York: United Nations, 1958).

20. W. S. Thompson, *Population and Progress in the Far East* (Chicago: University of Chicago Press, 1959).

21. *The Future Growth of World Population* (New York: United Nations, 1958).

22. I. B. Taeuber, "Population and Political Instabilities in Underdeveloped Areas," in *Population and World Politics,* P. M. Hauser, ed. (Glencoe, Ill: Free Press, 1958).

23. "The Population of Central America (Including Mexico), 1950-1980," *U.N. Rept. No. 1 on Future Population Estimates by Sex and Age* (New York: United Nations, 1954); "The Population of South America, 1950-1980," *U.N. Rept. No. 2 on Future Population Estimates by Sex and Age* (New York: United Nations, 1955); *The Future Growth of World Population* (New York: United Nations, 1958).

24. "Demographic Aspects of Urbanization in Latin America," UNESCO Seminar on Urbanization Problems in Latin America (Santiago, Chile, 1959).

25. *Social Implications of Industrialization in Africa South of the Sahara*

(London: UNESCO, 1956); Taeuber, "Population and Political Instabil-ities. . . ," *op. cit.*
26. K. Davis, "Population and Power in the Free World," in *Population and World Politics*, P. M. Hauser, ed. (Glencoe, Ill.: Free Press, 1958).
27. W. Lippmann, "China is No. 1 Problem," *Chicago Sun-Times*, Dec. 14, 1959; "To Live India Must Change Its Way of Life. . . .," *Chicago Sun-Times*, Dec. 15, 1959.
28. Nor is population a factor in political instability only in the under-developed areas. There are many other demographic dimensions of world politics which cannot be treated here because of limitations of space. The authors of a recent symposium volume which it was my privilege to edit in-clude further considerations of population as a factor in world politics. Espe-cially pertinent are the articles by Kingsley Davis, Frank Lorimer, Irene Taeu-ber, and Quincy Wright, from which material for this discussion has been drawn.
29. "Japan's Population Miracle," *Population Bull.*, 15, No. 7 (1959); "The Race Between People and Resources—in the ECAFE Region," pt. I, *Popula-tion Bull.* 15, No. 5 (1959), 89.
30. *Asia and the Far East, Seminar on Population* (New York: United Na-tions, 1957).
31. E. W. Notestein, "Knowledge, Action, People," *University—A Prince-ton Magazine*, No. 2 (1959); P. Streit and P. Streit, "New Light on India's Worry," *New York Times Magazine* (Mar. 13, 1960).
32. See, for example, G. Pincus et al., *Science* 130, (1959) 81; *idem*, "Field Trials with Norethynodrel as an Oral Contraceptive" (Shrewsbury, Mass.: Worcester Foundation for Experimental Biology, in preparation).
33. Data are based on the following: J. J. Spengler, *Proc. Am. Phil. Soc. 95 (1951)*, 53; original data (for 1937) from "Energy Resources of the World," *U.S. Dept. State Publ.* (Washington, D.C.: Government Printing Office, 1949), p. 102 ff.

### 7. Asian Populations: The Critical Decades

1. These overall figures for past, present, and projected future populations are broad approximations made on a world basis by the United Nations and published in 1958. See *The Future Growth of World Population* (New York: United Nations, 1958), Population Studies, No. 28 (prepared by Population Branch, Bureau of Social Affairs, Department of Economic and Social Affairs).
2. See "Population and Food," Chap. IV in *Economic Survey of Asia and the Far East 1961*, (Bangkok, Thailand: United Nations, Economic Commis-sion for Asia and the Far East, 1962), p. 119.
3. United Nations, Department of Economic and Social Affairs, *The Population of Asia and the Far East, 1950-1980*, p. 14.
4. The validity of the construct is attested by the results of the Indonesian census of 1961. The population at that time was 95.2 million.
5. In approximation, half the adult population consists of men, half of women, and the rates of change for the two groups are similar. This is crude, but the projected populations will also be more or less crude approximations to the true populations of the future.

### 8. Communist China and the Population Problem

1. Wang Ya-nan (President of Amoy University), "The Post-Liberation Population Problem of China," in *Marxist Population Theory and China's Population*, December, 1956; translated in *Extracts from China Mainland Magazines* (ECMM), No. 84 (May 27, 1957), p. 2.
2. Wu Ching-ch'ao, "A New Treatise on the Problem of China's Popula-

tion," *Hsin Chien She* (New Construction), No. 3, March 3, 1957; translated in *ECMM*, No. 78 (April 15, 1957).

3. *Ibid.*, p. 1.
4. *Ibid.*, p. 2.
5. *Ibid.*, p. 12.
6. *Ibid.*, p. 16.
7. Ma Yin-ch'u, "A New Theory of Population," *Jen-min Jih-pao*, Peking, July 5, 1957; translated in *Current Background*, No. 469 (July 25, 1957), p. 3.
8. *Ibid.*, p. 8.
9. Li Pu, "The Rightists Shall Not be Permitted to Take Advantage of the Population Problem for Political Scheming," *Jen-min Jih-pao*, Peking, October 14, 1957; translated in *Survey from China Mainland Press* (SCMP), No. 1644 (November 4, 1957), p. 2.
10. *Ibid.*, p. 2.
11. *Ibid.*, p. 3.
12. Wang Cho, "Way to Solve the Population Problem in China," *Jen-min Jih-pao*, Peking, February 1, 1958; translated in *SCMP*, No. 1721 (February 28, 1958), p. 2.
13. *Ibid.*, p. 2.
14. *Ibid.*, p. 2.
15. *Ibid.*, p. 3.
16. *Ibid.*, p. 3.
17. *Ibid.*, p. 4.
18. Chou Chia-pen and Chiang Chung-hua, "Comments on Ma Yin-chu's 'New Population Theory'," *Kuang Ming Jih Pao*, Peking, April 19, 1958; translated in *SCMP*, No. 1763 (May 2, 1958), p. 6.
19. *Ibid.*, p. 5.
20. Chu Pao-yi, "Refutation of Wu Ching-ch'ao's Slanderous Remarks Against The Chinese People on the Population Issue," *Tsai Ching Yen Chiu* (Finance and Economics), No. 1, February 15, 1958; translated in *ECMM*, No. 128 (May 12, 1958), p. 17.
21. *Ibid.*, p. 17.
22. *Ibid.*, p. 20.
23. Min Tzu, "It is Good to Have a Large Population," *Ch'i Hua Ching Chi* (Planned Economy), No. 6, June 9, 1958; translated in *ECMM*, No. 142 (Sept. 15, 1958), p. 25.
24. *Ibid.*, pp. 25-26.
25. *Ibid.*, p. 27.
26. *Ibid.*, p. 28.
27. *Ibid.*, p. 32.
28. *Ibid.*, p. 29.
29. Want Tso and Tai Yuan-chen, "Criticism and Appraisal of the 'New Theory of Population'," *Ching Chi Yen Chiu* (Economic Research), No. 2, February 17, 1958; translated in *ECMM*, No. 128 (May 12, 1958), p. 5.
30. Liu Shao-ch'i, "The Present Situation, the Party's General Line for Socialist Construction and its Future Tasks," *NCNA*, Peking, May 26, 1958. See *Current Background*, No. 507 (June 2, 1958), p. 24.
31. "Early Marriage is Harmful, Not Beneficial," *Nan-fang Jih-pao*, Canton, May 15, 1962; translated in *SCMP*, No. 2757 (June 13, 1962), p. 11.
32. "A Problem that Deserves Consideration by Unmarried Young People," *Chung-kuo Ch'ing-nien Pao*, Peking, May 10, 1962; translated in *SCMP*, No. 2745 (May 24, 1962), p. 15.
33. Yeh Kung-shao, "What is the Most Suitable Age for Marriage?" *Chung-kuo Ch'ing-nien Pao*, Peking, April 12, 1962; translated in *SCMP*, No. 2745. (May 24, 1962).
34. See Edgar Snow's five-hour interview with Chou En-lai, *Washington Post*, February 3, 1964, p. A12. (A portion of this interview is reprinted as Chapter 9 of the present volume.)

35. Cf. Ku Yi, "Contraception Will Not Impair One's Health," *Chung-kuo Ch'ing-nien Pao,* No. 14-15, July 28, 1963; translated in *SCMM,* No. 383 (Sept. 23, 1963), pp. 42-43; Wang Wen-pin (Professor of the Academy of Medical Science), "Will Contraception Affect Health?" *Kung-jen Jih-pao,* Peking, Sept. 4, 1962; "Planned Childbirth Must Not Depend on Artificial Abortion," *Kung-jen Jih-pao,* Peking, Sept. 27, 1962; Yao Shih-k'un, "Meeting on Planned Childbirth Held in Canton," *Nan-fang Jih-pao,* Canton, Aug. 26, 1962; translated in *SCMP,* No. 2829.

## 10. *The Population Explosion in Latin America*

1. See T. Lynn Smith, *Latin Americas Population Studies,* University of Florida Monographs, Social Sciences No. 8 (Fall 1960).

2. See W. Stanley Rycroft and Myrtle M. Clemmer, *A Study of Urbanization in Latin America* (1962).

3. For a hard-hitting attack on the failure of the Alliance for Progress to face up to the birth-control issue, see "Latin America and Population Growth. What Price Evasion?" *Population Bulletin,* XVIII, No. 6 (Washington, D.C.: Population Reference Bureau, Inc., October 1962).

4. The Family Planning Association operates clinics throughout Puerto Rico, distributes contraceptive pills free, and has legally sterilized some 100,000 men and women.

5. Yet, whatever the explanation, and with the exception of Costa Rica, the population explosion is concentrated in the areas where the living standards are lowest. See Carr B. Lavell, *Population Growth and the Development of South America,* Population Research Project of the George Washington University, (1959). See also in the same series Harold L. Geisert, *Population Problems in Mexico and Central America* (1959).

6. The population of Haiti, already hungry and crowded, will probably double to 8 million in 18 years.

7. Puerto Rico, with a population density of 702 per square mile, would collapse economically were it not for the built-in subsidy implicit in the so-called "Commonwealth" status, which is now being discussed by a specially appointed Status Commission.

8. The population pressure on the Mexican border will increase. Between 1920 and 1962 the population of Mexico increased from 14.5 million to 34.5 million. Irene B. Taeuber of Princeton University estimates that in 1980 there will be 64.4 million Mexicans and it is most unlikely that the land will be able to feed them.

9. For a protest against the Latin American conspiracy of silence on the population explosion, see Estanislau Fischlowitz, "Latinoamérica ante el vertiginoso crecimiento demográfico," *Combate* (San José, Costa Rica, July-August 1962), pp. 39-43. In 1962 the population of the world was estimated to be about 3 billion, that of Latin America 206 million—75 million more than two decades earlier. The population of Latin America is increasing at about 2.6% annually (or 5.3 million), while the gain in Africa is 2.2% and in Asia 1.9%. Per capita output of goods and services increases by only 1.6% annually. See *United Nations Demographic Yearbook,* 1962. With the restrictions on immigration imposed by the British Government in 1962, islands like Jamaica and Barbados will cease to have a convenient safety-valve, and population specialists like Dr. Richard Thoman of Queen's University (Kingston, Ontario) have warned them that they must take immediate steps to curb the birth-rate. The Catholic Church is not dominant in those islands and so could not block action easily.

## 11. *Housing and Population Growth in Africa, Asia, and Latin America*

1. Birth and death rates are in terms of 1,000 of the population per year.

2. The annual rural growth rates are: Africa, 1.7%; Asia, 1.5%; Latin America, 1%.

3. There is very little information available for individual African countries. In urban Africa as a whole, about 50 per cent of the total population "live in improvised housing, in slums, under bridges, and in all kinds of other shelters as well as overcrowded dwellings." The *United Nations Report on the World Social Situation* (1957) states: "While . . . in many African cities low-rent housing programs have been put into operation in recent years, formidable obstacles are created by the rapid increase of urban population, the limited capacity of Africans to pay even minimal rentals, and the rising cost of land and building materials."

4. The Ford Foundation has recently sponsored a project for improving conditions in this city.

5. United Nations, *Report on the World Social Situation*, 1957 and 1961.

### 16. *The Constructive Use of World Resources*

1. J. Edgar Pew, "Fifth Dimension in the Oil Industry," *Bulletin of the American Association of Petroleum Geologists*, 25, No. 7 (1941).

2. Eugene Holman, "Our Inexhaustible Resources," *The Atlantic*, June 1952.

3. W. Taylor Thom, Jr., "National and Regional Work Potentials, 1790-1938," *Trans. Am. Geophysical Union*, 26, No. 1 (1945), p. 4.

4. J. Douglas Brown, "Engineering as a Learned Profession," address delivered at Conference on Engineering Education, Oct. 11, 1962, published in *Mechanical Engineering*, 85, No. 4 (April 1963).

5. J. Edgar Pew, *op. cit.*

6. See original hardback edition on which this book was based, *The Population Crisis and the Use of World Resources*, Stuart Mudd, ed., (The Hague: Dr. W. Junk, 1964; Bloomington, Indiana University Press, 1964).

7. *Ibid.*, p. 514, Fig. 7.

8. *Ibid.*, pp. 511-516.

9. W. Taylor Thom, Jr., "Tectonic Team Research, Key to Social Progress and World Peace," address delivered before the New York Academy of Sciences, January 7, 1952.

10. John Kenneth Gailbraith. Warburg Professor of Economics, Harvard University, *The Affluent Society* (New York: The New American Library, 1958), p. 26, and Rev. Thomas Robert Malthus, "Essay on Population."

### 17. *Current Approaches to the Biological Control of Fertility*

1. W. O. Nelson, "Status of Research on the Control of Fertility," *Fertil. and Steril.*, 12 (1961), 109.

2. G. Pincus; C. R. Garcia; J. Rock; M. Paniagua; A. Pendleton; F. Laraque; R. Nicholas; R. Borno; and V. Pean, "Effectiveness of an Oral Contraceptive," *Science*, 130 (1959), 81; J. W. Goldzieher; L. E. Moses; and L. T. Ellis, "A Field Trial With a Physiological Method of Conception Control," *Research in Family Planning*, ed. C. V. Kizer (Princeton: Princeton University Press, 1962); E. T. Tyler, "An Oral Contraceptive—A 4-Year Study of Norethindrone," *Obstet. and Gynec.*, 18 (1961), 363.

3. E. J. De Costa, "Those Deceptive Contraceptives," *J.A.M.A.*, 181 (1962), 122.

4. M. G. Sevag and S. W. Colton, "Simple Chemical Method for the Determination of Ovulation Time in Women," *J.A.M.A.*, 170 (1959), 13.

5. J. B. Doyle; F. J. Ewers; and D. Sapit, "The New Fertility Testing Tape. A Predictive Test of the Fertile Period," *J.A.M.A.*, 172 (1960), 1744; C. H. Birnberg; R. Kurzrock; and A. Laufer, "Simple Test for Determining Ovulation Time," *J.A.M.A.*, 166: (1958), 1174.

6. L. Wide and C. A. Gemzell, "An Immunological Pregnancy Test," *Acta endocr.*, 35 (1960), 261.

7. S. J. Segal and W. O. Nelson, "An Orally Active Compound With Antifertility Effects in Rats," *Proc. Soc. exp. Biol. Med.*, 98 (1958), 431.

8. W. O. Nelson, "Current Research in the Regulation of Fertility," *J. Prosth. Dent.*, II (1961), 382.

9. R. B. Greenblatt, "Chemical Induction of Ovulation," *Fert. and Steril.*, 12 (1961), 402.

10. G. W. Duncan; J. C. Stuckl; S. C. Lyster; and D. Lednicer, "An Orally Effective Mammalian Antifertility Agent," *Proc. Soc. exp. Biol. Med.*, 109 (1962), 163.

11. E. Steinberger and W. O. Nelson, "The Effect of Furodroxyl Treatment and X-irradiation on the Hyaluronidase Concentration of Rat Testes," *Endocrinology*, 60 (1957), 105; E. Steinberger, A. Boccabella and W. O. Nelson, "Cytotoxic Effects of 5-Chlor-2-Acetyl Thiophen (BA 11044) on the Testis of the Rat," *Anat. Rec.*, 125 (1956), 312.

12. C. G. Heller; D. J. Moore; C. A. Paulsen; W. O. Nelson; and W. M. Laidlaw, Effects of Progesterone and Synthetic Progestins on the Reproductive Physiology of Normal Men," *Fed. Proc.*, 18 (1959), 1057.

13. W. O. Nelson and R. G. Bunge, "The Effect of Therapeutic Doses of Nitrofurantoin (Furandantin) Upon Spermatogenesis in Man," *J. Urol.*, 77 (1957), 275.

14. H. P. Drobeck and F. Coulston, "Inhibition and Recovery of Spermatogenesis in Rats, Monkeys, and Dogs Medicated with Bis (Dichloroacetyl) Diamines," *Exp. and Molecular Path.*, I (1962), 251; W. O. Nelson and D. J. Patanelli, "Inhibition of Spermatogenesis," *Fed. Proc.*, 20 (1961), 418.

15. Personal observations made in studies with C. G. Heller and J. MacCleod.

16. Personal communication.

17. D. J. Patanelli and W. O. Nelson, "A Quantitative Study of Inhibition and Recovery of Spermatogenesis," *Recent Advances in Hormone Research*, Academic Press, Vol. 20, 1964 (in press).

18. Albert Tyler, "Approaches to the Control of Fertility Based on Immunological Phenomena," *J. Reprod. Fertil.*, 2 (1961), 473.

19. J. Freund; M. M. Lipton; and G. E. Thompson, "Aspermatogenesis in the Guinea Pig Induced by a Single Injection of Homologous Testicular Material With Paraffin Oil and Killed Mycobacteria," *Bull. N.Y. Acad. Med.*, 29 (1953), 739.

20. K. A. Laurence and M. Perlbachs, "Studies on the Relationship of Delayed Hypersensitivity to Experimental Aspermatogenesis in Rats," *Bact. Proc.*, 88 (1962).

21. A. J. Weil; O. Kotsevalov; and L. Wilson "Antigens of Human Seminal Plasma," *Proc. Soc. exp. Biol. Med.* 92 (1956), 606.

22. A. Tyler, "Approaches to the Control of Fertility," *op. cit.*

23. S. Segal; E. T. Tyler; S. Rao; P. Rumke; and N. Nakabayashi, "Immunological Factors in Infertility," *Sterility*, ed. E. T. Tyler (New York: McGraw-Hill, 1961), p. 386.

24. S. J. Behrman; J. Buettner-Janusch; R. Heglar; H. Gershowitz; and W. L. Tew, "ABO(H) Blood Incompatibility As a Cause of Infertility: A New Concept," *Amer. J. Obstet. Gynec.*, 79 (1960), 847.

25. A. C. Menge; W. H. Stone; W. J. Tyler; and L. E. Casida, "Immunological Studies on Fertility and Sterility. IV. Fertility of Cattle and Rabbits Inseminated with Semen Treated with Antibodies Produced Against Semen, Spermatozoa and Erythrocytes," *J. Reprod. Fertil.*, 3 (1962), 331.

26. H. R. Cohen and A. J. Nedzel, "Specific Action on an Antiserum for Placental Proteins on Placenta and Normal Progress of Pregnancy," *Proc. Soc. exp. Biol. Med.*, 43 (1940), 249.

27. S. Lieberman; B. E. Erlanger; S. M. Beiser; and F. J. Agate, "Steroid Protein Conjugates: Their Chemical, Immunochemical and Endocrinological Properties," *Recent Progress in Hormone Research*, Vol. 15, ed. G. Pincus (New York: Academic Press Inc., 1959), p. 165.

28. N. R. Moudgal and C. H. Li, "An Immunochemical Study of Sheep Pituitary Interstitial Cell-Stimulating Hormone," *Arch. Biochem. Biophys.*, 95 (1961), 93; S. J. Segal; K. A. Laurence; M. Perlbachs; and S. Hakim, "Immunologic Analysis of Sheep Pituitary Gonadotrophin," *Gen. Comp. Endocr.* (Suppl.), I (1962), 12.

29. Atsumi Ishihama, "Clinical Studies on Intrauterine Rings Especially the Present State of Contraception in Japan and the Experiences in the Use of Intrauterine Rings," *Yokohama med. Bull.*, 10 (1959), 89.

30. W. Oppenheimer, "Prevention of Pregnancy by the Graefenberg Ring Method," *Amer. J. Obstet. Gyn.*, 78. (1959), 446.

31. Herbert H. Hall and Martin L. Stone, "Observations on the Use of the Intrauterine Pessary, with Special Reference to the Graefenberg Ring.," *Amer. J. Obstet. Gyn.*, 5 (1962), 683.

32. Intra-Uterine Contraceptive Devices: II (S. J. Segal, A. Southam, and K. Shafer, Eds.) Amsterdam: Excerpta Medica International Congress Series No. ———, 1965 (in press).

### 19. The Problems of Abortion: The Personal Population Explosion

1. G. Devereux, "A Typological Study of Abortion in 350 Primitive, Ancient and Pre-Industrial Societies," in *Therapeutic Abortion*, ed. H. Rosen (New York: Julian Press, 1954).

2. H. C. Warren, *Dictionary of Psychology* (Boston: Houghton Mifflin Co., 1934).

3. J. M. Kummer and Z. Leavy, "Criminal Abortion: A Consideration of Ways to Reduce Incidence," *Calif. Med.*, 95 (Sept. 1961), 170.

4. P. H. Gebhard; W. B. Pomeroy; C. E. Martin; and C. V. Christenson, *Pregnancy, Birth and Abortion* (New York: Harper and Bros., 1958); F. J. Taussig, *Abortion Spontaneous and Induced* (St. Louis: C. V. Mosby Co., 1936); M. E. Kopp, *Birth Control in Practice* (New York: McBride and Co., 1934); R. K. Stix, "A Study of Pregnancy Wastage," *Milbank Mem. Fd. Quart.*, 13 (1935), 347.

5. J. M. Kummer, "Value of Routine Psychiatric Examination in Treatment of Infertility," *Amer. Practic.*, 9 (March 1958), 383; Essen-Möller, quoted by E. E. Krapf, "Foreign Letters," *J.A.M.A.*, 118 (1942), 315; F. J. Kallman, *Heredity in Health and Mental Disorder* (New York: W. W. Norton and Co., 1953).

6. J. M. Kummer, "Post-Abortion Psychiatric Illness—a Myth?" *Amer. J. Psychiat.*, 119 (April 1963), 980; *idem,* "Psychiatric Contraindications to Pregnancy with Reference to Therapeutic Abortion and Sterilization," *Calif. Med.*, 79 (July, 1953), 31.

7. G. L. Timanus, Quoted in *Abortion in the United States*, ed. M. S. Calderone (New York: Hoeber-Harper, 1958).

8. Kummer and Leavy, *op. cit.*

9. F. J. Taussig, *op. cit.*

10. A. F. Guttmacher, "The Law that Doctors Often Break," *Redbook Magazine*, Aug., 1959, p. 24.

11. H. L. Packer and R. J. Gampell, "Therapeutic Abortion: A Problem in Law and Medicine," *Stanford Law Rev.*, II (May 1959), 417.

12. Z. Leavy and J. M. Kummer, "Criminal Abortion: Human Hardship and Unyielding Laws," *So. Calif. Law Rev.*, 35 (Winter 1962), 123.

## 22. *Public Health in an Overpopulated World*

1. J. E. Gordon, "Population Problems in a Contracting World," *Yale J. Biol. Med.,* 34 (1961), 60.
2. F. Osborn, *Population: An International Dilemma.* (New York: Population Council, 1958).
3. United Nations Department of Social Affairs, Population Division, *The Determinants and Consequences of Population Trends* (New York: United Nations, 1958).
4. A. J. Coale and E. M. Hoover, *Population Growth and Economic Development in Low-Income Countries* (Princeton, N.J.: Princeton University Press, 1958).
5. W. S. Woytinsky and E. S. Woytinsky, *World Population and Production: Trends and Outlook* (New York: Twentieth Century Fund, 1953).
6. P. M. Hauser and O. D. Duncan, eds., *The Study of Population: An Inventory and Appraisal* (Chicago: University of Chicago Press, 1959).
7. J. E. Gordon, J. B. Wyon, and T. H. Ingalls, "Public Health as a Demographic Influence," *Amer. J. Med. Sci.,* 227 (1954), 326.
8. Asia Family Planning Association, *Family Planning in Japan* (Tokyo: Asia Family Planning Association, 1961).
9. Y. Koya, H. Kubo, S. Yuasa, and H. Ogino, "Seven Years of a Family Planning Program in Three Typical Japanese Villages," *Milbank Mem. Fund Quart.* 34 (1958), 363.
10. *Report on Pilot Studies in Family Planning,* Vols. I and II (New Delhi: World Health Organization Regional Office for S. E. Asia, 1954).
11. J. E. Gordon and J. B. Wyon, "Field Studies in Population Dynamics and Population Control," *Amer. J. Med. Sci.,* 240 (1960), 361.

## 23. *Population, Space, and Human Culture*

1. Justus von Liebig, *Familiar Letters on Chemistry* (1844).
2. See Edmund Fuller, *Tinkers and Genius* (1955).
3. Harrison Scott Brown, James Bonner, and John Wier, *The Next Hundred Years* (1957), *passim.*
4. *U.S. Department of Agriculture Yearbook,* (1938), 84-110.
5. Brown, Bonner, and Wier, *op. cit.,* note 3, *passim.*
6. *Ibid.*
7. This remark has been ascribed to Henry A. Wallace.
8. *World Almanac* (1960), 303.
9. Whyte, "Urban Sprawl," *Fortune,* Jan. 1958, p. 103.
10. See President's Commission on Social Trends, *Report* (1933).

## 26. *United Nations General Assembly Resolution*

1. Presented in a report of the Second Committee (A/5354) with a report of the Fifth Committee (A/5375).
2. General Assembly resolution 1838 (XVII).
3. E/3451, para. 15.

# BIBLIOGRAPHY

### 2. Geography and the World's Population

Brown, H. *The Challenge of Man's Future.* New York: Viking Press, 1954.

Gourou, P. *The Tropical World.* New York: John Wiley and Sons, Inc. 1961.

——. "The Quality of Land Use of Tropical Cultivators," in *Man's Role in Changing the Face of the Earth.* Chicago: University of Chicago Press, 1956. Pp. 336-349.

Gould, L. M. *The Polar Regions in Their Relation to Human Affairs.* New York: American Geographical Society, 1958.

Gray, G. W. "Life at High Altitudes," *Scient. American* 193 (December, 1955), 58-68.

Issawi, Charles. *Egypt: An Economic and Social Analysis.* London: Oxford University Press, 1947.

Kellogg, C. E. *The Soils that Support Us.* New York: The Macmillan Company, 1941.

Monge, Carlos. *Acclimatization in the Andes.* Baltimore: Johns Hopkins University Press, 1948.

Kimble, G. H. T., ed. *Geography of the Northlands.* New York: John Wiley and Sons, 1955.

Notestein, F. W., "7 Billion People by the Year 2000." *Foreign Agric.,* 26 (July, 1962), 3-4; 22.

Pehrson, E. W. "Mineral Supply: There is Plenty of Everything We Need . . . If We Can Get It." *Int. Sci. and Technol.* (February, 1962), 23-27.

President's Materials Policy Commission. *Resources for Freedom.* 5 vols. Washington, D.C.: Government Printing Office, 1952.

Spengler, J. J. "Population Threatens Prosperity." *Harvard Business Rev.,* 34 (January-February, 1956), 85-94.

Stamp, L. Dudley. *Lands for Tomorrow.* Bloomington: Indiana University Press, 1952.

——. "The Measurement of Land Resources." *Geogr. Rev.,* 48 (January, 1958), 1-15.

"Symposium on World Food and Population." *Discovery,* 21 (October, 1960), 419; 456-457.

Taeuber, I. *The Population of Japan.* Princeton: Princeton University Press, 1958.

United Nations, Department of Social Affairs, Population Division. *Population Growth and the Standard of Living in Underdeveloped Countries,* No. 20. New York, 1954.

Wyllie, J. *Land Requirements for the Production of Human Food.* London: University of London Press, 1954.

### 3. How Many People Have Ever Lived on Earth?

Bennett, M. K. *The World's Food.* New York: Harper and Brothers, 1954.

Braidwood, Robert J. "Near Eastern Prehistory." *Science*, 127 (June 20, 1958).

Carr-Saunders, A. M. *World Population, Past Growth and Present Trends.* Oxford: Clarendon Press, 1936.

Durand, John. "Mortality Estimates from Roman Tombstone Inscriptions." *American Journal of Sociology*, 45 (January, 1960).

Russell, J. C. "Late Ancient and Medieval Population." *Transactions of the American Philosophical Society*, New Series 48, Part 3 (June, 1958).

Steward, Julian. "The Native Population of South America." *Bureau of American Ethnology Bulletin*, No. 143.

United Nations, Department of Social Affairs, Population Division. *The Determinants and Consequences of Population Trends.* New York, 1953.

United Nations, Department of Economic and Social Affairs, Statistical Office. *Demographic Yearbook, 1960.* New York, 1960.

————. *The Future Growth of World Population.* New York, 1958.

————. *Population and Vital Statistics Reports.* Statistical Papers, Series A, Vol. XIII, No. 1. New York, 1961.

Willcox, Walter F., ed. "Population of the Earth," in *International Migrations*, Vol. II, Part I. New York: National Bureau of Economic Research, Inc., 1931.

## 11. *Housing and Population Growth in Africa, Asia, and Latin America*

Butler, William F. "Housing in Latin America." Address at Latin American Housing Symposium. New York, April 1962.

Population Reference Bureau. *Population Bulletin*, XIII, No. 8 (December, 1957); XVIII, No. 6 (October, 1962); XVIII, No. 8 (December, 1962).

United Nations, Bureau of Social Affairs, Housing, Building and Planning Branch. *World Housing Conditions and Estimated Housing Requirements.* July, 1962.

United Nations, Demographic Center for Latin America. *Demographic Information Required for Housing Programs With Special Reference to Latin America.* July, 1962.

United Nations, Department of Economic and Social Affairs. *The Future Growth of World Population.* New York, 1958.

————. *The Population of Asia and the Far East, 1950-1980.* New York, 1959.

————. *Report on the World Social Situation.* New York, 1957 and 1961.

United Nations, Economic Commission for Asia and the Far East, *Urbanization and Housing in Asia and the Far East.* June, 1962.

United Nations, Economic Commission for Europe. *Report on the Seminar on Housing Surveys and Programs."* October, 1961.

United Nations, Statistical Office. *Demographic Yearbook.* New York, 1961.

————. *Statistical Yearbook.* New York, 1961.

Urban Land Institute. *World Urbanization.* Technical Bulletin, No. 43. Washington, D.C., 1962.

## 20. *The Protection and Improvement of Man's Genetic Inheritance*

American Eugenics Society. *Heredity Counseling*, ed. Helen G. Hammons. New York: Paul B. Hoeber, Inc., 1959.

Anastasi, Anne. *Differential Psychology.* New York: Macmillan, 1958.

Dobzhansky, Theodosius. *Evolution, Genetics and Man.* New York: Wiley & Sons, 1955.

Freedman, Ronald; Whelpton, Pascal K.; and Campbell, Arthur A. *Family Planning, Sterility and Population Growth.* New York: McGraw-Hill, 1959.

Newman, H. H.; Freeman, F. N.; and Holsinger, K. J. *Twins, A Study of Heredity and Environment*. Chicago: University of Chicago Press, 1937.
Osborn, Frederick. *Preface to Eugenics*. Revised Ed. New York: Harper & Bros., 1940.
Reed, Sheldon C. *Counseling in Medical Genetics*. Philadelphia: W. B. Saunders, 1955.
Schwesinger, Gladys. *Heredity and Environment*. New York: Macmillan, 1933.
Sinnott, Edmund W.; Dunn, L. C.; and Dobzhansky, Theodosius. *Principles of Genetics*. New York: McGraw-Hill, 1958.
Tyler, Leona E. *Psychology of Human Differences*. 2nd Ed. New York: Appleton Century Crofts, 1956.
Yaukey, David. *Fertility Differences in a Modernizing Country: A Survey of Lebanese Couples*. Princeton: Princeton University Press, 1961.

## 21. Better Genes for Tomorrow

Brewer, H. *Eugenics Rev.*, 27 (1935), 121.
———. *Lancet*, I (1939), 265.
———. *Balanced Living*, 17 (1961), 69.
Bunge, R. G., and Sherman, J. K. *Nature* (Lond.), 172 (1953), 767.
Bunge, R. G.; Keittel, W. C.; and Sherman, J. K. *Fertil. and Steril.*, 5 (1954), 520.
Dobzhansky, T. *Mankind Evolving: The Evolution of the Human Species*. New Haven and London: Yale University Press, 1962.
Dubos, R. *The Torch of Life*. New York: Simon and Schuster, 1962.
Guttmacher, A. F. *Babies by Choice or by Chance*. New York: Avon Books, 1961.
Hoagland, H. *Scient. Monthly*, 56 (1943), 56.
Hoagland, H., and Pincus, G. *J. Gen. Physiol.*, 25 (1942), 337.
Huxley, J. S. *Eugenics Rev.*, 1962.
———. *Current*, No. 29 (Sept., 1962), 58.
———. In: *Man and His Future*, ed. G. Wolstenholm. London: J. and A. Churchill; New York: Macmillan, 1963.
Iizuka, R., and Sawada, Y. *Jap. J. Fertil. and Steril.*, 3 (1958), 1.
Jahnel, F. *Klin. Wschr.*, 17 (1938), 1273.
Kline, C. W. *Balanced Living*, 17 (1961), 75.
Lederberg, J. In: *Man and his Future*, ed. G. Wolstenholm. London: J. and A. Churchill; New York: Macmillan, 1963.
MacKinnon, J. G. *The Humanist*, 20, No. 2 (1960), 89.
Medawar, P. B. *The Future of Man*. New York: Basic Books, 1960.
Montegazza, P. *Rend. reale Istit. Lomb.*, 3 (1866), 183.
Muller, H. J. *Out of the Night: A Biologist's View of the Future*. New York: Vanguard Press, 1935; London: Gollancz, 1936; Paris: Guillemard, 1938. (Fr. trans. by J. Rostand).
———. *Science*, 127 (1958), 625.
———. In: *Evolution after Darwin*. 2, "Evolution of Man," ed. S. Tax. Chicago: University of Chicago Press, 1960.
———. In: *Evolution after Darwin*. 3, "Issues in Evolution," ed. S. Tax. Chicago: University of Chicago Press, 1960.
———. *Science*, 134 (1961), 643.
———. *Perspectives in Biology and Medicine*, 4 (1961), 377.
———. In: *Evolution and Man's Progress*, ed. H. Hoagland and R. W. Burhoe. New York and London: Columbia University Press, 1962. p. 22.
———. In: *Man and His Future*, ed. G. Wolstenholm. London: J. and A. Churchill; New York: Macmillan, 1963.
Nakajima, K.; Iizuka, R.; Sawada, Y.; Yoshida, Y.; Ookubo, F.; and Isono,

M. Paper read at 4th World Cong. Internat. Fert. Assoc. in Brazil, 1962.

Polge, C.; Smith, A. V.; and Parkes, A. S. *Nature* (Lond.), 164 (1949), 666.

Rostand, J. Can Man Be Modified? New York: Basic Books, Inc., 1959.

Sawada, Y. *Jap J. Fertil. and Steril.*, 4 (1959), 1.

Sherman, J. K. *Fertil. and Steril.*, 5 (1954), 357.

———. *Fertil. and Steril.*, 49, No. 1 (1963), 14.

Sherman, J. K., and Bunge, R. G. *Proc. Soc. exp. Biol. Med.*, 82 (1953), 686.

Shettles, L. B. *Amer. J. Physiol.*, 128 (1940), 408.

Stokes, Walter R. *Marriage and Family Living*, 24 (1962), 269.

# LIST OF CONTRIBUTORS

EUGENE ROBERT BLACK, who was president of the World Bank from 1949 to 1962, is now a financial consultant to the United Nations. He has served on the boards of many companies and is chairman of the Board of Trustees of the Brookings Institution.

BROCK CHISHOLM, former director-general of the World Health Organization, has also served as an officer of the World Federalists and of the Canadian Peace Research Institute. His publications include *Prescription for Survival* (1957) and *Can People Learn to Learn?* (1958).

C. S. CHRISTIAN has headed scientific surveys in the underdeveloped areas of Australia and New Guinea to determine their potential for agricultural production. He also planned the Indian Central Arid Zone Research Institute at Jodhpur, India.

ROBERT CARTER COOK, president of the Population Reference Bureau, was editor of the *Journal of Heredity* and of the *Population Bulletin* for a number of years. He is a contributor to technical and popular journals and the author of *Human Fertility: The Modern Dilemma* (1951). Dr. Cook has been a lecturer at the School of Medicine at George Washington University since 1944.

LINCOLN H. DAY is a research associate with the Bureau of Applied Social Research at Columbia University. He is the author of a number of articles, and the co-author of two books, *Too Many Americans* and *Disabled Workers in the Labor Market.*

ANNABELLE DESMOND (MRS. ROBERT COOK) has worked with the Population Reference Bureau for the past twelve years. A science writer, she has edited a book on deafness and has co-authored several articles for professional and popular magazines.

HAZEL ELKINGTON is a research assistant in the Department of Demography and Human Ecology at the Harvard School of Public Health.

CLARENCE JAMES GAMBLE has been a research associate at Harvard since 1952. Since 1957 he has been president of Pathfinder Fund, which is dedicated to the expansion of contraceptive services in many countries. He is author of numerous technical articles on laboratory and clinical evaluation of contraceptives.

RICHARD NEWTON GARDNER, Deputy Assistant Secretary of State for International Organization Affairs since 1961, was formerly professor of law at Columbia University. He is author of *Sterling-Dollar Diplomacy* (1956) and *New Directions in U.S. Foreign Economic Policy* (1959).

JOHN EVERETT GORDON, professor emeritus of preventive medicine and epidemiology at Harvard School of Public Health, is a consultant to several national and international organizations. The author of a number of books and journal articles, Dr. Gordon received several U.S. awards for his army service during World War II, as well as awards for distinguished service from other countries.

MRS. KAVAL GULHATI has been a research assistant in demography at the Population Reference Bureau since 1960. A frequent contributor to Bureau publications, Mrs. Gulhati holds a first class M.A. degree in social work from Delhi University.

ALAN FRANK GUTTMACHER, president of Planned Parenthood/World Population, has served as director of the Department of Obstetrics and Gynecology at Mt. Sinai Hospital, and as director of the Margaret Sanger Research Bureau. Dr. Guttmacher is also a lecturer at Harvard and Columbia Universities. He has written widely on birth control and other socio-medical topics.

PHILIP MORRIS HAUSER is professor and chairman of the Department of Sociology at the University of Chicago. In addition to authoring and editing numerous publications, he has served as deputy director of the Bureau of the Census, U.S. representative to the U.N. Population Commission, and advisor to the governments of Burma and Thailand.

RONALD HILTON is professor of Romance languages at Stanford University. Until recently he was director of the Institute of Hispanic American and Luso-Brazilian Studies at Stanford. He is editor of *Who's Who in Latin America*, founder and former editor of *Hispanic American Report*, and author of numerous books and articles on Latin America.

SIR JULIAN HUXLEY is the renowned British biologist, naturalist, humanist and writer. Sir Julian, who was director-general of UNESCO from 1946 to 1948, was formerly professor of zoology at Rice Institute and at the University of London. Among the more recent of his numerous works are *The Story of Evolution* (1958) and *The Humanist Frame,* ed. (1961).

JEROME MELVIN KUMMER, associate clinical professor of psychiatry at the University of California at Los Angeles, is also senior attending psychiatrist at Santa Monica Hospital. Dr. Kummer has written a number of publications in his field.

F. L. LUCAS, well-known British literary critic, is a fellow of King's College, Cambridge, and University Reader in English. Among his many books are *The Decline and Fall of the Romantic Ideal* (1948); *The Search for Good Sense* (1958); *The Art of Living* (1959); and *The Greatest Problem* [world population] *and Other Essays* (1961).

HERMANN JOSEPH MULLER, professor emeritus of zoology and distinguished service professor at Indiana University, received the Nobel Prize in physiology and medicine in 1946. Some of his numerous writings appear in the book, *Studies in Genetics: The Selected Papers of H. J. Muller* (1962).

WARREN OTTO NELSON was medical director of the Population Council from 1954 until his death on October 19, 1964. He formerly served as professor of anatomy at Wayne University and the University of Iowa, and was the recipient of several scientific awards.

ROBERT CARVER NORTH has been professor of political science at Stanford University since 1962. He is author of *Moscow and the Chinese Communists* and *Kuomintang and Chinese Communist Elites,* and co-author of *Soviet Russia and the East* and of *M. N. Roy's Mission to China.*

FREDERICK OSBORN, president of the Population Council from 1952 to 1960, has had a varied career as a corporation and foundation executive and as a writer in the field of population studies. The author of *Preface to Eugenics* (1940), and *Population: An International Dilemma* (1958), he has written and co-authored many other publications.

EDGAR SNOW, noted author and journalist, has served as correspondent for numerous newspapers and magazines, including the *Chicago Tribune, New York Sun, London Daily Herald, Look,* and *Saturday Evening Post.* He is the author of several books on China, among them *Red Star Over China* (1961) and *The Other Side of the River* (1962).

J. MAYONE STYCOS is professor of sociology and director of the International Population Program at Cornell University. He has conducted and published studies of fertility and family planning in Caribbean and South American countries.

IRENE B. TAEUBER has been a demographer and sociologist with the Office of Population Research at Princeton University since 1936. She has been an officer of various scientific and professional organizations, and is the author of several books and numerous articles.

ARNOLD J. TOYNBEE is the world-renowned historian, humanist, and writer. He has been professor of Byzantine and Greek studies at London University, was director of research for the Foreign Office, and served as a member of the British delegation to the Paris peace conferences of 1919 and 1946. Among his many well-known books are *Study of History* (12 vols.); *War and Civilization; The World and the West;* and *Comparing Notes: A Dialogue Across a Generation,* which he co-authored with his son.

WILLIAM TAYLOR THOM, JR., is president of the American Institute of Geonomy and Natural Resources and chairman emeritus of the Department of Geological Engineering at Princeton University. He served on the staff of the U.S. Geological Survey for sixteen years, and has authored many publications, including *Science and Engineering and the Future of Man* (1961).

HENRY B. VAN LOON, an architect and planner with the firm of Perkins and Will, is a member of the American Institute of Architects, former executive director of the Pennsylvania State Planning Board, and co-author of *Urban Development Guidebook* (1955).

CHARLES LANGDON WHITE has been professor of geography at Stanford University since 1943. He has served as visiting professor at a number of U.S. and Latin American universities and as director of several field expeditions. He has contributed to various technical journals and recently co-authored a book on *World Economic Geography* (1964).

# INDEX

## A

Abortion:
  in other countries, 210, 250
  in U.S., 207–8, 211–12, 251
  medical attitudes toward, 211
  Therapeutic Abortion Statute
    (U.S.), 212
Acres per capita:
  in 17th century, 35
  in Japan today, 262
  in U.S. today, 262
Africa:
  income per capita estimates, 62,
    63
  population estimates, 30, 34, 37
Agency for International Development, 296
Amazonia:
  problem of inhabitation, 105
American Assembly:
  Final Report on the Population
    Dilemma, 317–22, 306
American College of Obstetrics and
  Gynecology:
  on birth control, 308–9
American Eugenics Society:
  activities of, 332
American Medical Association, 309
American Public Health Association:
  on population, 256, 309
Antarctica:
  problem of settlement, 15

Antispermatogenic agents:
  as contraceptives for males, 196–
    97
Antizygotic agents:
  as contraceptives, 195–96
Argentina:
  cities in, 106
  on birth control, 107–8
  housing situation in, 115
Artificially-controlled insemination:
  practice of, 229
Asia:
  population estimates, 30, 34, 37
  population estimates in selected
    countries, 80, 81, 83, 84, 85
  share of world income, 62
  standard of living, 63
Asian Population Conference, 1963:
  recommendations of, 299–300
  report on, 297–303
  resolution of, 301–2
Assortative mating:
  increase of, 221–22
Atomic fallout:
  effect of, 216–17

## B

Barbados:
  birth control clinics in, 253
  population policy of, 7
Bennett, M. K., 31

Birth control:
  among American Catholic wives, 219
  and public health, 251–53
  as a problem in underdeveloped countries, 70
  clinics, limitation of, 253
  in Communist China, 92, 93
  in U.S., 219, 312–13
  methods of, 250
  need for, 6, 318
Birth spacing:
  benefits of, 252
Black, Eugene R., 8, 39–44, 351
Bombay:
  housing problem in, 121
Brazil:
  immigrants to, 107
  population and per capita gross national product, 117
  population estimates, 120
Brush Foundation:
  activities of, 332

## C

Cairo Conference of Developing Countries (1962), 289
Calcutta:
  housing problem in, 121
Calories:
  countries with lowest intake, 150
Canada:
  population and per capita gross national product, 117
Catholic Church:
  influence in Latin America, 107
  in U.S., 309–10
  on birth control, 50
Ceylon:
  housing problem in, 115
  public health campaigns in, 40, 74, 248, 249
Chile:
  population estimates, 120

  practice of abortion in, 250–51
China (Mainland):
  family planning in, 101–2
  implications of population density, 65–66
  latest national census, 103
  official population policy of, 7, 98
  population estimates, 30, 80, 81, 83, 84, 85
  proportion of cultivated land in, 164
Chisholm, G. Brock, 279–81, 351
Chou En-lai:
  on family planning, 101–3
Christian, C. S., 157–77, 351
Cities:
  overcrowding of, 106, 118–22
Conference on Planned Parenthood (3rd International, 1952), 313
Conservation Foundation:
  activities of, 333
Contraception:
  approaches to, 191–200. *See also* Birth control, methods of
Contraceptives:
  field trials with, 254–55
  mechanical, 199–200
  oral, 192–94
Cook, Robert C., 114–24, 351
Cook, Mrs. Robert C. *See* Desmond, Annabelle
Costa Rica:
  population growth rate, 110–11, 120
Cuba:
  population estimates, 120

## D

Day, Lincoln H., 124–32, 351
DDT:
  use in Ceylon, 74

"Death Control":
  effect on population, 6, 70
De Castro, Josué:
  theory of, 49, 109
Denmark:
  housing situation in, 115, 116
Deserts:
  problem of cultivation, 15
Desmond, Annabelle (Cook, Mrs. Robert C.), 20–38, 297–303, 351
Deurbanization:
  a proposal for, 185
Developing countries:
  needs of, 41
Diabetes mellitus:
  eugenic considerations, 217
Dobzhansky, Th.:
  on germinal choice, 247. *See also* Dubos, R.
Dominican Republic:
  in comparison with Haiti, 109–10
  population estimates, 120
Dubos, R.:
  on germinal choice, 247. *See also* Dobzhansky, Th.

**E**

ECAFE (United Nations Economic Commission for Asia and the Far East), 297
ECOSOC (United Nations Economic and Social Council):
  recommendations to, 283, 284
Ecuador:
  population estimates, 120
Edaphological difficulties. *See* Latin America
Education:
  and the oncoming generation, 83–85
Eisenhower, Dwight D., 304, 305
El Salvador:
  population density, 108, 110
  population estimates, 120
Elkington, Hazel, 248–57, 351
Energy:
  consumed per capita, by continent, 60
England:
  family planning in, 53, 58, 250
Enovid:
  use of, 192–94
Epidemics:
  effect on population, 29, 30
Estrogen:
  inhibition of ovulation by, 192–94
Eugenics:
  and sterilization, 202
Europe:
  population estimates, 30, 33, 34, 37
  population, income and energy consumed per capita, 60
Evolution:
  man as leader of, 3

**F**

Family planning:
  in China (Mainland), 101–2
  in India, Pakistan, Barbados, Hong Kong, Korea, 253
  in Japan, 252–53
FAO (Food and Agricultural Organization of the United Nations):
  Freedom from Hunger Campaign of, 133 ff, 149 ff, 157
  International Rice Commission of, 164
  Report on Food Supplies, 149–56
Fertility control:
  problems in, 52–57. *See also* Family planning; Birth control
Fertilizers:
  use of, 158, 166, 260–1

Food supply:
overall index of needs, 152, 154.
FAO Report on Food Supplies, 149–56
Ford Foundation:
activities of, 327–28
aid to International Rice Institute, 164
Freedom from Hunger Campaign of FAO, 133 ff, 149 ff, 157

## G

Gamble, C. J., 312–17, 351
Gardner, Richard N., 285–97, 351
Genes:
defective, increase of, 216–19, 223–24
Germany:
West, housing situation in, 115, 116
Germinal choice:
case for, 230–35, 241–47
need for education in principles of, 227
Gordon, John E., 248–57, 352
Great Britain:
first national census, 34
Greenland:
inhabitation of, 15
Guatemala:
population estimates, 120
Gulhati, Mrs. Kaval, 114–24, 352
Guttmacher, Alan F., 201–6, 229, 304–12, 352

## H

Haiti:
compared with Dominican Republic, 109–10
population estimates, 120
Hauser, Philip M., 58–71, 352
High mountains:
inhabitation of, 15

Hilton, Ronald, 104–13, 352
Homo sapiens:
origin of, 24
Honduras:
conflict with El Salvador, 110
population estimates, 120
Hong Kong:
family planning in, 253
housing problem in, 121–22
Housing:
deficit in, 114–15
estimated needs, 123
Hugh Moore Fund:
activities of, 326–27
Human Betterment Association of New York:
work of, 204
Human germ cells:
banks of, 229
Hungary:
illegal abortions in, 250
Huxley, Julian, 3–8, 229, 352

## I

Ice-caps:
settlement of, 15
Illegitimacy:
and fertility, 51–52
and genetic inheritance, 219–20
Immunology:
in control of reproduction, 197–99
Income per capita:
by continent, 60, 116–17
India:
family planning in, 253, 254, 255
industrialization in, 6
population estimates, 30, 80–85
population policy of, 7, 70
sterilization programs in, 206, 251
Indonesia:
population trends and estimates, 78, 80–85

Indus River Agreement, 169
Industrialization:
  difficulties in developing countries, 18–19
International Planned Parenthood Federation. *See* IPPF
International Rice Institute, 164
International Union for the Scientific Study of Population:
  activities of, 331–32
Intrauterine devices:
  as contraceptives, 199–200, 205
IPPF (International Planned Parenthood Federation):
  activities of, 324–25
  Seventh World Conference of, 311
Irrigation:
  abuses of, 170
  importance of, 164, 170

**J**

Jamaica:
  birth control experimental program in, 57
Japan:
  abortions in, 250
  family planning in, 53, 57, 252, 253, 254
  land utilization in, 164
  migration to South America, 107
  population and per capita product, 117
  population estimates, 30, 80–85
  sterilization in, 205–6, 251
Java:
  population growth in, 80

**K**

Kennedy, John F., 296, 304, 305
Khrushchev, N., 294
Kinsey Report, 251
Korea:
  family planning in, 253
Kummer, Jerome M., 207–14, 352

**L**

Land:
  acres per capita (U.S.), 262
  cultivable, 164–65
  deterioration, 161–62
  "land systems" and "land units," 174
  reclamation, 261
  resources surveys, 173–74
  use and abuse of, 265, 387 ff
Lands:
  populous, 12–13
  sparsely settled, 13
Latin America:
  edaphological difficulties in, 105
  migration to, 106–7
  per capita income of, 61, 62
  population estimates for individual countries, 120
  population estimates by age, 117
  population estimates and per capita gross national product, 117
  total population estimates, 34, 37, 77
  urban growth in, 66–67, 119
Law of Increasing Returns:
  applicability of, 178, 180
Legalized abortion:
  in Japan, 57
Life expectancy:
  increase in, 22, 249
Liu Shao-Ch'i, 97, 98
Lower class:
  fertility, elite theories on, 49
  ignorance concerning sexual physiology, 55
Lucas, F. L., 267–76, 352

**M**

Ma Yin-Ch'u (President of Peking University):
  dismissal of, 100

Malaria:
eradication of, 17, 40, 107
Malthusianism:
compared with Marxism-Leninism, 73, 90, 91, 92
Mao Tse-Tung, 98
Marriage law in Communist China,
98
Marxism:
compared with Malthusianism,
73, 90, 91, 92
on population, 47–48
Mauritius:
housing situation in, 115
Megapoles:
typical of Latin America, 106
Mexico:
population estimates, 31, 120
population and per capita gross
national product, 117. *See
also* Telles, Raymond L.;
Rio Colorado Agreement
Mexico City:
housing problem in, 122
Migration:
in Asia, 86, 87
to South America, 107
Milbank Memorial Fund:
activities of, 328–29
Moore, Hugh. *See* Hugh Moore
Fund
Mt. Sinai Hospital, New York City:
sterilization program of, 203–4
Mudd, Stuart, vii
Muller, Hermann J., 223–47, 352

N

National Academy of Science
(U.S.), 306
National Committee on Maternal
Health:
activities of, 313, 333

National Institutes of Health:
the National Institute of Child
Health and Human Devel-
opment, 305
National Medical Association:
support of birth control programs, 309
Nationalism:
and fertility control, 47–48
Natural resources:
exploitation of, 4
plan for utilization of, 171–77
Nelson, Warren O., 191–200, 352
Neolithic Age:
population during, 25
Ng, Larry K. Y., v, vi
Nicaragua:
population estimates, 120
North, Robert C., 88–99, 353
North America:
share of world income, 60

O

Oceania:
population estimates, 34, 37
Old Stone Age:
population during, 23
Oral contraceptives:
types in use, 192–94
"Orthonovum," 193
Osborn, Frederick, 215–22, 353
Overpopulation:
and public health, 248–57
and writers, 267–76
concept of, 18
Ovulation:
detection of, 194
inhibition of, 192–94

P

Pakistan:
family planning in, 253

per capita income, 116, 117
population estimates, 80–85
population policy of, 7, 70
practice of sterilization in, 251
*See also* Indus River Agreement
Paleolithic Age. *See* Old Stone Age
Panama:
    housing situation in, 115, 116
    population estimates, 120
Paraguay:
    emigration from, 111
    estimated population, 120
    immigration into, 107
Pasture areas:
    reduction of, 165
Pathfinder Fund:
    activities of, 333
Perón, Juan, 108
Peru:
    family size in, 50
    high mountains of, 15
    Inca cereal of, 16
    population estimates, 120
Philippines:
    population and per capita gross
        national product, 117
    *See also* International Rice Insti-
        tute
Planned Parenthood Federation (In-
    ternal). *See* IPPF
Planned Parenthood–World Popu-
    lation:
    activities of, 323–24
    Report on, 304–12
Plant extractives:
    as contraceptives, 200
Pollution:
    of air and water, 186
Population:
    by regions, 34, 60
    doubling time, 23, 31–32, 59–60,
        286–87
    for Asia, 64, 78–87, 298
    for Latin America, 120
    growth and urban expansion,
        118 ff

in the productive ages (Asia),
    81
Population Association of Amer-
    ica:
    activities of, 331
Population Council:
    activities of, 329–30
Population Reference Bureau:
    activities of, 325–26
Population Study Centers (at Uni-
    versities): 333–36
"Pre-adoption":
    meaning of, 229
Puerto Rico:
    family planning in, 53, 57
    population policy of, 7
    sterilization in, 203, 251

**R**

Rainfall:
    average annual, 168, 171
Religion and birth control, 7, 50
Reproduction:
    physiology of, 192
Republic of South Africa:
    demographic problems of, 67
Rio Colorado Agreement, 169
Rio de Janeiro:
    population and housing in, 122
Rockefeller Brothers Fund:
    activities of, 330
Rockefeller Foundation:
    activities of, 330–31
    and the International Rice Insti-
        tute, 164
Russia:
    population estimates, 30, 77
    income per capita, 60
    *See also* U.S.S.R.; Marxism

**S**

Sanger, Margaret:
    and the Planned Parenthood
        movement, 53, 312, 313

Sanger, Margaret (*Cont.*)
Research Bureau, 313
Science:
and the population explosion, 6, 261
Sea water:
desalinization of, 15, 185
Sex relations:
and fertility, 50
Slums:
urban, 121–22
Snow, Edgar:
interview with Chou En-lai, 101–3, 353
Social Darwinists:
and genetic theory, 226
Solar energy:
harnessing of, 60
South America:
*See* Latin America
South Korea:
population explosion in, 65
Space:
a concept of, 258–67
Stanford University: 31, 109
Sterilization:
definition of, 201
in females, 57, 201–2
in males, 57, 201
in India, 206, 251
in Japan, 205–6, 251
in Pakistan, 251
in Puerto Rico, 203, 251
in U.S., 203–4
Stycos, J. Mayone, 44–58, 353
Sumatra:
migration to, 80, 86
Sweden:
farming in, 16
first census in, 34

**T**

Taboos:
remarriage of widows, 49

Taeuber, Irene, 66, 72–87, 118, 353
Taiwan:
importance of irrigation in, 164
population density of, 65
Tanganyika:
Olduvai gorge of, 24
Telles, Raymond L., 112
Thom, W. Taylor, Jr., 177–88, 353
Thompson, Warren S., 65–66
Thrombophlebitis:
and Enovid, 194
Tokyo:
oversize of, 6
Toynbee, Arnold J., 133–48, 353
Traffic jams:
problem of, 129
Trinidad-Tobago:
housing situation in, 115
Tropical medicine and the World Health Organization, 17
Tropical rivers of South America, 105
Trujillo, President (Dominican Republic), 109
Tuberculosis:
in early medieval Europe, 29
Tundras:
agriculture in, 15–16
Turkey:
abortion in, 251
malaria control in, 249

**U**

UNESCO:
mentioned, 4, 6, 303
recommendation to, 319
Underpopulation:
concept of, 18
United Kingdom:
family planning centers in, 313
population and per capita gross national product in, 117
*See also* England; Great Britain

United Nations:
ECAFE, 297
ECOSOC, 39, 284
General Assembly Resolution on Population Growth and Economic Development, 282–84, 285–95
need for population policy, 6
recommendations to, 302–3, 319
UNESCO, 303
UNICEF, 303
WHO, 302–3
*See also* FAO

United States:
abortion in, 207–8, 251
artificial insemination in, 229
fertility patterns in, 50, 124–32
housing situation in, 115, 116, 117
migrations to, 86–7, 109, 112
petroleum industry in, 178, 182
Planned Parenthood movement in, 53, 304–12, 313
policy on population, 305 ff
population estimates, 30, 34, 37, 77
use and abuse of water in, 168–69
use of contraceptives in, 192–93

Urban Expansion:
encroachment on valuable arable lands, 164
in Africa, 118, 119
in Asia, 63, 64, 65, 118, 119
in Latin America, 66, 118, 119, 120

Uruguay:
population estimates, 120

U.S.S.R.:
abortion in, 210
cultivation of tundras, 15–16
population estimates, 60, 77
*See also* Russia; Marxism

V

Van Loon, Henry B., 258–67, 353
Vasectomy:
technique of, 201
*See also* sterilization, male
Venezuela:
population estimates, 120
urbanization in, 66

W

Wang Ya-Nan (President of Amoy University):
on Marxist theory of population, 90–91
Water:
consumption by industry, 168
deficient areas, 171
fresh and desalinated, 166
transportable, 168
use and abuse of, 157 ff, 169
White, C. Langdon, 11–20, 353
WHO (World Health Organization of the United Nations):
fight against tropical diseases, 17, 249
recommendations to, 302–3, 319
World Food Congress of FAO, 133 ff, 157 ff
World population:
Conference, 283
distribution according to daily calorie intake, 144
estimates of, 30, 33, 34, 37, 77
per capita work potentials, 179
World resources:
constructive use of, 177 ff, 182–87
Writer, the:
in an overpopulated world, 267–76

X

X-rays:
on mutation rate, 216–17

## Y

Yaws:
  eradication of, 17
Yellow fever:
  eradication of, 107

## Z

Zinjanthropus:
  discovery of, 24